Proverbs within Cognitive Linguistics

Cognitive Linguistic Studies in Cultural Contexts (CLSCC)
ISSN 1879-8047

This book series aims at publishing high-quality research on the relationship between language, culture, and cognition from the theoretical perspective of Cognitive Linguistics. It especially welcomes studies that treat language as an integral part of culture and cognition, that enhance the understanding of culture and cognition through systematic analysis of language – qualitative and/or quantitative, synchronic and/or diachronic – and that demonstrate how language as a subsystem of culture transformatively interacts with cognition and how cognition at a cultural level is manifested in language.

For an overview of all books published in this series, please see
benjamins.com/catalog/clscc

Editors
Hans-Georg Wolf and Ning Yu
University of Potsdam / Pennsylvania State University

Founding Editor
Farzad Sharifian†
Monash University

Editorial Board

Antonio Barcelona
Universidad de Córdoba

Erich A. Berendt
Assumption University, Bangkok

Alan Cienki
VU University Amsterdam
& Moscow State Linguistic University

Alice Deignan
University of Leeds

Vyvyan Evans
Bangor University

Charles Forceville
University of Amsterdam

Roslyn M. Frank
University of Iowa

Raymond W. Gibbs, Jr.
University of California, Santa Cruz

Masako K. Hiraga
Rikkyo University

Zoltán Kövecses
Eötvös Loránd University

Zouhair Maalej
King Saud University

Fiona MacArthur
Universidad de Extremadura

Todd Oakley
Case Western Reserve University

Arne Peters
Universität Bremen

Frank Polzenhagen
RPTU Kaiserlautern - Landau

Chris Sinha
Hunan University

Gerard J. Steen
University of Amsterdam

Hans-Georg Wolf
Potsdam University

Volume 16
Proverbs within Cognitive Linguistics. State of the art
Edited by Sadia Belkhir

Proverbs within Cognitive Linguistics

State of the art

Edited by

Sadia Belkhir
Mouloud Mammeri University

John Benjamins Publishing Company
Amsterdam / Philadelphia

The paper used in this publication meets the minimum requirements of the American National Standard for Information Sciences – Permanence of Paper for Printed Library Materials, ANSI z39.48-1984.

DOI 10.1075/clscc.16

Cataloging-in-Publication Data available from Library of Congress:
LCCN 2024013394 (PRINT) / 2024013395 (E-BOOK)

ISBN 978 90 272 1484 3 (HB)
ISBN 978 90 272 4688 2 (E-BOOK)

© 2024 – John Benjamins B.V.
No part of this book may be reproduced in any form, by print, photoprint, microfilm, or any other means, without written permission from the publisher.

John Benjamins Publishing Company · https://benjamins.com

This book is dedicated to the memory of my parents,
Yamina and Si Moh Belkhir

Table of contents

Editor and contributors	IX
Acknowledgements	XIII
List of tables and figures	XV
Introduction: Proverbs from a cognitive linguistic perspective Sadia Belkhir	1

PART I. Theoretical discussions of proverbs in cognition and culture

CHAPTER 1. Proverbs in Extended Conceptual Metaphor Theory 26
 Zoltán Kövecses

CHAPTER 2. Metonymic layers in proverbs: A cross-linguistic and cross-cultural view 40
 Mario Brdar, Rita Brdar-Szabó & Daler Zayniev

CHAPTER 3. Contradiction in proverbs: The role of stereotypical metaphors 65
 El Mustapha Lemghari

PART II. A cognitive-cross-cultural linguistic approach on proverbs

CHAPTER 4. Metaphors of love before and after marriage in proverbs and anti-proverbs 88
 Anna T. Litovkina

CHAPTER 5. Proverbs of Latin and French origin in the history of English: A socio-cognitive analysis 112
 Julia Landmann

CHAPTER 6. Cognitive Linguistics and expressing/interpreting proverbs in a second language 132
 Gladys Nyarko Ansah

PART III. Cognitive categories in the proverbs of individual languages and cultures

CHAPTER 7. Emotion in Greek proverbs: The case of (romantic) love 174
 Maria Theodoropoulou

CHAPTER 8. LIVING IS MOVEMENT: A cognitive analysis of some
Akan proverbs   202
   Yaw Sekyi-Baidoo

CHAPTER 9. The role of Persian proverbs in framing Iran's nuclear program:
A cognitive linguistic approach   230
   Mohsen Bakhtiar

PART IV. Proverbs and related phenomena in a cultural-cognitive linguistic framework

CHAPTER 10. The only good snowclone is a dead snowclone:
A cognitive-linguistic exploration of the frayed ends of proverbiality   260
   Kim Ebensgaard Jensen

CHAPTER 11. A cultural linguistic study of embodied Hungarian proverbs
representing facial hair   298
   Judit Baranyiné Kóczy

CHAPTER 12. "We are in the same storm, not in the same boat":
Proverbial wisdom in environmental debates   328
   Anaïs Augé

Index   349

Editor and contributors

About the editor

Sadia Belkhir is Professor in the Department of English at Mouloud Mammeri University in Tizi-Ouzou, Algeria. She is particularly interested in animal-related proverbs, and metaphor in cognition, language, and culture. Her recent articles include Emotion and metaphor in Kabyle proverbs (2024, *Proverbium Online Supplement 3*), Metaphoric proverbs in EFL learners' translation (2022, *Cognitive Linguistic Studies*), Personification in EFL learners' academic writing: A Cognitive Linguistic Stance (2021, *Glottodidactica*), along with a book chapter entitled Cognitive Linguistics and proverbs (2021, *The Routledge Handbook of Cognitive Linguistics*). She is also the editor of *Cognition and Language Learning* (2020, Cambridge Scholars Publishing).

Contributors

Gladys Nyarko Ansah holds a PhD in Applied Linguistics, and a Master of Research degree in Cognitive Linguistics. She is Senior Lecturer at the Department of English, University of Ghana, Legon. Her research interests include language and culture, language and cognition, language use in bi/multilingual contexts, language in education, language and migration, and language and politics. Her recent papers include Exploring ethos in contemporary Ghana (2020, co-authored with A. E. Dzregah, *Humanities*), and Acculturation and integration: Language dynamics in the rural north-urban south mobility situation in Ghana (2018, *Legon Journal of the Humanities*). She also authored the book chapter Cultural conceptualisations of DEMOCRACY and political discourse practices in Ghana (2017, *Advances in Cultural Linguistics*).

Anaïs Augé is Post-doctoral Researcher affiliated to the University of Louvain, Belgium, at the Institute of Political Sciences Louvain-Europe. Her research interests are in the fields of environmental communication, Cognitive Linguistics, discourse analysis, and pragmatics. She published a monograph dedicated to metaphors in climate crisis discourse (2023, Routledge) and papers in several international journals such as *Environmental Communication, Metaphor and the Social World, Metaphor and Symbol,* and *Public Understanding of Science*.

Mohsen Bakhtiar is Lecturer of Linguistics at Ferdowsi University of Mashhad, Iran. His main research interests are figurative language, cultural key concepts, language and sexuality, and political discourse. He is the author of the journal article A cognitive linguistic view of control mechanism in Iranian culture: The case of *effat* 'chastity' in Persian (2019, *Review of Cognitive Linguistics*).

Judit Baranyiné Kóczy is Associate Professor of Linguistics at the University of Pannonia, Veszprém, Hungary. Her research focuses on language, conceptualisation, and culture within the framework of cognitive semantics, Conceptual Metaphor Theory and Cultural Linguistics. The main fields of her present linguistic investigation include embodiment via body-parts, embodied cultural metaphors, folk cultural metaphors, and corpus linguistics. She Chaired *The Third Cultural Linguistics International Conference* (2021, Budapest). She authored the monograph *Nature, Metaphor, Culture: Cultural Conceptualizations in Hungarian Folksongs* (2018 Springer Singapore) and various chapters on the figurative extensions of body-parts in Hungarian.

Mario Brdar is Professor of English Linguistics at Josip Juraj Strossmayer University, Osijek. He was the president of the Croatian Applied Linguistics Society in 2008–2010, and its vice-president in 2010–2012. From 2013 to 2017, he directed the postgraduate program in linguistics at the University of Osijek. Since 2014, he has been associate member of the Croatian Academy of Sciences and Arts. He was the editor of Jezikoslovlje and is a member of the editorial boards of Review of Cognitive Linguistics, ExELL, and Bosanski jezik. His main research interests include Cognitive Linguistics, morphosyntax, and lexical semantics.

Rita Brdar-Szabó is Full Professor of German Linguistics at Loránd Eötvös University (Budapest, Hungary). She was a guest lecturer at the University of Bamberg, Ludwig Maximilian University of Munich, Partium Christian University of Oradea, University of Wroclaw, University of Heidelberg, Complutense University of Madrid, and University of La Rioja at Logroño. She is Head of the Intercultural Linguistics Doctoral Programme at Loránd Eötvös University. Her main research interests include Cognitive Linguistics, morphology (in particular word formation), lexical semantics, and contrastive linguistics.

Kim Ebensgaard Jensen is Associate Professor of English Linguistics at the University of Copenhagen. His research falls under the rubrics of Cognitive Linguistics and corpus linguistics. He is a proponent of the Digital Humanities as well. He addresses the intersection between grammar, discourse, cognition, culture, and society. Furthermore, he has published articles on various cognitive and cultural aspects of English grammar and other linguistic phenomena.

Zoltán Kövecses is Professor Emeritus in the School of English and American Studies, Eötvös Loránd University, Budapest. His research focuses on conceptual metaphor theory and the role of context in the production of metaphors. His latest books include *Extended Conceptual Metaphor Theory* (2020, Cambridge UP) and *Where Metaphors Come From* (2015, Oxford UP).

Julia Landmann (née Schultz) works as Lecturer in Linguistics at the University of Basel, Switzerland. She has authored a number of studies with a specific focus on different language contact situations and their linguistic outcomes, such as the influence of French, German, Spanish and Yiddish on English. Julia is currently preparing a study on the dynamic lexicon of the English language from a socio-cognitive perspective. Her research interests focus on language contact, lexicology, lexical semantics and Cognitive Linguistics.

El Mustapha Lemghari is Professor of Linguistics at Cadi Ayyad University, Morocco. His work centers on such topics as mass/count distinction, proper names, proverbs, conceptual metaphor and conceptual blending. His latest papers include Constructing a broad model for proverb understanding (2021, *Metaphor and Symbol*), Metaphorical blending in complex proverbs. A case study (2021, *Metaphor and the Social World*), and La structure syntactico-sémantique de jouer dans la construction [Jouer + du + Nom d'instrument de musique] : une affaire de zone active massive (2020, *Travaux de linguistique*). He also authored the book chapters Les apparences sont trompeuses et L'habit ne fait pas le moine, synonymes ou antonymes ou les deux à la fois? (2020, *Liber Amicorum : Clins d'œil linguistiques en hommage à Emilia Hilgert*), and Traits massifs et traits comptables des noms propres métonymiques et/ou métaphoriques. Quelques problèmes de référence en suspens (2020, *Lexique et référence*).

Yaw Sekyi-Baidoo is Associate Professor in the Department of English Education, University of Education, Winneba. He did graduate work in both language and literature at the University of Ghana, Legon and the University of Cape Coast, both in Ghana. At the University of Education, Winneba, he has served variously as Dean of the Faculty of Languages Education, Dean, Centre for International Programmes and Member of the Governing Council. His current main research interest is Akan Names, and he has published a major monograph under the title *Akan Personal Names*, with the University of Ghana Press. He is currently on the Akan Personal Names Dictionary Project

Originally from Moscow, **Anna T. Litovkina** lives in Budapest (Hungary) and she is currently Professor in the Department of English Language and Literature at J. Selye University, Komárno, Slovakia. Her research interests include paremiology, paremiography, phraseology, and humour studies. Beyond more than one hundred scholarly articles, she is the author or co-author of 21 books on proverbs and humour, including *Twisted Wisdom: Modern Anti-Proverbs* (1999, co-authored with W. Mieder, DeProverbio.com), *Women Through Anti-Proverbs* (2018, Palgrave Macmillan), *Anti-Proverbs in Five Languages: Structural Features and Verbal Humor Devices* (2021, co-authored with H. Hrisztova-Gotthardt, P. Barta, K. Vargha, and W. Mieder, Palgrave Macmillan).

Maria Theodoropoulou is Assistant Professor at the Linguistics Department, School of Philology, Faculty of Philosophy, Aristotle University of Thessaloniki, Greece. Her research focuses on figurative language, language and emotion, the connection of Cognitive Linguistics and Psychoanalysis, as well as the linking of emotion to collective identity. Among her recent publications are Aspects of metaphor. Thematic section (forthcoming, *Review of Cognitive Linguistics*), FOOTBALL CLUB IS A FAMILY: Metaphor and the reconstruction of collective identity (forthcoming, *Review of Cognitive Linguistics*), "Has she got a mouth?" Metonymy, salience and experience in a child's speech (2021, *Proceedings of the ICGL14*), Comparing the Greek metaphors for fear and romantic love (2021, co-authored with T. Xioufis, *Proceedings of the ICGL14*), and Emotional aspects of collective identity–Part 1 (2020, co-authored with G. Paterakis and A. Loukas, *Studies in Greek Linguistics*).

Daler Zayniev is PhD Student in the Intercultural Linguistics Doctoral Programme of the Doctoral School of Linguistics at Eötvös Loránd University. He graduated from Samarkand State Institute for Foreign Languages in 2012. He obtained MA in General Linguistics in 2016. His current research deals with the use of colour terms in English, Russian, Tajik and Uzbek, with special emphasis on figurative uses of colour terms and expressions in the languages and cultures under study.

Acknowledgements

The editor is, foremost, grateful to the authors of the chapters in this volume for their commitment and endeavours. Without their contributions, this book would have never come to existence. Further sincere thanks go to the authors of the chapters who have earnestly participated in the peer-review process.

I also very gratefully acknowledge the assistance I received, in the peer-review process, from a number of scholars worldwide: Andreas Musolff, University of East Anglia, UK; Zouheir Maalej, retired professor, independent researcher; Gábor Győri, J. Sellye University, Komárno, Slovakia; Angeliki Athanasiadou, Aristotle University, Greece; Nadežda Silaški, University of Belgrade, Serbia; Ebru Türker, Arizona State University, USA; Maïa Ponsonnet, University of Western Australia; Žolt Papišta University of Novi Sad, Serbia; Inés Olza, University of Navarra, Spain.

I warmly thank Réka Benczes, Corvinus University of Budapest, Hungary and Sonja Kleinke, University of Heidelberg, Germany, for their support in suggesting contributors for the volume.

I also aknowledge the insightful feedback I received from anonymous reviewers and the very instructive comments from Klaus-Uwe Panther and Linda Thornburg on an earlier version of the manuscript.

Warmest thanks go to the CLSCC book series editors Ning Yu and Hans-Georg Wolf for their great professionalism.

I thank the publishers for their support in the publication process.

I also thank Wolfgang Mieder for the keen interest he has shown in this volume and for his kind and boosting words as well.

List of tables and figures

Tables

5.1	Chronological overview of Latin-and French-derived proverbs	117
6.1	English metaphoric proverbs	139
6.2	English non-metaphoric proverbs	139
6.3	Proverb response distribution	141
6.4	Response frequencies for Akan proverbs (Average response frequency: 8.6)	142
6.5	Response frequencies for English Proverbs (Average response frequency: 2.6)	142
6.6	Akan conceptual equivalents given for English proverbs	144
6.7	English conceptual equivalents given for Akan proverbs	145
8.1	Conceptual representation of LIVING IS MOVEMENT	212
9.1	List of Persian proverbs	256
9.2	Themes of the Persian proverbs	257
10.1	Overall frequencies	267
10.2	Overview of co-textual topics	268
10.3	Productivity profile of the only-good construction	269
10.4	Distribution of epistemic status categories in the only-good construction	275
10.5	Distribution of co-textual topics in the only-good construction	277
10.6	Productivity profile of the Mordor-construction	279

10.7	Distribution of transitivity patterns in the Mordor-construction	281
10.8	Distribution of epistemic status categories	282
10.9	Distribution of co-textual topics in the Mordor-construction	284
10.10	Productivity profile of the Ripley-construction	286
10.11	Distribution of epistemic status categories of the Ripley-construction	288
10.12	Distribution of co-textual topics in the Ripley-construction	291
12.1	General overview of the data	336

Figures

1.1	Proverbs based on shared schematicity structure	27
1.2	The GENERIC IS SPECIFIC ACCOUNT of proverbs	27
1.3	The structure of resemblance metaphors	27
2.1	Simplified illocutionary scenario for REQUEST	49
10.1	Lexemes in N1	270
10.2	Lexemes in N2	271
10.3	Lexemes in PrM	273
10.4	Distribution of discourse-pragmatic functions in the only-good construction	278
10.5	Lexemes in MVinf	280
10.6	Distribution of discourse-pragmatic functions in the Mordor-construction	283
10.7	Lexemes in Vinf2	287
10.8	Distribution of discourse-pragmatic functions in the Ripley-construction	290

Introduction
Proverbs from a Cognitive Linguistics perspective

Sadia Belkhir
Mouloud Mammeri University, Tizi-Ouzou, Algeria

1. Introduction

This volume focuses on Cognitive Linguistics[1] and its significance to the study of the proverb. Its objective is to present up-to-date research showing that this continuously evolving discipline can offer researchers essential tools to cope with the proverb in a theoretical or empirical way. The general theme of the volume is about the adeptness of Cognitive Linguistics at dealing with the proverb from cognitive and cultural perspectives altogether, thus allowing the attainment of fruitful research outcomes. Numerous scholars share the view that language has to be studied in relation to cognition and culture. Langacker (1994) argues that Cognitive Linguistics acknowledges cultural knowledge as the basis of vocabulary and grammar. Palmer (1996) contends that Cognitive Linguistics is skillful in the analysis of language and culture, underscoring the connectedness of Cognitive Linguistics and Cultural Linguistics. Kövecses (2005) places culture at the junction of cognition and language in the treatment of metaphorical variation. Additionally, it seems there is a connection between culture and embodiment. A number of studies emphasise that embodiment is not limited to the body only but goes far beyond it to involve the sociocultural environment as well. Yu (2015) underlines the relationship between bodily and socio-cultural dimensions characterising metaphor and realised in language, this yielding the notion of *extended embodiment* (Sinha 2021). Yu (2009, 2017) shows the role of culture in structuring metaphorical conceptualisation, and Sharifian (2015) reveals the relationship between language and cultural conceptualisation (as mentioned in Section 3.).

It should be pointed out that neither pre-cognitivist research into the proverb gave culture due consideration (see Section 4. below) nor did early Cognitive Linguistics (Lakoff and Turner 1989). In view of the lack of attention proverbs have

---

1. The term Cognitive Linguistics appears with capital C and L throughout the book, because it represents a name. The same goes for Cultural Linguistics, the Great Chain of Being, etc.

received as regards cognitive and cultural linguistic standpoints, the volume aims to make a kind of *rapprochement* of the two perspectives in order to advance understanding of the proverb with a view to cognition, language, and culture. The present contributions strive to respond to this aim, and this unites them within the broader context of the volume.

The chapters provide pioneering ideas about the proverb and contribute, from a Cognitive Linguistics interdisciplinary perspective, to the existing body of literature on the proverb. Indeed, the theoretical frameworks that the contributions draw on are quite diverse, ranging from the frameworks of purely Cognitive Linguistics to Cultural Linguistics/Anthropological Linguistics, Cognitive Sociolinguistics, and Construction Grammar – a theory of syntax that draws on principles of Cognitive Linguistics (see, for example, Lakoff 1987 and Filmore 1988). Furthermore, the book purports to show the theoretical implications of proverbs for cognitive linguistic theory. In this volume, it is believed that by taking a cognitive and cultural linguistic approach to proverbs, scholars could attain a deeper understanding of proverbial language use and thinking. This conviction is transparent not only in the contributors' investigations but also in the organisation of the volume described in Section 5.

In sum, the contributors to the volume endeavour to highlight the reason why a cognitive linguistic approach that gives consideration to the sociocultural dimension characterising linguistic phenomena is germane to an understanding of the cognitive mechanisms underlying proverbial language within various contexts. Particularly, this collective volume addresses the following questions: (i) Is the cognitivist approach compatible with pre-cognitivist research, or (ii) does it simply offer a different perspective in the subject matter of proverbs with regard to cognition and culture; (iii) Does it constitute a radical break from the tradition, and if so, what new insights does it offer? As aforementioned, it is believed that a Cognitive/Cultural Linguistics approach can provide gainful tools to remedy prevailing issues in paremiological research (see issues mentioned in forthcoming Sections 2. and 4.). Overall, it can be hoped that the present volume can contribute with efficacy to a profounder understanding of the proverb and its use.

The research volume focuses on a specialised topic. As such, the intended readership includes essentially academics and researchers willing to undertake research into proverbs within a cognitive linguistic framework. The book is also destined for scholars working in the areas of language studies, applied linguistics, language teaching and learning, and Cognitive Linguistics, and those who wish to refine their knowledge about the cognitive activities featuring proverb use and their interaction with sociocultural contextual variables. To respond to the needs of the target audience is a requisite in this volume, which offers original information about the proverb from a number of cognitive linguistic perspectives, and suggests future directions in both theoretical and empirical research in a wide range of contexts. It brings together scholars from different settings to discuss their contributions showing the diversity and richness of this germane area of research. Along these lines, the book not only mirrors the current state of the field of proverbs within Cognitive Linguistics but also aims to contribute to its upcoming advances.

This introductory chapter begins with an account on the proverb including its definitions, origin, and structural features. This is followed by some expedient background information about a number of fundamental and recurring conceptual notions including cultural model, cognitive model, image schema, cultural conceptualisation, among others. This is to guide the readers through the partially overlapping terminologies. It then moves on to a brief overview of previous research into the proverb before and after the advent of Cognitive Linguistics and a summary of the main findings. Finally, it describes the chapters enclosed in the volume, and draws conclusions.

2. On the proverb

The proverb is a traditional short saying that conveys some accepted truth grounded on shared experience. It is a linguistic fact and a socio-cultural cognitive phenomenon that belongs to the culture of people and to the patrimony of their country. It germinates inside society and travels through time from generation to generation by the word of mouth. The proverb is found in various places of the world and because it is a strong bit of speech characterised by imagery, it attracts so much attention among scholars. This leads to considerable amounts of research classified within a field of study known as paremiology (For more details about paremiology see Section 4 below). It seems that providing a precise definition to the proverb is not an easy task, as "no definition can both map all of proverbia and protect the neighbouring lands of clichés, maxims, slogans, and the like from unwanted annexation" (Hernadi and Steen 1999:1). In other words, "not even the most complex definition will be able to identify all proverbs" (Mieder 2004: 4). Earlier, Archer Taylor (1931: 3), the 'doyen' of modern proverb research, had acknowledged the difficulty of defining the proverb with precision and concluded on a positive note saying: "An incommunicable quality tells us that this sentence is proverbial and that one is not". Metaphor is one indicator of proverbiality, it is an extensively used image in proverbs; indeed, metaphorical proverbs make up a great portion. A definition that Mieder (1985:118) provided laid down the metaphorical nature of the proverb and its traditional frequent usage, among other aspects. He stated, "A proverb is a short, generally known sentence that expresses common, traditional and didactic views in a metaphorical and fixed form and which is easily remembered and repeated". Another definition (see Norrick 2014:14) emphasises the conversational trait of the proverb making of it a well-established speech act, "What we generally call proverbs are recurrent, pithy, often formulaic and/or figurative, fairly stable and generally recognizable units used to form a complete utterance, make a complete conversational contribution and/or to perform a speech act in a speech event".

With reference to the question of the origin of proverbs, Mieder (2014:28) considered that "every proverb begins with an individual whose keen insight is accepted and carried forth as a piece of proverbial wisdom by people of all walks of life". Every language has a rich store of proverbs that people use in their daily speech, and which originate from various sources: some were drawn from human experience and observation of the world around them, others from ancient languages, or from oral and written literary creation, from religion, or history.

Delineating proverbs from other expressions (such as, idioms, snowclones, and proverbial phrases) is still a debated issue. Scholars do not agree on the classification of such conventional fixed expressions. A problem of terminology is pointed out in the field of phraseology. It seems that general agreement is lacking as to how to name fixed expressions (proverbs, idioms, sayings, etc.). A number of notions happen to be used to refer to the same type of expressions, while one notion is used to name different kinds of expressions (Moon 1998). For Makkai (1995:vii), the idiom "is the assigning of a new meaning to a group of words which already have their own meaning". He provides three sets of idioms: the first, *lexemic idioms*, are verbal, nominal, adjectival, or adverbial, the second, *phraseological idioms*, are larger in size as they may come in the form of a clause that is entirely frozen, the third includes proverbs and sayings. The scholar thus sees the proverb as no more than one type of idiom. However, in a number of published works, proverbs and idioms are researched separately, this showing recognition of their being distinct types of expressions (see Gibbs and O'Brien 1990; Gibbs 1992; Gibbs, Strom, and Spivey-Knowlton 1997; Gibbs 2001). Gibbs and Beitel (1995) view the proverb as a fixed form in the same way as are idioms, clichés, and other expressions. Besides, they are characterised by meter, rhyme, alliteration, assonance, personification, paradox, and parallelism, while idioms are not. Proverbs are known to convey truths, socio-cultural values, and ethics (Mieder 1985). Flavel and Flavel (2000:24) recognise that proverbs and idioms belong to distinct classes of expressions. They, however, point out the difficulty of attaining a clear-cut between them. It is their contention that if a proverb is a complete sentence, whereas an idiom is a phrase, then, there is no reason that prevents a phrase (idiom) from becoming a whole sentence (proverb). It seems the sentential parameter is not sufficiently convincing for deciding whether a sentence is a proverb or not. Therefore, one needs to consider extra criteria, as for example, the moral-teaching function conveyed within the proverb, which is absent in the idiom. Furthermore, one needs to look deeper into the structure of the proverb to understand what it actually is. Structure represents a further indicator of proverbiality. That is, proverbs in any language are identified by their structure. For instance (see Mieder 2004:6), English proverbs are recognised by the structures 'Better X than Y', as in, *Better be the head of a dog than the tail of a lion*, "Like X, like Y, as in, *Like father, like son*, 'No X without Y', as in, *No smoke without fire*, 'One X doesn't make a Y', as in, *One swallow does not make a summer*, etc. In addition to structure, other indicators of proverbiality are considered, as for example 'self-containedness' (their important syntactic components cannot be substituted), 'traditionality' (they are elements of folklore rustic in character, which recur in discourse), 'didactic content' (they convey a collective directive), 'fixed form' (they have a static structure that make them recognisable, though variants do exist), and 'poetic features' (they are mostly characterised by metaphoricity) (see Norrick 2014:10–13). Overall, making a distinction between proverbs and other expressions constitutes a current problem that should be addressed in this introductory chapter. Explicitly, how in a cognitive linguistic framework can proverbs be delineated from other expressions that are also metaphorically motivated and may be derived from proverbs? An attempt to answering this question is forthcoming (see Section 6. Conclusions).

3. Fundamental conceptual terminology

Cognitive Linguistics is a science concerned with the study of language from a conceptual stance. Cognition is responsible for acquisition, storage, transformation, and use of knowledge. It is a mental construct characterised by cognitive activities including perception, memory, imagery, language, problem solving, reasoning, and decision-making (Matlin 2005). George Lakoff and Ronald Langacker are acknowledged among the leading figures of Cognitive Linguistics (see Geeraerts and Cuyckens 2007; Wen and Taylor 2021). This new science includes a range of linguistic theories sharing a common principle: language must be studied with respect to the cognitive processes involved in the interpretation and use of utterances rather than in relation to the syntactic forms of linguistic patterns. Language is seen as the perception and production of structured items symbolic in character. What is more, it is the contention of Cognitive Linguistics that human knowledge is conceptually arranged in the form of structures referred to as "Idealised Cognitive Models", ICMs for short. An ICM is described as a structured whole, or a "gestalt", having a "propositional structure", "image-schematic structure", "metaphoric mappings", and "metonymic mappings" (See Lakoff 1987:68). It is worth noting that, the conceptual structures characterising conceptual metaphors have been treated in terms of 'domains' in early CMT (Lakoff and Johnson 1980). Later, Kövecses (2017) provided an opinion of schematicity hierarchies different from that held within the standard view (see Lakoff 1993; David et al. 2016). The newly suggested hierarchy is four-levelled ending in a fifth (i.e., the linguistic expression) and arranged from most to least schematic.

Having clarified the idea of ICMs, further terms used in Cognitive and Cultural Linguistics need presentation, including 'cognitive model', 'cultural model', 'image schema', 'scenario', and 'cultural conceptualisation'. For Palmer (1996), cognitive models represent the form that cultural knowledge takes. The notion of cultural model has received various labels within a variety of scientific disciplines, such as, anthropology and linguistics (D'Andrade 1981; Lakoff 1987; Holland and Quinn 1987; Kövecses 2005; Sharifian 2015, 2017). Cultural models are regarded as systems of beliefs, values, and norms, conventionally organised and shaped by the experiences of particular community members living in one physical and socio-cultural environment. Kövecses (2005:7) uses the terms 'cognitive model' and 'cultural model' interchangeably. In his view, cultural models are often produced by conceptual metaphors. "These are structures that are simultaneously cultural and cognitive (hence, the term *cultural model*, or *cognitive model*), in that they are culturally specific mental representations of aspects of the world". It seems that "cultural models exist for both concrete and abstract concepts" (Kövecses 2005:193), and originate from the inherent characteristics of these concepts as well as the numerous functions assigned to them by the members of society. Understanding the functioning of the human conceptual system and cultures importantly depends on cultural models. The relationship between metaphors and metonymies with cultural models is demonstrated in the cultural model of anger characterised by five steps: Offending event, anger, attempt to control anger, loss of control, and retribution. (Lakoff and Kövecses 1987).

The term *image schema* is introduced within the scope of embodied cognition (Johnson 1987; Lakoff 1987) to describe how patterns of understanding and thinking about the world are organised. It refers to a recurring conceptual structure that emerges out of the bodily experience of both one's inner self and the external world. This conceptual structure is believed to feature the cognitive processes that motivate the mappings within conceptual metaphors. As such, "the image-schema structure of the source domain is used in reasoning about the target domain" (Lakoff and Johnson 1980 [2003]:253). Examples of image schemas arising from bodily experience include "CONTAINER, PATH, LINK, FORCES, BALANCE", while those relating to orientations and relations comprise "UP-DOWN, FRONT-BACK,

PART-WHOLE, CENTER-PERIPHERY, etc." (Lakoff 1987: 27). In Johnson's (1987: 29) terms, "in order for us to have meaningful, connected experiences that we can comprehend and reason about, there must be pattern and order to our actions, perceptions, and conceptions". These patterns can be conceived of as dynamic, and relating to states (e.g., being angry or sad) or motion (e.g., going up or down). Image schemas are claimed to structure certain ICMs wherein metaphorical mappings are used to map image schemas, e.g., CONTAINER, onto corresponding target domain concepts, e.g., ANGER (Lakoff 1987). In this particular instance of metaphor, the ICM has the structure of *cause and effect* (Kövecses 2002). A related notion is that of *scenario* or *scene* used to scrutinize the conceptual structures underlying metaphor use and capturing participants' roles, chain of events, and the setting involved in social discourse (Musolff 2006).

In Cultural Linguistics, the idea of *cultural schema* is advanced to account for the emergence of some aspect of cognition that is shared, in a distributive way, by the members of a community. The notion of *cultural conceptualisation* is claimed to refer to cultural schemas and categories representing collective cognitive systems, e.g., "worldviews". Cultural conceptualisations are considered dynamic as "they are developed through interactions between the members of a cultural group and enable them to think as if in one mind, somehow more or less in a similar fashion. These conceptualisations are negotiated and renegotiated through time and across generations" (Sharifian 2011: 5). As such, cultural conceptualisations are mostly thought of as "distributed representations" featuring people's minds in a given cultural community.

It is acknowledged that Cognitive Linguistics is characterised by a set of key tenets including the principle of viewing language primarily as a *conceptual phenomenon* (see Taylor 2012) studied within an *empirical corpus-based* approach. Besides, the concept of *embodiment* features the exploration of related manifestation of some authentic linguistic forms. Yet, embodiment seems not sufficiently relevant for the study of further natural occurring linguistic phenomena unless cultural-contextual factors are involved in the descriptions and analyses of these manifestations (see Deignan 2005; Kövecses 2005). Cognitive Linguistics is also known to abide by the principle of *empiricism*. It favours studies based on authentic data drawn from acknowledgeable sources (e.g., dictionaries, online corpora, newspapers, among others). This is to say, Cognitive Linguistics rests upon the principle that language study should be bound to empirical corpus-based type of research (Taylor and Littlemore 2014). Nonetheless, early explorations of metaphor and/or metonymy, in Cognitive Linguistics, particularly Conceptual Metaphor Theory (CMT), relied solely on created illustrative examples to sustain argumentative reasoning (Lakoff and Johnson 1980; Lakoff and Turner 1989; Lakoff and Kövecses 1987; Lakoff 1993). This way of proceeding has changed. Now, authentic data is favoured and used to substantiate discussions within research (e.g., Kövecses 2015, 2018). The principle of *embodiment* seems ubiquitous in research into figurative language (e.g., metaphor and metonymy) that presents a close-fitting relation between body-experience and thoughts. Human bodily experience shapes ways of thinking and affects cognitive processing of language. Rich exploration of this subject matter prevails in Cognitive Linguistics (see, for example, Lakoff 1987; Johnson 1987; Gibbs et al. 1996; Gibbs 2005; Kövecses 2002, 2005). Furthermore, the grounding of linguistic expressions, such as metaphors, is built upon the idea of an *experiential basis* that ensures "correlations in experience, various kinds of nonobjective similarity, biological and cultural roots shared by the two concepts [source and target], and possibly others" (Kövecses 2002: 69). In other words, conceptual metaphors though grounded in human experience of the body and the external world, making them universal, are affected by cultural components (for more information on the universality and culture specificity of metaphor, refer to Kövecses 2005). Besides, the idea of an existing mutual influence between embodied cognition and culture (Maalej 2008) has obviously led to advances in the exploration of conceptualisations within, for instance, proverbs including human body parts. The experiential-embodied nature characterising some patterns of ordinary language has been claimed to be over-emphasised in detriment of cultural and contextual influences whose utility has not been given the significance it deserves. Early version of CMT (Lakoff 1993; Lakoff and Turner 1989; Lakoff and Johnson 1980) received much criticism on the issue (see Deignan 2005; Kövecses 2005). Importantly, variation in conceptual metaphor across languages and cultures is a phenomenon that proponents of the theory overlooked. Due to this shortcoming and the growing need to study metaphor in relation to society and culture, aiming to explore the extent to which it is diverse and culture-specific, an improved version of CMT is introduced: the Cultural Cognitive Theory (CCT) (Kövecses 2005). In this theory, a number of issues are treated, such as, the social and cultural dimensions influencing human experience and metaphor use. In addition, the causes of metaphor variation and the aspects of conceptual metaphor being subject to variation are investigated. This new way of dealing with metaphor comes out of the central debated question of whether metaphor should be studied within a cognitive framework with the purpose of discovering universal conceptual metaphors, or be treated within a social-cultural and cognitive scope to reveal the diversity of conceptual metaphors. Further developments of the theory witness the emergence of a viewpoint devoting great importance to *context* in meaning making when dealing with metaphors (Kövecses 2015, 2020). Following this line of thought, Cultural Linguistics has apparently too much to offer to Cognitive Linguistics in the treatment of the proverb.

4. Previous studies into the proverb

The enterprise of proverb study bearing the label 'paremiology' began long before the advent of Cognitive Linguistics. Paremiology is a field of study mainly concerned with the definition, origin, history, dissemination, language, structure, meaning, use, and function of proverbs. Another associated domain of enquiry, known as paremiography, has a distinct focus: the collection and classification of proverbs (Mieder 2004: 125). It is worth noting in passing that early proverb collections provided sets of proverbs downplaying their use and function in concrete socio-cultural contexts and thus neglecting existing variations within different circumstances. Paremiology includes a vast array of published works, handbooks, and proverb collections in many languages. There exists a long history of proverb collections from classical antiquity to the present. The work achieved by paremiologists and paremiographers is so colossal. Primarily, research within paremiography from ancient age to the present has yielded countless numbers of collections of proverbs in varied world's languages (op. cit.: xii). In a similar vein, paremiological studies have been very dynamic and prolific. Most of those studies are recorded in *Proverbium: Yearbook of International Proverb Scholarship* (op. cit. xiii). Early research in paremiology in regards to English can be traced back to the volume *On the Lessons in Proverbs* (Trench 1853 [2003]) containing a study of the origin, nature, distribution, meaning, and significance of proverbs. In those past decades, proverbs were collected and classified according to prominent themes revealing variable cultural features. Emphasis was laid on explaining the way phenomena in the external world were used in proverb creation. At that time, metaphors were treated as forms of language inspired from ordinary people's state of affairs. For instance, *A burnt child dreads the fire* is a proverb involving a metaphor drawn from the household (see Taylor 1934: 6). Such paremiological methods of analysis focused mainly on proverb semantics, structure, and function thus failing to provide elucidations of the deep-rooted thinking activities underlying proverbial metaphor implications, as for example, the involvement of cognitive/cultural models in conceptual metaphors realised in proverbial discourse. This constitutes an issue within pre-cognitivist studies of the proverb.

Even after the advent of Cognitive Linguistics and its later development into theories sharing the converging purpose of studying language in relation to cognition, paremiological research carried on further the quest into the proverb without taking consideration of its underlying cognitive dimension. As for example, modern paremiology acknowledges the noteworthy *oeuvre* by Mieder (2004) entitled *Proverbs: A handbook*, a reference book treating paremiological subject matters including the use of proverbs in literature (novels and poems), plays, political discourse, mass-media, art, advertising, popular songs, caricatures, cartoons, and comics. The handbook, moreover, looks at the proverb from social, educational, religious, and psychological angles. Another edited work worthy of reference is the volume bearing the title *Introduction to paremiology. A comprehensive guide to proverb studies* (Hrisztova-Gotthardt and Varga 2014). This handbook introduces the basic premises of the study of proverbs along with an account of contemporary paremiological research. It comprises chapters written by leading scholars in the field of paremiology. The fundamental designs of the book include defining the proverb, describing its characteristics, providing its origin, dealing with the syntax, semantics, and pragmatics of proverbs, and accounting for the collection and classification of proverbs, among others. Pertinently, the seventh chapter of the handbook focuses on the cognitive dimension of the proverb and purports to question ideas held within CMT; specifically, Lakoff and Johnson's (1980) claim that everyday language is metaphorical in nature and their giving primacy to thought over language. The chapter concludes that concepts involved in proverbs are created not only via metaphors, but by means of language as well, as is the case with the creation of non-metaphorical proverbs (see Lewandowska and Antos 2014). In sum, those paremiological investigations did not account for the import of the thought processes governing proverbial language, such as, the cognitive/cultural functions motivating the use of one proverb instead of another in particular contextual discourse.

The Proverb has also been studied within a cross-cultural perspective to unveil metaphorical variations and gain a better understanding of the relationship between language and cultural conceptualisations (see Dabbagh 2016; Ben Salamh and Maalej 2018). From a purely cultural linguistic point of view, the cultural dimension of proverbs was investigated via cultural conceptualisations to offer substantiation in favour of the introduction of a 'cultural conceptualisation model' to the treatment of the facet characterising proverbs as elements of language endowed with the capacity of conveying socio-cultural beliefs and values (Dabbagh 2016). Yet, one thing lacking in the study was a cognitive linguistic exploration of cross-cultural metaphor variation within proverbs that would clarify the role of human cognitive processes together with cognitive-cultural models in understanding metaphoric proverbs across languages and cultures. Animal proverbs were also researched cross-culturally to demonstrate the effect of cultural features upon conceptualisations of humans as animals (see Ben Salamh and Maalej 2018). The study focused on four major aspects including the GENERIC IS SPECIFIC mappings, the GREAT CHAIN metaphor, the animals capitalised upon, and the evaluation of humans through animals. However, the emphasis put on the conceptual mappings involved within the animal-related metaphors could not illuminate the role played by cognitive mechanisms in proverb use in actual socio-cultural contexts, as is the case, for instance, in current international political discussions. Further cross-linguistic and cross-cultural research was conducted to highlight the structure of anti-proverbs and their humoristic features (see T. Litovkina et al. 2021). The author and her colleagues, in their *Anti-Proverbs in Five Languages: Structural Features and Verbal Humor Devices*, described a set of operational mechanisms underlying anti-proverbs, i.e., "parodied, twisted, or fractured proverbs that reveal humorous or satirical speech play with traditional proverbial wisdom" (Mieder 2004: 28). An anti-proverb is, in short, the alteration of an ordinary proverb for some humorous effect. The book contained discussions around four methods of alterations effected upon proverbs across some languages. These methods comprise 'addition', 'omission', 'substitution', and 'blending'. Although the book came with valuable information about proverbs formal structuring, it did not pay attention to the conceptual structures – cognitive models – that conceptual metaphors involve, and which proverbial language concretely instantiates.

In addition to proverb study within the area of rhetoric (see Mieder 2003, 2009), there has been attention in the proverb from other angles, such as semiotics (see Grzybek 1994) and pragmatics (see Yankah 1989; Norrick 1994; Briggs 1994). Yet, these studies focused either on the role of cultural devices characterising proverbs from a semiotic stance, or on proverb performances to highlight the pragmatics of social interaction. Essentially, a promising approach to the proverb would be one that is integrative of both cognitive and pragmatic dimensions, which would serve, on the one side, to enlighten proverbial conceptual nature within and/or across languages and cultures of the world, and on the other, to demonstrate, its socio-cultural pragmatic role.

In addition to the problem of defining the proverb (see Section 2. above), a further issue characterises research within paremiology; it is the task of dealing with proverb meaning. In this respect, Mieder (1997: 410) states,

> The vexing problem of proverb meaning continues to occupy semantic studies. Linguists and folklorists have repeatedly attempted to explain the semantic ambiguity of proverbs, which results to a large degree from their being used in various contexts with different functions. But proverbs also act as analogies, which adds to the complexity of understanding their precise meaning in a particular speech act.

Some attempts have been made to investigate proverb meaning (e.g., Kirshenblatt-Gimblett 1973; Honeck and Kibler 1984). Proverbs are intrinsically vague; hence, resorting to analogy is necessary to make their meaning clear (Mieder 1997). It goes without saying that further research in paremiology is required to resolve this issue.

With the advent of Cognitive Linguistics, the exploration of the proverb has observed a shift of focus from the study of its semantics, formal structure, and function to an unprecedented determination of understanding its conceptual nature via the investigation of the cognitive goings-on underlying proverb interpretation. In addition, usage has become the premise of most cognitive linguistic oriented research (see the notion of usage in Steen 2007). Studies into the proverb from a cognitive linguistic perspective are acknowledgeable (see Lakoff and Turner 1989; Lakoff 1993; Gibbs and Beitel 1995; T. Litovkina and Csábi 2002; Belkhir 2012, 2014, 2019, 2021, 2022; Lemghari 2019a, 2019b, 2021, among others). Two outstanding theories have marked the study of proverbs in Cognitive Linguistics: CMT (Lakoff and Turner 1989) and Extended Conceptual Base Theory (ECBT) (Honeck and Temple 1994). The latter theory suggests that proverb comprehension involves three stages: (i) a literal-meaning level, (ii) a figurative-meaning level, and (iii) an instantiation level. The scholars describe the process of ECBT in respect to two situations: irrelevant and relevant contexts. The former concerns a situation wherein a proverb is used out of context (i.e., the interlocutors do not share background information relevant to the proverb that is used, as for example, *A net with a hole in it won't catch any fish*), and the latter, a situation wherein a proverb is uttered in a definite context (i.e., sufficient contextual information is shared by speaker and listener allowing appropriate interpretation of the proverb).

A significant portion of proverbs represents authentic cultural instances of conventional metaphors that need exploration within a cognitive linguistic framework to understand the mental workings underlying proverbial metaphorical language and, accordingly, highlight the tight link between cognition, metaphor, and language. Research into this connection featured Lakoff and Johnson's (1980) *Metaphors We Live By*. Yet, very little or nothing was said about proverbs in this publication. Lakoff and Turner's (1989) *More than Cool Reason* introduced a theory of proverb interpretation called the Great Chain Metaphor Theory (GCMT), based on four requisite components – the *Maxim of Quantity* (Grice 1975), the *Great Chain*, the *Nature of Things*, and the GENERIC IS SPECIFIC metaphor. However, this theory was deemed very limited. While relying exclusively on the Great Chain of Being theory[2] and the GENERIC IS SPECIFIC metaphor to account for proverb understanding, they still presented a narrowed cognitive linguistic view of the proverb. They did not pay enough attention to the cognitive-social and cross-cultural dimensions characterising the proverb. These dimensions are worthy of consideration in their own right. In sum, their theory downplayed the status

---

2. See Lovejoy, A. O. (1936). *The Great Chain of Being*. Cambridge, MA: Harvard University Press.

of the proverb as a naturally occurring piece of language created within specific contextual cultural settings. Other publications treated the interplay between cognition, metaphor, and language from a wider stance including cross-cultural and contextual dimensions (see Kövecses 2005, 2015, 2020). However, a treatment of the proverb was lacking within the theory of cross-cultural metaphor variation and Kövecses' (2020) Extended Conceptual Metaphor Theory. Further published works that variedly treated this interconnection (e.g., Geeraerts and Cuyckens 2007; Gibbs 2008; Taylor and Littlemore 2014; Semino and Demjén 2017) unfortunately overlooked the proverb in their descriptions and analyses. Interestingly, Gibbs and Beitel, in a volume edited by Mieder (2003), offered an exploration of proverb understanding in relation to available works in psychology and cognitive sciences, and claimed that proverb comprehension depended highly on metaphorical cognitive processes. In addition, a recent publication by Wen and Taylor (2021) devoted a whole chapter to the discussion of the interplay between Cognitive Linguistics and the proverb (see Belkhir 2021). In this chapter, I set out to explore the contribution of Cognitive Linguistics to the study of proverbs. The focus was on CMT, starting from its early version (Lakoff and Johnson 1980; Lakoff and Turner 1989), and moving towards its more recent standard CCT (Kövecses 2005). The premise was that proverbs have not been researched from a cross-cultural perspective within this theory, and that research is needed to satisfy this lack. Examples of source-target domain mappings within some animal-related proverbs drawn from Kabyle, Arabic, French, and English in comparison and contrast revealed the central role played by the cultural dimension within the interplay between cognition and language in metaphoric variation. This can be viewed as a starting point for innovative research into this interrelationship aiming to demonstrate the import of a combinatory cognitive and cross-cultural approach to proverb study. This approach can handle the role of mental mechanisms involved in the interpretation and production of socio-culturally-based proverbial metaphors. This is what the present book is also intended for.

5. The present volume

The title *Proverbs within Cognitive Linguistics: State of the Art* has been chosen to spark off further curiosity in the study of the proverb from a cognitive linguistic perspective among scholars worldwide. Unlike the previous paremiological and cross-cultural type of research described in Sections 4., the chapters of the volume treat the proverb from a Cognitive Linguistics interdisciplinary viewpoint. In addition, the book does not contain chapters that have already been published. It thus presents only pioneering contributions that highlight new views of the proverb from a variety of stances that show how Cognitive Linguistics is a rich and intriguing field of research that allows the exploration of naturally produced language, such as the proverb.

Although each chapter deals with a specific aspect of the proverb, all the contributions are in some way linked to other chapters in the volume in that some chapters deal with a specific theoretical aspect in different ways, while others make use of different methodologies to treat a similar phenomenon. Therefore, the contributions can be seen as complementary to one another.

As was previously mentioned, the volume is contextualised with a view to the lack of attention proverbs have received as regards cognitive and cultural linguistic perspectives. It is thematically arranged into four main parts that acknowledge the significance of an interdisciplinary cognitive-cultural position in explorations of the proverb. These thematic sections are respectively labelled as: (1) Theoretical discussions of proverbs in cognition and culture, (2) A cognitive-cross-cultural linguistic approach on proverbs, (3) Cognitive categories in the proverbs of individual languages and cultures, and (4) Proverbs and related phenomena in a cultural-cognitive linguistic framework. Part I contains three chapters whose main concern lies in theoretical discussions of proverbs in cognition and culture. The contributions in this part examine the proverb from a cognitive linguistic stance recognising the importance of considering the cultural contextual dimension featuring proverb use. At the outset, the chapter by Zoltán Kövecses works as a presentation of an up-to-date approach to handling proverbs within the recent scope of Extended CMT that explicates the reason why numerous proverbs may show cultural differences, among other concerns. In this new view, the proverb is analysed with reference to four levels of schematicity; namely, image schema, domain, frame, and mental space structures. Besides, context is given due attention in the theory and so it is in the treatment of proverbs. The chapter shows how a set of related conceptual metaphors, referred to as a "schematicity hierarchy" (Kövecses 2020) can work as "conceptual pathways" (Kövecses 2020, 2021) that allow to conceptually relate a given literal meaning (e.g., 'leap') with a specific metaphorical meaning (e.g., 'in a quick and hasty way') in understanding the proverb *Look before you leap*. The scholar reminds readers of the fact that CMT, in its earlier version, is a cognitive theory that has not sufficiently considered context, and goes for highlighting the role of the contextual component.

The chapter by Mario Brdar, Rita Brdar-Szabó, and Daler Zayniev presents a cognitive-pragmatic approach in dealing with metonymy characterising proverbs. Relying on evidence from a number of languages and cultures, the scholars demonstrate that conceptual metonymy features the proverb and contributes to its meaning. The authors seek to identify several levels within proverbs, or more precisely 'metonymic layers' structuring the proverbs and contributing to meaning making. According to them, proverbs should be treated as instantiations of the metonymy SPECIFIC FOR GENERIC representing the first metonymic layer of the proverb. A second metonymic layer consists in its illocutionary force (i.e., statement, imperative, interrogative, etc.). A third metonymic layer is made possible by means of its reduced form. Another metonymic layer is the interpretation of a salient participant as standing for the implicit event in which it participates. The fifth metonymic layer is when a proverb employs a lexical item denoting a whole but one of its specific parts is targeted.

El Mustapha Lemghari, in chapter three, introduces the idea of stereotypical metaphors to explore proverbs exhibiting opposing meanings and thus aims at responding to a need within CMT in dealing with the cognitive devices featuring the meaning of proverbs. He conclusively argues that standard conceptual metaphors cannot account for contradictory proverbs while stereotypical ones can because of their capacity to deal with contradictory visions within a single conceptual domain. The researcher claims that contradiction emerges out of the opposition in the stereotypes lying behind concepts (or cognitive domains). He finally concludes that standard conceptual metaphor deals partly with the meanings of proverbs, while stereotypical metaphor is more useful as it clarifies why a given metaphorical expression exhibits contradiction.

The three chapters in Part II ponder proverbs within a cognitive-cross-cultural perspective. What they have in common is the intent to examine metaphorical conceptualisations involved in the proverbs of distinct languages and cultures to draw similarities and differences in both these conceptualisations and their actual usage in various societies. The chapter by Anna T. Litovkina discusses the ways how love after marriage is viewed and conceptualised in the body of Anglo-American proverbs and anti-proverbs, as well as in proverbs from around the world. The author treats models of love, which lead one to getting married: LOVE IS LOSS OF CONTROL and MADNESS, LOVE IS FOLLY, and LOVE IS LOSS OF EYESIGHT and BLINDNESS. This is followed by an exploration of three models of love after marriage picturing the sobering and eye-opening effect of marriage, loving shifting to war (LOVE IS WAR), and the diminished intensity of young love and lust in the course of matrimony, even leading to their complete disappearance, and very frequently to divorce.

The chapter by Julia Landmann explores, from a socio-cognitive perspective, proverbs borrowed from Latin and French into English, and shows how their use in dictionaries (e.g., OED) differs from their treatment in current newspapers' discourse. The author sets out to define the range of 'emotionally-affective' influences that potentially incite English speakers to choose loan proverbs in their discourse instead of already existing equivalents in their native language. The researcher considers the distribution, development, and contextual usage of the borrowed proverbs over centuries and concludes that most of the proverbs are linked to society, human nature, and behaviour. In addition, she reveals that the largest portion of loan proverbs has a Latin-based origin, this probably resulting from influence of an emergent interest in classical Latin within English Renaissance.

In chapter seven, Gladys Nyarko Ansah investigates the cognitive and cultural ability of Akan-English bilingual speakers to interpret and express proverbs across their L1 (Akan) and L2 (English). The research, carried out in Ghana, is based on Cognitive and Cultural Linguistics guidelines. The author's major aim is to highlight the role of cognitive-cultural models and cultural competence in understanding and interpreting metaphoric proverbs compared to the non-metaphoric ones. The author suggests that the bilingual speakers involved in the study would find non-metaphoric proverbs easier to understand than the metaphoric, in both languages. The findings of the research show that the bilinguals seem reliant not only on universal human cognitive processes but on Akan cultural models as well.

Part III of the volume includes three chapters that deal with the proverbs of individual languages and cultures. The purpose shared within the contributions is the investigation of cognitive categories including LOVE in Greek, LIFE and LIVING in Akan, and nuclear deal in Iranian, and show how cultural factors influence the conceptualisations of these categories. In chapter eight, Maria Theodoropoulou offers a study into Greek proverbs of love and romantic love containing *agape* 'love', *agapo* 'to love', and *agapitikia* 'lover'. The purpose of the research is to compare the conceptualisation of these emotions featuring proverbs with that of conventionalised expressions characterising ordinary language following cognitive models (Kövecses 1990). The cognitive devices at play in the proverbs along with their functions and linguistic patterns are also examined. The research reveals that the number of proverbs on romantic love is higher than that of proverbs on love, and figurativity features the former category more than it does for the latter. This is largely because of the importance attributed to this emotion in Greek culture. In addition, it is shown that the two sets of proverbs do not perform similar pragmatic functions.

In the chapter by Yaw Sekyi-Baidoo, the conceptual categories of LIFE and LIVING in Akan proverbs are examined from a cognitive and sociocultural angle. The focus of the research is to examine the LIVING IS MOVEMENT conceptual schema in a number of Akan proverbs, and contribute to the growing interest of Cognitive Linguistics in cultural specificity in meaning making and understanding. Finally, the research concludes that Akan contains some proverbs involving the metaphor LIVING IS MOVEMENT. These proverbs seem to be realisations of metaphors reflecting 'sustenance', 'progress', and 'security' together with views about the role of MOVEMENT in reaching those dimensions. Another conclusion pertains to the contribution of image-schematic structures of space, such as INSI-

DENESS and OUTSIDENESS to an understanding of how, in Akan proverbs, LIFE and LIVING are perceived in terms of MOVEMENT.

In the chapter by Mohsen Bakhtiar, the use of a number of Persian proverbs relating to Iran's nuclear program is examined via the tools of CMT. The aim of the investigation is to demonstrate that proverbs play various roles in political discourse other than their actual conventional role. Further functions are found to be assigned to these proverbs, such as fabricating a new political reality, manipulating the content and courses of action, expressing sarcasm, humiliating the opponents, among others. These communicative functions, in the author's view, can be attained only if a cognitive linguistic study of proverbs as active metaphorical linguistic expressions rather than static elements within discourse is considered along ideological, social, political, and economic perspectives. The researcher makes use of a sample of popular Persian proverbs available at www.daneshchi.ir and searches them on the net to gather instances of usage in natural occurring discourse. This is to categorise them, on the one side, following the themes they convey, and on the other, according to whether their use is in favour of the deal or against it. The findings indicate an unbalanced use of the proverbs, because views opposing the deal are overwhelming compared to those supporting it.

Finally, the focus of the three chapters making up Part IV is the study of proverbs and/or related phenomena from a cognitive and cultural perspective. Precisely, three types of phenomena are dealt with: snowclones, idioms, and proverbial phrases. The three contributions provide information contributing to the clarification of the issue of delineation of proverbs from these expressions. Kim Ebensgaard Jensen's chapter is devoted to the analysis of snowclones from the perspective of construction grammar and cognitive semantics. The researcher explores, within current usage of English, some cognitive linguistic patterns and examines productivity, epistemic status marking, and co-occurrence with co-textual topics involved in constructions of the types '*the only good X is a dead X, one does not simple X into Y,* and *in X no one can hear you Y*'. This is in order to claim that they are potentially endowed with a proverbial nature. The author concludes that though proverbial snowclones happen to share proverb features and functions, they cannot be considered proverbs proper. Additionally, skilful use of proverbial snowclones depends on one's comprehensive cultural knowledge.

The chapter by Judit Baranyiné Kóczy relies on an approach matching Cultural Linguistics (Sharifian 2011, 2017) and Cognitive Linguistics, and examines Hungarian proverbs containing *szakáll* 'beard' and *bajusz* 'moustache'. The scholar has also recourse to other linguistic data (idioms) to sustain her argumentation. The investigation uncovers seven metaphorical or metonymic target domains associated with the two concepts including PERSONALITY, MANLINESS, INDEPENDENCE, PATRIOTISM, AGE, DIGNITY, and WISDOM. The findings of the study additionally verify that the two concepts hold distinct ranks in Hungarian culture; while the concept of MOUSTACHE is viewed positively within its metaphorical usages, the concept of BEARD is looked at from both a positive and a negative viewpoint. In sum, the discrepancy in the positions held by the two concepts results from the influence of cultural models.

In chapter twelve, Anaïs Augé investigates the varied uses and inferences of the proverbial expression *to be in the same boat* featuring international discussions around climate change. The scholar explores the manifestation of the EARTH IS A BOAT metaphor in the form of the proverbial expression and draws the conclusion that the expression plays a rhetorical role in international debates on climate change. In addition, implicit references to war can reveal the historical background characterising the expression. The author also concludes that choice of the source domain BOAT in discourse can be prompted by purposes other than the historical inferences featuring the concept. The study reveals that the proverb *We are in the same storm, but not in the same boat* can appear in a reduced/truncated form and become a proverbial phrase largely used in contemporary worldwide discussions to achieve socio-cultural communicative functions.

All in all, the contributions of the volume deal with the proverb from a cognitive linguistic interdisciplinary perspective, as aforementioned. What unites them is their quest into metaphors and/or metonymies within the proverb and/or related phenomena from a cognitive and cultural stance highlighting the idea that cognition and culture cannot be held separate in explorations of real linguistic manifestations.

6. Conclusions

The chapters making up the volume can be seen as a major step forward, as they rely upon sound theoretical and methodological approaches and well-grounded analytical frameworks that are essential to an ample understanding of the part that Cognitive Linguistics plays in the study of proverbs. The contributions have drawn from varied methodological perspectives and investigative contexts. Of note, current Cognitive Linguistics increasingly relies on large-scale empirical data. In this volume, however, intuition-based studies like in traditional, pre-corpus Cognitive Linguistics (e.g., Chapters 1, 2, 3), and studies based on qualitative analyses of relatively small samples of proverbs (e.g., Chapters 7, 8, 9, 11) outnumber studies based on large (electronic) databases such as corpora and dictionaries or experimental data that typically feature empirical studies framed within the usage-based approach (Chapters 5, 6, 10, 12). It would perhaps be favourable to see more such data-driven or data-based studies in this book.

Nonetheless, this is not necessarily a flaw of the volume, in general. It can thus be hoped that it has allowed highlighting the challenging enterprise of researchers interested in the connection between Cognitive Linguistics and proverbs in their scholarly quests. In addition, the chapters of the book have hosted inspiring ideas for future research into proverbs within Cognitive Linguistics. They have showed that explorations of proverbs provide stimulating prospects for the development of original lines that could significantly unveil how much Cognitive Linguistics is profitable to proverb study.

The contributions to this volume have successfully revealed the purport of a cognitive and cultural linguistic approach to proverb study conveying new insights about proverb understanding and use for communication purposes in concrete contextual situations. They have grounded the description and analysis of proverbs in aspects of cognition, have dealt with proverb semantics from a conceptual stance instead of a syntactic-structural view, and have shown how social-cultural context influences underlying conceptual structures or schemas. Looking back, the work achieved by paremiologists and paremiographers, in pre-cognitivist time, is truly impressive, and serves, to some extent, scholars in their explorations of the proverb. However, the lacks in paremiological research pointed out earlier necessitate a remediation by implementing relevant cognitive linguistic methods to attain satisfactory outcomes in respect to proverb interpretation and use in varied sociocultural contexts. As far as contemporary paremiology is concerned, this area of research can co-exist along with the cognitive-cultural linguistic approaches to proverbs. The two fields of study can progress in parallel to attain a sufficient treatment of proverbs.

With regard to the problem of delineating proverbs from other metaphoricatically-motivated expressions (idioms, snowclones, or proverbial phrases), Cognitive Linguistics appears to be helpful in clarifying this issue. In a cognitive linguistic framework, proverbs are recognisable by their underlying conceptual structure. They can furthermore be analysed with regard to their schematicity hierarchy revealing a set of conceptual metaphors that make possible the connection between their literal meanings with their corresponding metaphorical meanings (Kövecses this volume). In addition, cognitive processes featuring conceptual metonymy and metaphor are acknowledged to be at the origin of the emergence of proverbs as traditional conventional pieces of wisdom bearing a didactic function and having a fixed form. These features of proverbs can be treated from a cognitive linguistic point of view. The traditional aspect characterising the proverb can be enlightened via the SPECIFIC FOR GENERIC conceptual metonymy wherein the specific is relevant for other situations as well. Besides, the didactic function, which is a property of proverbs but not of other expressions, such as idioms, can be explicated in terms of "illocutionary metonymic shifts", understood in terms of performing indirect speech acts that are operated on proverbs. Cognitive Linguistics can also account for how proverb truncation is a phenomenon that may lead to the emergence of idiomatic expressions or proverbial phrases, such as, *to be in the same boat* (Augé this volume), simply by looking at the role of conceptual metonymy within proverbs (Brdar et al. this volume). Cognitive Linguistics, specifically, construction grammar is able to show the distinction between proverbs and snowclones. The property of fixedness featuring proverbs seems absent in snowclones because of their productivity. What is more, the investigation of snowclones from the perspective of construction grammar shows that proverbial snowclones, though they share proverb characteristics, cannot form proverbs proper (Jensen this volume).

All things considered, the present volume is no way comprehensive of research into the proverb within Cognitive Linguistics. Further research is requisite. Even so, it can be hoped that the contributions represented will serve to trigger scholarly thinking and research advance on proverbs within a cognitive linguistic framework, and encourage researchers to take over where this book left and continue to support research in the thought-provoking discipline of Cognitive Linguistics and the no less intriguing aspect of naturally occurring language as the proverb.

References

Belkhir, S. (2012). Variation in source and target domain mappings in English and Kabyle dog proverbs. In S. Kleinke, Z. Kövecses, A. Musolff, & V. Szelid (Eds.), *Cognition and culture – The role of metaphor and metonymy* (pp. 213–227). Budapest: Eötvös University Press, Tàlentum 6.

Belkhir, S. (2014). Cultural influence on the use of DOG concepts in English and Kabyle proverbs. In A. Musolff, F. MacArthur, & G. Pagani (Eds.), *Metaphor and intercultural communication* (pp. 131–145). London: Bloomsbury.

Belkhir, S. (2019). Animal-related concepts across languages and cultures from a cognitive linguistic perspective. *Cognitive Linguistic Studies*, 6(2). 296–325.

Belkhir, S. (2021). Cognitive Linguistics and proverbs. In X. Wen & J. R. Taylor (Eds.), *The Routledge handbook of Cognitive Linguistics* (pp. 599–611). New York & London: Routledge.

Belkhir, S. (2022). Metaphoric proverbs in EFL learners' Translation. *Cognitive Linguistic Studies*, 9(1), 110–127.

Ben Salamh, S., & Maalej, Z. A. (2018). A cultural linguistics perspective on animal proverbs, with special reference to two dialects of Arabic. *Arab World English Journal for Translation & Literary Studies*, 2(4), 21–40.

Briggs, C. L. (1994). The pragmatics of proverb performances in New Mexican Spanish. In W. Mieder (Ed.), *Wise words* (pp. 143–158). London & New York: Routledge.

Dabbagh, A. (2016). Cultural linguistics as an investigative framework for paremiology: comparing *time* in English and Persian. *International Journal of Applied Linguistics*, 27(3), 577–595.

D'Andrade, R. G. (1981). The cultural part of cognition. *Cognitive Science*, 51, 179–195.

David, O., Lakoff, G., & Stickles, E. (2016). Cascades in metaphor and grammar. *Constructions and Frames*, 8(2), 214–255.

Deignan, A. (2005). *Metaphor and corpus linguistics*. Amsterdam & Philadelphia: John Benjamins.

Fillmore, C. (1988). The mechanisms of construction grammar. In S. Axmaker, A. Jassier & H. Singmaster (Eds.), *Proceedings from the Fourteenth Annual Meeting of the Berkeley Linguistics Society* (pp. 35–55). Berkeley, CA: Berkely Linguistics Society.

Flavel, L., & Flavel, R. (2000). *Dictionary of idioms and their origins*. Leicester: Bookmark Limited.

Geeraerts, D., & Cuyckens, H. (Ed.). (2007). *The Oxford handbook of cognitive linguistics*. Oxford: Oxford University Press.

Gibbs, R. W. (1992). What do idioms really mean? *Journal of Memory and Language*, 31, 485–506.

Gibbs, R. W. (2001). Proverbial themes we live by. *Poetics*, 29, 167–188.

Gibbs, R. W. (2005). *Embodiment and cognitive science*. Cambridge: Cambridge University Press.

Gibb, R. W. (Ed.). (2008). *The Cambridge handbook of metaphor and thought*. Cambridge: Cambridge University Press.

Gibbs, R. W., & O'Brien, J. E. (1990). Idioms and mental imagery: The metaphorical motivation for idiomatic meaning. *Cognition*, 36, 35–68.

Gibbs, R. W., and Beitel, D. (1995). What proverb understanding reveals about how people think. *Psychological Bulletin*. 118(1), 133–154.

Gibbs, R. W. Colston, H. L., & Johnson, M. D. (1996). Proverbs and the metaphorical mind, *Metaphor and Symbolic Activity*, 11(3), 207–216.

Gibbs, R. W. Strom, L. K., & Spivey-Knowlton, M. (1997). Conceptual metaphor in mental imagery for proverbs. *Journal of Mental Imagery*, 21, 3/4, 83–110.

Gibbs, R. W., & Beitel, D. (2003). What proverb understanding reveals about how people think. In W. Mieder (Ed.), *Cognition, comprehension, and communication. A decade of North American proverb studies (1990-2000)* (pp. 109–163). Baltmannsweiler: Schneider Verlag Hohengehren.

Grice, H. P. (1975). Logic and conversation. In P. Cole & J. L. Morgan (Eds.), *Syntax and semantics 3: Speech acts* (pp. 41–58). New York: Academic Press.

Grzybek, P. (1994). Foundations of semiotic proverb study. In W. Mieder (Ed.), *Wise words* (pp. 31–72). London & New York: Routledge.

Hernadi, P. & Steen, F. (1999). The Tropical landscapes of proverbia: A crossdisciplinary travelogue, *Style*, 33(1), 1–20.

Holland, D., & Quinn, N. (Eds.) (1987). *Cultural models in language and thought*. Cambridge: Cambridge University Press.

Honeck, R. P., & Kibler, C. T. (1984). The role of imagery, analogy, and instantiation in proverb comprehension. *Journal of Psycholinguistic Research*, 13, 393–414.

Honeck, R. P., & Temple, J. G. (1994). Proverbs: The extended conceptual base and great chain metaphor theories. *Metaphor and Symbolic Activity*, 9(2), 85–112.

Hrisztova-Gotthardt, H., & Varga, M. A. (Eds.). (2014). Introduction to paremiology: A comprehensive guide to proverb studies. Berlin: De Gruyter Open.

Johnson, M. (1987). *The body in the mind: The bodily basis of meaning, imagination, and reason*. Chicago: University of Chicago Press.

Kirshenblatt-Gimblett, B. (1973). Toward a theory of proverb meaning, *Proverbium*, 22, 821–827.

Kövecses, Z. (1990). *Emotion concepts*. New York: Springer/Verlag.

Kövecses, Z. (2002). *Metaphor: A practical introduction*. Oxford: Oxford University Press.

Kövecses, Z. (2005). *Metaphor in culture: Universality and variation*. Cambridge: Cambridge University Press.

Kövecses, Z. (2015). *Where metaphors come from. Reconsidering context in metaphor*. Oxford: Oxford University Press.

Kövecses, Z. (2017). Levels of metaphor. *Cognitive Linguistics*, 28(2), 321–347.

Kövecses, Z. (2018). Metaphor in media language and cognition: A perspective from conceptual metaphor theory. *Lege Artis. Language yesterday, today, tomorrow. The journal of University of SS Cyril and Methodius in Trnava*, 3(1), 124–141.

Kövecses, Z. (2020). *Extended conceptual metaphor theory*. Cambridge: Cambridge University Press.

Kövecses, Z. (2021). Metaphoric conceptual pathways. *Cognitive Semantics*, 7(1), 135–153.

Lakoff, G. (1987). *Women, fire, and dangerous things: What categories reveal about the mind*. Chicago: University of Chicago Press.

Lakoff, G. (1993). The contemporary theory of metaphor. In A. Ortony (Ed.), *Metaphor and thought*. Second edition. (pp. 202–251). Cambridge & New York: Cambridge University Press.

Lakoff, G., & Johnson, M. (1980). *Metaphors we live by*. Chicago: University of Chicago Press.

Lakoff, G., & Johnson, M. (1980 [2003]). *Metaphors we live by*. Chicago: University of Chicago Press.

Lakoff, G., & Kövecses, Z. (1987). The cognitive model of anger inherent in American English. In D. Holland & N. Quinn (Eds.), *Cultural models in language and thought* (pp. 195–221). New York and Cambridge: Cambridge University Press.

Lakoff, G., & Turner, M. (1989). *More than cool reason: A field guide to poetic metaphor*. Chicago: University of Chicago Press.

Langacker, R. W. (1994). Culture, cognition, and grammar. In M. Pütz (Ed.), *Language contact and language conflict* (pp. 25–53). Amsterdam & Philadelphia: John Benjamins.

Lemghari, M. (2019a). A metaphor-based account of semantic relations among proverbs. *Cognitive Linguistic Studies*, 6(1), 158–184.

Lemghari, M. (2019b). A metonymic-based account of the semiotic status of proverbs: Against the "deproverbialization thesis". *Linguistics Journal*, 13(1), 30–51.

Lemghari, M. (2021). Constructing a broad model for proverb understanding. *Metaphor and Symbol*, 36(4), 265–287.

Lewandowska, A., & Antos, D. (2014). Cognitive aspects of proverbs. In H. Hrisztova-Gotthardt, & M. A. Varga. *Introduction to paremiology: A comprehensive guide to proverb studies* (pp. 162–181). Berlin: De Gruyter Open.

Lovejoy, A. O. (1936). *The great chain of being.* Cambridge, MA: Harvard University Press.

Maalej, Z. (2008). The heart and cultural embodiment in Tunisian Arabic. In F. Sharifian, R. Dirven, N. Yu, & S. Niemeier (Eds.), *Culture, body, and language: conceptualizations of internal body organs across cultures and languages* (pp. 395-428). Berlin & New York: Mouton de Gruyter.

Makkai, A. (1995). *A dictionary of American idioms.* Hauppauge, NY: Barron's Educational Series.

Matlin, M. W. (2005). *Cognition.* Hoboken, NJ: John Wiley and Sons.

Mieder, W. (1985). Popular views of the proverb. *Proverbium: Yearbook of International Proverb Scholarship,* 2, 109-143.

Mieder, W. (1997). Modern paremiology in retrospect and prospect. *Paremia,* 6, 399-416

Mieder, W. (2003). "It's not a president's business to catch flies": Proverbial rhetoric in inaugural addresses of American presidents. In W. Mieder (Ed.), *Cognition, comprehension, and communication. A decade of North American proverb studies (1990-2000)* (pp. 325-366). Baltmannsweiler: Schneider Verlag Hohengehren.

Mieder, W. (2004). *Proverbs: A handbook.* Westport Connecticut & London: Greenwood Press.

Mieder, W. (2009). "We must pick ourselves up, dust ourselves off" president Barack Obama's proverbial inaugural address. *Paremia,* 18, 31-42.

Mieder, W. (2014). Origin of proverbs. In H. Hrisztova-Gotthardt, & M.A. Varga (Eds.), *Introduction to paremiology: A comprehensive guide to proverb studies.* Berlin: De Gruyter Open.

Moon, R. (1998). *Fixed Expressions and Idioms in English. A corpus-based approach.* Oxford: Clarendon Press.

Musolff, A. (2006). Metaphor scenarios in public discourse. *Metaphor and Symbol,* 21(1), 23-38.

Norrick, N. R. (1994). Proverbial perlocutions. How to do things with proverbs. In W. Mieder (Ed.), *Wise words* (pp. 143-158). London & New York: Routledge.

Norrick, N. R. (2014). Subject area, terminology, proverb definitions, proverb features. In H. Hrisztova-Gotthardt, & M.A. Varga. *Introduction to paremiology: A comprehensive guide to proverb studies* (pp. 7-25). Berlin: De Gruyter Open.

Palmer, G. B. (1996). *Toward a theory of Cultural Linguistics.* Austin: University of Texas Press.

Semino, E., & Demjén, Z. (Eds.). (2017). *The Routledge handbook of metaphor and language.* London & New York: Routledge.

Sharifian, F. (2011). *Cultural conceptualisations and language: Theoretical framework and applications.* Amsterdam & Philadelphia: John Benjamins.

Sharifian, F. (Ed.) (2015). *The Routledge handbook of language and culture.* Milton Park: Routledge.

Sharifian, F. (2017). *Cultural linguistics.* Amsterdam & Philadelphia: John Benjamins.

Sinha, C. (2021). Culture in language and cognition. In X. Wen & J.R. Taylor (Eds.), *The Routledge handbook of Cognitive Linguistics* (pp. 387-407). New York & London: Routledge.

Steen, G. J. (2007). *Finding metaphor in grammar and usage.* Amsterdam & Philadelphia: John Benjamins.

Taylor, A. (1931). *The proverb*. Cambridge: Harvard University Press.

Taylor, A. (1934). Problems in the study of proverbs. *The Journal of American Folklore*, 47(183), 1–21.

Taylor, J. R. (2012). *The mental corpus: How language is represented in the mind*. Oxford: Oxford University Press.

Taylor, J. R., & Littlemore, J. (Eds.). (2014). *The Bloomsbury companion to cognitive linguistics*. London & New York: Bloomsbury.

T. Litovkina, A., & Csábi, S. (2002). Metaphors we love by: The cognitive models of romantic love in American proverbs. *Proverbium: Yearbook of International Proverb Scholarship*, 19, 369–398.

T. Litovkina, A., Hrisztova-Gotthardt, H., Barta, P., Vargha, K., & Mieder, W. (2021). Anti-proverbs in five languages. Structural features and verbal humor devices. Cham, Switzerland: Palgrave Macmillan.

Trench, R. C. (1853 [2003]). *Proverbs and their lessons*. London: Parker. Ed. by W. Mieder. Burlington: University of Vermont.

Wen, X., & Taylor, J. R. (Eds.). (2021). *The Routledge handbook of cognitive linguistics*. London & New York: Routledge.

Yankah, K. (1989). The Proverb in the context of Akan rhetoric: A theory of proverb Praxis. Bern: Peter Lang.

Yu, N. (2009). *The Chinese Heart in a cognitive perspective: Culture, body and language*. Berlin: Walter de Gruyter.

Yu, N. (2015). Embodiment, culture and language. In Sharifian, F. (Ed.). *The Routledge handbook of language and culture*. New York: Routledge.

Yu, N. (2017). Life as opera: A cultural metaphor in Chinese. In F. Sharifian (Ed.), *Advances in Cultural Linguistics* (pp. 65–87). Singapore: Springer.

PART I

Theoretical discussions of proverbs in cognition and culture

CHAPTER 1

Proverbs in Extended Conceptual Metaphor Theory

Zoltán Kövecses
Eötvös Loránd University, Budapest, Hungary

In the chapter, I provide an account of metaphorical proverbs within the new framework of extended conceptual metaphor theory, or ECMT, for short (Kövecses 2020). I rely especially on the multilevel and contextualist aspects of this view. I argue that ECMT can account for why many proverbs are widespread in the world's languages; why, at the same time, many proverbs can also exhibit cultural differences; and why proverbs can have very specific meanings in particular discourse situations. Finally, I show that context plays a very different role in metaphorical proverbs than in non-proverbial uses of metaphor.

Keywords: conceptual metaphor, extended conceptual metaphor theory, schematicity hierarchy, context in proverbs, correlation vs. resemblance in proverbs

1. Proverbs in Cognitive Linguistics

Major work on proverbs in a cognitive linguistic framework has been done by George Lakoff, Mark Turner, and Ray Gibbs. In their book, *More than Cool Reason*, Lakoff and Turner (1989) postulate a broad, general metaphor, GENERIC IS SPECIFIC, to account for the understanding of many proverbs. On their account, a proverb, like *The early bird catches the worm*, has some generic structure that is applicable to a large number of situations beyond the one described by the proverb. The generic structure is something like 'If you do something first, you will get what you want before others get it'. For example, if you stand in line early enough to get a ticket to a popular show on Broadway, you will succeed in getting a ticket.

We can represent this example as follows:

https://doi.org/10.1075/clscc.16.01kov
© 2024 John Benjamins Publishing Company

Chapter 1. Proverbs in Extended Conceptual Metaphor Theory

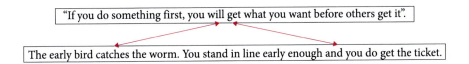

More generally, what we have here is some schematic structure, a specific instance of the schematic structure, that is, the situation that the proverb describes, and another specific instance of the same schematic structure, that is, the situation to which the proverb applies. In diagrammatic form:

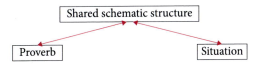

Figure 1. Proverbs based on shared schematicity structure

On the Lakoff-Turner view, the shared schematic structure would correspond to the target domain and the proverb to the much more specific and concrete source domain. This target could then apply to any number of source situations that share the schematic structure:

Figure 2. The GENERIC IS SPECIFIC ACCOUNT of proverbs

However, Figure 1. can also be interpreted as a resemblance-based metaphor (see Grady 1999) where the contextually relevant situation would become the target domain, the proverbial situation the source, and the shared schematic structure would be the structural similarity that brings the two situations into correspondence:

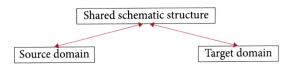

Figure 3. The structure of resemblance metaphors

The question would then be whether the solution represented in Figure 3. could still be considered a metaphor, let alone a *conceptual* metaphor. After all, the two situations here are both concrete ones, which would allow for a nonmetaphorical interpretation based on literal similarity.

The latter view would be in line with Honeck and Temple's (1994) "Conceptual Base Theory", where what is called here "shared schematic structure" would correspond to what Honeck and his colleagues call "conceptual base". The conceptual base is some abstract, schematic structure that emerges from the literal meaning of a proverb and that is applicable to a new situation. On the Honeck-Temple view, the interpretation of proverbs depends on these core ideas.

By contrast, Gibbs et al. (1997) suggest that proverbs like *The early bird catches the worm* are actually motivated by conventional conceptual metaphors that exist independently of the literal meaning of the proverb. According to Gibbs et al. (1997), there are two conceptual metaphors here that play a role in the interpretation of the proverb; LIFE IS A STRUGGLE AGAINST AN OPPONENT and ACHIEVED PURPOSES ARE ATTAINED POSSESSIONS. These two conceptual metaphors further specify and constrain the interpretation of the proverb, as based on the GENERIC IS SPECIFIC metaphor. (Cieslicka 2002, provides a good comparison of Gibbs' and Honeck's views on proverbs.)

Let me now turn to a brief introduction to Extended Conceptual Metaphor Theory and see how this view of metaphor would handle metaphorical proverbs. The aspects of ECMT that I utilise for this purpose are (1) that it is a multilevel view of metaphor and (2) that the notion of context plays a major role in the theory.

2. The multilevel view

The original Lakoff-Johnson view saw metaphor on the domain level. Later discussions of metaphor often used frames as the conceptual structures involved in metaphor. In blending theory, Fauconnier and Turner (2002) predominantly talk about mental spaces in relation to metaphorical blends. Lakoff (1993), David, Lakoff, and Stickles (2016), and Dancygier and Sweetser (2014) take into account two or three hierarchically interrelated layers of conceptual metaphors according to the various levels of the schematicity of metaphors. Kövecses (2017, 2020) proposes a four-level view, where a conceptual metaphor is constituted of a schematicity hierarchy composed of image schema-, domain-, frame-, and mental space-level metaphors.

Conceptual metaphors and the conceptual structures that they involve are discussed under many different names in Cognitive Linguistics. Lakoff and Johnson preferred to use *domain* (as in the definition of conceptual metaphors; i.e., "one domain understood in terms of another domain"), but they also talked about *experiential gestalts* in their early work (Lakoff and Johnson 1980). Lakoff (1996) mostly refers to conceptual metaphors as a relationship between two *frames*. Lakoff and Kövecses (1987) use the term *cognitive model*, and many cultural anthropologists called the same conceptual structure *cultural model* (Holland and Quinn 1987). The term *schema* also became popular in the wake of Lakoff and Turner's (1989) work, together of course with *image schema* that originated in Johnson's (1987) book. More discourse-oriented recent work (e.g., Musolff 2006) found the term *scenario*, or *scene*, as more appropriate in describing metaphor-related phenomena in discourse. In addition, researchers in conceptual integration theory adopted such further designations to the conceptual structures involved in conceptual metaphors as *space, mental space* or, even simply, *input (space)*. And, the list could no doubt be continued.

What unifies all the terms that became available in the CMT literature was a simple but powerful idea: we experience aspects of the world in terms of coherent mental organisations of our experience. Domain, frame, schema, model, scenario, space, and so on, all capture the gestalt character of how we experience the world. Conceptual metaphor as a way of experiencing the world can involve any one of these constructs.

It was recognised early on that conceptual metaphors could be stated at various levels of generality. (On this, see, e.g., Clausner and Croft 1997). For example, Lakoff and Johnson (1980) observed that the TIME IS MONEY metaphor can also be given as TIME IS A RESOURCE, and this way more general metaphorical expressions, such as *use* time or *give* time, can be accommodated within the same metaphor. The RESOURCE metaphor is more general or schematic than the MONEY metaphor. The question is whether concepts like RESOURCE and MONEY constitute domains or frames, or whether one is a domain and the other is a frame.

What was initially less clear in connection with such gestalt-like conceptual structures used in metaphor was that the various conceptual structures (designated by the mnemonics A IS B, such as LOVE IS A JOURNEY) tend to occupy different levels on a scale of specificity-schematicity. In his 1993 paper, Lakoff distinguished a number of conceptual metaphors in a hierarchy of three tiers:

The Event Structure metaphor

LIFE IS A JOURNEY
LOVE IS A JOURNEY

He states that they are different in their degree of schematicity; that is, life events are special cases of events in general, and the events in a love relationship are subcases of life events. Lower level metaphors inherit higher level metaphorical structures.

Dancygier and Sweetser (2014: 43–49) adds to this that at the level of the Event Structure metaphor we are dealing with image schema frames (as they refer to more complex image schemas) that can be elaborated by frames at lower levels. For instance, the JOURNEY frame is a rich subframe of the image-schematic frame DIRECTED MOTION ON A PATH (composed of the basic image schemas of MOTION, PATH, and LOCATION). The frame of JOURNEY can then be used to structure various domains, including life, relationships, careers, projects, etc. – almost any long-term activity. What this means is not only that the particular conceptual metaphors themselves can form "schematicity hierarchies," but also that the conceptual structures that constitute these conceptual metaphors form such hierarchies:

Image schema structures (most schematic)
Domain structures (less schematic)
Frame structures (less schematic)

We can call all of them frames or domains (in that they all represent coherent organisations of experience), but when we see these conceptual structures (and the corresponding metaphors) as being relatively more or less schematic, the structures on top (i.e., the most schematic ones) will always be image schemas, with domains below them, and with frames below domains. (On the issue of distinguishing these conceptual structures, see Kövecses 2017.)

In this recent work (Kövecses 2017), I made it clear that my view of schematicity hierarchies differs from the standard view (see Lakoff 1993; David et al. 2016) in two ways. The first is that in my conception the least schematic conceptual structure in a hierarchy is not a frame but a *mental space*. (Dancygier and Sweetser 2014, share this view.) Mental spaces elaborate on frames, making them as specific as required by the given discourse situation. In other words, I suggest a four-level hierarchy (in addition to the level of linguistic expression):

Image schema structures (most schematic)
Domain structures (less schematic)
Frame structures (less schematic)
Mental space structures (least schematic)
(Linguistic expression)

Mental spaces usually foreground a single metaphorical mapping between two frames, but this mapping, which expresses the contextual meaning at a given point in discourse, evokes the entire hierarchy "above" it. This way, it can be shown that the functioning of schematicity hierarchies is not limited to conceptual structures in long-term memory (such as image schemas, domains, and frames), but is closely linked to how these structures are mobilised in working memory.

The second way my treatment of schematicity hierarchies is different from the standard view is that I see each hierarchy that emerges in particular discourse situations as functioning within a rich context. Various aspects of the contexts (i.e., the contextual factors; on which, see next section) can have an influence on which conceptual metaphor (and the hierarchy that goes with it) is utilised to conceptualise the situation. The same factors can also be crucial in the (unconscious) choice of the linguistic metaphors that can best express the conceptual metaphor in the situation of discourse.

3. Proverbs in the multilevel view

Imagine a situation in which your son walks up to you and says that he would like to marry a particular girl. Imagine, further, that you think that the girl would not be a very good choice for your son for some reason. In this situation, it would be perfectly appropriate for you to use the proverb: *Look before you leap.*

In their 1997 paper, Gibbs et al. suggest that this proverb is based on two conceptual metaphors: KNOWING IS SEEING and LIFE IS A JOURNEY, where the LIFE IS A JOURNEY metaphor is related to the 'leaping' part of the proverb and KNOWING IS SEEING to the 'looking' part. In other words, the verbs 'look' and 'leap' in the proverb are linguistics examples of the two well-established conceptual metaphors ('look' instantiates KNOWING IS SEEING and 'leap' instantiates LIFE IS A JOURNEY), and these conceptual metaphors considerably constrain and facilitate the understanding of the proverb in the given situation.

Extended CMT (as elaborated by Kövecses 2020) would add to this that the conceptual metaphors involved in the proverb are constituent metaphors of two "schematicity hierarchies" that the metaphorically used verbs evoke. Let us start with 'leap'. 'Leap' is conceptually connected to and evokes the image schema of MOTION, which is the source domain of the independently existing generic metaphor ACTION IS (SELF-PROPELLED) MOTION. Self-propelled motion can take a variety of forms, one of them being TRAVEL. TRAVEL is the source domain of a major conceptual metaphor for life: LIFE IS TRAVEL.[1] Travel is a large category that consists of various elements – both static institutions and dynamic actions. The most characteristic dynamic element of travel is JOURNEYING. This element shows up in conceptual metaphor LEADING A LIFE IS JOURNEYING (or LIFE IS JOURNEY,

---

1. I use LIFE IS TRAVEL here, instead of the more commonly used LIFE IS A JOURNEY, for the reasons given below.

for short, as Gibbs et al. (1997) put it). Finally, it is clear in the given use of the proverb that a particular aspect of life is discussed (marrying the right person), not life in general. In other words, we have a very specific conceptual metaphor at work in this situation; namely, that GETTING MARRIED IN A QUICK AND HASTY WAY IS LEAPING TO A PLACE THAT MAY NOT BE SAFE. This can be regarded as the metaphorical meaning of the 'leaping' part of the proverb *Look before you leap* in the circumstances.

However, how can this meaning possibly arise? After all, the LEADING A LIFE IS JOURNEYING metaphor does not have as one of its instances the verb 'leap'; this simply not being the way we usually travel. Yet, it does occur in the proverb! Leaping is a quick action whereby one jumps free from the ground and moves through the air from one location to another. The quick movement can be dangerous if one does not know where one leaps (i.e., the destination). This element of meaning justifies the use of the verb in the proverb. To see this, let us take the conventional mappings of the LEADING A LIFE IS JOURNEYING frame-level metaphor:

the traveller → the person leading a life
the travel motion → an action in life
the initial location → a stage where you are in life
the destination → the desired stage in life
reaching the destination → achieving the desired stage in life

The verb 'leap' in the proverb is related to the travel motion, that is, the action you plan to do (the second mapping from the top). When the action is quick and hasty, the corresponding metaphorical travel motion will be quick and hasty (since the person may not know where he leaps), resulting in a submapping of 'the travel motion → an action in life': 'quick and hasty (travel) motion → quick and hasty action in life'.

In other words, as regards the verb 'leap' the proverb is based on a submapping of a more general conventional mapping of the LEADING A LIFE IS JOURNEYING metaphor. The submapping "quick and hasty (travel) motion (i.e., leaping) → quick and hasty action in life" constitutes the conceptual content of the mental space of the person who uses the proverb in the discourse situation at hand. Thus, we have a hierarchy of conceptual metaphors that the verb 'leap' evokes:

ACTION IS MOTION
LIFE IS TRAVEL
LEADING A LIFE IS JOURNEYING
GETTING MARRIED IN A QUICK AND HASTY WAY IS LEAPING TO A PLACE THAT MAY NOT BE SAFE

This set of conceptual metaphors is called a "schematicity hierarchy" (see Kövecses 2020). Such schematicity hierarchies function as "conceptual pathways" (see Kövecses 2020, 2021), i.e., as ways of conceptually connecting a particular literal meaning (like that of 'leap') with a particular metaphorical meaning (like 'in a quick and hasty way'). The 'leaping' part of the proverb's meaning emerges from being able to connect conceptually the literal meaning of 'leap' with the metaphorical meaning of 'leap' in the proverb by means of a hierarchical structure that involves schematically related conceptual metaphors on four distinct levels of organisation: the image schema level, domain level, frame level, and mental space level.

What about the 'look' part of the proverb? We can analyse the verb 'look' in much the same way as we did 'leap'. However, the schematicity hierarchy, and the metaphorical conceptual pathway that is connected with it, will inevitably be different. The highest-level conceptual metaphor for 'look' will be COGNITION IS PERCEPTION (see Ibarretxe-Antuñano 2013). This generic-level metaphor links cognition with perception. Cognition is not imaginable without perception in the case of natural systems, such as human beings. However, of course, animals also have both cognition and perception. For this reason, the two domains to which COGNITION IS PERCEPTION applies and brings into a metaphorical relationship are HUMAN THOUGHT (MIND) and the HUMAN BODY. Human thought involves a large number of mental activities, such as knowing, understanding, considering, and suspecting. As is well known from the CMT literature, these mental actions are commonly conceptualised metaphorically by means of conceptual metaphors like KNOWING / UNDERSTANDING IS SEEING, CONSIDERING IS LOOKING, and SUSPECTING IS SMELLING. Thus, the domain-level metaphor here is THE (HUMAN) MIND IS THE BODY (see Johnson 1987; Sweetser 1990), and the frame-level metaphor that is relevant to the proverb "Look before you leap" is CONSIDERING IS LOOKING. In the situation under discussion, the object of consideration is getting married without paying attention to, or being aware of, (potentially unwelcome) consequences that is metaphorically conveyed as looking ahead (which assumes the FUTURE IS AHEAD metaphor). Thus, we have the very specific mental space-level metaphor: GETTING MARRIED WITHOUT CONSIDERING (THE POTENTIALLY UNWELCOME) CONSEQUENCES IS LEAPING WITHOUT LOOKING AHEAD (WHERE YOU LEAP).

The conceptual metaphors discussed above each form a part of the following schematicity hierarchy:

COGNITION IS PERCEPTION
THE HUMAN MIND IS THE BODY
CONSIDERING IS LOOKING

GETTING MARRIED WITHOUT CONSIDERING (THE POTENTIALLY UNWELCOME) CONSEQUENCES IS LEAPING WITHOUT LOOKING AHEAD (WHERE YOU LEAP)

In other words, the two schematicity hierarchies I have discussed above merge an action hierarchy (the one for 'leap') with a cognition (or thought) hierarchy (the one for 'look'), where the object of the looking-considering is the leaping-action (of getting married).

Nevertheless, obviously, the proverb does not only work at the metaphorical conceptual level; it also works on a socio-pragmatic level. Specifically, it functions as an *admonishment* that urges a person to consider the potentially unwelcome consequences of his actions. Moreover, very importantly, it urges the person to perform the mental action (of considering) *first* and the real-world action (of getting married) *second*. This is explicitly indicated by the conjunction 'before'.

4. The contextualist view of metaphor in extended CMT

Conceptual metaphor theory has been primarily formulated as a cognitive theory – lacking a contextual component. In *Where Metaphors Come From* (Kövecses 2015), using examples from naturally occurring discourse, I presented a large amount of evidence to show that the use of metaphors in discourse is influenced by a variety of contextual factors. These contextual factors can be grouped into four large categories: situational context, discourse context, conceptual-cognitive context, and bodily context.

4.1 Situational context

The situational context comprises a variety of different contextual factors. Most commonly, this type of context can be thought of as including the physical environment, the social situation, and the cultural situation. To take one example, the *cultural situation* involves both the global context (the shared knowledge represented in the conceptual system) and the local context (the specific knowledge in a given communicative situation). For example, we have ANGER IS HEAT (OF FLUID OR SOLID) in a large number of languages such as English and Hungarian, whereas in Chinese the metaphor can also involve GAS as its source domain – because of the influence of Yin and Yang theory (see Yu 1998).

4.2 Discourse context

The discourse context involves the surrounding discourse, knowledge about the main elements of discourse, the previous discourses on the same topic, and the dominant forms of discourse related to a particular subject matter. We can illustrate this with the contextual factor of how conceptualisers often rely on their *knowledge concerning the main elements of a discourse* in the course of an act of metaphorical conceptualisation: the speaker, hearer, and the topic. For instance, in an article about former soccer star David Beckham a journalist remarked, "*Los Angeles Galaxy are sardines not sharks in the ocean of footy*" (Kövecses 2010). Here the relevant contextual knowledge includes that Beckham played for the Los Angeles Galaxy soccer team and that Los Angeles is located on the ocean with all kinds of fish in it.

4.3 Conceptual-cognitive context

This type of context includes the metaphorical conceptual system at large, ideology, knowledge about past events, and the characteristic interests and concerns of a community or individual. Concepts can stand in a metaphorical relationship with one another (e.g., LIFE IS A JOURNEY, ARGUMENT IS WAR) in long-term memory. Given such metaphorical relationships between concepts (such as between, say, ARGUMENT and WAR), their presence or absence in the *metaphorical conceptual system* may lead to the production and comprehension of particular metaphors. *Ideology* can also be a formative factor in how metaphors are used in discourse. One's ideological stance concerning major social and political issues may govern the choice of metaphors (as work by, for instance, Lakoff 1996 and Goatly 1997, shows).

4.4 Bodily context

A particular state of the body can produce particular metaphorical conceptualisations in specific cases, such as a poet's or writer's illness. Such cases illustrate, more broadly, that people's bodily specificities influence which metaphors they tend to use. There is experimental evidence (Casasanto 2009) that left-handers prefer to use the GOOD IS LEFT, as opposed to the BAD IS RIGHT, conceptual metaphor. Such metaphors contrast with the metaphors that evolve because of universal properties of the human body (i.e., the correlation-based primary metaphors; see Grady 1997). In other words, the body can lead to the production of metaphors in discourse in the same way as the other contextual factors previously mentioned can. Given this, we can think of the body as an additional context type.

In general, we can suggest that contextual influence is strongest and immediate at the mental spaces level in particular local discourse situations. In the case of frame and domain level metaphors, contextual influence is not direct and immediate. These metaphors (conceptual structures) appear to be stable in given speech communities and change over longer periods because of historical changes in context. (On this, see, e.g., Trim's work on the evolution of several conceptual metaphors in European languages and cultures (Trim 2007, 2011)). At the image schema level, the metaphors tend to be universal and they emerge unnoticeably in the course of ontogeny and phylogeny.

5. Metaphorical proverbs and context

What is the role of context in using metaphorical proverbs? Interestingly, the role of context in the use of metaphorical proverbs is very different from that in the use of non-proverbial metaphors. As the brief description in the previous section above makes it clear, the use of non-proverbial metaphors depends heavily on contextual factors subsumed under *all* four large context types. Non-proverbial metaphors emerge in specific communicative situations on the level of mental spaces. Given a target domain (and a particular target domain meaning), contextual factors of various sorts will prompt the speaker to use a given linguistic and conceptual metaphor. This applies also to cases where speakers rely on well-entrenched linguistic and conceptual metaphors in their mental lexicon and their default conventional metaphor system that forms part of what I refer to above as the conceptual-cognitive context.

However, in the case of proverbs, the situation is remarkably different. When we use proverbs, we do not have a choice regarding which proverbial metaphor (linguistic and conceptual) we can employ in the situation, *except for the choice prompted by the topic of discourse*. As we saw above, the topic of discourse is a major element of discourse and a contextual factor subsumed under what was called discourse context. This contextual factor is the only one that has influence on the choice of a proverb. In other words, the topic of discourse can influence *both* the choice of a *metaphorical proverb* and the choice of *non-proverbial metaphors* in discourse.

When we want to admonish someone to consider the consequences of a potentially damaging action before they actually perform it, we do not have much choice other than using the proverb *Look before you leap*. The fact that we use the metaphorical expressions 'look' and 'leap' and the source domains of LOOKING and LEAPING (JOURNEYING) is not a matter of choice and no contextual factors can influence it. What does influence the choice, however, is the target domain meaning, the topic of discourse (CONSIDERING THE CONSEQUENCES in the course of LEADING ONE'S LIFE). A given target domain meaning plays the crucial role in the selection of the proverb and, hence, the proverbial metaphors that come with it automatically and ready-made. These conceptual and linguistic metaphors are *not* prompted by the topic of discourse; they are a *consequence* of the choice of a proverb, which results from the topic of discourse.

Maybe this is a trivial distinction to draw concerning the role of context in the production of metaphorical proverbs and non-proverbial uses of metaphors. I only mention it to show that the 'ready-made character' of metaphorical proverbs is (almost) diametrically opposed to the flexibility and freedom resulting from the variability of context in the use of non-proverbial metaphors.

6. Conclusions

In the paper, I showed how a set of proverbs could be analysed within a new framework of conceptual metaphor theory – extended CMT. The new framework applies to those metaphorical proverbs that rely on correlation-based metaphors, such as *Look before you leap*, where we find such basic, primary metaphors as COGNITION IS PERCEPTION and ACTION IS MOTION at a very high level of schematicity. Given this grounding, the schematicity hierarchies will be highly motivated all the way down the hierarchy and they make the proverbs utilising them equally well motivated in a community of speakers. Many other proverbs could be analysed this way. Actually, the proverb *The early bird catches the worm*, also discussed in the introduction, is another instance of the same multilevel structure (but utilising a different basic correlation metaphor: ACHIEVED PURPOSES ARE ATTAINED POSSESSIONS).

A major advantage of the multilevel view of proverbs is that many proverbs can be accounted for from various perspectives, such as their embodied character, social-cultural embeddedness, and their situational meaning. First, the highly schematic primary metaphors provide experiential grounding for the proverbs and can explain their often universal, or widespread, status in the world's languages. Second, the domain- and frame-level metaphors underlying proverbs involve less schematic concepts that are combined into particular conceptual metaphors in a given culture and society. Third, the very specific mental-space level metaphors reveal a large portion of the conceptual content of the proverbs in a given discourse situation.

However, we should bear in mind that correlation-based metaphors are just one major type of metaphor; many other metaphors are based on shared schematic structures. The latter are resemblance metaphors. These can also form the basis of many metaphorical proverbs. I have not discussed proverbs of this kind in the paper.

As regards the issue of context, I pointed out that context plays a very different role in metaphorical proverbs than in non-proverbial uses of metaphor. While in the case of non-proverbial uses of metaphor context supplies the metaphorical source domains and the corresponding linguistic metaphors, the topic of discourse evokes the metaphorical proverbs that come with independently existing conceptual metaphors and the corresponding metaphorical expressions. In other words, this specific aspect of context (the topic of discourse) influences the choice of metaphorical proverbs. The rest of the contextual factors that characterise non-proverbial uses of metaphors do not seem to play any role in the process.

References

Casasanto, D. (2009). Embodiment of abstract concepts: Good and bad in right- and left-handers. *Journal of Experimental Psychology: General*, 138(3), 351–367.

Cieslicka, A. (2002). Comprehension and interpretation of proverbs in L2. *Studia Anglica Poznaniensia*, 37, 173–200.

Clausner, T., & Croft, W. (1997). Productivity and schematicity in metaphors. *Cognitive Science*, 21(3), 247–282.

Dancygier, B., & Sweetser, E. (2014). *Figurative language*. Cambridge & New York: Cambridge University Press.

David, O., Lakoff, G., & Stickles, E. (2016). Cascades in metaphor and grammar. *Constructions and Frames*, 8(2), 214–255.

Fauconnier, G., & Turner, M. (2002). *The way we think*. New York: Basic Books.

Gibbs, R. W., L. K. Strom, & M. Spivey-Knowlton. (1997). Conceptual metaphor in mental imagery for proverbs. *Journal of Mental Imagery*, 21, 3/4, 83–110.

Goatly, A. (1997). *The language of metaphors*. London: Routledge.

Grady, J. E. (1997). *Foundations of meaning: Primary metaphors and primary scenes*. Ph.D. diss., University of California at Berkeley.

Grady, J. E. (1999). A typology of motivation for conceptual metaphor. In R. Gibbs, & G. Steen, (Eds.), *Metaphor in cognitive linguistics* (pp. 79–100). Amsterdam & Philadelphia: John Benjamins.

Holland, D. & Quinn, N., (Eds.) (1987). *Cultural models in language and thought*. Cambridge: Cambridge University Press.

Honeck, R. & Temple, J. G. (1994). Proverbs: The extended conceptual base and great chain metaphor theories. *Metaphor and Symbolic Activity*, 9(2), 85–112.

Ibarretxe-Antuñano, I. (2013). The power of the senses and the role of culture in metaphor and language. In R. Caballero, & J. Diaz-Vera (Eds.), *Sensuous cognition: Explorations into human sentience – imagination, (e)motion and perception* (pp. 109–133). Berlin: Mouton de Gruyter.

Johnson, M. (1987). *The body in the mind*. Chicago: University of Chicago Press.

Kövecses, Z. (2010). A new look at metaphorical creativity in cognitive linguistics. *Cognitive Linguistics*, 21(4), 663–697.

Kövecses, Z. (2015). *Where metaphors come from. Reconsidering the role of context in metaphor*. New York & Oxford: Oxford University Press.

Kövecses, Z. (2017). Levels of metaphor. *Cognitive Linguistics*, 28(2), 321–347.

Kövecses, Z. (2020). *Extendedconceptual metaphor theory*. Cambridge: Cambridge University Press.

Kövecses, Z. (2021). Metaphoric conceptual pathways. *Cognitive Semantics*, 7(1), 135–153.

Lakoff, G. (1993). The contemporary theory of metaphor. In A. Ortony (Ed.), *Metaphor and thought*. Second edition. (pp. 202-251). Cambridge & New York: Cambridge University Press.

Lakoff, G. (1996). *Moral politics*. Chicago: University of Chicago Press.

Lakoff, G. & Johnson, M. (1980). *Metaphors we live by*. Chicago: The University of Chicago Press.

Lakoff, G., & Kövecses, Z. (1987). The cognitive model of anger inherent in American English. In D. Holland & N. Quinn (Eds.) *Cultural models in language and thought*. (pp. 195–221). Cambridge & New York: Cambridge University Press.

Lakoff, G., & Turner, M. (1989). *More than cool reason: A field guide to poetic metaphor*. Chicago: University of Chicago Press.

Musolff, A. (2006). Metaphor scenarios in public discourse. *Metaphor and Symbol*, 21(1), 23–38.

Sweetser, E. (1990). *From etymology to pragmatics*. Cambridge: Cambridge University Press.

Trim, R. (2007). *Metaphor networks. The comparative evolution of figurative language*. Houndmills, Basingstoke: Palgrave Macmillan.

Trim, R. (2011). *Metaphor and the historical evolution of conceptual mapping*. Houndmills, Basingstoke: Palgrave Macmillan.

Yu, N. (1998). *The contemporary theory of metaphor. A perspective from Chinese*. Amsterdam & Philadelphia: John Benjamins.

CHAPTER 2

Metonymic layers in proverbs
A cross-linguistic and cross-cultural view

Mario Brdar, Rita Brdar-Szabó & Daler Zayniev
University of Osijek, Croatia | ELTE, Budapest, Hungary

Metonymy can be manifest at several levels in proverbs. In this chapter, we identify five such metonymic layers. We first examine whole proverbs as instances of the SPECIFIC-FOR-GENERIC metonymy. Secondly, proverbs can be seen as indirect speech acts in which an element of a speech act scenario can stand metonymically for the whole of the associated illocutionary category. Proverbs can also appear in reduced form, and the part that is retained is capable of metonymically evoking the whole. A phrase within a proverb can occasionally be interpreted as an instance of the metonymy PARTICIPANT FOR EVENT. Finally, a part of a proverb can receive a non-event metonymic interpretation that may even happen systematically, as in the case of weather proverbs.

Keywords: metonymy, generic-specific mapping, illocutionary metonymy, indirect speech act, usage-based model, truncated proverb, topic-comment

1. Introduction

The fact that proverbs are ubiquitous in all cultures and linguistic communities is due to their use in discourse, where they have several important functions, but also to how they come into being in the course of assuming these functions. We could in fact say that they are the outcome of the constant process of the crystallisation or sedimentation of human experiences gained in the interaction with their physical and social environment as well as of the dynamic processes of their adaptation in use.

It is our contention that what makes possible this crystallisation or sedimentation of folk wisdom; i.e., generalisation, as well as their adaptation, often leading to flexible and creative use, are basic cognitive operations of conceptual metonymy and conceptual metaphor, the former possibly playing an even more important part than the latter. Cognitive linguistic approaches to proverbs have often stressed the role of conceptual metaphor, e.g., Gibbs and Beitel (1995), Litovkina and Csábi (2002), Lewandowska and Antos (2001), Nuessel (2003), Szpila (2005), Buljan and Gradečak-Erdeljić (2013), Belkhir (2014 and 2021), or Lemghari (2019a). Lewandowska and Antos (2015:167) stress the role of proverb concepts that they see as being parallel to conceptual metaphors, both sharing "a similar or even identical cognitive structure" based on pre-conceptual imagery. What is more, "both metaphor and proverb have a similar function in *bridging* new concepts with known ones: They are linguistically stereotyped models for a standardizing organization of new concepts (situational or other)" (Lewandowska and Antos 2015:168). Incidentally, as Grzybek (1998:133) points out, Aristotle's *Rhetoric* already refers to proverbs as metaphors, even if it is not explicitly said that metaphoricity is an obligatory feature of proverbs, or only optional (though common).

In this chapter, we are concerned with the role conceptual metonymy plays in proverbs. It has been discussed in a number of articles; e.g., in Krikmann (1984, 1998), Buljan and Gradečak-Erdeljić (2013) Molnar and Vidaković Erdeljić (2016), or Lemghari (2019b). We show, however, that it is systematically present in proverbs and contributes to their meaning at several levels across languages and cultures.

The chapter is organised as follows. We first contextualise proverbs by identifying their structural and functional-pragmatic aspects in Section 2. Section 3 is a brief overview of the state-of the-art of cognitive linguistic research into metonymy. This cognitive operation, as we show below, can be manifest at several levels in proverbs, from the most general one, at the level of the whole proverb, to very specific metonymies at lower levels, where it operates on smaller segments. In this chapter, we identify five such metonymic layers. Consequently, in Section 4, we discuss these five layers one by one, basing our analysis on examples from a variety of languages, but focussing on English, German, Croatian, Russian, Hungarian, Uzbek, and Tajik. Our conclusions are summed up in Section 5.

2. Defining proverbs: Structural and functional-pragmatic aspects

Surprisingly, in spite of the fact that proverbs are a frequent phenomenon in language that speakers recognise relatively easily, a universally accepted inclusive definition of proverb is practically impossible to find, as pointed out by Norrick (2015:14). Rather, it is a fuzzy phenomenon, exhibiting Wittgensteinian family resemblance. A proverb may exhibit a number of properties typically found with many other tokens of the category, but not necessarily all of them (Norrick 2007:382). This idea is also reflected in Arora's notion of proverbiality, denoting proverbial style constituted by frequently occurring poetic and structural features. The results of Mieder's (1985) survey of 55 definitions of proverbs indicate that they "are thought to express human wisdom and basic truths in a short sentence". A working definition by Norrick concatenates five such properties: "Proverbs have repeatedly been characterized as self-contained, traditional units with didactic content and fixed, poetic form, whereby all these characterizations have been cast in varying terminologies with various nuances and connotations" (2015: 8).

It is easy to see that these properties are all interconnected in more than one way, but we will try to disentangle them as much as possible. We may as well start with the second property above. Proverbs can be seen as traditional units in the original etymological sense of the word *tradition*, 'statement, belief, or practice handed down from generation to generation', ultimately derived from the Latin verb *tradere* 'deliver, hand over'. This is something that is very easy to handle within Cognitive Linguistics with the help of the usage-based model, as explained in more detail in 4.1.1 below. The basic idea is that proverbs, like any other construction, originate from concrete utterances produced by concrete people in concrete situation tied to concrete time points, as for example, the proverb *Time is money* (that also happens to express a conceptual metaphor), originally published in 1748 as an aphorism attributed to Benjamin Franklin (according to Gallacher 1949: 250). Members of the linguistic and cultural (sub) community may accept such an utterance as a useful addition to their collective repertoire. The more outstanding, the more poetic the formulation, the higher is its aesthetic appeal, and therefore better chances for survival. Provided the cost of its keeping in the system as formal load compares favourably with its functional load; i.e., its didactic value. Its didactic function emerges because of illocutionary metonymic shifts, as we explain briefly in 4.1.2 below.

As a proverb becomes entrenched, it may undergo some changes but will tend to remain stable after some time, although of course many proverbs exhibit variants. This at the same time explains why proverbs are more or less fixed. On the one hand, it must preserve a high degree of resemblance to the original slogan, aphorism, allusion, quotation, etc. in order to be recognised as such and to keep the same message. On the other hand, once it has attained the status of a proverb, it must remain stable in order to make it easily memorisable and reproducible. Proverbs, however, are not different from other idiomatic structures because they are not absolutely fixed. There may be some lexical and/or grammatical variation, but they can also be enriched and further modified; e.g., to create so-called anti-proverbs, or to be turned into idioms. As we show in 4.2.1, they can be truncated to just a part and still be recognised as bearing a link to the whole. We claim that this is due to a metonymic link between the whole utterance and a part of the whole utterance, typically the beginning part of a proverb.

In a further step, we might link the fixed form of proverbs with the property of being self-contained and with its traditional character. As proverbs develop from some specific utterances, they tend to preserve their form that was originally, something very close to having the size of a sentence. The sentence in question may have been, be finite or non-finite (or even verbless), and may consist of a single clause, or of more clauses, typically two clauses. These can be two independent or main clauses, or an independent clause and a dependent clause, or two (or more) dependent clauses, linked syndetically or asyndetically. Both monoclausal and multiclausal proverbs can generally be broken down to two parts that are in a sort of topic-comment relationship, as discussed in 4.1 and 4.2 below.

3. On metonymy as a cognitive operation

In order to understand fully the role metonymy plays in proverbs, we have to briefly introduce this basic cognitive process; i.e., define it and introduce its main types. Despite a whole volume devoted to the problem of defining metonymy (see Benczes, Barcelona, and Ruiz de Mendoza 2011), there is still no consensus on the issue. As Barcelona (2011: 8) stresses, the fact that there is something most researchers would agree to call a "standard" cognitive-linguistic notion of conceptual metonymy that contains core elements of the cognitive view of metonymy, "it is by no means a completely uniform notion, as there is some disagreement among these authors over a number of issues". Various definitions of metonymy that have been proposed can only be appreciated if we first consider how it was treated in the traditional rhetoric as well as how it differs from metaphor. Within the cognitive linguistic framework, both these processes have been contrasted with respect to five central points of difference, although it has been repeatedly claimed that the borderline between the two is blurred (see Barcelona 2000a and 2000b; Ruiz de Mendoza 2000).

The first of these four points of difference concerns the nature of the relationship involved. A standard ingredient of traditional definitions of metonymy is a statement on what makes it different from a non-figurative expression, viz. that metonymy is a stand-for type of relationship. In other words, a linguistic expression denoting a part of a larger whole is substituted by another expression denoting the whole, or the other way around. The relationship holding between the two is one of contiguity, association, or proximity (Ullmann 1962: 212, Taylor 1989: 122), whereas metaphor is based on similarity. This means that metonymies are expressions that are used instead of some other expressions because the latter are associated with or suggested by the former, as illustrated in the following examples:

(1) *Buckingham Palace* has washed its hands of Prince Harry and Meghan Markle after they 'told Americans to vote out Trump'.
(https://www.dailymail.co.uk/news/article-8762603/Meghan-Markle-labels-November-vote-important-lifetime.html)

(2) Here, though, it seemed as if it was just the *first violin*, Edward Dusinberre, who was really contributing ideas.
(https://www.theguardian.com/music/2021/nov/09/takacs-quartet-review-wigmore-hall-london-beethoven-janacek-haydn)

Metaphors are in fact often considered shortened similes; i.e., two entities are brought into correlation as exhibiting some similarity, but there are no function words that would make this comparison explicit. In other words, something is described by mentioning another thing with which it is assumed to implicitly share some features.

The two also differ in terms of the number of conceptual domains involved. The standard view is that a metonymic shift occurs within a single domain, while metaphoric mappings take place across two discrete domains. Conceptual metaphors typically employ a more concrete concept or domain as their source in order to structure a more abstract concept or domain as their target. They typically rest on a whole set of cross-domain mappings, while conceptual metonymies are said to involve only a single link (see Ruiz de Mendoza and Peña 2002).

Thirdly, metaphor and metonymy are generally different with respect to the directionality of conceptual mappings involved. Metaphors typically employ a more concrete concept or domain as source in order to structure a more abstract concept or domain as target. In the majority of cases, elements from the physical world are mapped onto the social and mental world. Metaphorical mappings are thus normally unidirectional, and the source and target are not reversible (see Kövecses 2010: 7). Metonymic mappings, in principle, can proceed in either direction, from the more concrete part of the domain (subdomain) to the more abstract one and the other way around, but of course not simultaneously. According to Radden and Kövecses (1999: 22), "[i]n principle, either of the two conceptual entities related may stand for the other, i.e., unlike metaphor, metonymy is basically a reversible process".

Metaphor and metonymy are also said to have different functions. Lakoff and Johnson (1980: 36) say that metaphor is "principally a way of conceiving of one thing in terms of another, and its primary function is understanding", while metonymy "has primarily a referential function, that is, it allows us to use one entity to stand for another". However, both of the above statements have to be relativised. While Lakoff and Johnson see metonymy as having primarily referential function they are aware of its additional functions and point out not only that metonymy is "naturally suited for focussing" (Lakoff and Johnson 1980: 37), but that it can just like metaphor have a role in construal. It makes it possible for us to see and understand things in alternative ways.

Lakoff and Johnson (1980: 35) describe metonymy as the use of "one entity to refer to another that is related to it". Kövecses and Radden (1998: 39) refine this by explicitly shifting everything to the conceptual level when they say "a cognitive process in which one conceptual entity, the vehicle, provides mental access to another conceptual entity, the target, within the same domain, or ICM [Idealized Cognitive Model]".

In view of the complex nature of conceptual metonymy, it can be seen, taking into account most of the relevant insights in the literature (see Ruiz de Mendoza and Otal Campo 2002; Ruiz de Mendoza and Díez Velasco 2004; and Panther 2005), as a cognitive operation of conceptual elaboration based on the part-whole relationship that is triggered by the use of an expression (or metonymic vehicle) that is associated with a certain conceptual cluster (or metonymic source) within a conceptual domain so that the activation of the source conceptual cluster opens up a mental space. This space is dynamically expanded or reduced so as to come as close as possible to fitting the conceptual frame provided by the co(n)text of use, in the course of which the mental space thus opened and elaborated also comes very close in terms of its contents to another conceptual cluster (or metonymic target) within the same conceptual domain that may be or is typically associated with another expression (Brdar 2017; Brdar-Szabó and Brdar 2021; Brdar and Brdar-Szabó 2022).

It is also assumed in Cognitive Linguistics that metonymy can involve a range of relationships, not only the WHOLE FOR PART relationship (as asserted in the traditional approach), but also the PART FOR WHOLE relationship (in which case we have a subtype traditionally called synecdoche). What is more, the PART FOR PART type of relationship has also been assumed (which comes in numerous subtypes; e.g., CAUSE FOR EFFECT, PRODUCER FOR PRODUCT, CONTAINER FOR THE CONTAINED, etc.), although the viability of this type is disputed by Ruiz Mendoza and his collaborators (see Ruiz de Mendoza 2000; Ruiz de Mendoza and Díez Velasco 2002; Ruiz de Mendoza and Mairal 2007, Ruiz de Mendoza and Pérez 2001). They are better analysed as the outcome of the interaction between two or more successively used metonymies.

4. Metonymic layers in proverbs

The most general metonymic layer at which metonymy works in proverbs is the whole proverb as such. We briefly discuss this in 4.1. However, proverbs can be reduced in actual usage to just one part. In very many cases the initial segment of a proverb can stand metonymically in discourse for the whole metonymy, as discussed in 4.2.1, Metonymy can also be detected within parts of proverbs that are downgraded to lower-level grammatical units (4.2.2). Finally, certain elements within lower-level units, e.g., modifiers, or heads of phrases, can also be the locus of metonymic shifts (4.2.3).

4.1 Metonymy at the level of the whole proverb

4.1.1 *Proverbs as results of metonymy*

As claimed by Radden and Kövecses (1999 and 2006), metonymy underlies our interpretation of proverbs. While Lakoff and Turner (1989, Chapter 4) see proverbs as instances of the metaphor GENERIC IS SPECIFIC within the metaphor system they call the Great Chain of Being, we rather embrace the approach by Krikmann (1984) and Radden and Kövecses, who analyse them as cases of the metonymy SPECIFIC FOR GENERIC. This metonymy is very frequently found in many languages and comes in several subtypes (e.g., SPECIFIC BRAND FOR A GENERIC PRODUCT, as in *scotch tape* standing for any adhesive tape, or AN INDIVIDUAL FOR A CATEGORY, as in *every Tom, Dick, and Harry*). It is also at work in many idioms, as shown by Negro (2019).

The state of affairs described in a proverb applies originally to a specific situation but becomes applicable to a wider number of situations. Sullivan and Sweetser (2010) attempt to avoid deciding between the two analyses and suggest that all cases of specific-generic mappings involve conceptual blending.

It is true that proverbs typically involve a metaphorical layer, too, because of the didactic transfer from one type of situation to another. In other words, there are mappings between two discrete domains, and this leads to some problematic issues. First, the labels used to refer to the two domains in this metaphor are very different from what we see in the rest of cognitive linguistic work on conceptual metaphors. It is well known that the target domain is as a rule more abstract than the source domain, but both of them are typically well delineated, it is TIME IS JOURNEY and IDEAS ARE OBJECTS, and not SOMETHING TIME-LIKE IS JOURNEY, and SOMETHING IDEA-LIKES ARE OBJECTS. Further, in order for mappings to make sense, and even to establish them, we should be clear about the meaning of the proverb, and about the two situations being correlated, and this is not always necessarily the case. This is why we think that the whole process of a proverb's coming into being is apparently metonymic.

Another argument in favour of the metonymic approach is the genesis of proverbs, i.e., their rise, entrenchment and development that, as mentioned in the introduction, can be best appreciated within a usage-based model. The term was coined and first used by Langacker (1987: 494). It was described there as giving substantial importance to:

> ... the actual use of the linguistic system and a speaker's knowledge of this use; the grammar is held responsible for a speaker's knowledge of the full range of linguistic conventions, regardless of whether these conventions can be subsumed under more general statements.

This model is bottom-up oriented, as it follows how linguistic structures arise in actual use. For cognitive linguists, the speaker's linguistic system is fundamentally grounded in usage events, i.e., instances of a speaker's use of language. Rules can only be arrived at in an inductive way; i.e., they are abstracted from concrete usage events because of the repetition of similar instances of use. Many a complex fabricated phenomenon, system or activity may appear at first blush rather chaotic and unregulated, but in the course of time/the workings of the system, certain patterns of regularity emerge and are recognised (and often socially accepted) by the participants and/or external observers.

More or less the same applies to various types of syntactic constructions and of fixed or idiomatic expressions. The latter have been evolving over decades, centuries, or millenniums, some of them emerging and undergoing modifications, some gradually disappearing, etc., simply because people have found communication, and life, easier when things were said in a particular way. This of course is very much true of the expressions we focus on in this chapter; i.e., of proverbs. They emerged as a crystallised folk wisdom built into language to enable a dynamic development of the society while safeguarding its stability.

What we have said above applies very well to proverbs, too, in a double sense. Proverbs are, on the one hand, after all linguistic structures arising as originally particular utterances or parts of utterances of particular people, but which over time, if accepted by the linguistic community, generalise to become part of the repertoire of more or less fixed expressions, while they, on the other hand, accompany much of human daily activities. More or less the same ideas were formulated by Firth (1926: 262–263), who talks about three stages of their development, the central being "[a]cceptance by the people at large as being appropriate to a more general situation".

In conclusion, we may say that proverbs are not something that has just waited to be used metaphorically; their meanings have been abstracted away from specific situations.

4.1.2 *Metonymy and the illocutionary force of proverbs*

Another way in which metonymy can work on the whole proverb concerns its illocutionary force. As is well known, proverbs, which are typically realised as whole sentence, can appear as various sentence types; i.e., as declaratives (statements), directives (imperatives), or sometimes as questions (interrogatives). In order to fulfil their didactic function they have to be understood as something else, as other than what they look like; i.e., not as the speech act that they seem to exemplify. In other words, a statement may come to be understood as an indirect warning, a directive as a piece of advice, etc.

The indirectness of proverbs has been recognised in a series of studies (Norrick 1982; Nahberger, 2000, 2004). Norrick (1982) even talks about proverbs as doubly indirect speech act. Indirect speech acts have been discussed widely in pragmatic literature. In a classical Searlean account, indirect speech acts are speech acts by which the speaker appears to perform a speech act A (a primary speech act), while actually performing another speech act B (a secondary speech act). In other words, this is a speech act "performed by means of another" (see Searle 1975:60).

According to Searle, the central problem is as follows: How does the speaker understand the nonliteral primary illocutionary act from understanding the literal secondary illocutionary act? What he proposes is a sequence of steps in reconstructing the primary speech act. The problem with these is that, although the individual steps are supposed to be unconscious, the nonliteral primary act is somehow derived from the literal secondary act. Some other accounts; e.g., Grice (1975), Bach and Harnish (1979), or Sperber and Wilson (1986) also assume that the hearer can infer the indirect speech act; i.e., arrive at the proper interpretation of its propositional contents and illocutionary force by going through several steps in which inferential rules are ordered. As far as paremiology is concerned, Grzybek (2015:78–79) recognises that "it might eventually be appropriate to classify a proverb as an indirect speech act", but concludes that whether "such classifications are helpful for semantic purposes (…), is an entirely different matter".

More recently, a more radical approach that appears well applicable to proverbs, too, has been advanced in Cognitive Linguistics, the interpretation of indirect speech acts being based on the activation of a certain part of a cognitive model. Specifically, the interpretation of the indirect speech act is based on the metonymic evocation of the whole model or one of its parts through a previous activation of another part of the model. This idea about the metonymic motivation of indirect speech acts, first formulated by Gibbs (1994: 351),[1] has been worked out in more detail in a series of studies, especially by Panther and Thornburg. Illocutionary metonymy is one of the three major types of metonymies in their typology, next to referential metonymy and predicational metonymy, as two subtypes of propositional metonymies. Their speech act scenario model (Thornburg and Panther, 1997; Panther and Thornburg, 1998, 1999) is the most elaborate account of the role of metonymy in indirect speech acts. It has been applied to a wide range of constructions, as can be seen in Brdar and Brdar-Szabó (2002), Brdar-Szabó (2006, 2007, 2009), Kosecki (2007), or Pérez Hernandez (2013).

The speech act scenario model by Panther and Thornburg is based on the assumption that any element of an illocutionary scenario or a speech act scenario can stand metonymically for the whole of the associated illocutionary category. The central component of the model is the idea that our knowledge about illocutionary categories is organised in the form of so-called illocutionary scenarios as information package. They are stored in our long-term memory, and are accessible to all members of a linguistic community, so that a brief hint at a particular component of the associated scenario suffices to activate the whole illocutionary category, or at least to point in its direction. The model can be demonstrated on a simplified REQUEST scenario (Figure 1):

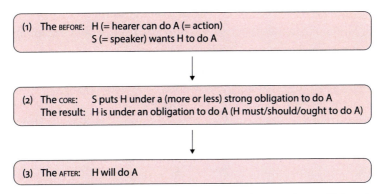

Figure 1. Simplified illocutionary scenario for REQUEST (see Panther and Thornburg 1998: 759)

Starting from this scenario for REQUEST, Panther and Thornburg assume that those instances of indirect REQUESTS, such as the examples in (3) and (4), can be

---

1. "[...], speaking and understanding indirect speech acts involves a kind of metonymic reasoning, where people infer wholes (a series of actions) from a part".

understood without problems due to the fact that they activate certain components of the above scenario.

(3) *Will you close the door?*

(4) *Can you pass the salt?*

The utterance in (3) is a conventionalised expression in English, used in order to realise a request. One component of the illocutionary scenario for REQUEST, viz. the question about the future action of the hearer, stands here for the request to perform a given action. Example (3) is referred to by Panther und Thornburg (1998) as "a pragmatic substitute for the explicit request *Close the door*".

The component *H will do A* as part of the scenario for REQUEST is so close to the CORE component that it can activate the whole scenario. The modal auxiliary *can* in (4) links the utterance to the information in the BEFORE component, viz. the precondition for the sequence of actions of the whole scenario, so that the illocutionary category REQUEST is activated.

Let us now demonstrate how this applies to proverbs. If we take the example of the English proverb *The early bird catches the worm* and its counterparts in various languages (*Tko rano rani, dvije sreće grabi*, lit. 'He who gets up early, takes two pieces of luck', in Croatian, Кто рано встает, тому Бог подает, Kto rano vstaet, tomu Bog podaet', lit. 'He who gets up early, to him the God gives', in Russian, *Morgenstunde hat Gold im Munde*, lit. 'The morning hour has gold in its mouth', in German, etc.), we see that the proverb, realised as a declarative statement, is reinterpreted as indirect advice.

The Speaker (= S) is convinced that getting up early can help to have more success in life. He thinks that the potential readers or hearers (= H) of his text are not aware of the fact that they are not in an optimal situation or state of mind. He seems to know that it would be better for H to get up earlier. S draws H's attention to the fact that it would be better to follow the model of behaviour depicted in the proverb because, by means of a metaphorical transfer, successful people also get up early and gain extra time allowing them to do many good things. Therefore, getting up early can lead to positive emotional, mental, physical, and spiritual experiences. By making this statement, S puts H under weak expectation-type obligation, as S cannot control the reaction of H directly. The foregrounded element of the AFTER component in the comment part of the proverb,[2] the desirable

---

2. The concepts of topic and comment as two functional (and often structural) parts within proverbs are taken over from Georges and Dundes (1963) and Dundes (1975). Dundes (1975: 970) defines the proverb as "a traditional propositional statement consisting of at least one descriptive element, a descriptive element consisting of a topic and a comment". This echoes the Praguian functional approach where the topic or theme of a sentence is an entity

state of affairs, and the BEFORE component in the topic part, thus jointly activate the advice scenario, overriding the formally declarative force of the statement.

Similarly, the English proverbs *Make hay while the sun shines* and *Strike the iron while it is hot*, take the form of directives, but actually are metonymically reinterpreted as indirect advice. The relationship between the topic and comment parts is exactly the reverse. Here the comment parts of the proverbs foreground the BEFORE or the PRECONDITION for the CORE and the AFTER components. The sun shining and the iron being hot make possible to perform successfully the respective activity. The two are not pure directives, as the additions in the comment parts would be pragmatically speaking superfluous. If the speaker wants the hearer to just literally strike the iron (in the metonymic sense of striking meaning to form iron into something, to give it a particular form, or prepare it for this), then it is not one of his concerns whether the iron is hot or not. It is rather a concern of the hearer, because the ultimate goal of the action can be realised only if the piece of iron being processed reaches and keeps a certain temperature; if the hearer stops striking it, the metal cannot be processed further. Apparently, the addition in the comment serves as a hint or advice for the hearer to keep striking.

A phenomenon related to this, something that we can see as an additional, interim metonymic layer operating at the level between the whole proverb and the level of its parts can be observed here. The comment and the topic parts are in a metonymic presupposition relationship. Making hay normally (when done by a rational person) presupposes good weather that is in turn metonymically conveyed by the reference to the sun shining. Similarly, transforming a piece of iron, giving it a new form presupposes a particular temperature range, i.e., when it is white-hot. Saying simply that it is hot is a metonymic understatement (the whole scale stands for a particular range on the scale, specifically its upper part).

A similar situation can be observed in the case of the proverb *A lie has no feet* (next to its variants *Lies don't travel far* and *Truth will out*), and its counterparts in other languages, e.g., *Lügen haben kurze Beine*, lit. Lies have short legs, in German. Having short or no feet/legs metonymically implies the inability to travel far and fast, which in turn implies that whoever is running will be caught in short time and close to the starting point. Therefore, the proverb points out in the comment part an element that paints a negative outcome, and thus creates a negative

---

about which something is said or predicated. It thus forms the point of departure of the message, while the rest of the sentence, called comment or rheme, tells the hearer/reader something about the theme. The term topic is not to be confused with Honeck's use of it when he talks about the interpretation of proverbs, distinguishing between the "literal meaning model and the proverb topic" (1997: 132).

or loss frame. This framing is also a factor that makes it possible to activate the most appropriate speech act scenario.

4.2 Metonymic layers within a proverb

4.2.1 *Truncated proverbs and metonymy*

One of the defining features of proverbs is that they are typically complete sentences (Belkhir 2021). What is more, they can be seen as distinct or texts of their own texts within larger texts. Specifically, we propose that they constitute one type of what Halliday (1985: 392) called little texts. They are short texts like telegrams, newspaper headlines, titles, product labels, signboards, or some recipes. This character of proverbs has also been recognised by Norrick (2015: 7) when he talked about proverbs "as little texts complete in themselves". However, like many other types of little texts, they are embedded into or linked to larger texts. Many little texts can be expanded or shortened.

It has often been observed that proverbs can appear in a reduced form, just like many other idiomatic multi-word structures. They can be truncated (Mieder 2004) to just one part in discourse; e.g., when *A stich in time saves nine* ('a timely effort that will prevent more work later') is reduced to just *A stich in time*, or the German proverb *Kommt Zeit, kommt Rat* (lit. 'comes time, comes advice', 'Time will tell, we'll cross that bridge when we come to it'), when shortened to just *Kommt Zeit...* This truncation is shown in Excerpts (5) and (6) hereafter:

(5) *Railway track* is an *elastic structure* and when the *track is subjected* to *stresses* by the train moving at high speed it is *adversely affected* by the vibrations resulting in loosening of sleeper fittings and reduction in elasticity of supporting ballast. *A stitch in time should* therefore be the policy of maintenance crew, i.e., defect should be rectified as soon as it is noticed.
(https://books.google.hu/books/about/T_B_On_Transportation
_Engineering.html?id=cbZ-fuq_RUkC&redir_esc=y)

(6) *Wo gehobelt wird...*
betr.: „Zurück zur Sache!" (Die grüne Bosnien-Debatte droht zu verkommen), taz vom 28. 11. 95 u.a.   (https://taz.de/Wo-gehobelt-wird/!1480501/)

The complete form of the German proverb in the title of a journal article in (6) is *Wo gehobelt wird, fallen Späne* (lit. Where wood is chopped, splinters fall, 'You cannot make an omelette without breaking eggs').

We claim that this is another metonymic layer in proverbs because, as argued in Barcelona (2005), one salient part of form can metonymically stand for the whole form, or still better, a salient part of the complex construction can stand for the whole construction. Because proverbs are generally learned and used as echoes; i.e., as repetitions of utterances previously heard as used by other people, we can also treat such elliptical structures as instances of the metonymy PART OF AN ECHO FOR THE WHOLE ECHO. This metonymy is discussed in Ruiz de Mendoza and Lozano-Palacio (2019) and Galera Masegosa (2020).

Such truncation is of course made possible by the structure of the proverbs in question. It works best if the proverb clearly divides into two syntactically similar parts, two phrase or two clauses linked by a copula verb or coordinated.

That claim that the part of a proverb can metonymically stand for the whole proverb is supported by several facts. First, some proverbs may develop into idiomatic expressions over time through the process of their reduction to just one part, typically their beginning. The case in point is *A stitch in time*, which is also listed, along with the full proverb in some dictionaries, carrying the meaning of the whole proverb, e.g., in *Oxford Learner's Dictionaries* (https://www.oxfordlearnersdictionaries.com/definition/english/stitch_1?q=stitch), or *Collins Dictionary* (https://www.collinsdictionary.com/dictionary/english/a-stitch-in-time), 'said to mean that it is better to deal with a problem in its early stages, in order to prevent it getting worse'. Another common example is the expression *an early bird*, from *An early bird catches the worm*.

Secondly, in tests of the so-called paremiological minimum linguists may use, among others, proverb completion tasks that prove that subjects are familiar with a given proverb (see Grzybek 1991; Chlosta, Grzybek and Roos 1994; Tóthné Litovkina 1996; Haas 2008; Aleksa Varga and Matovac 2016; Ďurčo 2015; Aleksa Varga and Keglević 2018, 2020). Subjects may be either presented with the initial or with the final part of a proverb and are required to supply what is missing. As shown by Aleksa Varga and Keglević (2020: 45), subjects perform better when they are presented with the initial part of the proverb, which proves that it is capable of the metonymic recall of the whole.

Further, initial parts may be shared by several more or less related proverbs, as in the following pair of Russian proverbs:

(7) a. *Время красит, (безвременье старит)*
Vremya krasit, (bezvremen'e starit)
Time paints timelessness makes-old
Lit. 'Time paints (timelessness ages)'.
b. *Время красит, (а безвремянье чернит)*.
Vremya krasit, (a bezvremyan'e chernit).
Time paints and timelessness blackens
Lit. 'Time paints (and timelessness blackens)'

(8) a. Время придет, и час пробьет.
    Vremya pridet, i chas prob'et.
    time comes and hour strikes
    Lit. 'The time will come and the hour will strike'.
  b. Придет время – будет и наш черед (и наша пора)
    pridet vremya – budet i nash chered (i nasha pora).
    come time – will.be and our turn (and our time)
    Lit. 'The time will come – it will be our turn (and our time)'.

This means that a complex semantic relationship may exist between related proverbs, involving polysemy, antonymy, synonymy, etc. In any case, the first part is apparently capable of metonymically recalling something, be it this or that idea, depending on the context or the speaker's knowledge.

Finally, the part that can metonymically stand for the whole proverb is the part that is usually kept intact in various creative and playful modifications of proverbs because it can recall the whole that thus serves as the baseline against which to appreciate the whole. This is often the case in so-called anti-proverbs, transformations of standard proverbs for humorous effects (Mieder 1982; Mieder and Tóthné Litovkina 1999; Tóthné Litovkina and Mieder 2006). We can illustrate this point with the Biblical proverb *Eat, drink and be merry, for tomorrow we die*. It can be truncated to just *Eat, drink and be merry*, but it can be playfully changed to *Eat, drink and be merry, for tomorrow you may not be able to afford it* (Litovkina 2015: 334). The German proverb *Andere Länder, andere Sitten*, lit. 'Other countries, other customs' meaning *When in Rome, do as Romans do*) is reported in Lewandowska and Antos (2015: 176) as *Andere Länder, gleiche Auskunft*, lit. 'Other countries, the same response'. In some cases, the humorous effect of the anti-proverbs stem from the fact that an element in the first part that is kept is actually used as a homonym. This becomes obvious when the new second part is supplied, as when *Where there's a will, there is a way* is changed to *When there's a will, there is an inheritance tax/there's a delay*, etc. (Litovkina 2015: 336).

The phenomenon of proverb truncation that we have seen above is found in many languages, as can be seen from examples from Tajik (9) and Uzbek (10):

(9) *Ангур аз ангур гирад ранг, (ҳамсоя зи ҳамсоя панд).*
    angur az angur girad rang, (hamsoya zi hamsoya pand).
    grape from grape take colour, (neighbour from neighbour advice).
    Lit. 'Grapes take on colour from other grapes, (the neighbour take advice from another neighbour)'.

(10) Гул   тиконсиз бўлмас, (гўшт   суяксиз).
      gul   tikonsiz bo'lmas, (go'sht suyaksiz).
      flower thorn   without (flesh/meat bone)
      Lit. 'A flower cannot be without thorns (a flesh without bones)'.

Some more or less universally present proverbs; e.g., those of Biblical origin, can be reduced in practically all languages in which they occur, as for example *An eye for an eye* (*and a tooth for a tooth*):

Croatian
(11) Oko za oko nije   kršćanski.
      eye for eye NEG-is Christian
      Lit. 'An eye for an eye is not the Christian way'.

Portuguese
(12) Ele pratica a   técnica   do *olho por olho.*
      he practices the technique of eye for eye
      Lit. 'He practices an eye for an eye technique'.

Hungarian
(13) A szem a szemért nem oldja meg a   társadalom bajait.
      the eye the eye-for not solves PREF the society   problems-of
      Lit. 'An eye for an eye does not solve the problems of the society'.

4.2.2 *Metonymic interpretation of a word group within a proverb: Events as metonymic targets*

Because of this truncation, proverbs are very often downgraded in the sense of Moon (1998:131); i.e., "traditional proverbs and sayings [are] downgraded from their canonical or earliest forms to lower-level grammatical units: a compound sentence to a single clause, or a clause to a group". We have seen this happening in the previous section, when whole proverbs are reduced to just one part, e.g., from two clauses to a single clause, or the whole clause to just the phrase functioning as the subject. We suggest that there is another metonymic layer exhibiting an implicit or logical reduction. In the above example, *A stich in time (saves nine)*, the noun phrase followed by a prepositional phrase, or perhaps a verbless clause (see Quirk et al. 1985), can be interpreted as an instance of the metonymy SALIENT PARTICIPANT FOR THE EVENT IN WHICH IT PARTICIPATES. The first part of the proverb stands for the action of 'performing a stich in time'. Similarly, *an apple a day*, as the first part of *An apple a day keeps the doctor away*, stands for 'eating an apple a day'.

The metonymy SALIENT PARTICIPANT FOR THE EVENT IN WHICH IT PARTICIPATES is a relatively common type of metonymy, described in Dirven (1999), Brdar and Brdar-Szabó (2004, 2014), Brdar (2005, 2007) or in Choi (2016). In Example (14), the adjective *fond* is clearly used in two different ways, the second token together with the noun phrase following it means something like 'fond of eating zebra':

(14)   *Like you, I am very fond of lions, though in a sociogenetically distanced manner, not at all the same way that your lions are fond of zebra…*
            (http://lchc.ucsd.edu/MCA/Mail/xmcamail.2011_09.dir/msg00090.html)

In *An apple a day keeps the doctor away*, the two parts of the proverb, the topic (*an apple a day*) and the comment (*keeps the doctor away*) relate to each other as cause and effect, where the latter is also capable of metonymically standing, as an effect, for the whole situation of enjoying good health. By further extension, i.e., by telescoping the two metonymies, the salient participant can also stand for the whole situation.

This type of metonymy is not so frequent in proverbs, in part because the participant in question may be interpreted as non-metonymic as well. The following two proverbs are thus parallel in terms of their structure, but while the topic in (15) may indeed be in need of metonymic expansion ('eating grain, one by one'), this is not necessarily the case in (16), where 'step by step' is more convincing as a manner adverbial:

(15)   *Grain by grain, the hen fills her crop.*

(16)   *Step by step, the ladder is ascended.*

The SALIENT PARTICIPANT FOR THE EVENT IN WHICH IT PARTICIPATES metonymy is found in proverbs of other languages as well, as shown Example (17) from Croatian:

(17)   *Čizma glavu čuva,   šubara je   kvari.*
          boot   head protects fur-hat AUX spoils
          Lit. 'The boot protects the head, and the fur-hat spoils it'.

In both the topic and the comment part, the first element can be expanded to 'wearing X', i.e., boot or fur hat.

4.2.3 *Metonymic interpretation of constituents (within phrases)*

Finally, as a fifth metonymic layer, we find cases where a particular part of a proverb, of the whole proverb, or of its truncated, or downgraded variant, can receive a metonymic interpretation, the target not being an event. The apple in the above example is of course not the whole tree, but just its fruit. Humans however do not eat the fruit as a whole, but just a part of it, i.e., just its mesocarp of pulp, without its stem, stamen, calyx, and endocarp or core with pips. It appears that we have the metonymy of the type FRUIT FOR A PART OF THE FRUIT. This metonymy apparently works in Uzbek:

(18) *Олманинг тагида олма ётар, (Довчанинг тагида довча ётар).*
Olmaning tagida olma yotar, (Dovchaning tagida dovcha yotar).
apple-GEN under apple lie-3SG, (apricot-GEN under apricot lie-3SG)
Lit. The likes of an apple lie under an apple (the likes of an apricot lie under an apricot)

'Under the apple (tree) lies the apple, (under the apricot tree lies the apricot), used in the sense of keeping the tradition of doing the same thing within the family'

However, in some languages the tree and its fruit can be denoted by two separate words, either unrelated or morphologically related (by means of suffixation or compounding). In other words, the polysemy is resolved. This is the case in Russian proverbs (19) and (20):

(19) *От яблоньки яблочко, а от ели шишка.*
ot yablon'ki yablochko, a ot yeli shishka.
from appletree, apple, and from pine cone.
Lit. 'From an apple tree, an apple, and from a pine, a cone'.

(20) *Яблоко от яблони недалеко падает.*
yabloko ot yabloni nedaleko padaet.
apple from apple tree not-far falls
Lit. 'Apple does not fall far from the tree'.

Yablon 'tree' and *yabloko* 'fruit' are obviously morphologically related, unlike *yel'* (pinetree) and *shishka* 'cone'.

However, there are many more obvious, and more systematic, cases of certain condensation of constituents of phrases within proverbs; e.g., proverbs about weather that mention sky and objects in the sky as well as certain colours. A case in point is the English proverb *Red sky in morning, sailors take warning/Red sky at night, sailors' delight*, and the Spanish counterpart of the former, *Cielo rojo al amanecer, el mar se ha de mover*. The phenomena mentioned do not involve the whole sky; it is just the part of the sky in the east, or in the west. A further condensation can be seen in the Italian pair *Rosso di sera, bel tempo si spera, Rosso di mattina, la pioggia si avvicina*, lit. 'red of evening' and 'red of morning'. Here the red colour is used to metonymically refer to the sky, or part of the sky with the sun, or the sun itself. In Russian, we find:

(21) *Красному утру не верь!*
Krasnomu utru ne ver'!
red morning not trust
Lit. 'Do not trust the red morning!'

Similarly, in the Portuguese proverb *Melhorérosto vermelhoque coração negro*, lit. 'better a red face than a black heart', the red colour metonymically indicates anger.

5. Conclusion

Using a proverb as a metaphor, we could say that not everything that glitters in proverbs is metonymic gold but it can be found in considerable quantities at more than one level. In this chapter, we have uncovered five such levels or metonymic layers in various proverbs. Metonymy is thus systematically present in proverbs and contributes to their meaning at various levels across languages and cultures

First, we have demonstrated that two metonymic layers can operate on the whole proverb. On the one hand, proverbs can be seen as exemplifying the SPECIFIC FOR GENERIC METONYMY, as claimed by Krikmann (1984) and Radden and Kövecses (1999, 2006). We have also adduced some arguments that apparently support this claim that is consonant with the usage-based approach to proverbs. On the other hand, we have shown that metonymy can work on the whole proverb when it helps constituting its illocutionary force. The interpretation of proverbs as indirect speech acts is based on the activation of a certain part of a cognitive model. Specifically, the interpretation of the indirect speech act is based on the metonymic evocation of the whole model or one of its parts through a previous activation of another part of the model.

Metonymy can be detected at three levels within the proverb. Firstly, a proverb can be truncated to just a part, typically the beginning part of a proverb or topic, and still be recognised as bearing a link to the whole. We claim that this is due to a metonymic link between the whole the beginning part of a proverb or topic. Sometimes a noun phrase in the topic or in the comment can be interpreted as an instance of the metonymy SALIENT PARTICIPANT FOR THE EVENT IN WHICH IT PARTICIPATES. Finally, there are also some cases where a particular part of a proverb, i.e., an element within a phrase, can receive a metonymic interpretation, but where the metonymic target is not an event. These metonymies can be incidental, but also more systematic in proverbs tied to certain topics, such as proverbs about weather, where celestial objects and meteorological phenomena, as well as their colour may undergo a metonymic shift.

It is interesting that several metonymies can occur simultaneously within a single proverb, at various levels. The relationship between these metonymies is not always the same. Sometimes they are unrelated, but sometimes they occur embedded within each other, like Russian dolls, producing layered or complex metonymies. However, they can also form a metonymic complex, with one and the same vehicle (and the source concept) linked with different target concepts.

How these metonymies interact with each other, as well as with conceptual metaphors, is an important task for future research.

Funding

This publication is part of the R&D&i project PID2020-118349GB-I00 funded by MICIU/AEI/ 10.13039/501100011033 (Spain)

References

Aleksa Varga, M., & Matovac, D. (2016). Kroatische Sprichwörter im Test. *Proverbium*, 33, 1–28.

Aleksa Varga, M., & Keglević, A. (2018). Kroatische und deutsche Antisprichwörter in der Sprache der Jugendlichen. *Proverbium: Yearbook of International Proverb Scholarship*, 35(1), 343–360.

Aleksa Varga, M., & Keglević, A. (2020). Hrvatske poslovice u slavenskome okruženju: određivanje hrvatskoga paremiološkog minimuma i optimuma. *Slavia Centralis*, 13(1), 40–51.

Arora, S. (1984). The perception of proverbiality. *Proverbium: Yearbook of International Proverb Scholarship*, 1, 1–38.

Bach, K., & Harnish, R. M. (1979). *Linguistic communication and speech acts*. Cambridge: Cambridge University Press.

Barcelona, A. (2000a). Introduction. The cognitive theory of metaphor and metonymy. In A. Barcelona (Ed.), *Metaphor and metonymy at the crossroads. A cognitive perspective* (pp. 1–28). Berlin & New York: Mouton de Gruyter.

Barcelona, A. (2000b). On the plausibility of claiming a metonymic motivation for conceptual metaphor. In A. Barcelona (Ed.), *Metaphor and metonymy at the crossroads. A cognitive perspective* (pp. 31–58). Berlin & New York: Mouton de Gruyter.

Barcelona, A. (2005). The multilevel operation of metonymy in grammar and discourse, with particular attention to metonymic chains. In F. J. Ruiz de Mendoza & S. Peña Cervel (Eds.), *Cognitive linguistics: Internal dynamics and interdisciplinary interaction* (pp. 313–352). Berlin & New York: Mouton de Gruyter.

Barcelona, A. (2011). Reviewing the properties and prototype structure of metonymy. In R. Benczes, A. Barcelona, & F. Ruiz de Mendoza Ibáñez (Eds.), *Defining metonymy in cognitive linguistics: Towards a consensus view* (pp. 7–57). Amsterdam & Philadelphia: John Benjamins.

Belkhir, S. (2014). *Proverb use between cognition and tradition in English, French, Arabic and Kabyle*. PhD diss., Sétif 2 University, Sétif.

Belkhir, S. (2021). Cognitive linguistics and proverbs. In X. Wen & J. R. Taylor (Eds.). *The Routledge handbook of cognitive linguistics* (pp. 599–611). New York & London: Routledge.

Benczes, R., Barcelona, A., & Ruiz de Mendoza Ibáñez, F. (Eds.). (2011). *Defining metonymy in cognitive linguistics: Towards a consensus view*. Amsterdam & Philadelphia: John Benjamins.

Brdar, M. (2005). What is compatible with what? Or, reducing the collocational chaos in the predicate-argument structure, with a little help from metonymy. In F. Kiefer, G. Kiss, & J. Pajzs (Eds.), *Papers in computational lexicography. COMPLEX 2005* (pp. 40–49). Budapest: Linguistics Institute of the Hungarian Academy of Sciences.

Brdar, M. (2007). *Metonymy in grammar: Towards motivating extensions of grammatical categories and constructions*. Osijek: Faculty of Philosophy.

Brdar, M. (2017). *Metonymy and word-formation: Their interactions and complementation*. Newcastle upon Tyne: Cambridge Scholars Publishing.

Brdar, M., & Brdar-Szabó, R. (2002). Indirect speech act metaphtonymies and diagrammatic iconicity. *Strani jezici*, 31(2), 45–54.

Brdar, M., & Brdar-Szabo, R. (2014). Metonymies we (don't) translate by: The case of complex metonymies. *Argumentum*, 10, 232–247.

Brdar, M. & Brdar-Szabó, R. (2022). Targetting metonymic targets. In M. Brdar & R. Brdar-Szabó (Eds.), *Figurative thought and language in action* (pp. 59–86). Amsterdam & Philadelphia: John Benjamins.

Brdar-Szabó, R. (2006). Stand-alone dependent clauses functioning as independent speech acts: A crosslinguistic comparison. In R. Benczes & S. Csábi (Eds.), *The Metaphors of Sixty. Papers Presented on the Occasion of the 60th Birthday of Zoltán Kövecses* (pp. 84–95). Budapest: Department of American Studies, School of English and American Studies, Eötvös Loránd University.

Brdar-Szabó, R. (2007). The role of metonymy in motivating cross-linguistic differences in the exploitation of stand-alone conditionals as indirect directives. In K. Kosecki (Ed.), *Perspectives on metonymy* (pp. 175–198). Frankfurt am Main: Peter Lang.

Brdar-Szabó, R. (2009). Metonymy in indirect directives: Stand-alone conditionals in English, German, Hungarian, and Croatian. In K.-U. Panther, L.L. Thornburg, & A. Barcelona (Eds.), *Metonymy and metaphor in grammar* (pp. 323–336). Amsterdam & Philadelphia: John Benjamins.

Brdar-Szabó, R., & Brdar, M. (2004). Predicative adjectives and grammatical-relational polysemy: The role of metonymic processes in motivating cross-linguistic differences. In G. Radden & K.-U. Panther (Eds.), *Studies in linguistic motivation* (pp. 321–355). Berlin & New York: Mouton de Gruyter.

Brdar-Szabó, R., & Brdar, M. (2021). Metonymic indeterminacy and metalepsis: Getting two (or more) targets for the price of one vehicle. In A. Soares da Silva (Ed.), *Figurative language – Intersubjectivity and usage* (pp. 211–247). Amsterdam & Philadelphia: John Benjamins.

Buljan, G., & Gradečak-Erdeljić, T. (2013). Where cognitive linguistics meets paremiology: A cognitive–contrastive view of selected English and Croatian proverbs. *ExELL. Explorations in English Language and Linguistics*, 1(1), 63–83.

Chlosta, C., Grzybek, P., & Roos, U. (1994). Wer kennt denn heute noch den simrock? Ergebnisse einer empirischen untersuchung zur bekanntheit deutscher sprichwörter in traditionellen sammlungen. In C. Chlosta, P. Grzybek, & E. Piirainen (Eds.), *Sprachbilder zwischen Theorie und Praxis. Akten des Westfälischen Arbeitskreises "Phraseologie/Parömiologie" (1991/1992)* (pp. 31–60). Bochum: Universitätsverlag Dr. N. Brockmeyer.

Choi, Y. (2016). How metonymy influences grammar: The case of concrete-noun-plus-*hata* constructions in Korean. *Discourse and Cognition*, 23(4), 137–158.

Dirven, R. (1999). Conversion as a conceptual metonymy of event schemata. In K.-U. Panther & G. Radden (Eds.), *Metonymy in language and thought* (pp. 275–287). Amsterdam & Philadelphia: John Benjamins.

Dundes, A. (1975). On the structure of the proverb. *Proverbium*, 25, 961–973.

Ďurčo, P. (2015). Empirical research and paremiological minimum. In H. Hrisztova-Gotthardt & M. Aleksa Varga (Eds.), *Introduction to paremiology* (pp. 183–205). Warsaw & Berlin: De Gruyter Open.

Firth, R. (1926). Proverbs in native life, with special reference to those of the maori, I. *Folklore*, 37(2), 134–153.

Galera Masegosa, A. (2020). The role of echoing in meaning construction and interpretation: A cognitive-linguistic perspective. *Review of Cognitive Linguistics*, 18(1), 19–41.

Gallacher, S. A. (1949). Franklin's "way to wealth": A florilegium of proverbs and wise sayings. *The Journal of English and Germanic Philology*, 48(2), 229–251.

Georges, R. A., & Dundes, A. (1963). Toward a structural definition of the riddle. *The Journal of American Folklore*, 76(300), 111–118.

Gibbs, R. W. (1994). *The poetics of mind: Figurative thought, language, and understanding*. Cambridge: Cambridge University Press.

Gibbs, R. W., & Beitel, D. (1995). What proverb understanding reveals about how people think. *Psychological Bulletin*, 118(1), 133–154.

Grice, H. P. (1975). Logic and conversation. In P. Cole & J. L. Morgan (Eds.), *Speech Acts* (pp. 41–58). New York: Academic Press.

Grzybek, P. (1991). Sinkendes kulturgut? Eine empirische pilotstudie zur bekanntheit deutscher sprichwörter. *Wirkendes Wort*, 41(2), 239–264.

Grzybek, P. (1998). Prolegomena zur Bildhaftigkeit von Sprichwörtern. In A. Hartmann & C. Veldhues (Eds.), *Im Zeichen-Raum: Festschrift für Karl Eimermacher* (pp. 133–152). Dortmund: Projekt Verlag.

Grzybek, P. (2015). Semiotic and semantic aspects of the proverb. In H.-G. Hrisztalina & V. Melita Aleksa (Eds.), *Introduction to paremiology* (pp. 68–111). Warsaw & Berlin: De Gruyter Open.

Haas, H. A. (2008). Proverb familiarity in the United States: Cross-regional comparisons of the paremiological minimum. *The Journal of American Folklore*, 121(481), 319–347.

Halliday, M. A. K. (1985). *An introduction to functional grammar*. London: Edward Arnold.

Honeck, R. P. (1997). *A proverb in mind: The cognitive science of proverbial wit and wisdom*. New York: Psychology Press.

Kosecki, K. (2007). On multiple metonymies within indirect speech acts. *Research in Language*, 5(1), 213–219.

Kövecses, Z. (2010). *Metaphor: A Practical Introduction*. 2nd edition. Oxford & New York: Oxford University Press.

Kövecses, Z., & Radden, G. (1998). Metonymy: Developing a cognitive linguistic view. *Cognitive Linguistics*, 9(1), 37–77.

Krikmann, A. (1984). 1001 frage zur logischen struktur der sprichwörter. Semiotische studien zum sprichwort. Simple forms reconsidered I. *Kodikas*, 7(3–4), 387–408.

Krikmann, A. (1998). On the relationships of the rhetorical, modal, logical, and syntactic planes in Estonian proverbs. Part 1. *Folklore: Electronic Journal of Folklore*, 06, 99–127.

Lakoff, G., & Johnson, M. (1980). *Metaphors We Live by*. Chicago; London: University of Chicago Press.

Lakoff, G., & Turner, M. (1989). *More than cool reason: A field guide to poetic metaphor*. Chicago & London: University of Chicago Press.

Langacker, R. W. (1987). *Foundations of cognitive grammar. Volume 1. Theoretical prerequisites*. Stanford: Stanford University Press.

Lemghari, E. (2019a). A metaphor-based account of semantic relations among proverbs. *Cognitive Linguistic Studies*, 6(1), 158–184.

Lemghari, E. (2019b). A metonymic-based account of the semiotic status of proverbs: Against the "deproverbialization thesis". *Linguistics Journal*, 13(1), 30–51.

Lewandowska, A. & Antos, G. (2001). Sprichwörter, metaphorische Konzepte und Alltagsrhetorik: Versuch einer kognitivistischen Begründung der Sprichwortforschung. *Proverbium*, 18, 167–183.

Lewandowska, A., & Antos, G. (2015). Cognitive aspects of proverbs. In H.-G. Hrisztalina & V. Melita Aleksa (Eds.), *Introduction to paremiology* (162–182). Warsaw & Berlin: De Gruyter Open.

Litovkina, A. (2015). Anti-proverbs. In H.-G. Hrisztalina & V. Melita Aleksa (Eds.), *Introduction to paremiology* (326–352). Warsaw & Berlin: De Gruyter Open.

Litovkina, A. T. & Csabi, S. (2002). Metaphors we love by: The cognitive models of romantic love in American proverbs. *Proverbium*, 19, 369–398.

Mieder, W. (1982). *Antisprichworter. Band I*. Wiesbaden: Verlag fur deutsche Sprache.

Mieder, W. (1985). Popular views of the proverb. *Proverbium: Yearbook of International Proverb Scholarship*, 2, 109–143.

Mieder, W. (2004). *Proverbs: A handbook*. Westport: Greenwood Press.

Mieder, W. & Tóthné Litovkina, A. (1999). *Twisted wisdom: Modern anti-proverbs*. Burlington: The University of Vermont.

Molnar, D., & Vidaković Erdeljić, D. (2016). An orchard invisible: Hidden seeds of wisdom in the English and Croatian proverbial apples. *European Journal of Humour Research*, 4(1), 34–58.

Moon, R. (1998). *Fixed expressions and idioms in English: A corpus-based approach*. Oxford & New York: Clarendon.

Nahberger, G. (2000). *Morgen ist auch noch ein tag*. Baltmannsweiler: Schneider-Verlag Hohengehren.

Nahberger, G. (2004). „eine schwalbe macht noch keinen sommer" – eine empirische Untersuchung zur Bedeutungsgenerierung und illokutionären Schlagkraft von Sprichwörtern. In C. Földes & J. Wirrer (Eds.), *Phraseologismen als Gegenstand sprach- und kulturwissenschaftlicher Forschung* (pp. 309–324). Baltmannsweiler: Schneider-Verlag Hohengehren.

Negro, I. (2019). Metaphor and metonymy in food idioms. *Languages*, 4(3), 47.

Norrick, N. R. (1982). Proverbial perlocutions: How to do things with proverbs. *Grazer Linguistische Studien, 17–18*, 169–183.

Norrick, N. R. (2007). Proverbs as set phrases. In H. Burger, D. Dobrovolskij, P. Kühn, & N. R. Norrick (Eds.), *Phraseologie/Phraseology. Volume 1* (pp. 381–393). Berlin & Boston: De Gruyter Mouton.

Norrick, N. R. (2015). Subject area, terminology, proverb definitions, proverb features. In H.-G. Hrisztalina & V. Melita Aleksa (Eds.), *Introduction to paremiology* (pp. 7–27). Warsaw & Berlin: De Gruyter Open.

Nuessel, F. (2003). Proverbs and metaphoric language in second-language acquisition. In W. Mieder (Ed.) *Cognition, comprehension, and communication. A decade of North American proverb studies (1990–2000)* (pp. 395–412). Baltmannsweiler: Verlag Hohengehren.

Panther, K.-U. (2005). The role of conceptual metonymy in meaning construction. In F. J. Ruiz de Mendoza & S. Peña Cervel (Eds.), *Cognitive linguistics: Internal dynamics and interdisciplinary interaction* (pp. 353–386). Berlin & New York: Mouton de Gruyter.

Panther, K.-U., & Thornburg, L. (1998). A cognitive approach to inferencing in conversation. *Journal of Pragmatics*, 30(6), 755–769.

Panther, K.-U., & Thornburg, L. (1999). The potentiality for actuality metonymy in English and Hungarian. In K.-U. Panther & G. Radden (Eds.), *Metonymy in language and thought* (pp. 333–357). Amsterdam & Philadelphia: John Benjamins.

Pérez Hernandez, L. (2013). Illocutionary constructions: (multiple source)-in-target metonymies, illocutionary icms, and specification links. *Language & Communication*, 33(2), 128–149.

Quirk, R., Greenbaum, S., Leech, G., & Svartvik, J. (1985). *A comprehensive grammar of the English language*. London: Longman.

Radden, G., & Kövecses, Z. (1999). Towards a theory of metonymy. In K.-U. Panther & G. Radden (Eds.), *Metonymy in language and thought* (pp. 17–59). Amsterdam & Philadelphia: John Benjamins.

Radden, G., & Kövecses, Z. (2006). Towards a theory of metonymy. In V. Evans, B. K. Bergen, & J. Zinken (Eds.), *The Cognitive linguistics reader* (pp. 335–359). Hereford, U.K.: Equinox Publishing.

Ruiz de Mendoza, F. J. (2000). The role of mappings and domains in understanding metonymy. In A. Barcelona (Ed.), *Metonymy and metaphor at the crossroads* (109–132). Berlin & New York: Mouton de Gruyter.

Ruiz de Mendoza, F. J., & Díez Velasco, O. I. (2002). Patterns of conceptual interaction. In R. Dirven & R. Pörings (Eds.), *Metaphor and Metonymy in Comparison and Contrast* (pp. 489-532). Berlin & New York: Mouton de Gruyter.

Ruiz de Mendoza, F. J., & Díez Velasco, O. I. (2004). Metonymic motivation in anaphoric reference. In G. Radden & K.-U. Panther (Eds.), *Studies in linguistic motivation* (pp. 293–320). Berlin & New York: Mouton de Gruyter.

Ruiz de Mendoza Ibáñez, F. J., & Lozano-Palacio, I. (2019). A cognitive-linguistic approach to complexity in irony: Dissecting the ironic echo. *Metaphor and Symbol*, 34(2), 127–138.

Ruiz de Mendoza, F. J., & Mairal Usón, R. (2007). High-level metaphor and metonymy in meaning construction. In G. Radden, K.-M. Köpcke, T. Berg, & P. Siemund (Eds.), *Aspects of meaning construction* (pp. 3–49). Amsterdam & Philadelphia: John Benjamins.

Ruiz de Mendoza, F. J., & Pérez Hernández, L. (2001). Metonymy and the grammar: Motivation, constraints and interaction. *Language and Communication*, 21(4), 321–357.

Ruiz de Mendoza, F. J., & Otal Campo, J. L. (2002). *Metonymy, grammar, and communication*. Albolote, Spain: Editorial Comares.

Ruiz de Mendoza, F. J., & Peña Cervel, S. (2002). Cognitive operations and and projection spaces. *Jezikoslovlje*, 3(1–2), 131–158.

Searle, J. R. (1975). Indirect speech acts. In P. Cole & J. L. Morgan (Eds.), *Speech acts* (pp. 59–82). New York: Academic Press.

Sperber, D., & Wilson, D. (1986). *Relevance: Communication and cognition*. Oxford: Blackwell.

Sullivan, K., & Sweetser, E. (2010). Is "generic is specific" a metaphor? In F. Parrill, V. Tobin, & M. Turner (Eds.), *Meaning, form, and body* (pp. 309–328). Stanford: Center for the Study of Language and Information.

Szpila, G. (2005). Metonymic operations in Polish proverbs. *Proverbium*, 22, 403–414.

Taylor, J. R. (1989). *Linguistic categorization: Prototypes in linguistic theory*. Oxford: Clarendon Press.

Thornburg, L., & Panther, K.-U. (1997). Speech act metonymies. In W.-A. Liebert, G. Redeker, & L. R. Waugh (Eds.), *Discourse and perspective in Cognitive Linguistics* (205–219). Amsterdam & Philadelphia: John Benjamins.

Tóthné Litovkina, A. (1996). Parömiológiai felmérés Magyarországon. *Magyar Nyelv*, 92(4), 439–457.

Tóthné Litovkina, A., & Mieder, W. (2006). *Old proverbs never die, they just diversify. A collection of anti-proverbs*. Veszprém & Burlington: University of Vermont & The Pannonian University of Veszprém.

Ullmann, S. (1962). *Semantics: An introduction to the science of meaning*. Oxford: Blackwell.

CHAPTER 3

Contradiction in proverbs
The role of stereotypical metaphors

El Mustapha Lemghari
Cadi Ayyad University, Morocco

> Contradiction in proverbs has been noted over centuries. As a culture-specific phenomenon, contradiction is an important research topic for Conceptual Metaphor Theory. It must be asked why given proverbs contradict. The likely answer is that they express opposite meanings. Granted the metaphoricity of proverbs' meanings, contradictory proverbs must be assumed to be motivated via opposite metaphors. This hypothesis is workable, but with the proviso that the metaphorical conceptualisations concerned are not standard conceptual metaphors but rather stereotypical metaphors – a kind of metaphors that emerge from stereotypes, that is, stereotypical thoughts that speakers within a speech community attach to concepts.
>
> **Keywords:** conceptual metaphor, contradiction, proverbs, stereotypical metaphor

1. Introduction

The extensive research in Cognitive Linguistics in the last four decades has created much clarity regarding the hidden mechanisms behind everyday conceptualisation. The main emphasis has been on the cognitive operations involved in the process of meaning construction (see Fauconnier 1985[1994]; Langacker 1987, 1999, 2008; Talmy 2000; Croft and Wood 2000; Fauconnier and Turner 2002; among others). One operation that received much attention since the early 1980s is conceptual metaphor, the study of which has evolved into what has been known as Conceptual Metaphor Theory (CMT) (Lakoff and Johnson 1980, 1999). This notion has been exploited in various areas of research mainly to show that the most part of concepts are metaphor-based in nature.

Another important claim of CMT is that conceptual metaphor is used "to govern reasoning and behaviour based on that reasoning" (Lakoff 1993: 210).

https://doi.org/10.1075/clscc.16.03lem
© 2024 John Benjamins Publishing Company

In other words, since we reason about various cognitive domains in terms of metaphors, the latter appear to influence considerably our behaviour that shows up in the stands we take about different concerns (Lakoff 2002, 2004). In this sense, the study of proverbs from the standpoint of CMT may prove a promising avenue for gathering new insights into the cognitive function of metaphors. As social products, indeed, proverbs lend themselves as vehicles of cultural and ancestral knowledge. For this reason, their study is crucial to casting some light on how their underlying metaphors shape patterns of thinking and behaving.

That proverbs have an influence on people's behaviour is intrinsic to their semiotic status as poly-lexical generic sentences that convey folk truths and allow for default inferences (see Kleiber 1994, 2000; see also Lemghari 2019a). In addition, it is no surprise that conceptual metaphors play a key part in proverbs' multiple readings (see Gibbs and Beitel 1995). Notwithstanding, the issue of how we understand proverbs cannot be accounted for with regard to standard conceptual metaphor only. Another kind of metaphor is required that is more instrumental in framing their meanings, that is, *stereotypical metaphor* (Lemghari *forthcoming*). Such a metaphor calls mostly on the notion of stereotype, that is, the open-ended set of stereotypical thoughts that can be attached to concepts within a speech community (Putnam 1975; Fradin 1984; Anscombre 2001).

The main aim of the chapter is to highlight the import of stereotypical metaphors to the study of proverbs. It is thus more of a theoretical than an empirical contribution. I make the claim that stereotypical metaphors are more crucial than standard conceptual metaphors in the process of proverb understanding. The focus is on contradictory proverbs in particular, the investigation of which would help comprehend why some cognitive domains are prone to opposite metaphorical conceptualisations.

The chapter is divided into three parts. The first one offers a brief overview of some relevant views on contradiction in proverbs. The emphasis is on the interrelation between some foundational notions in the paremiological literature, namely wisdom, truthfulness and contradictoriness. The second presents and illustrates the notion of stereotypical metaphor and shows how it stems from the stereotypical thoughts that define concepts within a speech community; it also emphasises the difference between stereotypical metaphor and standard conceptual metaphor. The final part is dedicated to analysing a set of contradictory proverbs. The main goal is, on the one hand, to demonstrate how they are commonly interpreted and what kind of semantic relations they bear to one another, and on the other, to identify, and to explain the emergence of, the stereotypical metaphors that crucially participate in their individual meanings.

2. Truth, wisdom, and contradiction in proverbs: A brief overview

Contradiction in proverbs is a passionate topic for discussion and research from the standpoint of Cognitive Linguistics. Given that they are commonly conceived as repositories of condensed folk-wisdom, and to the extent that wisdom "should at least contain a kernel of truth" (Teigen 1986: 4), one may expect that they have some bearing on people's way of thinking and behaving. People using proverbs can be assumed to be somehow influenced and accordingly shaped by the statements they convey.

The point being emphasised here is that the notion of wisdom in proverbs appears to be inconsistent with the fact that some of them are contradictory. This would suggest that there is certain lack of logic in speakers' attitudes. However, that individual stances might be self-contradicting raises no serious problem for the semiotic status of proverbs. But that contradictoriness goes along with truthfulness presents indeed a challenge to the wisdom of proverbs, one of the basic definitional features of the category, and this is where the rubber hits the road. Overall, as regards folk knowledge, there seems to be a tendency to understand wisdom generally in terms of truthfulness.

Wisdom and truthfulness are tightly intertwined. They both play a considerable part in the diverging stands researchers take on proverbs. Furnham (1987: 47) observed that there are two main groups of researchers within the broad paradigm of psychological research on proverbs. The first group of linguistically-oriented psychologists is interested more particularly in such topics as "the comprehensibility and interpretability of proverbs (...), their familiarity versus novelty (...), and the visual images associated with them (...)". The second group comprises social psychologists whose focus is on the truthfulness of proverbs. Within the latter group, as Furnham pointed out, several social psychologists showed only little interest in proverbs, due to their ambiguity, vagueness, and contradictoriness. Many others, however, paid much heed to proverbs, focusing more particularly on what makes them be perceived as true (see mainly Yankah 1984[1994]; Teigen 1986; Furnham 1987).

In this line of research, in particular, special emphasis has been on the conflicting relationship between truthfulness and contradictoriness. The main debate concentrated on the issue of finding a way to talk in a consistent fashion of contradiction for proverbs, commonly accounted true statements. In light of some experimental studies conducted on contradictory proverbs (Teigen 1986; Furnham 1987), there seems to be a tendency to favour the property of truthfulness over that of contradictoriness. For instance, Teigen (1986: 47) showed that participants accepted pairs of contradictory proverbs as generally true. However, he noticed that such an acceptance cannot be taken as evidence that people reject the principle of contradiction; most statements can be interpreted in more than one way and, according to the 'logic of conversation' (Grice, 1967), the interpreter will tend to choose a meaning that makes the message as sensible and informative as possible.

This view is explicitly assumed and advocated by Furnham (1987) who showed on the basis of two experiments that truthfulness in contradictory proverbs is a matter of context. To the extent that the role of proverbs is social interaction, contextual features are crucial to interpreting opposite proverbs in the appropriate way, that is, without contradiction. In a word, contradictory proverbs are accepted as true because they can be interpreted in different contexts as meaning different things, that is, as applying to different specific situations.

A rather radical version of such a thesis is found in Yankah (1984 [1994]). To argue for the unlikelihood of contradiction in proverbs, the author drew a clear-cut distinction between "proverb concept" and "proverb context". His main claim was that contradiction characterises the proverb concept, not the proverb context. At the level of concept, the meaning of a proverb is a fact or truism; say a cultural truth that is, by its very nature, prone to contradiction. At the level of context, however, the proverb acquires the nature of an opinion that corroborates or validates the speaker's judgment or point of view. As such, the proverb context is not liable to contradiction, since the opinion it assumes cannot be contested or denied; only can it be accepted or rejected. Yankah (1984 [1994]: 139) concluded that "the whole idea of proverbs in opposition seems to be merely a scholarly construct, of little or no relevance in the free flow of discourse". In sum, the main idea is that proverbs' meanings are context-dependent and, consequently, that proverbs cannot be contradictory in normal discourses where they are just used and interpreted appropriately.

This view poses at least two serious problems. Firstly, the discrepancy between 'proverb concept' and 'proverb context' is radical, in such a way that the same proverb seems to split into two distinct proverbs, each with a particular meaning. In other words, the meaning of a proverb as 'concept' and its meaning as 'context' turn out to be unrelated. The question is how speakers can use a proverb in a discourse context in a meaning that may somehow be unconnected to the meaning she associates to the proverb in her mental lexicon. We would all agree that context helps pin down the speaker's intended meaning – this task context achieves for all lexical units, not only for proverbs –, but what we will have much difficulty understanding is that the specific situation the proverb applies to in discourse context would not be taken to instantiate the proverb as a concept, say as a category. This is to say, the relevance of a proverb in the specific situation that makes it leap to the speaker's mind (see White 1987) is ensured in particular by the continuum between the schematic meaning of the proverb as a concept and the more specific one that is activated in the free flow of discourse.

Secondly, the claim that contradiction characterises proverbs only at the level of concept is questionable, in that not all opposite proverbs cease to behave as antonyms in discourse contexts. Such a flaw might reside in the method of accounting pairs of proverbs as contradictory. It seems that opposition in proverbs is generally delineated because of the meanings they express in isolation. In the latter case, more particularly, proverbs serve rather as schematic categories for a range of potential specific situations (Lakoff and Turner 1989). The problem is, then, that the more schematic the meanings of proverbs the more ambiguous they might be. Because of schematicity, it sometimes happens that pairs of proverbs function in relevant situations either as opposite or non-opposite. As an illustration, the following proverbs are commonly cited as examples of proverbial contradiction (see, for instance, Furnham 1987).

(1) *Never too old to learn.*

(2) *You cannot teach an old dog new tricks.*

The proverb in (1) raises no problem, mainly for the following reason. As a category, that is, as a concept, the proverb exhibits a schematic meaning that fits only one kind of specific situations, those that meet the schematic meaning of the category. In other words, the proverb is unambiguous, its meaning being univocal.

Things are not that simple as regards the proverb in (2). The reason is that its schematic meaning is equivocal, being open indeed to two interpretations. One interpretation (the most common one) that is attested by most dictionaries is that old people are unable to learn new skills or methods. The other, often overlooked, is that old people are rather reluctant to be taught already mastered skills, which means that they are well experienced and thus hate being despised or ridiculed chiefly when reminded how to act or to work. Surprisingly, it is the latter meaning that the French equivalent proverb in (3) foregrounds.

(3) Ce n'   est pas à un vieux singe   qu' on apprend des   grimaces.
    it NEG is not to an old   monkey that we learn   ART.INDF.PL funny faces
    'You cannot teach an old monkey funny faces.'

The basic point here is that the proverbs in (1) and (2) are only partially contradictory at the level of concept. This is to say, *You cannot teach an old dog new tricks* is antonymous with *Never too old to learn* in view of its first meaning, that is, "old people are unable to learn new skills or methods". As a result, unless the discourse context is highly specific, these proverbs would naturally contradict. In contrast, there seems to be no good reason why they would be antonyms when the proverb in (2) means in the flow of discourse rather "old people dislike being taught already mastered skills".

In the paremiological literature, opposition, as well as similarity, in meaning between proverbs is described on intuitive grounds. Such a method leads to disagreement on whether some related proverbs are synonyms or antonyms. A case in point concerns the kind of semantic relations the proverbs below bear to one another:

(4) *Appearances are deceiving.*

(5) *Clothes do not make the man.*

My focus here is mainly on Anscombre's analyses (2012, 2016). To the best of my knowledge, he is the first scholar to have drawn our attention to the subtle semantic relationships between the proverbs in (4)–(5). They are commonly regarded as synonyms. However, Anscombre considers them rather antonyms. Central to his claim is the test he refers to as *conclusive sequences*. This test states that the characterisation of given pairs of proverbs as synonyms or antonyms crucially depends on whether they are substitutable with each other or not in conclusive sequences. The mutual exclusion of these proverbs in the conclusive sequences in (6)–(7) led Anscombre (2016: 47) to conclude that they are antonyms rather than synonyms.

(6) To enter the bank, the thief disguised himself as a policeman, relying on the fact that "Appearances are deceiving" + * "Clothes do not make the man".

(7) To enter the bank, the thief disguised himself as a policeman, but he was quickly unmasked: * "Appearances are deceiving + "Clothes do not make the man".

I attempted in a series of papers to describe the semantic relationships between proverbs from the standpoint of CMT. In doing so, I concentrated mainly on proverbs that pertain to the cognitive domain of APPEARANCE (see Lemghari 2019b, 2020, 2021a), and found out that the kind of semantic relationships holding between the proverbs *Appearances are deceiving* and *Clothes do not make the man* prove more intricate than Anscombre expected them to be. Once again, the reason is that the proverb *Appearances are deceiving* lends itself as a schematic superordinate category for all the appearance-related proverbs that instantiate it. Granted its high-level schematicity, the proverb is ambiguous, in that it works, paradoxically, as synonym for some contradictory proverbs. This conclusion is evidenced by Anscombre's test itself, as shown in conclusive sequences (8) and (9) (see for more details Lemghari 2020, 2021a).

(8) To rescue a child, a firefighter hesitated for a long time before entering the burning house: "Appearances are deceiving" and "Clothes do not make the man", but not "There is many a good cock come out of a tattered bag".

(9) To rescue a child, an old neighbor hurried off to the burning house and saved it: "Appearances are deceiving" and "There is many a good cock come from a tattered bag", but not "Clothes do not make the man".

What these conclusive sequences reveal is that the three proverbs are not related to one another via the same semantic relationship, which casts doubt on their common lexicographical characterisation as synonyms. Of note, only in different conclusive sequences can the proverb *Appearances are deceiving* substitute for both *Clothes do not make the man* and *There is many a good cock come out of a tattered bag*. Such behaviour indicates that the latter proverbs contradict each other. However, they both are synonymous with *Appearances are deceiving*, each in terms of one of its two opposite meanings that are: (i) "judgments formed according to good appearances are inaccurate", and (ii) "judgments formed according to bad appearances are inaccurate" (see Lemghari 2019b for details).

Overall, the semantic network organising appearance-related proverbs includes not only synonymy but also antonymy and hyperonymy relations. Still, the challenge is to account for the hidden cognitive mechanisms behind the semantic subtleties in related proverbs. My focus in the remainder of the chapter is on one of these mechanisms, namely stereotypical metaphor, and its role in proverbial contradiction.

3. Presenting the framework of stereotypical metaphor

3.1 Conceptual metaphor/stereotypical metaphor

CMT originated with the publication by Lakoff and Johnson of *Metaphors We Live By* in early 1980. It quickly evolved into a promising theory for the study of everyday metaphorical thoughts. Since then, CMT experienced important developments as it extended its scope of application to diverse spheres (see Kövecses 2010, 2020). The divergence between scholars notwithstanding, the standard definition of conceptual metaphor is as follows: "The essence of metaphor is understanding and experiencing one kind of thing [one domain of experience] in terms of another" (Lakoff and Johnson 1980: 5). As such, it designates the mapping itself, that is, the set of systematic correspondences between two distinct domains of knowledge: the source and the target. In general, the source domain is somewhat more concrete, while the target is rather abstract. For instance, in the LOVE IS

A JOURNEY metaphor at work in such linguistic expressions as *Our relationship is at a crossroads*; *Love is a two-way street*; *Our relationship has hit a dead-end street*, the source domain JOURNEY is more familiar to, thus directly experienced by, speakers than the target LOVE. As Kövecses (2020: 5) points out, the particular direction of generally conceptualising less accessible target domains via more tangible source domains "makes a lot more sense" than the reverse.

The notion of *stereotypical metaphor* is a new model within the paradigm of metaphor-based approaches. It refers to a kind of conceptual metaphor that, despite being conceptual in character, differs from standard conceptual metaphor in a number of crucial respects. It crucially relies on the construct of stereotype as defined within the framework of Stereotype Theory (Anscombre 2001, 2012, 2016, 2020). The foundational tenet of this theory, in short, is that semantic structures of lexical units are highly complex, being made up not only of lexical meanings but also of various culture-specific stereotypes. The theory borrows the notion of stereotype from Putnam (1975)'s, but uses it most importantly in line with Fradin (1984)'s construct of "stereotypical statement". In this perspective, stereotypes are open-ended sets of stereotypical statements that are conventionally attached to concepts within a speech community. According to Anscombre (2020: 20), the understanding of a word calls on the stereotypical statements it activates in the appropriate context. For instance, the stereotypical statement "monkeys like bananas" the word *monkey* conventionally activates in relation with the word *banana* helps explain its different behaviour with the adjective *normal* and *curious* in the following sentences:

(10)   My monkey is (normal + *curious): it likes bananas.

(11)   My monkey is (curious + * normal): it does not like bananas.

In a word, the use of *normal*, unlike *curious*, is relevant in (10), because there is no inconsistency between its meaning and the stereotypical statement activated by *monkey*. In contrast, in (11), *curious* proves rather compatible with *monkey* than *normal*. The reason is that its meaning matches the negation of the stereotypical statement evoked.

Stereotype Theory has an important implication on the semantic structure of cognitive domains. It provides us with a good theoretical basis for describing domains not only as structurally complex, but also as consisting of various concepts, some of which might entail opposite conceptions because of being characterised via contradictory stereotypes.

Nonetheless, to the extent that the most of concepts are metaphorical in character, there is every reason to believe that speakers' culture-specific conceptualisations are governed by a particular kind of metaphors referred to as *stereo-

typical metaphors (Lemghari *forthcoming*). The latter can be defined as a kind of conceptual mapping that is more concerned with explaining the motivation of the metaphorical extension of concepts. In this sense, it differs from standard conceptual metaphor in specifically emerging from stereotypical thoughts speakers within a speech community attach to concepts. It must be noted, furthermore, that such stereotypical thoughts, unlike metaphorical expressions, are not metaphorical in themselves. Their cognitive function is, indeed, to give rise, as a consequence of their recurrence, to conceptual patterns that capture the emergence of metaphorical senses from the basic meanings of corresponding categories. The metaphoricity of these senses can be evidenced by the fact that the domains they activate are distinct from the ones evoked by their categories. In this regard, the schematic categories constitute the source domains for the target domains. On this view, stereotypical metaphor may fall within the kind of metaphors Kövecses (2010: 84) calls "Source as the root of target".

3.2 Ambiguous metaphorical expressions: A case in point

Let us look, for the purpose of illustration, at a widely discussed expression in the cognitive literature, namely *This surgeon is a butcher* (see Coulson 2001; Glucksberg and Keysar 1990; Grady, Oakley and Coulson 1999; Kövecses 2011; Lakoff 2008; Lemghari 2021b). Kövecses (2011) assumed that two of the conventionalised meanings of the word *butcher* carry main meaning foci. They are the following (according to Merriam-Webster Online Dictionary).

(12) One that kills ruthlessly or brutally.

(13) One that bungles or botches.

The author pointed out, furthermore, that speakers may make two different interpretations of the expression, depending on whether they make use of the main meaning focus in (12) or that in (13). In the first case, speakers would understand the expression as meaning that a surgeon has 'killed one or several patients as a result of an unsuccessful operation'. In the second, they would rather interpret it as meaning that a surgeon is sloppy, carless, and thus incompetent. In short, the expression proves ambiguous.

On the view that both meanings are metaphorical, a double problem arises: there is a need, on the one hand, to identify the metaphors that can be taken to structure the metaphorical senses in (12) and (13), and on the other, to set forth the basis on which such metaphors are posited. The notion of stereotypical metaphor provides a plausible solution to the issue; it mostly sheds light on the way these metaphorical senses arise by extension from the schematic meaning of the category denoted.

My suggestion is that since the meanings in (12) and (13) are distinct, they must be taken to be structured via different metaphors. These metaphors, moreover, must not only be conceived of as conceptual but also as stereotypical in nature, for they do not emerge from linguistic realisations, but rather from the stereotypical thoughts that are part of the semantic characterisation of the concept *butcher*. In a word, each sense arises from a metaphor that is generalised over a set of stereotypical thoughts revolving around a particular scene in the domain of BUTCHERY.

The sense in (12) refers to the act of killing animals for food. This act is awful for all of us who are not in the business of slaughtering animals, and thus prompts the emergence of a number of stereotypical thoughts in terms of what we seem to conceive of butchers as cruel animal-killers. Some of these are:

(14) a. Butchers kill animals.
 b. Butchers have no mercy, no compassion for animals.
 c. Butchers are not repulsed or disgusted by the spectacle of blood being shed.
 d. Butchers are bloodthirsty.

The sense in (12) obtains indeed once the meaning 'a butcher is a pitiless animal-killer' is mapped onto the sense 'a butcher is a pitiless people-killer', and hence the reason it is metaphorical in character. As we can see, the schematic category of butcher serves as the source domain, whereas the metaphorical sense "a butcher is a pitiless people-killer" as the target domain. Clearly, although the concept of butcher denotes one single category, the metaphorical sense it gives rise to by extension invokes a rather different domain, that is, KILLING PEOPLE PITILESSLY. In sum, the stereotypical conceptualisation at work here can be put in the form of the metaphor PITILESS PEOPLE-KILLERS ARE BUTCHERS.

Why should it be regarded as a stereotypical rather than a standard conceptual metaphor? The answer is that it mainly serves to capture the stereotypical mapping between the literal conception "a butcher is a pitiless animal-killer" and the metaphorical conception "a butcher is a pitiless people-killer". As such, it is claimed to arise from the recurring stereotypical pattern our conceptualisation of butchers slaughtering animals activates.

The sense in (13) refers rather to the act of cutting carcasses and preparing meat for sale. Such a scene is not terrible in itself, for it does not foreground the domain of LIFE. Our attention is therefore drawn mostly to the way s/he dismembers carcasses with butchery-specific tools. Such a scene, wherein butchers work on dead rather than live animals, triggers a set of stereotypical thoughts that all partake of the paradigm of carelessness and sloppiness. Among these are:

(15) a. Butchers rip carcasses to bits.
 b. Butchers tear carcasses limb to limb.
 c. Butchers use cleavers to chop meat.
 d. Butchers debone and defat meat.

These thoughts prompt the literal stereotypical conception 'a butcher is a carcass-careless cutter'. Such a conception provides indeed the basis for thinking metaphorically of a person who carries out tasks in a sloppy fashion as a butcher. Its metaphorical character is due in principle to the fact that the domain it conjures up is distinct from the one evoked by the schematic category of butcher. Thus, it is motivated via a stereotypical metaphor that encapsulates the commonality inherent in its underlying stereotype, that is, TASK-BUNGLERS ARE BUTCHERS.

To conclude this section, one last question suggests itself: why is it important for CMT to distinguish stereotypical metaphor in addition to standard conceptual metaphor? There might be many reasons for that; the following ones are readily apparent.

In general, in identifying a conceptual metaphor, scholars focus on metaphorical expressions as a whole. In other words, although identification of conceptual metaphors depends on specific source and target items, their formulation tends to take into account the overall meanings of the expressions. Therefore, most conceptual metaphors identified in the literature are of a high level of generality. This is not a flaw in itself, but it seems that the principle of generality makes researchers overlook the main meaning foci involved in the metaphorical meanings of the linguistic expressions. In this case, even though the source word may exhibit some entrenched figurative senses, the source domain is identified in view of the literal meaning of the category instead of the potential figurative senses that might participate in the metaphorical conceptualisation. Stereotypical metaphor helps sort out such a problem. To the extent that it is concerned with not only the literal but also the metaphorical senses of source words, it helps explain why the expressions allow for different interpretations. That is to say, it disambiguates them by accounting for the main meaning focus that is involved in the appropriate interpretation.

In particular, one crucial implication of stereotypical metaphor is that it provides the grounding for contradiction in statements relating to the same cognitive domain. The question that must be asked is: why is it that some cognitive domains can be assessed in a contradictory way? For instance, why is the domain of PRUDENCE conceived of in the proverbs in (16)–(17) both as a wise and unwise precaution? (see Lemghari 2019b).

(16) *Look before you leap.*

(17) *He who hesitates is lost.*

A piece of answer to this question lies in the main claim that contradiction arises from the opposition in the stereotypes underlying concepts. This claim also leads to a better understanding of why a number of proverbs contradict.

4. How stereotypical metaphors account for contradiction in proverbs

Lakoff and Tuner's (1989) *More than cool reason* highlighted the part conceptual metaphor plays in the way proverbs are understood. The authors developed the GREAT CHAIN metaphor to account for the mapping of the forms of a given level on the Great Chain of Being onto the forms of another one. To the extent that proverbs are essentially connected with human concerns, the lower-level forms (object, plants, animals, etc.) are mapped onto the higher-level properties of human beings. The GREAT CHAIN metaphor serves thus the function of inducing proverbs' metaphoricity. In this sense more particularly, it is akin to many other conceptual metaphors such as PERSONS ARE INANIMATE OBJECTS (see Gibbs and Beitel 1995), PEOPLE ARE PLANTS, PEOPLE ARE COMMODITIES, and so on (see Kövecses 2010).

Despite their crucial effect on proverb understanding, these kinds of metaphors fail to explain how their meanings are related to the readings we make of proverbs, either in isolation or in appropriate contexts. For instance, according to Gibbs and Beitel (1995), people understand the proverb *A rolling stone gathers no moss* in terms of the metaphors LIFE IS A JOURNEY and PERSONS ARE INANIMATE OBJECTS. They showed in an experiment that its various interpretations, thanks to these metaphors, could not boil down to the literal paraphrase "A restless person keeps few possessions".

A body of evidence was adduced to indicate that these metaphors are instrumental in the multiple interpretations of the proverb (see Lemghari 2021a for details). In short, the mapping of the lower-level forms *rolling stone* and *moss* onto higher-level properties of human beings are motivated via the PERSONS ARE INANIMATE OBJECTS metaphor. Similarly, the LIFE IS A JOURNEY metaphor is activated because of the domain of MOVEMENT evoked by the form *rolling stone*.

Yet, it remains unclear how the meanings of such metaphors are connected with the various interpretations of the proverb. Putting aside the details of the previous study, I would suggest that the metaphors that play a key role in the meanings of the proverb are stereotypical metaphors, not conceptual metaphors of the sort suggested by Gibbs and Beitel (1995). The main idea is that once the GREAT

CHAIN metaphor (or even the metaphors PERSONS ARE INANIMATE OBJECTS and the LIFE IS A JOURNEY) has achieved its task, the focus should be put on the higher-level properties onto which they are projected.

It must be first acknowleged that the GREAT CHAIN metaphor is not an arbitrary mechanism that maps any form of being onto any other form. Rather, it abides by the general tenet that conceptual mapping within the framework of CMT is motivated. How conceptual mappings between different forms of being are motivated depends on how their properties are apprehended. Accordingly, it makes sense that the forms *rolling stone* and *moss* bring to mind the domains of RESTLESSNESS and ABUNDANCE, respectively. Such mappings must come as no surprise. The form *rolling stone* can be found to denote the domain of RESTLESSNESS, if only because of the lexical meaning of the word *rolling*. Likewise, the form *moss* readily invokes the domain of ABUNDANCE, granted our knowledge about the development and reproduction of this plant: we experientially know that it grows luxuriantly in urban areas, on driveways, sidewalks, and various other man-made structures. Furthermore, it is a mass substance, and consequently satisfies the ontological properties of homogeneity, continuity, and the like (Pelletier 1975, 1979; Quine 1960; among others). Thus, even if it may cover only a limited area, it is perceived to some extent as intrinsically plentiful. This explains why the word *moss* collocates with verbs that denote continuous extension and/or quantity in space such as *spread, overgrow*, etc. It is no accident, therefore, that stones can be described as overgrown with moss. In this way, the verb *gather*, because of its salient meaning (i.e., amass, collect), proves to be supportive of the notion of profusion evoked by *moss*. Overall, the proverb understanding is crucially grounded in our knowledge that moss grows abundantly over motionless stones.

Far more central to the way the proverb is understood, however, are the stereotypes the domains of RESTLESSNESS and ABUNDANCE are attached as a result of a number of stereotypical behaviours restless persons exhibit in causal relation to abundance. Two of such stereotypes turn out to be opposite in character, as illustrated by the following assumptions:

(18) a. Restless persons are satisfied /They are not bothered with material possessions.
 b. Restless persons are free from social worry/ They are not stuck in a rut.

(19) a. Restless persons are unsatisfied, always running around to enjoy further profits.
 b. Restless persons are stressed/unwise, etc.

(20) a. Plenty is no plague.
 b. Abundance feeds our confidence and helps us stay resilient during the tough time

(21) a. Too much is hard to enjoy.
　　 b. Abundance of things turns into a burden.

As we can see, the stereotypes in (18)–(19) and in (20)–(21) provide alternatively a positive and a negative conception of RESTLESSNESS and ABUNDANCE, respectively. They are taken to be structured by the following stereotypical metaphors:

(22)　RESTLESSNESS IS GAIN

(23)　RESTLESSNESS IS WASTE

(24)　ABUNDANCE IS WELL-BEING

(25)　ABUNDANCE IS BURDEN

The conceptual integration of these metaphors yields the contradictory meanings that are commonly associated with the proverb, that is: "moving all the time is efficient" and "moving all the time is inefficient" (see Lemghari 2021a for details).

The proverb *A rolling stone gathers no moss* is metaphorically complex because it combines the stereotypical metaphors of two cognitive domains, RESTLESSNESS and ABUNDANCE. In most cases, however, the proverbs we deal with exhibit simple metaphorical potential. I limit myself to the following:

(26)　*Many hands make light work.*

(27) a. *Too many cooks spoil the broth.*
　　 b. *With seven nurses the child loses an eye.*

(28) a. *A heavy purse makes a light heart.*
　　 b. *A light purse makes a heavy heart.*

(29) a. *Much coin, much care.*
　　 b. *Money cannot buy happiness.*

The main claim is that contradiction in these sets of proverbs includes opposite views of the same cognitive domains. Granted that cognitive domains are metaphor-based, each view is assumed to be structured via a metaphor. The latter is stereotypical in nature, for it derives from a particular underlying stereotype. It makes sense in this way to state, incidentally, that metaphors do not primordially arise from linguistic expressions; the latter only instantiate structuring metaphors. In other words, linguistic expressions serve the function of reflecting a metaphor-based view about a given domain that already exists in the form of a metaphorical pattern in the speaker's mind. This may explain why many proverbs, despite their different forms of being, are similar in meaning. This is the case of the proverbs in (a–b).

Actually, there seems to be a crucial difference between stereotypical metaphors and standard conceptual metaphors. While conceptual metaphors require – at least according to Stefanowitsch (2006) – that metaphorical expressions constitute "metaphorical patterns" in that they contain explicit source and/or target items, stereotypical metaphors need not abide by such a constraint. For instance, there is every reason that the proverbs in (26)–(27), mostly because of the idea of *joint effort and/or work* they display, pertain to the domain of ASSISTANCE, but none of them could be taken to comprise items that evoke it overtly. The question now is: what does make us understand those proverbs as expressing opposite meanings about assistance, that is, respectively, 'assistance makes work easy' and 'assistance makes work difficult'? I believe stereotypical metaphor does. Of note, assistance is assessed in general as positive. Nonetheless, there are many situations where it is rather unnecessary, or at least over what is needed, and hence the reason it may be considered negative.

It is noteworthy that the proverbs in (26)–(27) do not invoke the domain of ASSISTANCE as an undifferentiated whole; the focus is particularly on one of its sub-domains, namely QUANTITATIVE ASSISTANCE, as is evidenced by the very meaning of the quantifiers *many* and *too*. In this sense, a given amount of assistance can be seen either as positive or negative, depending on whether the quantity of aid afforded in particular circumstances makes a worthwhile contribution to, or has an adverse effect on, the work under way. On this view, therefore, the sub-domain QUANTITATIVE ASSISTANCE breaks down into two separate aspects that contradict along the positive/negative dimension.

On its positive aspect, QUANTITATIVE ASSISTANCE remains within the limits of what is desirable or permissible. This is exactly the quantity of help the proverb in (26) emphasises. In view of this, the proverb can be suggested to be structured by the positive metaphor QUANTITATIVE ASSISTANCE IS RELIEF that is abstracted from the stereotypical assumptions in (30).

(30) a. Much help makes quick progress.
 b. Much help realises unexpected results.
 c. Much help is a delightful aid.

On its negative aspect, however, QUANTITATIVE ASSISTANCE is viewed as a rather excessive or undesirable support, as show the proverbs in (27a)–(b). Crucial to the way we interpret them is our common understanding that a large number of people taking part in a common project might be pulling in different directions, thereby hindering its progress or achievement. There is hence evidence to suggest that QUANTITATIVE ASSISTANCE is conceptualised here in terms of the negative metaphor QUANTITATIVE ASSISTANCE IS AN ENCUMBRANCE that is generalised over such stereotypical thoughts as the following:

(31) a. Much help is a hindrance to rapid work.
 b. Much help ends up in unwelcome outcomes.
 c. Much help is a rather bothersome service.

This account still hits two snags. First, why are the domains of RELIEF and ENCUMBRANCE preferentially singled out as source domains? Second, why are the stereotypical thoughts not accounted mere metaphorical expressions?

As regards the first question, it is legitimate to state, in light of the statements' content, that QUANTITATIVE ASSISTANCE can be metaphorically thought of as either RELIEF or ENCUMBRANCE, depending on whether it is positively or negatively evaluated. The reason for selecting these concepts over many possible domains is simply that QUANTITATIVE ASSISTANCE is commonly experienced either as a kind of comfort that makes hard work much easier to do, or as a brake that is put on the progress of a project. Therefore, the source domains RELIEF and ENCUMBRANCE are evoked because of the commonality inherent in the recurring stereotypical thoughts attached to ASSISTANCE. The answer to the second question is that the propositions in (30) and (31) are mere instances of the underlying stereotypes at the root of QUANTITATIVE ASSISTANCE. In this sense, it is the stereotypes that are metaphorical, not the instantiating individual thoughts.

The proverbs in (28)–(29) afford a fascinating case for addressing their intricate semantic relationships, as well as providing additional evidence in support of the model of stereotypical metaphor. Before going any further, clarification of the kind of semantic relationship the proverbs *A heavy purse makes a light heart* and *A light purse makes a heavy heart* bear to each other is of importance here. They are commonly considered synonyms (see Manser 2007). Such a claim sounds reasonable from the perspective of CMT. Overall, it can be argued that their synonymy is grounded in a common underlying stereotypical metaphor, namely the WEALTH IS HAPPINESS metaphor. What distinguishes this metaphor is that it originates in two somehow distinct sets of stereotypical thoughts. Both sets underscore the numerous merits of wealth either in positive or negative terms, as shown in (32) and (33), respectively.

(32) a. Plenty of money helps people develop a sense of self-confidence and self-esteem.
 b. Plenty of money makes people happy and carefree.
 c. Plenty of money provides the feelings of certainty and security.

(33) a. Lack of money makes people self-doubting.
 b. Lack of money generates trouble and anxiety.
 c. Lack of money produces a heightened sense of insecurity and isolation.

Rather than contradicting, these stereotypical thoughts turn out to complement and reinforce each other, in that they all emphasise some qualities of wealth. Still, the kind of synonymy the proverbs present is somehow special, and could best be referred to as *complementary synonymy*. Crucial to synonymy relation in general is the fact that the connection of synonyms with the coordinating conjunction *and* is somehow redundant: a pair of synonymous words cannot be appropriately joined with *and* unless one of them adds further information. Likewise, synonymous proverbs cannot be joined together unless they are complementary. For the purpose of comparison, connecting the proverbs in (27a)–(b) would result in tautology, as is shown in this example.

(34) The project failed because, as we say, too many cooks spoil the broth and with seven nurses, the child loses an eye.

However, no such redundancy would be observed in joining the proverbs in (28a)–(b), as illustrated by (35). Here the information the second proverb brings about is the confirmation that wealth promotes well-being.

(35) His new opulent situation promises him comfort and prosperity, and as we say, a heavy purse makes a light heart and a light purse makes a heavy heart.

In light of the WEALTH IS HAPPINESS stereotypical metaphor, the proverbs *A heavy purse makes a light heart* and *A light purse makes a heavy heart* lend themselves as contradictory with the proverbs *Much coin, much care* and *Money cannot buy happiness*, given in (29a)–(b). Granted that proverbial contradiction stems from opposite underlying metaphors, it stands to reason that the latter set of proverbs rely on a contradictory stereotypical metaphor that provides a rather negative opinion of the domain of WEALTH. This metaphor can be formulated as WEALTH IS ANNOYANCE. As such, it is expected to be generalised over a set of stereotypical thoughts that cast wealth in tones of negativity, overall, as a source of worry and anxiety. Some of such thoughts are:

(36) a. Too much money causes too much trouble.
b. Keeping too much money puts one's security at risk.
c. Too much money wrecks the ties of love and friendship.

I would refer, for further evidence, to one famous fable by Jean de La Fontaine (1971), *Le Savetier et le Financier* (The Cobbler and the Financier), that best exploits the WEALTH IS ANNOYANCE metaphor, and also summarises the main stereotypical thoughts it emerges from (an English version of the fable is available at the link https://readandripe.com/the-cobbler-and-the-financier).

5. Conclusion

Many rounds of metaphor investigation have been achieved in the last four decades, and have greatly contributed to improving our understanding of the conceptual nature of metaphor, as well as its bearing on people's way of thinking and behaving. The brief round the chapter accomplished is meant to call attention to a different kind of metaphor that stands some chance to elucidating some less clear aspects of everyday metaphorical thoughts. This kind is referred to as stereotypical metaphors. They are highly culture-specific in the sense that they derive from the stereotypes speakers within a speech community attached to the most of concepts. As such, they open up new perspectives for tackling at least three serious challenges to CMT. These are: (i) how the metaphorical senses of words arise by extension from the schematic meanings of their categories; (ii) why some metaphorical expressions are ambiguous; and (iii) how to account for the fact that some concepts allow for opposite metaphorical conceptualisations.

The first and the second issues turned out to be tightly interrelated, in that ambiguity in metaphorical expressions appears to follow from the coexistence of two or more main meaning foci. The problem then is what fosters multi-main meaning foci in ambiguous expressions. Stereotypical metaphors afford a convincing answer to this issue. On the assumption that they motivate semantic extension of words, they entail that metaphorical expressions containing polysemous source words may be open to several interpretations, depending mostly on which metaphorical senses, indeed which underlying stereotypical metaphors, participate in the conceptualisations involved.

The chapter focused mainly on the third issue, and sought to provide a theoretical basis for handling contradiction in proverbs. Such a phenomenon presents indeed an interesting case for investigating the issue of why the existence of contradictory proverbs does not seriously question their semiotic status both as wise and truthful statements. In this respect, it was shown that standard conceptual metaphors only partially account for proverbs' meanings. A brief survey of the proverb *A rolling stone gathers no moss* reveals that the conceptual metaphors LIFE IS A JOURNEY and PEOPLE ARE INANIMATE OBJECTS play a less crucial role in the way speakers interpret it as expressing two opposite meanings. Stereotypical metaphor proves rather instrumental in indicating in general why a given metaphorical expression might give rise to contradiction. Granted the hypothesis that a concept may be attached a number of stereotypes, there is likelihood that it may have a variety of senses, some of which can contradict at least along the positive/negative dimension. Therefore, a metaphorical expression that evokes such a concept is likely to be understood in opposite meanings.

It must be noted, furthermore, that self-contradicting proverbs as *A rolling stone gathers no moss* are extremely rare. Contradiction characterises rather separate proverbs. The account of a series of examples at the end provided additional evidence in support of the claim that stereotypical metaphors serve the function of capturing and motivating opposite views about the same cognitive domains. In a word, the contradiction in pairs of proverbs amounts to the opposition in the stereotypes underlying the cognitive domains activated.

There is still much to be learnt about stereotypical metaphors. However, the main goal of the chapter seems to have been reached: stereotypical metaphors have been shown to play a crucial role in framing proverbs' meanings, and hence provide a good basis for explaining why their folk truths come sometimes to contradict.

References

Anscombre, J. C. (2001). Dénomination, sens et référence dans une théorie des stéréotypes nominaux [Denomination, meaning and reference within a theory of nominal stereotypes]. *Cahiers de Praxématique*, 36, 43–72.

Anscombre, J. C. (2012). Le problème de l'antonymie dans le champ parémique [The problem of antonymy in the paremic field]. In J. C. Anscombre, A. Rodríguez Somolinos, & S. Gómez-Jordana Ferary (Eds.), *Voix et marqueurs du discours: Des connecteurs à l'argument d'autorité [Voices and discourse markers: From connectors to the argument from authority]* (pp. 121–140). Lyon: ENS Editions.

Anscombre, J. C. (2016). Sur la détermination du sens des proverbes [On determining the meaning of proverbs]. *Etudes et Travaux d'Eur'ORBEM*, 1, 39–53.

Anscombre, J. C. (2020). La théorie des stéréotypes: Référence, représentation du monde et morphologie lexicale [Theory of stereotypes: Reference, representation of the world and lexical morphology]. In E. Hilgert, S. Palma, G. Kleiber, P. Frath, & R. Daval (Eds.), *Lexique et référence [Lexicon and reference]* (pp. 13–32). Reims: Editions et Presses Universitaires de Reims.

Coulson, S. (2001). *Semantic leaps. Frame-shifting and conceptual blending in meaning construction*. Cambridge: Cambridge University Press.

Croft, W., & Wood, E. (2000). Construal operations in linguistics and artificial intelligence. In L. Albertazzi (Ed.), *Meaning and cognition. A multidisciplinary approach* (pp. 51–78). Amsterdam & Philadelphia: John Benjamins.

Fauconnier, G. (1985[1994]). *Mental spaces*. Cambridge: Cambridge University Press.

Fauconnier, G., & Turner, M. (2002). *The way we think: Conceptual blending and the mind's hidden complexities*. New York: Basic Books.

Fradin, B. (1984). Anaphorisation et stéréotypes nominaux. *Lingua*, 64(4), 325–369.

Furnham, A. (1987). The proverbial truth: Contextually reconciling and the truthfulness of antonymous Proverbs. *Journal of Language and Social Psychology*, 1, 49–55.

Gibbs, R., & Beitel, D. (1995). What proverb understanding reveals about how people think. *Psychological Bulletin*, 1, 133–154.

Glucksberg, S., & Keysar, B. (1990). Understanding metaphorical comparisons: Beyond similarity. *Psychological Review*, 97, 3–18.

Grady, J., Oakley, T., & Coulson, S. (1999). Blending and metaphor. In R. W. Gibbs, & G. Steen (Eds.), *Metaphor in cognitive linguistics* (pp. 101–124). Amsterdam & Philadelphia: John Benjamins.

Grice, H. M. (1967). The logic of conversation. *William James Lectures*. Cambridge, MA: Harvard University

Kleiber, G. (1994). *Nominales. Essais de sémantique référentielle [Nominals. Essays on referential semantics]*. Paris: Armand Colin.

Kleiber, G. (2000). Sur le sens des proverbes [On the semantics of proverbs]. *Langages*, 139, 39–58.

Kövecses, Z. (2010). *Metaphor: A practical introduction*. Second edition. Oxford & New York: Oxford University Press.

Kövecses, Z. (2011). Recent developments in metaphor theory: Are the new views rival ones? *Review of Cognitive Linguistics*, 9(1), 11–25.

Kövecses, Z. (2020). *Extended conceptual metaphor theory*. Cambridge: Cambridge University Press.

La Fontaine, J. (1971). *Fables [Fables]*. Paris: Le Livre de Poche.

Lakoff, G. (1993). The contemporary theory of metaphor. In A. Ortony (Ed.), *Metaphor and thought*. Second edition. (pp. 202–251). Cambridge: Cambridge University Press.

Lakoff, G. (2002). *Moral politics. How liberals and conservatives think*. Second edition. Chicago, IL: The University of Chicago Press.

Lakoff, G. (2004). *Don't think of an elephant! Know your values and frame the debate*. White River Junction, VT: Chelsea Green Publishing.

Lakoff, G. (2008). The neural theory of metaphor. In R. W. Gibbs (Ed.), *The Cambridge handbook of metaphor and thought* (pp. 17–38). Cambridge & New York: Cambridge University Press.

Lakoff, G., & Johnson, M. (1980). *Metaphors we live by*. Chicago, IL: The University of Chicago Press.

Lakoff, G., & Johnson, M. (1999). *Philosophy in the flesh: The embodied mind and its challenge to western thought*. New York: Basic Books.

Lakoff, G., & Turner, M. (1989). *More than cool reason: A field guide to poetic metaphor*. Chicago, IL: The University of Chicago Press.

Langacker, R. W. (1987). *Foundations of cognitive grammar: Theoretical prerequisites* (Vol. 1). Stanford, CA: Stanford University Press.

Langacker, R. W. (1999). *Grammar and conceptualization*. New York: Mouton de Gruyter.

Langacker, R. W. (2008). *Cognitive grammar: A basic introduction*. Oxford & New York: Oxford University Press.

Lemghari, E. (2019a). A metonymic-based account of the semiotic status of proverbs: Against the "Deproverbialization Thesis". *The Linguistics Journal*, 13, 30–51.

Lemghari, E. (2019b). A metaphor-based account of semantic relations among proverbs. *Cognitive Linguistic Studies*, 6(1), 158–184.

Lemghari, E. (2020). *Les apparences sont trompeuses* et *L'habit ne fait pas le moine*, synonymes ou antonymes ou les deux à la fois? [*Appearances are deceiving* and *Clothes do not make the man*, synonyms or antonyms, or both?]. In M. Meulleman, S. Palma, & A. Theissen (Eds.), *Liber Amicorum: clins d'œil linguistiques en hommage à Emilia Hilgert* [Liber Amicorum: linguistic winks in homage to Emilia Hilgert] (pp. 15–30). Reims: Editions et Presses Universitaires de Reims.

Lemghari, E. (2021a). Constructing a broad model for proverb understanding. *Metaphor and Symbol*, 36(4), 265–287.

Lemghari, E. (2021b). Metaphorical blending in complex proverbs. A case study. *Metaphor and the Social World*, 11(1), 72–98.

Lemghari, E. (forthcoming). Stereotypical metaphor: a missing piece in Conceptual Metaphor Theory.

Manser, M. (2007). *The facts on file dictionary of proverbs: Meanings and origins of more than 1,700 popular sayings*. Second edition. New York: Infobase Publishing.

Pelletier, F. J. (1975). Non-Singular reference: Some preliminaries. *Philosophia*, 5(4), 451–465.

Pelletier, F. J. (Ed.) (1979). *Mass terms: Some philosophical problems*. Dordrecht: Reidel Publishing Company.

Putnam, H. (1975). *Philosophical papers* (Vol. 2). Cambridge: Cambridge University Press.

Quine, W. V. (1960). *Word and object*. Cambridge, MA: MIT Press.

Stefanowitsch, A. (2006). Words and their metaphors: A corpus-based approach. In A. Stefanowitsch & S. Gries (Eds.), *Corpus-based approaches to metaphor and metonymy* (pp. 63–105). Berlin & New York: Mouton de Gruyter.

Talmy, L. (2000). *Toward a cognitive semantics* (Vol. 1). Cambridge, MA: MIT Press.

Teigen, K. (1986). Old truths or fresh insights? A study of students' evaluations of proverbs. *British Journal of Social Psychology*, 25(1), 43–49.

White, G. M. (1987). Proverbs and cultural models: An American psychology of problem solving. In D. Holland & N. Quinn (Eds.), *Cultural models in language and thought* (pp. 151–172). Cambridge & New York: Cambridge University Press.

Yankah, K. (1984[1994]). Do proverbs contradict? In W. Mieder (Ed.), *Wise words. Essays on the proverb* (pp. 127–142). London & New York: Routledge.

PART II

A cognitive-cross-cultural linguistic approach on proverbs

CHAPTER 4

Metaphors of love before and after marriage in proverbs and anti-proverbs

Anna T. Litovkina
J. Selye University, Komárno, Slovakia

In the present chapter I am going to discuss the ways how love after marriage is viewed and conceptualised in the body of Anglo-American proverbs and anti-proverbs (or proverb transformations), as well as in proverbs from around the world. My discussion is organised in two parts. While in the first part of the chapter I treat the paremiological issue of the metaphorical nature of proverbs, in the second part I address the relation between love and marriage in proverbs from around the world and Anglo-American anti-proverbs. I treat various metaphors of love which lead one to getting married (e.g., LOVE IS FOLLY), as well as some metaphors of love after marriage (e.g., LOVE IS WAR).

Keywords: anti-proverb, proverb, Anglo-American, love, marriage, metaphor

1. Addressing the paremiological issue of the metaphorical nature of proverbs

1.1 Metaphor as one of the most powerful markers of proverbiality

One of the most exciting and complex issues that emerge in connection with research in paremiology (i.e., proverb science) concerns the metaphorical nature of proverbs. According to Shirley Arora (1984: 12), metaphor is "one of the most effective indicators of proverbiality" and (along with personification, hyperbole, rhyme, parallelism, paradox, alliteration, irony, etc.) serves as a major device for creating figurativeness in proverbs. The role of metaphor is so pervasive in proverbs, that many of the definitions of the genre employ the word 'metaphor'; consider Wolfgang Mieder's: "A proverb is a short, generally known sentence that expresses common, traditional and didactic views in a metaphorical and fixed form and which is easily remembered and repeated" (Mieder 1985: 118). It has

https://doi.org/10.1075/clscc.16.04lit
© 2024 John Benjamins Publishing Company

also been observed that "By translating a realistic situation into a metaphorical proverb, we can generalize the unique problem and express it as a common phenomenon of life" (Mieder 1989a: 20). As Mieder (1989a: 20) points out, "metaphors comprise an important marker for many proverbs, and it is exactly this vivid imagery of most proverbs which makes them so appealing to us." Thus, metaphorical proverbs are remarkably common (see the extensive lists of bibliography on various markers of proverbiality in Tóthné Litovkina 1993; T. Litovkina and Mieder 2005). For instance, my analysis of 5 randomly selected pages from "A Dictionary of American Proverbs" (see Mieder et al. 1992) has shown that 49% of American proverbs lend themselves to metaphorical interpretation, while 51% of them are to be understood literally (see Tóthné Litovkina 1994, 1998). Furthermore, my research on 40 American subjects has shown that figurativeness has proved to be one of the most powerful markers of proverbiality (see Tóthné Litovkina 1994).

As far as the metaphor is concerned, several proverb scholars have discussed the matters of distinguishing metaphorical expressions from non-metaphorical ones, and have regarded metaphoricalness as an indispensable trait of the proverb, e.g., G. L. Permyakov (1979: 12–14) distinguished proverbs from folk aphorisms, or aphorisms, Nigel Barley – from maxims (1972: 738–739); Archer Taylor (1962: 5–15) – metaphorical proverbs from proverbial apothegms. But proverbs without their actualisation could hardly be divided into two clearly distinguished classes: metaphorical and non-metaphorical ones. Metaphorical meaning manifests itself only in concrete text actualisation. Grzybek's comment (1987: 61), according to which "a distinction between metaphorical and non-metaphorical sayings is assumed to exist not as such, but only in language use", is relevant here. Galit Hasan-Rokem (1982: 15) supports the same idea, demanding that the metaphorical-literal character of proverbs should be analysed in context: "This is a distinction not referring to text, but to use. Thus, proverb *x* may be in a metaphorical relationship to context *a*, but in literal relationship to context *b*, and so forth". Barley (1974: 991) states, "It seems that we cannot at one moment take one of our proverbs literally and at another metaphorically".

Kirshenblatt-Gimblett has addressed the problem of proverb meaning from the perspective of the multiple contexts in which each proverb can be used. She explains the multiple meaning and usage of three common Anglo-American proverbs (*A friend in need is a friend in deed*, *Money talks*, and *A rolling stone gathers no moss*). Let us observe here only the findings concerning the last proverb. When asked about the meaning of the proverb *A rolling stone gathers no moss*, the class of about 80 Texas students came up with the following three possibilities (Kirshenblatt-Gimblett 1973: 821–822):

(1) a rolling stone gathering no moss is like a machine that keeps running and never gets rusty and broken; (2) a rolling stone is like a person who keeps on moving, never settles down, and therefore never gets anywhere; (3) a rolling stone is like a person who keeps moving and is therefore free, not burdened with a family, and material possessions and not likely to fall into a rut.

Kirshenblatt-Gimblett points out that her students were surprised, because in most cases, each of them was familiar with one, or at most, two of the possible meanings. She gives four sources for the multiple meaning of the proverb (Kirshenblatt-Gimblett 1973: 822):

(1) what is understood by the image presented in the metaphor (stone roller, stone in brook); (2) what is understood as the general principle expressed by the metaphor (movement promotes efficiency, stability promotes tangible gains); (3) how the general principle is evaluated (tangible gains are worthwhile, tangible gains are not worthwhile); (4) the requirements of the situation in which the proverb is used regardless of what one actually believes in principle (does one want to console or criticize the stable person; does one wants to console or criticize the wanderer).

1.2 Addressing the paremiological issue of the metaphorical nature of proverbs from a cognitive linguistic view

Cognitive linguistic studies on proverbs have shown that proverbs are interpreted mainly with the help of conceptual metaphors. As Gibbs and Beitel (1995: 136) propose, "[t]he conceptual metaphor hypothesis for proverb understanding states that many proverbs arise from and are understood in terms of different conceptual metaphors that are ubiquitous in everyday thought". As a result, conceptual metaphors can provide partial motivation for the figurative meanings of proverbs. In addition, this metaphorical process in the case of proverbs does not exclusively apply to one language alone, but to a variety of languages. Gibbs and Beitel (1995: 136) illustrate this statement with the example of the proverb *One rotten apple spoils the whole barrel*, which is available in German as well, in the linguistically different form *One bad potato ruins the whole bag*. These proverbs are reflections of the conceptual metaphor PEOPLE ARE INANIMATE OBJECTS. The important claim here is that "[t]he possibility that people in different cultures may draw similar kinds of complex inferences for these expressions suggests that conceptual metaphors might underlie what many proverbs mean" (Gibbs and Beitel 1995: 136).

One of the claims proposed by George Lakoff and Mark Turner (1989: 162) in connection with the link between proverbs and metaphors is that "there exists a single generic-level metaphor, GENERIC IS SPECIFIC, which maps a single specific-level schema onto an indefinitely large number of parallel specific-level schemas that all have the same generic-level structure as the source domain schema". For instance, the proverb *It is no use crying over spilt milk* can be applied to various situations, like breaking a vase, failing an exam, or even manslaughter. There is, however, something common in these very different specific situations. The focus of all these situations can be captured with a generic definition of the meaning of the proverb, which is the following: "Don't get upset about something that has already happened and can't be changed" (T. Litovkina and Mieder 2006: 128).

The role of metaphor in proverbs and proverb understanding has been in the focus of attention within the cognitive linguistic framework. There have also been cognitive linguistic studies on the relationship of conceptual metaphors, conceptual metonymies and specific emotion concepts, such as love, the topic the present chapter is concerned with. A detailed study of the metaphors and metonymies of love was made by Zoltán Kövecses in his book entitled *The Language of Love. The Semantics of Passion in Conversational English* (1988). In his work, Kövecses examines the attitude to romantic love in conversational English. Since language reflects our conceptual system, it is possible to draw conclusions about our conceptual network from language. Kövecses discusses the major conceptual metaphors of love that are manifest in language, and groups them as well. He analyses the cognitive models of love that the various metaphors and metonymies jointly converge on. Idealised cognitive models, or ICMs, are structures with the help of which we organise our knowledge (Lakoff 1987). ICMs may be of various types, such as ideal, typical, stereotypical, and many others (see Lakoff 1987). A concept can be characterised by a cluster of converging models. Thus, the concept of love, as Kövecses (1988) notes, can be characterised by the ideal, the typical, and other alternative cognitive models. The different cognitive models may fit our understanding of the world to various degrees. What is important is that these models are present in language as well as in thinking – thus, the analysis of love proverbs reveal the conceptual metaphors and metonymies of love, which in turn, point to the existent ICMs of love (Tóthné Litovkina and Csábi 2002).

Cognitive Linguistics offers promising methods to contextualise paremiological problems such as the exact role of metaphors in proverbs. However, some paremiologists criticise Cognitive Linguistics as employed in paremiology claiming that there are elemental problems with the metaphor analysis such as that proposed by Lakoff and Johnson (1980), Lakoff (1987), Lakoff and Turner (1989), Gibbs and Beitel (1995). Krikmann (1994: 122), for example, states that the cognitive linguistic approach, concepts, and metaphors "can hardly solve any of the related fundamental problems long ago recognized and researched in paremiology".

However, the cognitive approach to metaphors in proverbs is fruitful and effective, as the studies *Metaphors we love by: The cognitive models of romantic love in American proverbs* (see Tóthné Litovkina and Csábi 2002), *Cognitive Linguistics and proverbs* (see Belkhir 2021) and *Metaphoric proverbs in EFL learners' translation* (see Belkhir 2022) have shown.

2. "Matrimony is the root of all evil"

For centuries, proverbs have provided a framework for endless transformation. In recent decades, the modification of proverbs has taken such proportions that sometimes we can even meet more proverb transformations than traditional proverbs. Wolfgang Mieder has invented a term *anti-proverb* (or in German *Antisprichwort*) for such deliberate proverb innovations, also known as alterations, parodies, transformations, variations, wisecracks, mutations, or fractured proverbs. This term has been widely accepted by proverb scholars all over the world as a general label for such innovative alterations and reactions to traditional proverbs. Although proverb transformations arise in a variety of forms, several types stand out (which are by no means mutually exclusive), e.g., adding a tail to the original text; replacing a single word; substituting two or more words; changing the second part of the proverb; melding two proverbs; punning; and, last but not least, adding literal interpretations (for more, see T. Litovkina 2005; T. Litovkina et al. 2021).

All's fair for anti-proverbs – there is hardly a topic that anti-proverbs do not address. Among the most frequent themes discussed in proverb alterations are women (see T. Litovkina 2005; 2018a), sexuality (see T. Litovkina 2011b; 2018a: 149–170; T. Litovkina and Mieder 2019: 65–79), professions and occupations (see T. Litovkina 2011a, 2013, 2016).

Without any doubt, marriage and love are two of the most frequent themes in Anglo-American anti-proverbs (T. Litovkina 2017; 2018a; T. Litovkina and Mieder 2019). The focus of Subchapter 2 is the relation between love and marriage in Anglo-American anti-proverbs and proverbs, as well as in proverbs from around the world. In Section 2.1. I briefly address four of my publications treating love and marriage in proverbs and (or) anti-proverbs. Then, in Section 2.2., I discuss the metaphors of love and marriage in proverbs and anti-proverbs. In particular I attempt to answer the following question: What happens to love before marriage and after marriage, according to these nuggets of wisdom and their transformations? In order to show how the different aspects of love connected to marriage are conceptualised in different languages, proverbs from various languages will be also quoted. We will try to see the evidence of cross-cultural similarity in the conceptualisation of love leading to marriage, as well as love after marriage manifested in proverbs of different languages.

The material for the investigation of American proverbs comes primarily from the largest dictionary of American proverbs: *A Dictionary of American Proverbs* (1992) by Wolfgang Mieder et al., as well as the following proverb collections compiled and edited by Wolfgang Mieder: *Love: Proverbs of the Heart* (1989b), and *The Prentice Hall Encyclopedia of World Proverbs: A Treasury of Wit and Wisdom Through the Ages* (1986). The examples cited from languages other than American English mainly come from the following proverb collections: Mieder 1986, 1989b.

The anti-proverbs discussed in the present chapter were taken primarily from American and British written sources. The texts of anti-proverbs were drawn from hundreds of books and articles on puns, one-liners, toasts, wisecracks, quotations, aphorisms, maxims, quips, epigrams, and graffiti the vast majority of which have been published in two dictionaries of anti-proverbs compiled by Wolfgang Mieder and Anna Tóthné Litovkina: *Twisted Wisdom: Modern Anti-Proverbs* (Mieder and Tóthné Litovkina 1999) and *Old Proverbs Never Die, They Just Diversify: A Collection of Anti-Proverbs* (T. Litovkina and Mieder 2006).

2.1 Anna T. Litovkina's publications on love and marriage

In Section 2.1., I will focus on four of my main publications treating love and marriage in proverbs and (or) anti-proverbs: two articles (Tóthné Litovkina and Csábi 2002; T. Litovkina 2017) and two books (T. Litovkina 2018a; T. Litovkina and Mieder 2019).

2.1.1 *"Metaphors we love by: The cognitive models of romantic love in American proverbs" (Tóthné Litovkina and Csábi 2002)*

In order to start the examination of the metaphorical nature of proverbs – especially American proverbs – Szilvia Csábi and I decided to look at proverbs about love, especially romantic love. The study *Metaphors we love by: The cognitive models of romantic love in American proverbs* (Tóthné Litovkina and Csábi 2002) employs a cognitive approach to proverb metaphors. This study examines more than two hundred proverbs dealing with American attitudes toward romantic love; the authors concentrate on conceptual metaphors and metonymies to discover the cognitive models of love, which these metaphors and metonymies jointly constitute. The study attempts to clarify the nature of the metaphorical structure of love proverbs. Despite the fact that the emphasis is on American proverbs about love, we also wanted to illustrate that the phenomena present in American love proverbs are also present in proverbs of other languages. The study focuses on American English proverbs first; and the issue of universality is undertaken from the perspective of American English proverbs as contrasted with proverbs in other languages.

Our work demonstrated the potential of cognitive approaches to proverb metaphors, and generally supports Zoltán Kövecses's work in establishing cognitive models of love (see Kövecses 1988).

The ideal model of love (see Kövecses 1988) is constituted by a number of conceptual metaphors, like LOVE IS A UNITY, LOVE IS AN OBJECT, LOVE IS FIRE, LOVE IS A NUTRIENT, LOVE IS INSANITY, LOVE IS A FORCE. The various metaphors, which are illustrated with proverbs from both American English and other languages, map onto various parts of the ideal model, as we have seen in our study.

Metaphors of the typical model of love are as follows: LOVE IS A HIDDEN OBJECT, LOVE IS AN OPPONENT, and AFFECTION IS WARMTH. It is worth noting that there are some deviations from the typical model that Kövecses discovers from everyday language use. Firstly, the entailments of the LOVE IS A UNITY metaphor are missing from this model as well, since the unity metaphor, as shown in the study, is primarily concerned with the end of the unity. Secondly, instead of emphasising the real fulfilment of love in marriage, proverbs focus on the fact that marriage may bring the decrease of love's intensity.

Besides the ideal and the typical model mentioned above, there are other, "alternative" models of love as well. The alternative models are based on metaphors that are different from the ones mentioned above: LOVE IS WAR, LOVE IS A LIVING ORGANISM, and LOVE IS A DISEASE.

All in all, the study advances the fact that cognitive linguistic metaphor analysis is helpful in paremiology to systematically analyse the metaphorical structure of proverbs about romantic love.

2.1.2 "'Make love, not war … Get married and do both': Negative aspects of marriage in anti-proverbs and wellerisms" (T. Litovkina 2017)

The study "'Make love, not war … Get married and do both': Negative aspects of marriage in anti-proverbs and wellerisms" explores negative aspects of marriage and the ways it is viewed and conceptualised in the body of Anglo-American anti-proverbs and wellerisms.[1] Another aim of the study is also to depict those who adhere to the institution of marriage, that is, wives and husbands, and

---

1. Wellerisms is a form of folklore normally made up of three parts: (1) a statement (sometimes a proverb or proverbial phrase), (2) a speaker who makes this remark, and (3) a phrase that places the utterance into an unexpected, contrived situation. The meaning of the proverb, proverbial phrase or other statement is usually distorted by being placed into striking juxtaposition with the third part of the wellerisms. E.g., *"Every man for himself and God for us all,"* said the farmer who saw his wife drown, without lifting a finger (Dutch) (Schipper 2003: 122).

analyse their nature, qualities, attributes and behaviours as revealed through Anglo-American anti-proverbs and wellerisms. The study briefly comments what marriage is associated with in anti-proverbs and wellerisms, and touches upon the topic of hostility towards spouses. There is a wide range of aspects of marriage discussed in anti-proverbs and wellerisms. Most of them diminish the institution of marriage. To name just a few, matrimony is conceptualised as bossiness and dominance, constant blaming and arguing, slavery and imprisonment, the tomb of love and diminishing of lust, madness and folly, seeing and enlarging each other's shortcomings, hiding and lying. Furthermore, matrimony in the corpus of Anglo-American anti-proverbs and wellerisms is very often associated with a burden and torture. Marriage is also shown in our material as a form of slavery. Matrimony also constitutes a prison. Matrimony in our examples is frequently associated with constant fighting and war. Not surprisingly, both spouses instead of being engaged in passionate sexual activities are frequently shown as simply wishing to kill their partners.

2.1.3 *"Women through anti-proverbs" (T. Litovkina 2018a)*

The main aim of the book "Women through Anti-Proverbs" is to address stereotypical traits of women as they are reflected in Anglo-American anti-proverbs. The book also makes an attempt to analyse the surface meanings of the anti-proverbs with a view to establishing the image of the woman, her qualities, attributes and behaviours. The book treats American proverbs about women in various roles (wife, mother, daughter, widow, mother-in-law, grandmother, etc.). It also explores how women in various roles are constructed in the corpus of Anglo-American anti-proverbs. The overwhelming majority of Anglo-American anti-proverbs depicting women in a role deal with women as wives. Women in the role of mother-in-law, spinster, widow, daughter, young girl, fiancée, bride, mother, grandmother, and many other roles are also a frequent subject of ridicule and mockery in Anglo-American anti-proverbs. The book concentrates on the most common themes appearing in sexual proverb transformations about females, such as sex acts, female parts of body, culturally taboo and less accepted erotic pleasures, monogamy, adultery, bigamy, procreation, pregnancy, and birth control. The book also reviews anti-proverbs about various female professions and occupations, such as housewife and actress, whore and driver, maid and babysitter, teacher and secretary, hairdresser and beautician, among many others. Last but not least, various aspects of love and marriage are also discussed are exemplified.

2.1.4 *"Marriage seen through proverbs and anti-proverbs"* (T. Litovkina and Mieder 2019)

The main aim of the book *Marriage Seen Through Proverbs and Anti-Proverbs* is to explore various aspects of marriage and the ways it is viewed and conceptualised in the body of Anglo-American anti-proverbs. The book also makes an attempt to depict those who contribute to the institution of marriage (that is, husbands and wives), and analyses their nature, qualities, attributes, and behaviours as revealed through Anglo-American anti-proverbs. Furthermore, the book also briefly explores those who remain single and do not belong to the institution of marriage (that is, spinsters and bachelors), as well as brides and bridegrooms, parents and children, mothers-in-law and children-in-law, widows and widowers, and divorced women and men), but contribute to the institution of marriage.

Similar to traditional proverbs in general, Anglo-American anti-proverbs do not paint a rosy portrait of matrimony. The vast majority of our texts give the most unpleasant, disappointing, pessimistic, and denigrating picture of marriage, emphasising its most negative and dark sides. First, having a gambling nature, marriage is perceived as a lottery; similar to this, there is only a very slight chance that one can have a successful and happy marriage. Marriage is very often associated with torture and trouble. Hence, the fate of married couples is often to repent, especially if they rush into marriage without proper thought. A very large group of Anglo-American anti-proverbs concerning marriage discuss its financial side. Matrimony is seen as an economic exchange or financial unit. Marriage is also conceptualised as a state of having arguments and quarrels leading to constant fighting and even marital war. Marriage is shown as a form of slavery, and matrimony constitutes prison. Spouses are frequently depicted as wishing to kill or even actually killing their partners. Matrimony is very often portrayed as prey or a catch, and perceived as a mechanism, which needs repair. Furthermore, matrimony is seen as hiding, lying, and inventing excuses. Last but not least, marriage is very often associated with disillusion, misery, unhappiness, and evil, which is summarised in the witty proverb transformation *Matrimony is the root of all evil* (Edmund and Workman Williams 1921: 275){*Money is the root of all evil*}.[2] Furthermore, numerous anti-proverbs point out that marriage is predestined to failure.

---

2. For the reader's ease, all anti-proverbs in this chapter are followed by their original forms, given in { } brackets.

2.2 "'Tis better to have loved and lost than to have loved and married"

As Tóthné Litovkina and Csábi (2002: 384) have already mentioned, a related concept that often links coldness to love is marriage. Eleven proverbs from Tóthné Litovkina and Csábi's corpus (more than two hundred proverbs) are related to marriage. Let us see in this subchapter what happens according to proverbs from around the world and American anti-proverbs if people who are in love get married. Section 2.2. attempts to answer this question. The focus of this section is the relation between love and marriage in proverbs from around the world and Anglo-American anti-proverbs.

2.2.1 Metaphors of love leading to marriage

Section 2.2.1. discusses three metaphors of love leading one to marriage. Such metaphors are: LOVE IS MADNESS and LACK OF CONTROL, LOVE IS FOLLY, and LOVE IS LOSS OF EYESIGHT and BLINDNESS. While Section 2.2.1.1. depicts LOVE IS LOSS OF CONTROL and MADNESS, Section 2.2.1.2. shows it IS FOLLY. Last but not least, Section 2.2.1.3. focuses on love associated with PARTIAL OR ENTIRE LOSS OF EYESIGHT and BLINDNESS.

2.2.1.1 "Marriages are made in heaven knows what state of mind"

Although some American proverbs (*To be successful in love, one must know how to begin and when to stop*; *Love wisely but not too well*) suggest that one has to be rational in one's love experience, we know that a person in love is sometimes unable to function normally and loses control over love: *You can't control your love* (for more on the conceptualising of LOVE IS CRAZINESS and MADNESS in proverbs, see Tóthné Litovkina and Csábi 2002: 380–381). Love is often considered a "mad" state of mind that can drive people into such a state that they act in strange and unpredictable ways. The highest degree of lack of control is when love makes you mad, as formulated in the proverb *Lovers are madmen*. This idea is supported by the anti-proverb below, which emphasises that those who get married are considered crazy and mindless:

(1) *Marriages are made in heaven knows what state of mind.*   (Berman 1997: 264)
 {Marriages are made in heaven}

2.2.1.2 "Fools rush in where bachelors fear to wed"

People often say that lovers are fools and lack wisdom. In fact, love and wisdom seem not to go together, as the following American proverbs show: *To love and be wise is impossible*; *Lovers are fools*; *It is a fool who loves a woman from afar*. Let us see some examples from other cultures: *To love and to be wise are two different things* (French); *When passionately in love, one becomes stupid* (Japanese); *When passion enters at the foregate, wisdom goes out at the postern* (English); *Love has made heroes of many and fools of many more* (Swedish).

If a man gets married, no matter what qualities he possesses, inevitably he will feel like a fool due to the persistent efforts of his wife. This might be one of the reasons why bachelors might not wish to get married (for bachelors in anti-proverbs, see T. Litovkina 2015). Matrimonial union is frequently depicted as a fight between spouses, and consequently spouses are seen as enemies and not as allies (see Section 2.2.2.2. below on marriage and LOVE IS WAR metaphor). Such a fight might also include fooling each other, and wives undoubtedly manage to triumph over their husbands in this fight.

Not surprisingly, a number of proverb alterations claim that getting or being married is seen as the biggest folly (for more on marriage as folly, see T. Litovkina and Mieder 2019: 52–54). Therefore, spouses, independently of their gender (but most frequently, men), might be viewed as foolish. Have a look at the numerous mutations of the proverb *Where [When] ignorance is bliss, 'tis folly to be wise*:

(2) a. *When singleness is bliss, it's folly to be wives.* (Bill Counselman)[3]
     b. *When spooning is bliss, 'tis folly to get married.* (Loomis 1949: 355)
     c. *Where ignorance is bliss, 'tis folly to be wives.* (Loomis 1949: 355)
     d. *When spinsterhood is bliss, 'tis folly to be wived.* (Esar 1968: 760)

Spouses' folly is also reflected in the four anti-proverbs below. In all of them, husbands are treated as fools, and moreover, in the first two examples, not only husbands but also wives are portrayed as foolish.

Our first example portrays the foolishness of both spouses. Why is this so? The husband is a fool since he has married a foolish woman:

(3) *One man's folly is another man's wife.* (Helen Rowland)[4]
     {One man's meat is another man's poison}

Our second example plays with the proverb *There's no fool like an old fool*. This anti-proverb employs the usage of antonyms (the *old* and *young*), which is very symptomatic for proverbs:

(4) *There's no fool like an old fool who marries a young fool.* (Esar 1968: 318)

From the anti-proverb above, we do not know if this is the first time the old man is getting married. The following example, the transformation of the same proverb,

---

3. http://www.anvari.org/fortune/Miscellaneous_Collections/312257_when-singleness-is-bliss-its-folly-to-be-wives-bill-councelma.html (accessed August 18, 2015).

4. http://www.quotegarden.com/marriage.html (accessed September 15, 2015).

however, portrays the image of an old man who commits the same foolish mistake (gets married) for the fourth time:

(5) *"There's no fool like an old fool,"* as the old man said when he married his fourth wife. (Mieder and Kingsbury 1994: 49)

Similarly to the proverb *Honest men marry soon, wise men not at all*, the following proverb mutation depicts the foolishness of married men, who, contrary to a bachelor wisely thinking before proposing, do not think and rush into marriage without considering its terrible consequences:

(6) *Fools rush in where bachelors fear to wed.* (Esar 1968: 59)
 {Fools rush in where angels fear to tread}

2.2.1.3 *"When the blind lead the blind, they both fall into – matrimony"*

If we are in love, we are often unable to function normally and might have an inaccurate perception of reality. This means that we may be "blinded" by love and perceive the world in a way which does not correspond to the facts. Possibly the most important proverb that captures this aspect of love is *Love is blind*, which is also found in many other languages, for example, in Latin: *Amor (est) caecus*, as well as Hungarian, Russian, and German (for more on proverbs conceptualising LOVE IS BLINDNESS, see Tóthné Litovkina and Csábi 2002: 378). We often see the object of love as being wonderful. However, it does not have to be beautiful at all in reality. He or she may even be the ugliest person in the world; still, they will always be considered beautiful, as the following American proverbs show: *Love is all beautiful*; *Blind love mistakes a harelip for a dimple*; *In the eye of the lover, pockmarks are dimples*; *Love takes away the sight, and matrimony restores it*; *There are no ugly loves nor handsome prisons*; *Hatred is blind, as well as love*; *Love covers many faults*; *Love sees no faults*.

The following proverbs show that the same attitude is true in many other societies: *Love turns pimples into dimples* (Japanese); *That which is loved is always beautiful* (Norwegian); *She who loves an ugly man thinks him handsome* (Spanish); *Love blinds* (Danish, African /Swahili/); *If Jack's in love, he's no judge of Jill's beauty* (English); *Nobody's sweetheart is ugly* (Dutch); *Love and blindness are twin sisters* (Russian); *The toad thinks his bride beautiful* (African /Kongo/). *Love is blind to blemish and faults* (Irish); *He who loves you won't see your faults* (African /Hausa/); *Love conceals ugliness, and hate sees a lot of faults* (Irish); *Love overlooks defects and hatred magnifies shortcomings* (Lebanese); *Whomever we love is clean even when unwashed* (Russian); *Love blinds itself to all shortcomings* (Lebanese); *Love looks through spectacles that make copper look like gold, poverty like riches, and tears like pearls* (Peruvian); *The jealous eye brings out every fault, but the loving eye sees none* (Arab); *Love is a cover: it hides all shortcomings* (African /Shona/).

According to one of the most well-known proverbs in the United States and many other cultures about love, *Love is blind*, and in its numerous transformations (see T. Litovkina and Mieder 2006: 205–207), a person in love ceases to see any faults in their beloved:

(7) *It's a good thing that love is blind, otherwise it would see too much.*
(Esar 1968: 490)

The following mutation humorously describes the institution of matrimony:

(8) *Marriage: An institution. Marriage is love. Love is blind. Therefore marriage is an institution for the blind.* (Prochnow and Prochnow 1964: 175)

While another internationally known proverb about blind people of biblical origin – *When the blind lead the blind, both shall fall into the ditch* (Matth. 15: 14) – points out that if a person lacking in understanding, knowledge, or expertise attempts to guide an ignorant person like themselves, both of them will suffer serious consequences, the proverb transformation below claims that such blind people are those who are in love with each other, and the ditch they fall into is nothing but matrimony:

(9) *When the blind lead the blind, they both fall into – matrimony.*
(George Farquhar, in Myers 1968)

2.2.2 Metaphors of love after marriage

Let us examine below what happens to love after wedding, according to our proverbs and anti-proverbs. While Section 2.2.2.1. focuses on the sobering and eye-opening effect of marriage, Section 2.2.2.2. addresses love as war. Last but not least, in Section 2.2.2.3., we explore the diminished intensity of young love and lust in the course of matrimony, even leading to their complete disappearance, and, consequently, very frequently to divorce.

2.2.2.1 "Love is blind – and when you get married you get your eyesight back"

It has just been discussed in the previous section, a person in love might be blinded. Since love causes interference with our accurate perception, we do not see the faults of the beloved when we are in love.

The opposite is true as well, with the lack of love immediately leading to seeing even the smallest faults in a partner: *Where there is no love, all faults are seen; Faults are thick when love is thin.* Proverbs from other cultures treating this topic are: *One who does not like his wife, finds pebbles in his butter-milk*

(Indian /Konkani/); *Other men can see her beauty, but only her husband knows her faults* (African /Mali/). Since marriage – according to both proverbs and anti-proverbs – is associated with the constant decrease of love (see the Section 2.2.2.3. below), a fault in a spouse will be discovered very quickly. This is not surprising; indeed, after the honeymoon is over, both spouses regain their sight at once: *Love intoxicates a man; marriage sobers him*; *Love takes away the sight, and matrimony restores it*. Therefore, marriage is associated in American proverbs with partial or entire loss of eyesight, and consequently spouses might be depicted as having no eyes or shutting their eyes, or even being blind: *Discreet wives have sometimes neither eyes nor ears*; *A deaf husband and a blind wife are always a happy couple* (for more on LOVE IS BLINDNESS, see T. Litovkina and Mieder 2019: 54–55).

A score of alterations of the proverb *Love is blind* claim that, after blinded lovers get married and start living together, they gradually start seeing all the faults of their second halves, that is, get their "eyesight back" (for more on marriage as getting one's eyesight back, see T. Litovkina and Mieder 2019: 56–57):

(10) a. *Love is blind, and marriage is an eye doctor.*   (Lawson 1924: 110)
      b. *Love is blind, and marriage is an eye-opener.*   (Esar 1968: 491)
      c. *Love is blind – and when you get married you get your eyesight back.*
                                                                                   (Kilroy 1985: 261)

Marriages, therefore, would be so much happier if spouses were still constantly blinded by each other, similarly to the phase of courtship, when no faults of their beloved were seen:

(11) *Were the husband as blind to the faults of the wife, as the lover to the faults of the maiden, few unhappy marriages would follow happy courtships.*
                                                                                 (Ivan Panin, Thoughts)[5]

2.2.2.2   "'Every little bit helps,' as the old lady said when she pissed in the ocean to help drown her husband"

As stressed elsewhere (Tóthné Litovkina and Csábi 2002: 388), the "love is war" metaphor belongs to the most prevalent metaphorical conceptualisations of love in American proverbs. Indeed, one of the most popular proverbs about love in America is *All is fair in love and war*, which states that in courtship, just as on the battlefield, you are allowed to take advantage of every opportunity (for more on marriage as war, see T. Litovkina 2017; T. Litovkina and Mieder 2019: 94–107). There are some proverbs in other cultures as well, in which the aspect of love is captured by the war metaphor: *All is fair in love and war* (Danish). *No rose without a thorn, no love without a rival* (Turkish). *War, hunting, and love are as full*

---

5. http://www.notable-quotes.com/m/marriage_quotes.html (accessed September 15, 2010).

of troubles as pleasures (English). According to Kövecses (1988: 72), the LOVE IS WAR metaphor "highlights those instances of love where the idea of love's mutuality is absent in some way". This is due to the fact that the person who is in love has to fight in order to have their love returned. It belongs to the most prevalent metaphorical conceptualisations of love.

Let us view three additional American proverbs, which link love and war: *In love and war no time should be lost*; *In love, as in war, each man must gain his own victories*; and *Make love, not war*. We should not be surprised to discover that marriage is also conceptualised as constant war and fighting in a number of our anti-proverbs as well.

The following two examples – both transformations of *Make love, not war*, the anti-war slogan from the 1960s, which has become proverbial – besides addressing the ups and downs in marriage, also emphasise the warlike aspects of marriage. When the spouses feel up to it, they might be engaged in making love, but there is also another side of a marital union – the side of war:

(12) a. *Make love, not war.*
    I'm married, I do both. (Rees 1980: 80)
  b. *Make love, not war … Get married and do both.* (Berman 1997: 251)

The two mutations above reflect the dual nature of marriage – it can cure and kill, it might bring you happiness and unhappiness, it can be both war and peace at the same time. The anti-proverb below, however, emphasises the great dangers of marriage as well, depicting it as a battlefield in which anyone can be wounded (or even killed):

(13) *Marriage is like life in this – that it is a field of battle, and not a bed of roses.*
    {Life is not a bed of roses} (Robert Louis Stevenson, *Virginibus Puerisque*)[6]

Numerous anti-proverbs (many of them in the form of wellerism) depict spouses wishing for the demise of their other half (for more, see T. Litovkina 2017; T. Litovkina and Mieder 2019: 104–107). Let us start with one of the "favourite" ways of eradicating one's husband in our corpus, namely drowning. The following wellerisms reflect women's fantasies about getting rid of their husbands. By employing the proverb *Every little bit helps*, they show desperate women who have suffered so much during their marriages that they are ready to do the most absurd things in order to contribute at least a little bit to their husbands' death. Even something very small such as a little bit of her urine or some water, which is really grotesque, can help a woman to drown her husband:

---

6. http://www.notable-quotes.com/m/marriage_quotes (accessed September 25, 2017).

(14) a. *"Every little bit helps," as the old lady said when she pissed in the ocean to help drown her husband.* (Mieder and Kingsbury 1994: 76)
 b. *"Every little bit helps," said the old woman as she threw the water on the ceiling to drown her husband with.* (Mieder and Kingsbury 1994: 76)

Men in our corpus also want their spouses' death, although not as frequently. The following examples reflect males' wishes to kill their wives. Again, husbands, similarly to wives, also like murdering their spouses by drowning. The proverb *Every little bit helps* is also used as a base for this wellerism:

(15) *"Every little helps," as the captain said when he threw his wife overboard to lighten the ship.* (Mieder and Kingsbury 1994: 75)

By throwing his wife overboard, the captain of the wellerism above shows very clearly that she has become an unbearable burden for him. This is not surprising, since one's marriage is frequently seen in anti-proverbs and wellerisms as a burden, especially by men (for marriage as burden see T. Litovkina and Mieder 2019: 87–94). Naturally, it is also assumed that it will not be a problem for the captain to replace his wife with another woman.

A wish to kill one's spouse is jokingly expressed in wellerisms from many other cultures as well, either from the perspective of the wife, or from that of the husband:

(16) *"Every little bit lightens," said the skipper, and he threw his wife overboard.*
  (Frisian)
  "That clears a space," said Grietje, when her husband died. (Dutch)
  (Schipper 2003: 122)

2.2.2.3 *"The course of true love never runs smooth – it usually leads to marriage"*

Many American proverbs state that love passes, e.g., *Love at first sight is cured by a second look. Love lasts seven seconds; the fantasia lasts seven minutes; unhappiness lasts all one's life.* One of the primary reasons for the end of love may be time e.g., *Love makes time pass; time makes love pass*, lack of money, e.g., *The love light goes out when the gas bill comes in. When want comes in at the door, love flies out of the window*, absence, e.g., *Absence is love's foe: far from the eyes, far from the heart. Absence kills a little love but makes the big ones grow* or some other problems, e.g., *When doubt comes in, love goes out.* It goes without saying that matrimony is one of the most important reasons for the end of love: *Love takes away the sight, and matrimony restores it.*

In the typical model of love proposed by Kövecses, the intensity of love is lower than in the ideal model. Fire is less frequently used in the typical cases of love. It is rather the concept of warmth that is used to refer to love or affection (see Kövecses 1988: 64). Thus, body heat becomes lower as time passes. Mild affection is more likely to be long-lived than a love known as "flame" or "infatuation" which may soon burn itself out: *Love me little, love me long.*

The proverb *Where there is marriage without love, there will be love without marriage* states that, if you marry without love, you will find a lover outside your marriage. But what happens according to American proverbs if people who are in love get married? To make one's relationship in marriage good, a lot of love is needed: *It is not the house that makes the home, it's the love that is inside. It takes a lot of loving to make a home.*

Two proverbs comment on the sobering effect of married life, which gives rise to the decrease of intensity of young love: *Love takes away the sight, and matrimony restores it; Love intoxicates a man; marriage sobers him.* Love cools very quickly in marriage: *Marriage is a romance novel in which the hero dies in the first chapter; The lover is often lost in the husband.* The cooling of love with time is likened to the cooling of hot water: *Marriage is like a tub of water: after a while, it is not so hot.*

The proverb *Marry first and love will follow* reflects the old belief that an emotion such as love is not a necessity for marriage at first and that love will develop after the marriage has taken place. In Icelandic, they say: *Love comes after marriage.* (But we also know that *He who forces love where none is found remains a fool the whole year round.*). But among the American proverbs under the headings *marriage/marry* (see Mieder et al. 1992: 406–408), no proverb was found to express that love is fulfilled in marriage.

The decrease and disappearance of love in marriage is shown not only in American proverbs: *Marriage is the tomb of love* (Russian); *Marriage is the sunset of love* (French); *There is no cure for love but marriage* (Irish); *Marriage will sober love* (Irish); *Love has wings on its shoulders; matrimony has crutches under its arms* (Russian); *There is no such fiery love that would not be cooled down by marriage* (Russian); *Love is a fair garden, and marriage a field of nettles* (Finnish). The fast cooling of love in marriage is claimed in: *Love provides wings, but wings of wax melt with the torch of marriage* (Russian); *A dish of married love soon grows cold* (Scottish). Mere love is not enough for a good marriage: *One who marries for love alone will have bad days but good nights* (Egyptian); *Who marries for love has good nights and sorry days* (English; French). Whereas love is intrinsic for couples' sexual activities, money is essential for their everyday life: *Who marries for love without money hath good nights and sorry days* (English). Marriage is particularly bad for a man, as the following Polish proverb states: *The woman cries before the wedding and the man after.* Marriage and love are considered to be two separate and unrelated issues: *A man is often too young to marry, but a man is never too old to love* (Finnish).

Chapter 4. Metaphors of love before and after marriage in proverbs and anti-proverbs

There are very few positive proverbs about the relation of love and marriage. In Icelandic they say: *Love comes after marriage*. The following proverbs spread the message that love is fulfilled in marriage: *Love is often the fruit of the marriage* (French); *Love is a flower that turns into fruit at marriage* (Finnish). Although Kövecses claims that the conversational English language emphasises that love is fulfilled in marriage, that "marriage is the highest, the most desired point – indeed the fulfilment – of love" (1988: 65), proverbs and anti-proverbs – in accordance with the quote "If you want to read about love and marriage, you've got to buy two separate books" (Alan King)[7] – do not seem to emphasise the real fulfilment of love in marriage.

Not surprisingly, a lot of people enjoy only one phase of their matrimonial union, "the honeymoon phase". After the "honeymoon phase" is over the real marriage begins, with all its problem, in the vein of the proverb *The honeymoon is over; now the marriage begins*. As scores of American proverbs claim, not only love but also lust disappears in marriage: *The lover is always lost in the husband* (for more on the diminishing of love and lust in marriage, see T. Litovkina and Mieder 2019: 57–63).

One of the reasons for the disappearance of love, lust, and infatuation after the honeymoon is over might be explained by the fact that, after the novelty of a new passionate relationship is gone, its place is taken over by everyday routine, habit, and boredom.

Now, after analysing how love and marriage are connected in proverbs from various cultures, let us look at Anglo-American anti-proverbs treating the relationship between love and marriage.

A number of anti-proverbs comment on the sobering effect of married life, which can lead not only to the diminished intensity of young love and lust, but even its utter disappearance and eventual divorce (see T. Litovkina 2018b; T. Litovkina and Mieder 2019: 131–145). Thus, having mere love affairs and later on losing your partner might be considered more fruitful and enjoyable than eventually becoming committed (that is, getting married), from both the female and male perspectives:

(17) *The course of true love never runs smooth – it usually leads to marriage.*
{The course of true love never runs smooth}   (Esar 1968: 491)

Let us now look at one of the most popular American proverbs about love, and also one of the most frequently transformed in our corpus – *It's better to have loved and lost than never to have loved at all* (thirty mutations have been identified – see T. Litovkina and Mieder 2006: 190–191]). All of its mutations, explicitly

---

7. http://www.quotegarden.com/marriage.html (accessed November 19, 2012).

or implicitly treating marriage with only three exceptions, spread the message that love disappears in marriage, and do not recommend one get married.

In a number of our examples, we do not know the gender of the people who "have loved and lost":

(18) a. *'Tis better to have loved and lost than to be married and divorced.*
(Berman 1997: 251)
b. *'Tis better to have loved and lost than to have loved and married.*
(Metcalf 1993: 143)

Getting out of a relationship without having even a slight thought of getting married might be entirely justified, especially when one partner (generally a man, see T. Litovkina 2017: 117–119; T. Litovkina and Mieder 2019: 97–100) doesn't want to be bossed:

(19) *'Tis better to have loved and lost than to marry and be bossed.* (Esar 1968: 90)

Bachelors prefer having affairs without commitment and obligation. They quit rather than get married:

(20) *Bachelors*
'Tis better to have loved and lost – indeed, lots better. (Safian 1967: 47)

Almost all the transformations of the proverb *It's better to have loved and lost than never to have loved at all* give a very negative, doomy picture of marriage, and warn one of tying oneself down with matrimonial bonds.

The positive picture of marriage is hardly ever found in transformations of this proverb. Exception, however, proves the rule, see the following two mutations:

(21) a. *It is better to have loved your wife than never to have loved at all.*
(Edgar Saltus, in Lieberman 1984: 141)
b. *Occasionally you meet a man who thinks it is better to have loved and married than never to have loved at all.* (Esar 1968: 491)

It is an interesting fact that both examples above treat a happy husband and not a happy wife.

According to the wellerism below, addressing a very popular category of old woman (or wife), the disappearance of sexual infatuation and passion towards one's wife might be due to the fact that almost nothing natural is left in her:

(22) *"Wife is just one sham thing after another,"* thought the husband, as his spouse placed her teeth, hair, shape, and complexion on the bureau.
{Life is just one damned thing after another} (Mieder and Kingsbury 1994: 151)

Similar to the husband from this wellerism, the husband from the anti-proverb below does not seem too enthusiastic about his old wife either:

(23) *It's used to be wine, women and song. Now it's beer, the old lady, and TV.*
 {Wine, women, and song will get a man wrong} (Berman 1997: 452)

As discussed earlier in this section and elsewhere (see T. Litovkina 2011b; T. Litovkina and Mieder 2019: 67–77), many anti-proverbs state that love and lust frequently disappear in marriage. Their disappearance frequently leads to divorce (for the main causes of the divorce, according to anti-proverbs, see T. Litovkina 2018b; T. Litovkina and Mieder 2019: 131–145). Naturally, in the proverb mutation below, it is not love among spouses but love towards the third person, which will conquer all obstacles and "will find a way – out":

(24) *Divorced couples*
 Love will find a way – out. (Safian 1967: 48)
 {Love will find a way}

Conclusion

In the first part of the chapter, I explored the paremiological issue of the metaphorical nature of proverbs. After my discussion of metaphor as one of the most powerful markers of proverbiality (Section 1.1), I treated the paremiological issue of the metaphorical nature of proverbs from a cognitive linguistic view (Section 1.2.). Then in the second part of the chapter I introduced four of my publications addressing love and (or) marriage in proverbs and (or) anti-proverbs (Section 2.1.). Afterwards, using the corpus of various proverb and anti-proverb dictionaries, I made an attempt to explore the relation between love and marriage in the course of a couple's life, according to proverbs and anti-proverbs. In particular, I tried to analyse various metaphors manifested in them (Section 2.2.). Furthermore, I also grouped the proverbs and anti-proverbs under the various metaphors of love (e.g., LOVE IS MADNESS and LACK OF CONTROL, LOVE IS FOLLY, and LOVE IS LOSS OF EYESIGHT and BLINDNESS, LOVE IS WAR, etc.) proposed by Kövecses.

We have seen that, while love at its beginning is conceptualised as loss of control and even madness, it can also be depicted as folly. Love is also associated as partial or entire loss of eyesight and blindness. After the honeymoon phase is over and spouses get close to each other, marriage opens their eyes, enlarging and over exaggerating each other's shortcomings and faults. By numerous examples, we have proven that love is conceptualised as war. Last but not least, we have also discovered the diminished intensity of young love and lust in the course of matrimony.

The overall picture we get from our corpus about the relationship between marriage on the one side, and love and lust on the other, is more than disappointing. Proverbs and anti-proverbs mostly focus on the fact that love becomes less intense and the emotion gets colder after wedding. Thus, marriage frequently leads to the utter disappearance of love. Scores of anti-proverbs (especially numerous transformations of the proverb *It's better to have loved and lost than never to have loved at all*) claim that love and marriage, or lust and marriage, are entirely incompatible things. Indeed, as we have seen, marriage frequently becomes the tomb of love.

In order to show how various aspects of love are conceptualised in different languages, besides Anglo-American anti-proverbs and proverbs, proverbs from various languages have been quoted. We have seen the evidence of cross-cultural similarity in the conceptualisation of love manifested in proverbs not only from American English but also from numerous other languages. In this way, I have shown that there are possible universal phenomena and conceptual metaphors of love, which are shared among, and used in a similar way by various cultures. Thus, there are universal or near-universal experiences which are very similar in various cultures, and this causes the striking similarity of the conceptualisation of emotions, such as love, in various, often unrelated languages (for more, see Kövecses 1986, 1988, 2000, 2005). This is why there are a remarkably large number of proverbs that work in a similar way in unrelated languages as instantiations of similar conceptual metaphors.

The present chapter, continuing Tóthné Litovkina and Csábi's research published in 2002, argues for the fact that cognitive linguistic metaphor analysis is helpful in paremiology to systematically analyse the metaphorical structure of not only proverbs about love but anti-proverbs about love as well.

I hope that the present chapter will project some implications for further research into this field of study not only in American culture but also in other cultures. Thus, it would be important to do a detailed cross-cultural analysis of anti-proverbs in American and other societies, and to compare and contrast basic attitudes towards love reflected in anti-proverbs from different languages. Such analysis of anti-proverbs might help to answer the question in exactly what ways the conceptual metaphors of romantic love are universal in anti-proverb use.

References

Arora, Sh. L. (1984). The perception of proverbiality. *Proverbium: Yearbook of International Proverb Scholarship*, 1, 1–38.

Barley, N. (1972). A structural approach to the proverb and maxim with special reference to the Anglo-Saxon corpus. *Proverbium*, 20, 737–750.

Barley, N. (1974). Some comments on Krikmann. *Proverbium*, 25, 991–992.

Belkhir, S. (2021). Cognitive linguistics and proverbs. In X. Wen, & J. R. Taylor (Eds.), *The Routledge handbook of cognitive linguistics* (pp. 599–611). New York & London: Routledge.

Belkhir, S. (2022). Metaphoric proverbs in EFL learners' translation. *Cognitive Linguistic Studies*, 9(1), 110–127.

Berman, L. A. (1997). *Proverb wit & wisdom: A treasury of proverbs, parodies, quips, quotes, clichés, catchwords, epigrams and aphorisms*. Berkeley: A Perigee Book.

Edmund, P., & Workman Williams, H. (1921). *Toaster's handbook: Jokes, stories and quotations*. New York: The H. W. Wilson Company.

Esar, E. (1968). *20,000 quips and quotes*. Garden City, New York: Doubleday & Company.

Gibbs, R. W., Jr. & Beitel, D. (1995). What proverb understanding reveals about how people think. *Psychological Bulletin*, 118(1), 133–154.

Grzybek, P. (1987). Foundations of semiotic proverb study. *Proverbium: Yearbook of International Proverb Scholarship*, 4, 39–85.

Hasan-Rokem, G. (1982). *Proverbs in Israeli folk narratives: A structural semantic analysis*. (=FFC No.232). Helsinki: Suomalainen Tiedeakatemia.

Kilroy, R. (1985). *Graffiti: The scrawl of the wild and other tales from the wall*. London: Gorgi Books.

Kirshenblatt-Gimblett, B. (1973). Toward a theory of proverb meaning. *Proverbium*, 22, 821–827.

Kövecses, Z. (1986). *Metaphors of anger, pride and love: A lexical Approach to the structure of concepts*. Amsterdam & Philadelphia: John Benjamins.

Kövecses, Z. (1988). *The language of love. The semantics of passion in conversational English*. Lewisburg: Bucknell University Press.

Kövecses, Z. (2000). The concept of anger: Universal or culture-specific? *Psychopathology*, 33(4), 159–170.

Kövecses, Z. (2005). *Metaphor in culture: Universality and variation*. Cambridge: Cambridge University Press.

Krikmann, A. (1994). The great chain metaphor: An open sesame for proverb semantics. *Proverbium: Yearbook of International Proverb Scholarship*, 11, 117–124.

Lakoff, G. (1987). *Women, fire, and dangerous things*. What categories reveal about the mind. Chicago: The University of Chicago Press.

Lakoff, G., & Johnson, M. (1980). *Metaphors we live by*. Chicago: University of Chicago Press.

Lakoff, G., & Turner, M. (1989). *More than cool reason: A field guide to poetic metaphor*. Chicago: University of Chicago Press.

Lawson, G. J. (Ed.). (1924). *The world's best epigrams: Pungent paragraphs*. London: Hodder & Stoughton.

Lieberman, G. F. (1984). *3,500 good quotes for speakers.* Wellingborough: Thorsons.

Loomis, C. G. (1949). Traditional American wordplay: The epigram and perverted proverbs. *Western Folklore, 8,* 348–357.

Metcalf, F. (1993). *The Penguin dictionary of jokes, wisecracks, quips and quotes.* London: Viking.

Mieder, W. (1985). Popular views of the proverb. *Proverbium: Yearbook of International Proverb Scholarship, 2,* 109–143.

Mieder, W. (1986). *The Prentice Hall encyclopedia of world proverbs: A treasury of wit and wisdom through the ages.* New Jersey: Prentice-Hall, Inc.

Mieder, W. (1989a). *American proverbs: A study of texts and contexts.* New York: Peter Lang.

Mieder, W. (1989b). *Love: proverbs of the heart.* Shelburne: The New England Press.

Mieder, W., Kingsbury, S. A., & Harder, K. B. (Eds.) (1992). *A dictionary of American proverbs.* New York & Oxford: Oxford University Press.

Mieder, W., & Kingsbury, S. A. (Eds.). (1994). *A dictionary of wellerisms.* New York: Oxford University Press.

Mieder, W., & Tóthné Litovkina, A. (1999). *Twisted wisdom: Modern anti-proverbs.* Burlington: The University of Vermont.

Myers, R. (1968). *The spice of love: Wisdom and wit about love through the ages.* Kansas City: Hallmark Cards, Inc.

[Permyakov] ПермяковГ. Л. (1979). *Пословицы и поговорки народов Востока. Систематизированное собрание изречений двухсот народов [Proverbs and sayings of peoples of the East. Systematized collection of proverbs and sayings of two-hundred peoples].* Москва: Наука.

Prochnow, H. V., & Prochnow, H. V. Jr. (1964). *A dictionary of wit, wisdom and satire.* New York: Popular Library.

Rees, N. (1980). *Graffiti 2.* London: Unwin Paperbacks.

Safian, L. A. (1967). *The Book of updated proverbs.* New York: Abelard-Schuman.

Schipper, M. (2003). *Never marry a woman with big feet: Women in proverbs from around the world.* New Haven: Yale University Press.

Taylor, A. ([1931] 1962). *The Proverb.* Cambridge: Harvard University Press.

T. Litovkina, Anna. (2005). *Old proverbs cannot die: They just fade into paroDY: Anglo-American anti-proverbs.* Habilitációs dolgozat. Budapest: ELTE. (manuscript)

T. Litovkina, A. (2011a). "Where there's a will there's a lawyer's bill": Lawyers in Anglo-American anti-proverbs. *Acta Juridica Hungarica, 52*(1), 82–96.

T. Litovkina, A. (2011b). Sexuality in Anglo-American anti-proverbs. In M. Dynel (Ed.), *The pragmatics of humour across discourse domain, pragmatics and beyond* (pp. 191–213). Amsterdam & Philadelphia: John Benjamins.

T. Litovkina, A. (2013). Politicians in Anglo-American anti-proverbs. In E. Grodzki, Sh. Rehman, C. Calma, & K. Colombo (Eds.), *International issues from wars to robots* (pp. 95–109). Linus Publications.

T. Litovkina, A. (2015). To marry or not to marry, that is the question: Marriage and singleness as revealed through Anglo-American anti-proverbs. In Ch. Grandl, K. J. McKenna, E. Piirainen, & A. Nolte, (Eds.) *"Bis dat, qui cito dat" – Gegengabe in paremiology, folklore, language, and literature: Honoring Wolfgang Mieder on his seventieth birthday*, (pp. 239–48). Frankfurt am Main: Peter Lang.

T. Litovkina, A. (2016). *"Do you serve lawyers and politicians here?": Stereotyped lawyers and politicians in Anglo-American jokes and anti-proverbs*. Komárno: J. Selye University Faculty of Education.

T. Litovkina, A. (2017). "Make love, not war ... Get married and do both": Negative aspects of marriage in anti-proverbs and wellerisms. *The European Journal of Humour Research*, 5(4), 112–135.

T. Litovkina, A. (2018a). *Women through anti-proverbs*. Cham: Palgrave Macmillan.

T. Litovkina, A. (2018b). Positive and negative sides of divorce as reflected in Anglo-American anti-proverbs. *Вестник Карагандинского Университета. Серия Филология*, 4(92), 29–33.

T. Litovkina, A., & Mieder, W. (2005). *"A közmondást nem hiába mondják". Vizsgálatok a proverbiumok természetéről és használatáról ["A proverb is not said in vain": A study of the nature and use of proverbs]*. Budapest: Tinta Könyvkiadó.

T. Litovkina, A., & Mieder, W. (2006). *Old proverbs never die, they just diversify: A collection of anti-proverbs*. Burlington: The University of Vermont – Veszprém: The Pannonian University of Veszprém.

T. Litovkina, A., & Mieder, W. (2019). *Marriage seen through proverbs and anti-proverbs*. Newcastle upon Tyne: Cambridge Scholars Publishing.

T. Litovkina, A., Hrisztova-Gotthardt, H., Barta, P., Vargha, K., & Mieder, W. (2021): *Anti-proverbs in five languages: Structural features and verbal humor devices*. Cham: Palgrave Macmillan.

Tóthné Litovkina, A. (1993). *Felmérés a magyar közmondások ismeretére vonatkozóan és a felmérésben legismertebbeknek bizonyult közmondások elemzése [A survey concerning knowledge of Hungarian proverbs and an analysis of the best-known proverbs thus established]*. PhD dissertation. Kandidátusi disszertáció. Budapest: ELTE (manuscript).

Tóthné Litovkina, A. (1994). The most powerful markers of proverbiality. Perception of proverbiality and familiarity with them among 40 Americans. *Semiotische Berichte*, 1–4, 327–353.

Tóthné Litovkina, A. (1998). An analysis of popular American proverbs and their use in language teaching. In Heissig, W., & Schott, R. (Eds.), *Die heutige bedeutung oraler traditionen – Ihre archivierung, publikation und index-erschließung [The Present-Day Importance of Oral Traditions: Their Preservation, Publication and Indexing]* (pp. 131–58). Opladen: Wetdeutscher Verlag.

Tóthné Litovkina, A., & Csábi. Sz. (2002). Metaphors we love by: The cognitive models of romantic love in American proverbs. *Proverbium: Yearbook of International Proverb Scholarship*, 18, 369–98.

CHAPTER 5

Proverbs of Latin and French origin in the history of English
A socio-cognitive analysis

Julia Landmann
University of Basel, Switzerland

The present study deals with proverbs of Latin and French origin adopted into English throughout its history. Dictionaries such as the *Oxford English Dictionary Online* (*OED Online*) serve as valuable sources to identify the different lexical units. The treatment of proverbs in lexicographical resources is compared to their current usage as reflected by a multitude of recent newspaper articles. This raises the question of how the uses of the various proverbs as described in dictionaries such as the *OED* differ from those in recent newspapers. A socio-cognitive perspective is paramount in order to determine the variety of emotionally-affective forces which may account for English speakers' motivations for using the borrowed proverb instead of a native translation equivalent.

Keywords: borrowed proverbs, socio-cognitive approach, Latin, French, English

1. Introduction

Proverbs are often seen as clues that make it possible to better understand a given culture. Buja (2018: 86) points out that

> [i]n almost every culture, proverbs offer a set of instructions/pieces of advice for people to follow. These **words of wisdom** [author's emphasis] seem to stand the test of time; thus, each and every generation learns what a culture considers relevant. The reasons behind the fact that proverbs have such a long life and are remembered and employed so frequently is that they depict issues that people consider important through vivid and simple language. We could say that, to a certain extent, proverbs, just like specific objects or food items, represent a cultural symbol.

https://doi.org/10.1075/clscc.16.05lan
© 2024 John Benjamins Publishing Company

Chapter 5. Proverbs of Latin and French origin in the history of English

The question of implicit *wisdom* is crucial to the nature of proverbs. Buja (2018: 86) rightly draws attention to the fact that "[p]roverbs came into being a long time ago, and the reason why nowadays they are still considered an important living genre is that they embody the wisdom of the cultures that have created them".

Proverbs have so far been defined from different angles in different fields of research such as anthropology, philosophy, psychology, and linguistics. A generally accepted definition can be found in Finnegan (2006: 14), who surveys proverbs in Africa. According to Finnegan, a proverb "is a saying in more or less fixed form, marked by 'shortness, sense, and salt' and distinguished by the popular acceptance of the truth tersely expressed in it". It should be noted that the formula advanced by Finnegan also underlies the conception of *proverb* in the present chapter.

Most of the studies on proverbs published so far are of a general nature and do not concentrate on those of foreign origin. Examples of earlier analyses are Holbek (1970), Barley (1972), Abrahams (1975), and Norrick (1985). Of these, Holbek examines proverb style. Barley (1972) provides a structural approach with a specific focus on proverbs in the Anglo-Saxon corpus, while Abrahams (1975) assumes a sociolinguistic perspective. Norrick offers a book-length study of meaning in proverbs, comparing literal readings and figurative uses.

A few recent studies examine proverbs in different languages from a comparative point of view. Comparative linguistics is the study of the differences, similarities, or relationships between different languages and the methods used to analyse them. The focus of the comparative method in historical linguistics is on the analysis of an earlier state of a language by means of an investigation of correspondences between words and expressions in two or more languages. This approach was initially developed in the nineteenth century for the study of Proto-Indo-European (see also Hock and Joseph 2019: 1–16). Examples of recent comparative studies of proverbs are Smith (2011), Iyalla-Amadi (2014), and Buja (2018). Smith investigates cultural identity as reflected by proverbs and idioms in French, Spanish, and English. Iyalla-Amadi takes a different approach: she examines translational techniques in teaching using the example of French-English proverbs. Buja compares cultural values and attitudes as revealed by Romanian and Korean proverbs.

The focus of linguistic concern of the present study is on an area that has so far been considered little if at all in earlier surveys. It sets out to examine proverbs of Latin and French origin in the history of English from a socio-cognitive point of view, a perspective that accounts for linguistic variation in social contexts based on a cognitive explanatory framework. The aim of Socio-cognitive Linguistics is to research the complex interaction between usage, meaning and the mind of a speaker. Since the foundation of Cognitive Sociolinguistics as a linguistic discipline, social factors which may influence language use have moved into the focus of interest (see, for example, Kristiansen and Dirven 2008; Croft 2009; Geeraerts, Kristiansen, and Peirsman 2010 and others). Zenner, Backus, and Winter-Froemel (2019: 3) point out that

> The interplay between the individual and the community, the tension between language variants and language varieties, and the importance of adequate methods to study empirically these fundamental relations acquired a central position in the study of categorization in and through language. However, contact-induced variation and change largely stayed under the radar, despite the wealth of learning opportunities offered by the bi- and multilingual mind.

Cognitive Linguistics implies a usage-based perspective. A significant premise of this perspective is that language competence is associated with usage (see also Tomasello 2003: 5–6). Such a perspective is also paramount in the present study, the two main objectives of which are provided here together with their related research questions (abbreviated as RQs):

(1) To analyse the treatment of the Latin- and French-derived proverbs in dictionaries in comparison with their actual usage in English.

RQs: How does the treatment of borrowed proverbs in dictionaries such as the *OED* differ from their use as depicted in recent newspaper corpora? How is the use of the proverbs under review described in dictionaries from a historical point of view; i.e., from their first recorded usage in the receiving language to the present day? Do newspaper corpora reveal additional contextual usages (comprising new connotations) of borrowed proverbs that cannot be determined according to the linguistic documentary evidence in the dictionaries consulted?

(2) To investigate the interplay between linguistic use and social or cognitive attitudes and evaluations.

RQs: What social or socio-cognitive attitudes and valuations can be determined which influence linguistic use? What are the relevant socio-cognitive factors that have contributed to the spread of the proverbs under scrutiny?

2. Data and methodology

For the present analysis, the following methodological steps have been carried out:

Step (1): Identification of the proverbs of Latin and French origin in dictionaries

To identify the various proverbs of Latin and French origin that were introduced into English over the centuries, the *OED Online* was consulted. In addition to the data retrieved from the *OED*, the comprehensive lexicographical collection of proverbs in Speake's 2015 *Oxford Dictionary of Proverbs* (henceforth referred to as *ODP*) was taken into account.

The *OED*, accessible online via <http://www.oed.com>, is being completely overhauled. It consists of the second edition from 1989, the complete texts of the 1993 and 1997 *OED Additions Series* and a diversity of new and revised lexical entries from the third edition currently in progress (see also Durkin 1999: 1–49). The electronic version of the *OED* includes a search option by means of which all dictionary entries with a 'foreign' etymology can be identified. To capture all the lexical entries that have a Latin or French origin in their etymological analysis, the following search is necessary: Entries containing 'Latin' (or 'French') in 'Etymology'. Besides a multitude of words and phrases borrowed from Latin or French throughout the centuries, the entries collected in this manner also included a number of proverbs taken over from these languages.

ODP is a compilation of the diversity of proverbs currently used in English. It also includes proverbs with a *possible* foreign origin. An example is *absence makes the heart grow fonder*, which shows a semantically accordant expression in Latin which may have influenced the relevant use in English, i.e., *semper in absentes felicior aestus amantes*, "passion [is] always warmer towards absent lovers" (*ODP*). The reader should note that proverbs showing a possible foreign origin in the dictionaries consulted were not taken into account. The focus of the present study is on direct loans with Latin or French as the *immediate* donor language. Hence, *festina lente*, 'more haste, less speed', 'slow and steady wins the race', is classified as a direct loan from Latin despite the fact that it ultimately reflects synonymous Hellenistic Greek σπεῦδε βραδέως (see *OED*). The lexicographical sample presented herewas compiled in June 2021.

Dictionaries such as *OED* and *ODP* comprise a number of proverbs unknown to the 'average' native speaker of English, while others have made it into common usage. To differentiate between comparatively rare proverbs and those that have become relatively common, two EFL (English as a Foreign Language) dictionaries (i.e., the electronic versions of the *Oxford Advanced Learner's Dictionary* (*OALD*) and the *Longman Dictionary of Contemporary English* (*LDOCE*)) were used because they record words and expressions that belong to a certain core area of frequent lexical units. Within the study itself, both the widespread and the less common proverbs have been selected for research. Proverbs that are included in the *OALD* and/or the *LDOCE* are printed in bold in the present chapter.

Step (2): Analysing the interplay between linguistic use and socio- cognitive attitudes and valuations

To analyse socio-cognitive attitudes and valuations underlying language use, the linguistic evidence collected from the *OED* and English newspaper corpora available at *Nexis Uni* has been examined. *Nexis Uni* includes a plethora of electronic editions of newspapers ranging from *The Times, The Independent, The Guardian* to *The New York Times*, and revealing language use from the 1980s to the present day.

The investigation of synonymy has long been the focus of interest in Cognitive Linguistics. Examples of (early) empirical surveys are Dirven *et al.* (1982), Lehrer (1982), Schmid (1993), Geeraerts, Grondelaers and Bakema (1994) and Rudzka-Ostyn (1995). Recent studies concentrate on near-synonymous lexical units (e.g., Newman and Rice 2004a, 2004b; Divjak and Gries 2006) and syntactical variation (e.g. Grondelaers et al. 2007; Speelman and Geeraerts 2009).

From a cognitive perspective, an analysis of the use of synonyms or near-synonyms is crucial because it offers a method for determining conceptual structures resulting from speakers' preferences. According to Glynn (2010: 91), variation in language use is to be interpreted taking into account extra-linguistic factors and the social situations in which the lexical units in question occur:

> [i]f we assume that speakers have knowledge of their language and culture and make their judgements based on that knowledge, this entails that their choices will reflect such knowledge. In Cognitive Linguistics, where entrenched language structure (or knowledge of language use) equates conceptual structure, by identifying the patterns of similar and distinctive usage, we chart the conceptual structure that motivates those patterns.

Among the proverbs under scrutiny, some already have a synonymous English translation equivalent. An example is *tempus fugit* that is much more often documented in its translated form *time flies* in present-day English. It was formed after *sed fugit interea, fugit inreparabile tempus*, lit. 'but meanwhile it is flying, irretrievable time is flying', a phrase from Virgil's *Georgics* (see also *OED*). To explain speakers' choices of synonyms, proverbs of Latin and French origin with native translation equivalents have been qualitatively examined to determine socio-cognitive motivations that may underlie their use. To determine relations between the (preferred) use of a borrowed proverb instead of an English synonym and socio-cognitive attitudes, analyses of culture-specific valuations have been undertaken.

Chapter 5. Proverbs of Latin and French origin in the history of English 117

3. Latin and French proverbs in the history of English

3.1 The distribution, development, and contextual usage of Latin and French proverbs over the centuries

The present chapter is concerned with the distribution, development, and contextual usage of the proverbs of Latin and French origin down the ages. Table 1 gives a chronological overview of the different proverbs collected from the *OED* and the *ODP*. Their English translations that can be found in the *OED* are also provided. Proverbs printed in bold have made it into common usage; i.e., they are also recorded in EFL dictionaries such as the *OALD* and/or the *LDOCE*.

Table 1. Chronological overview of Latin- and French-derived proverbs

Time	Latin-derived proverbs	French-derived proverbs	Numbers and proportions of proverbs
1501–1600	*nosce te ipsum* 'know yourself' (might have been first recorded in English in 1527); *festina lente* 'make haste slowly' (1537); *quot homines tot sententiae* 'there are as many opinions as there are men' (1539); *facilis descensus Averni* 'the descent into Avernus (i.e., hell) is easy' (might have been first recorded in English in 1566); *tempora mutantur* 'times change' (1577)		Latin proverbs: 5; i.e., 20.0%
1601–1700	*nemo dat quod non habet* 'no one gives what he or she does not have' (about 1674); *post hoc ergo propter hoc* 'after this, therefore because of this' (1685)	*reculer pour mieux sauter* 'to draw back in order to leap better' (1616)	Latin proverbs: 2; i.e., 8.0% French proverbs: 1; i.e., 4.0%
1701–1800	*morituri te salutant* 'those about to die salute you' (1704); *noscitur a sociis* 'he is known from his companions' (1749); *quieta non movere* 'do	*chacun à son goût* 'each to his own taste' (1784)	Latin proverbs: 4; i.e., 16.0% French proverbs: 1; i.e., 4.0%

Table 1. *(continued)*

Time	Latin-derived proverbs	French-derived proverbs	Numbers and proportions of proverbs
	not move settled things' (1754); *tempus fugit* 'time flies' (1792)		
1801–1900	*res non verba* 'things not words'(1805); *pacta sunt servanda* 'agreements must be kept' (1836); *solvitur ambulando* '(the problem) is solved by walking' (1852); *dulce et decorum est (pro patria mori)* 'it is sweet and fitting (to die for one's country)'(1863); *tertium non datur* 'no third possibility exists' (1887)	*pour encourager les autres* 'to encourage others' (1804); *après nous le déluge* 'after us the flood' (1809); **noblesse oblige** 'noble rank entails responsibility' (1837); *c'est la vie* 'that's life' (1854); *cherchez la femme* 'seek out the woman' (1863); **plus ça change (plus c'est la même chose)** 'the more it changes (the more it stays the same)' (1893)	Latin proverbs: 5; i.e., 20.0% French proverbs: 6; i.e., 24.0%
1901–2000		*les jeux sont faits* 'the games are made' (1922)	French proverbs: 1; i.e., 4.0%
TOTALS	16; i.e., 64.0%	9; i.e., 36%	25

The sources consulted contain a variety of multi-word phrases that do not represent proverbs in the proper sense and thus had to be excluded from the present study. An example is *pas devant les enfants*, lit. 'not in front of the children', an idiomatic expression used as a request to avoid inappropriate statements and utterances (see *OED*). The number of genuine, non-assimilated proverbs from Latin and French is relatively small. As can be seen from Table 1, it amounts to 25 lexical units. Of these, 16 (i.e. 64.0%) were introduced from Latin, nine (36.0%) from French. The number of Latin proverbs peaked in the sixteenth and nineteenth centuries (with 20% each); the highest proportion of French proverbs was borrowed in the nineteenth century (i.e., 24%).

The English Renaissance as an artistic and socio-cultural movement in England from the early sixteenth to the early seventeenth century, having its heyday during the Elizabethan age, may account for the increased adoption of Latin-derived proverbs at that time. The humanist movement during this period led to a revival of interest in classical Latin language and culture. Greek and Roman literary works were held in high esteem; the style of authors such as Virgil assumed a role model function (see also Orgel 2021). As will be seen, some proverbs were first recorded in Latin texts before they were adopted into English. The Latin works thus served as a medium for the introduction of these types of lexical units. From a cognitive point of view, one might argue that the evaluation of Latin as a prestigious language could have enhanced the borrowing process.

Similarly, the nineteenth century is characterised by a special appreciation of classical education. Throughout Europe, specific attention was also paid to the French language and culture. French culture was considered a sign of sophistication with Paris as an internationally appreciated centre of refined culture and art (Hellmuth 2020: 7–27). Like in other European countries, French served as the preferred means of conversation for the English aristocracy and upper middle class. The status of French as well as the number of English speakers who had a competent knowledge of this language certainly contributed to the adoption of French proverbs in the course of the nineteenth century.

In the sample of proverbs under review, only two, *noblesse oblige* and *plus ça change*, belong to a certain core field of well-used lexical units that can also be found in EFL dictionaries such as *OALD*. Others have become established in general English in their translated form. For example, this holds for the above-mentioned *time flies*, a loan translation of the Latin *tempus fugit* and *that's life* or *such is life*, which reflect the French *c'est la vie* (for a comparison between the use of a borrowed proverb instead of a synonymous English translation equivalent, see 2.2 below).

Most of the proverbs under consideration are related to society, human nature, and behaviour. An example from Latin is *quot homines tot sententiae*, lit. 'there are as many opinions as there are men', used with reference to the fact that among people there usually is a diversity of opinions that are difficult to reconcile. It was first documented in *Phormio*, a comedy by the Roman playwright Terence. Its English synonym or near-synonym is *so many men, so many minds* (see *OED*). This category of Latin proverbs also comprises a variety of worldly wisdoms, such as *nosce te ipsum*, *res non verba* and *solvitur ambulando*. The Latin equivalent of *nosce te ipsum*, '[k]now yourself', reflects an inscription at the Temple of Apollo of Delphi, the author of which is assumed to be Chilon of Sparta, regarded as one of the Seven Wise Men of ancient Greece. In ancient Greek thought, this demand is attributed to the god Apollo (see *OED*). *Res non verba*, literally translating as 'things not words', implies a request for less conversation and more action, and *solvitur ambulando*, lit. 'it is solved by walking', constitutes an appeal for a practical approach to solving a problem. The latter ultimately goes back to the Greek philosopher Diogenes (see *OED*).

All the worldly wisdoms as revealed by the Latin proverbs in question still function as tips and instructions for modes of behaviour or ways of life in manifold contexts in present-day usage. Yet, their use is mostly confined to elevated style, as is illustrated by Examples (1), (2), and (3) retrieved from newspaper corpora:

(1) *The Times*, October 21, 2020: "The secret of success in life and sport"
As a manager Wenger thrived on obsessiveness, something he knew was core to his being. One could say the same for Margaret Thatcher, who worked 16-hour days and whose relentlessness was central to her efficacy as a politician. [...] The problem, of course, is that it is far from easy to penetrate one's self, to understand the motivations, drives and neuroses that sit deep within each of us, a point (like so many) first articulated by the Ancient Greeks. This is why the Latin phrase **nosce te ipsum**[1] may serve as a useful motto for ambitious people of all kinds. The translation? Know thyself. (*Nexis Uni*)

(2) *The Belfast Telegraph*, April 24, 2015: "Why people of Belfast should snub Sinn Fein"
The ability to vote in the upcoming Westminster election is a right to be cherished and defended. By voting, you have the ability to affect who will be elected in your constituency in the hope that the successful MP will promote and support all within the constituency. [...] However, if you aren't content with the here-and-now and want to improve the outlook for future generations, then vote for a candidate who will use every avenue available to them – including within the corridors of Westminster. **Res non verba** Belfast
(*Nexis Uni*)

(3) *The Guardian*, May 18, 2016: "Why I'm walking in my father's footsteps, retracing the People's March for Jobs; In 1981, 280 people set off from Liverpool protesting at the Thatcher revolution. I hope to join the dots that have led to the state we're in now"
Even at the time, the first months of 1981 felt momentous. In January the Social Democratic party split from Labour. February saw Rupert Murdoch Rupert buying the Times and the Sunday Times, and in March the IRA prisoner Bobby Sands began his hunger strike. [...] I plan to write about my experiences, and I'd love to hear from you, to get your views on Britain in 2016. If you'd like to walk with me for a mile or more, or even let me kip on your couch, please get in touch. If you were on the original march orknew somebody on it, or remember it passing through your town, I'd loveto hear from you too. As Diogenes said, **solvitur ambulando** (it is solved by walking). Well, I'm about to find out whether that's true. (*Nexis Uni*)

---

1. All the proverbs under scrutiny are printed in bold in the various usage examples (the author's emphasis).

As might have been expected, sources reflecting informal language such as the tabloid *The Sun* include hardly any usage examples of Latin-derived proverbs. A certain classical education is necessary to understand the relevant newspaper articles in which they appear. Such texts seem to be written for the discerning reader who understands the connotations and allusions the different proverbs imply.

Similarly, a decent knowledge of French is required to make sense of English texts in which French-derived proverbs are documented. Of the proverbs to do with 'society, human nature, and behaviour', only *noblesse oblige* has become widespread enough to occur in tabloids, too, see

(4) *Daily Mail* (London), May 13, 2002: "Camilla, David Beckham and the Di factor"
What do Mr Beckham and Mrs Parker Bowles have in common? They are embarked on the strategy of **noblesse oblige** - the much-admired French maxim that those privileged by rank are obliged to help others less fortunate. **Noblesse oblige**, in the case of Mr Beckham and Mrs Parker Bowles, also means helping themselves. Earning almost GBP 5million a year for playing football could make Mr Beckham an object of public envy. Being seen to reach out to unfortunate children gives him a princely air. (*Nexis Uni*)

The French original was first recorded in *Maximes et Réflexions sur Différens Sujets de Morale et de Politique, Suivies de Quelques Essais* (1808), a treatise written by the French politician and author G. Duc de Levis (see *OED*). The other proverbs in this field are far less common. As to *reculer pour mieux sauter*, for instance, lit. 'to draw back in order to leap better', English newspaper articles sometimes include an explanation of its meaning. It seems as if the authors of the relevant texts doubt whether the proverb is understood by their entire readership and thus add a definition, as in the following article dealing with Brexit as a political strategy:

(5) *The Guardian*, September 18, 2017: "Carney warns fall in migrant workers could push up wages and inflation [...]"
Stock markets have begun the week on a positive note, as investors shrugged off any lingering worries about geopolitical tensions and central bank actions. [...] In his speech on Monday, Carney also said Britain was unlikely to immediately offset any weakening of trade ties with its EU partners by striking new trade agreements with other countries. "But Brexit is an example of '**reculer pour mieux sauter**'", Carney said, using a French expression which means stepping back in order to jump better. (*Nexis Uni*)

There are also lexical units referring to life in general and the way of the world. For example, *tempora mutantur*, more fully *tempora mutantur nos et* (or *et nos) mutamur in illis*, lit. 'times change and we change with them', is "[a] statement emphasizing the inevitability of change in human affairs and customs" (*OED*). An additional example is *post hoc ergo propter hoc*, lit. 'after this, therefore because of this', used with reference to the false assumption that one thing that results from another might be a logical, inevitable consequence. Again, a number of newspaper articles include paraphrases of the meanings of these proverbs in the corresponding contexts; e.g.,

(6) *The Times*, August 3, 2002: "Incredible life of Fry is stuff of sporting legend"
It is impossible to imagine a C. B. Fry in the modern sporting universe. [...] Of course, a C. B. Fry would not have emerged a century on: to play for Southampton in the FA Cup Final (as he did in 1902) and to represent Sussex and England at cricket is now impossible. To break the long jump world record into the bargain (while at Oxford in the 1890s) and to turn out for Blackheath – then one of the powerhouses in the sport – and the Barbarians at rugby union demonstrates both Fry's wonderful gifts and how much times have changed. Fry, were he alive today, would have understood better than most, as a classics scholar, the old Latin tag that **tempora mutantur** – times change. (*Nexis Uni*)

(7) *The Guardian*, June 23, 2019: "Black Cats: Curse of the Bye strikes again but there's little mystery to latest loss; Forget superstitions and hoodoos, like all sporting curses the reasons for Geelong's surprise defeat to Port Adelaide are much more mundane"
If there is one thing our game lacks, it is a decent curse – the invocation of an otherworldly power to punish a club or player. [...] But is a sporting curse nothing more than **post hoc ergo propter hoc** - an excuse pulled from the figment of our collective imagination to reconcile an intolerable truth? (*Nexis Uni*)

One proverb, *plus ça change*, belongs to the category of fairly widespread expressions. It is a shortening of the French *plus ça change, plus c'est la même chose*, lit. 'the more it changes, the more it stays the same', "used to suggest that human nature, institutions, etc., are always fundamentally the same, despite apparent changes" (*OED*), as in:

(8) *The Times*, March 18, 1993: "**Plus çachange**"
Plus ça change: "The Budget should be balanced, the Treasury refilled, public debt reduced, the arrogance of officialdom tempered and controlled, and assistance to foreign lands reduced lest the state become bankrupt. The people should be forced to work and not depend on government for assistance." Stafford Cripps? Metternich? Churchill? No, Marcus Cicero (106–20 B.C.) (*Nexis Uni*)

Chapter 5. Proverbs of Latin and French origin in the history of English

'Combat, war and the military' is another field to which some of the proverbs under scrutiny belong. An example is the Latin *morituri te salutant*,[2] literally 'those about to die salute you', initially served as an address to the emperor by gladiators in ancient Rome before the beginning of a battle, as is illustrated in the *OED*:

(9) 1704 B. Kennett Rom. Antiq. (ed. 3) ii. iii. 269 The Naumachiæ of Claudius which he presented on the Fucine Lake before he drain'd it, deserve to be particularly mention'd, not more for the greatness of the Show, than for the Behaviour of the Emperour: who when the Combatants pass'd before him with so melancholy a Greeting as, Ave imperator, morituri te salutant, return'd in Answer, Avete vos.

The proverb came to be used more generally in anticipation of impending calamity or death, see

(10) *The Daily Telegraph*, November 6, 2010: "Life is best lived at a full gallop; My perfect weekend Captain Ian Forquhar Huntsman"
To sit at the meet with a pack of hounds you trust and a horse you are happy on, and with the knowledge that the homework has been comprehensively done is a comfortable feeling.
I often cross myself at the meet and mutter: "**morituri te salutant**" ("those who are about to die salute you"). Since this is the perfect weekend, I am talking here about pre-ban, when good scenting conditions immediately thrill the senses and produce a feeling of wellbeing. Hunting is an inexact science and luck plays such a large part in things going your way. (*Nexis Uni*)

'Law' as well as 'entertainment and leisure activities' are additional areas comprising certain proverbs. An example restricted in its use to legal contexts is *pacta sunt servanda*, which translates as "[a]greements must be kept" (*OED*). Since 1998, the usage of Latin in court proceedings in England and Wales has been prohibited by the Civil Procedure Rule (see *OED*), which may account for the lack of usage examples of the proverb since the late 1990s. Its latest attested usage in the *OED* dates from 1992.

One individual French proverb has been assigned to 'entertainment and leisure activities'. This is *les jeux sont faits*, lit. 'the stakes are made', originally representing a type of call in roulette. Usage examples are scarce. It occasionally occurs in a transferred meaning, sometimes in combination with *rien ne va plus*, an additional call in roulette. In a 2014 article taken from *The Irish Times*, for

---

[2]. For additional examples of proverbs related to 'combat, war and the military', see Section 2.2.

instance, it is part of an extended metaphor, used in allusion to the typical behaviour/attitude of the Irish politician Albert Reynolds:

(11) *The Irish Times*, August 22, 2014: "Johnson lays out alternative manifesto for Brexit"
"I am a risk-taker." At first, I thought this was just harmless bravado on Albert's part, but I soon learned he would hazard all, even being Taoiseach, on what might amount to a mere hunch. I jotted in a diary: "Albert is a born gambler – at the track, in business and politics … When the chips are finally down and there's nothing more that can be done, he just stands and watches – fascinated, fatalistic, almost stoic. **Les jeux sont faits.** Rien ne va plus!" (*Nexis Uni*)

3.2 Motivations for the use of proverbs including socio-cognitive valuations and attitudes

In the following, some representative examples of contextual usages are adduced, pointing to possible motivations for the use of Latin- or French-derived proverbs by speakers of English (instead of the corresponding English synonyms).

Galinsky, who examines stylistic uses of Americanisms in German, concludes that local colour is an important function of borrowed lexical items (see Carstensen and Galinsky 1975: 37). Local colouring also represents a crucial function of foreign-derived proverbs. That is, they are (consciously) used to portray the typical features of a foreign setting and contribute to the creation of a culture-specific ambience. Local colouring occurs in British English, but also in any other variety of English, such as American English. The following recent article from *The New York Times* about the French fashion worldis a typical example.

(12) *The New York Times*, July 1, 2021: "The Imperial editor goes the way of the Dodo"
Business and culture have conspired to kill off a passé persona.
On Monday, when the fashion world will gather in Paris for the first live couture shows […] and assorted editors will take their socially distanced seats en masse, the front row – that power chain of often instantly recognizable individuals who set the tone for trends and style setters for the world – will look very different. […] By 2017, the #Me Too movement had pulled back the velvet curtain to reveal the complicity of the fashion world in the abuse of its least powerful citizens – its models – and the **noblesse oblige** of the editors began to look more like exploitation and willful blindness. (*Nexis Uni*)

Apart from the French place name *Paris*, the above extract comprises French borrowings such as the adjective *passé*, the noun *couture* and the adverb *en masse* as well as the French-derived proverb *noblesse oblige*. From a cognitive point of view, one might argue that the various foreign-derived elements allow the writer to present the depicted scene in the mind's eye of the reader even more vividly and authentically than the corresponding native vocabulary could do (e.g., *couture* instead of *fashion*, *en masse* instead of *in a body* and *noblesse oblige* instead of its English translation equivalent *noble rank entails responsibility*).

In some cases, a borrowed proverb is preferentially used to offer the culturally specific tone[3] of a speech or an utterance. *Après nous le déluge*, for example, lit. 'after us the flood,' goes back to an alleged declaration by Madame de Pompadour to Louis XV after the French defeat against the Prussian army at the Battle of Rossbach in 1757 (see *OED*). It now usually occurs in any context in general English, meaning 'what comes after, what it looks like afterwards, we do not care', see

(13) *The Independent*, May 12, 2011: "A regime's defiance fails to conceal its weakness; One crucial point is that today's turmoil is causing huge damage to the Syrian economy"
In the face of overwhelming odds, the popular revolt against the Assad regime continues. Many hundreds have been killed, and thousands more, maybe tens of thousands, have beenrounded up. Yesterday, tanks shelled residents in Homs, Syria's third largest city, and protest continues in half a dozen or more towns across the country. [...] In an interview yesterday with The New York Times, Rami Makhlouf – Syria's most powerful businessman, a first cousin of President Assad and an emblem of the corruption and economic injustice which fuels the protest movement – spelt that determination out. The regime was treating the protests as "afight to the end" and, he warned, "when we suffer we will not suffer alone". Such is the argument of dictators throughout the ages: "**Après nous, le deluge**." (*Nexis Uni*)

Yet, newspaper corpora also include several examples in which the proverb is put into the mouth of a French speaker, as in:

(14) *The Times*, June 26, 1987: "Brussel's View: EEC's financial wrangle persists"
'The trouble with summits is that people expect them to come up with dramatic solutions,' one official of the European Economic Community complained this week. [...] M Delors puts this plan firmly within the context of the amendments to the Treaty of Rome recently adopted as 'the single European Act', which inched the enlarged EEC of 12 closer to eventual union by ceding further power to the Commission and the European Parliament and providing for a common foreign policy (something else which unsettles the Danes).

---

3. From a stylistic point of view, certain implications or connotations of a speech or piece of writing may be due to a speaker's humorous, positive, negative, etc. tone emerging from the relevant context(s). For tone as a stylistic function of borrowed lexical items, see Carstensen and Galinsky 1975: 59.

> In other words, the battle is not only about cash (this year's deficit and farm price cuts) but also about political power and sovereignty, as struggles for the purse strings have so often been in history. [...] In his final pre-summit talks in Paris yesterday and in Bonn today M Delors is in effect echoing Madame de Pompadour: '**Après nous, le déluge.**' (*Nexis Uni*)

As can be seen, the utterance of the politician Jacques Delors is provided in its actual French voice, which heightens the immediacy of the described situation.

The lexicographical sample under review also includes some proverbs that occur in contexts revealing an ironical or humorous tone of the speaker or writer. *Dulce et decorum est*, an abbreviation of Latin *dulce et decōrum est prō patriā morī*, lit. 'it is sweet and fitting to die for one's country', is a proverb which goes back to Horace's *Odes* (see *OED*). It initially served as an inscription on tombs of fallen soldiers before it came to be used more generally in English "to assert (now frequently ironically) that to give one's life in this way is glorious or noble" (*OED*), as in:

(15) 2010 M. Robinson Absence of Mind ii. 69 Why war? **Dulce et decorum est.** Why altruism? It is more blessed to give than to receive. (*OED*)

Some of the proverbs in question were translated into English some time after their adoption. Examples are the Latin-derived proverbs *tempus fugit* (translated as *time flies*) and *quieta non movere* (*let sleeping dogs lie*). A look at corpora of recent usage reveals that the English synonyms or near-synonyms are used much more frequently than the Latin forms. The question arises as to what motivates the speaker or writer to resort to the foreign-language structure in a given context (instead of using the much more common English translation equivalents). The analysis of the available linguistic evidence suggests that the use is related to the evaluation of Latin as the prestige donor language *par excellence*. Sources reflecting informal English contain hardly any evidence of the original Latin proverbs. Most usage examples can be found in resources reflecting 'Standard' English; for example, they are comparatively often used in texts that appear to be written for the 'educated' reader. They can act as linguistic clues to attract the reader's attention and to give the impression that the relevant text reflects a sophisticated level of language use. Typical usage examples are:

(16) *The Independent*, May 26, 1999: "Leonardo's lost supper"
Consider [...] the words of Carlo Pedretti, Italy's foremost Leonardo expert. "I have some perplexities about the overall philosophy of intervention. We have lost a repainting that started a century after Leonardo's death and was part of the historical context of the work", he says. "Pinin Brambilla has destroyed the historical thread of the painting," concludes Michael Daley of Art Watch UK.

Even the world's most famous art historian, Ernest Gombrich, is reported to have obliquely criticised the restoration with a Latin phrase, **Quieta non movere**, which could be roughly translated as let sleeping dogs lie. (*Nexis Uni*)

(17) *The Guardian*, August 9, 2021: "The forgotten city review: sliding into your diems"
The genesis of The Forgotten City can be traced back to the day a stranger decided to punch its writer and creator, Nick Pearce, in the face. This unprovoked attack led him, then a tech lawyer, to pen his first short story. [...] For me, the moment that it got its hooks into me was when I used my foreknowledge of an impending accident to ensure that an assassin met an unfortunate end without my having to raise a finger. After that I was sunk, and the credits arrived too soon. **Tempus fugit**, indeed. (*Nexis Uni*)

In addition, some Latin proverbs are used to add more emphasis to a statement or an utterance, which at the same time increases linguistic expressiveness and vividness. An example is *facilis descensus Averni*, lit. 'the descent of (or to) Avernus (is) easy', a proverb first recorded in Virgil's *Aeneid*. Avernus was the name of a lake in the west of Naples, Italy, the supposed entrance to the underworld. The meaning of the proverb can be paraphrased as 'the descent into an immoral way of life is easy'. In Extract (18), it is used as a maxim with reference to the abuse of medical research and knowledge, enhancing the overriding statement of the article; i.e., that people can easily go astray in this regard.

(18) *The Scotsman*, February 1, 2001: "When medicine turns into the devil's work"
ON THE night the report on Alder Hey was published, we watched an episode of All Creatures Great and Small. (The series is being repeated on one of the digital channels, and my daughter had recorded it.) I couldn't help thinking, not for the first time, that vets seem to care more deeply for their patients than many doctors. Certainly, James Herriot and Siegfried Farnon seemed infinitely preferable to Professor Dick van Velzen.
Of course, it's ridiculous to compare them, just as it's ridiculous to compare Professor van Velzen to your ordinary overworked and conscientious GP. No doubt, too, some vets who work in animal laboratories develop a callousness equal to van Velzen's. All the same, the comparison between Herriot and van Velzen should remind us of this: that medical (or indeed veterinary) practice may sink into a moral wilderness whenever the natural impulses of humanity are stifled.
Facilis descensus Averni, wrote Virgil: the way down to Hell is easy, the return journey laborious and difficult. Nobody reading of what went on at Alder Hey can fail to have been reminded of Dr Josef Mengele and the other Nazi medical monsters. (*Nexis Uni*)

The above passage points to another motivation of the speaker for using a foreign-derived proverb. One might argue that *facilis descensus Averni* can also be used due to decency/linguistic politeness in order to express the given subject matter in a rather allusive and metaphorical manner without having to say it explicitly, so as not to offend the interlocutor. In the article cited above, it serves as a kind of euphemism[4] for the conscious and easy abuse of medical knowledge.

Another proverb that shows allusive as well as euphemistic implications is the French *pour encourager les autres*, first used with reference to the execution of Admiral John Byng during the Seven Years War. According to the indictment, Byng had failed to do his utmost to defend Menorca against the French and was thus shot on March 14, 1757 (see *OED*). In present-day English, the proverb is used allusively in remembrance of the killing of the admiral, relating to "a punishment or sacrifice: as an example to others; to encourage or deter others" (*OED*). Examples from recent newspaper articles are:

(19) *The Guardian*, October 12, 2018: "Infantino's jetsetting contrasts grimly with migrant worker's Fifa case; A $5,000 legal challenge over exploitation of workers building for the 2022 World Cup in Qatar pales next to the value of private flights accepted by Fifa's president"
In the grim scheme of things, it is the modesty of the sum that gets you. With the formal backing of the Netherlands Trade Union Confederation, a Bangladeshi man named Nadim Sharaful Alam is to sue Fifa for its alleged complicity in the mistreatment of those migrant workers in Qatar who are charged with building its World Cup venues and infrastructure. [...] As I say, that little jolly consumed 17 backbreaking and cruelly fruitless months of Alam's existence. In contrast, let us consider the figures attached to a mere four days – four days! – in the life of Gianni Infantino, the Solomon Grundy of a Fifa president who was appointed on a Monday and embroiled in an ethics investigation by the Tuesday, before being cleared on the Wednesday. I paraphrase only slightly. Still, what does 10 grand buy you in the world of the chap who will undoubtedly bat away Alam's request for compensation, **pour encourager les autres?**   (*Nexis Uni*)

(20) *The Times*, May 6, 2021: "Who's to blame for our shoddy building culture? An industry riddled with corner-cutting is possible only because so many of us try to get our homes built on the cheap"
Four years ago next month a fire turned a London tower block into a vertical pyre which killed 72 people. [...] The problem is baked in. The incentives to behave well and build well are, the odd catastrophe apart, simply not there.

---

4. For the use of borrowed euphemisms as a result of intentional disguise, see Carstensen and Galinsky 1975: 47.

They'd even created euphemisms for cheap, shoddy work, such as "value engineering". Perhaps if we sent someone at the top of a big company to prison for this, **pour encourager les autres**, then things might change. But so far the bosses have blamed the workers further down the food chain. (*Nexis Uni*)

4. Summary and conclusion

Of the two donor languages under investigation, Latin provided the largest number of proverbs in the history of English: 64% were borrowed from Latin, only 36% from French. The analysis of borrowed proverbs in dictionaries such as *OED* makes it possible to reconstruct the socio-cultural or historical context in which they were originally used and to account for their chronological distribution down the ages. We established that the English Renaissance with its associated revival of interest in classical Latin language and culture as well as the increased appreciation of authors such as Virgil might have enhanced the borrowing of Latin proverbs. The status of French as a prestige donor language especially in the nineteenth century accounts for the peak of French proverbs during that time. A comparison between the treatments of proverbs in historical dictionaries with their use in recent newspaper articles revealed that numerous Latin- and French-derived proverbs related to 'society, human nature and behaviour' as well as 'life and the way of the world' still serve as valuable worldly wisdoms in present-day English. As emerged from the present survey, some proverbs that were first used in martial conflicts have developed extended or transferred uses in current English. This does not hold for the Latin-derived proverbs in the field of law, all of which are confined to (historical) legal situations. Only one proverb of French origin, *les jeux sont faits*, is initially and mostly recorded in contexts to do with 'entertainment and leisure activities'. Like the majority proverbs in question, it shows manifold uses in English, including figurative meanings.

As was seen, newspaper corpora reflect a number of further contextual usages that cannot be identified by means of the lexicographical resources consulted. The borrowed proverbs tend to be used in elevated style. Based on the linguistic data collected from newspapers, several additional extra-linguistic aspects including socio-cognitive forces were determined, pointing to speakers' motivations for using the borrowed proverbs instead of a semantically accordant English equivalent. Among them are emotionally-affective forces, ranging from the pursuit of prestige and decency, to linguistic vividness, authenticity, expressiveness and emphasis.

References

Abrahams, R.D. (1975). A sociolinguistic approach to proverbs. *Midwestern Journal of Language and Folklore*, 1, 60–4.

Barley, N. (1972). A structural approach to the proverb and maxim with special reference to the Anglo-Saxon corpus. *Proverbium*, 20, 737–50.

Buja, E. (2018). Proverb as a means of crossing cultural borders. *Acta Universitatis Sapientiae, Philologica*, 10, 85–97.

Carstensen, B., & Galinsky, H. (1975). *Amerikanismen in der deutschen Gegenwartssprache*. Heidelberg: Winter.

Croft, W.A. (2009). Toward a social cognitive linguistics. In V. Evans, & S. Pourcel (Eds.), *New directions in cognitive linguistics* (pp. 395–420). Amsterdam & Philadelphia: John Benjamins.

Dirven, R., Goossens L., Putsey, Y., & Vorlat E. (1982). *The scene of linguistic action and its perspectivization by SPEAK, TALK, SAY, and TELL*. Amsterdam & Philadelphia: John Benjamins.

Divjak, D., & Gries S.Th. (2006). Ways of trying in Russian: Clustering behavioral profiles. *Journal of Corpus Linguistics and Linguistic Theory*, 2, 23–60.

Durkin, P. (1999). Root and Branch: Revising the etymological component of the OED. *Transactions of the Philological Society*, 97, 1–49.

Finnegan, R. (2006). Proverbs in Africa. In W. Mieder, & A. Dundes (Eds.): *Wisdom of manny: essays on the proverb* (pp. 10–42). Wisconsin: The University of Wisconsin Press.

Geeraerts, D., Grondelaers, S., & Bakema, P. (1994). *The structure of lexical variation. Meaning, naming, and context*. Berlin: Mouton de Gruyter.

Geeraerts, D., Kristiansen, G., & Peirsman, Y. (2010). *Advances in Cognitive Sociolinguistics*. Berlin: Mouton de Gruyter.

Glynn, D. (2010). Synonymy, lexical fields, and grammatical constructions. A study in usage-based cognitive semantics. In H. Schmid, & S. Handl (Eds.): *Cognitive foundations of linguistic usage patterns. Empirical studies* (pp. 89–117). Berlin: Mouton de Gruyter.

Grondelaers, S., Speelman D., & Geeraerts, D. (2007). A case for a cognitive corpus linguistics. In M. Gonzalez-Marquez, I. Mittelberg, S. Coulson, & M. Spivey (Eds.), *Methods in cognitive linguistics*. (pp. 149–70). Amsterdam & Philadelpha: John Benjamins.

Hellmuth, T. (2020). *Frankreich im 19. Jahrhundert. Eine Kulturgeschichte*. Wien: Böhlau Verlag.

Hock, H., & Joseph, B. (2019). *Language history, language change, and language relationship. An introduction to historical and comparative linguistics*. Berlin: Mouton de Gruyter.

Holbek, B. (1970). Proverb style. *Proverbium*, 15, 54–6.

Iyalla-Amadi, P.E. (2014). Translational techniques as a teaching tool using culture-specific units: the case of French-English proverbs. *Sino-US English Teaching*, 11, 111–8.

Kristiansen, G., & Dirven, R. (Eds.) (2008). *Cognitive sociolinguistics. Language variation, cultural models, social systems*. Berlin: Mouton de Gruyter.

Lehrer, A. (1982). *Wine and conversation*. Bloomington: Indiana University Press.

Newman, J., & Rice, S. (2004a). Patterns of usage for English SIT, STAND, and LIE: A cognitively-inspired exploration in corpus linguistics. *Cognitive Linguistics*, 15, 351–96.

Newman, J., & Rice, S. (2004b). Aspect in the making: A corpus analysis of English aspect-marking prepositions. In S. Kemmer, & M. Achard (Eds.): *Language, culture and mind* (pp. 313–27). Stanford, CA: CSLI.

Norrick, N. R. (1985). *How proverbs mean. Semantic studies in English proverbs.* Berlin: Mouton.

Orgel, S. (2021). *Wit's treasury. Renaissance England and the classics.* Philadelphia: University of Pennsylvania Press.

Rudzka-Ostyn, B. (1995). Metaphor, schema, invariance: the case of verbs of answering. In L. Goossens, P. Pauwels, B. Rudzka-Ostyn, A. Simon-Vandenbergen, & J. Vanparys (Eds.): *By word of mouth, metaphor, metonymy and linguistic action in a cognitive perspective* (pp. 205–44). Amsterdam & Philadelphia: John Benjamins.

Schmid, H. (1993). *Cottage, idea, start: Die Kategorisierung als Grundprinzip einer differenzierten Bedeutungsbeschreibung.* Tübingen: Niemeyer.

Smith, A. (2011). Exploring cultural identity through proverbs and idioms in English, French and Spanish. *Revista de Lenguas Modernas*, 15, 261–72.

Speake, J. (2015). *Oxford Dictionary of Proverbs.* Oxford: Oxford University Press.

Speelman, D., & Geeraerts, D. (2009). Causes for causatives. The case of Dutch *doen* and *laten*. In T. Sanders, & E. Sweetser (Eds.): *Causal categories in discourse and cognition* (pp. 173–204). Berlin: Mouton de Gruyter.

Tomasello, M. (2003). *Constructing a language. A usage-based theory of language acquisition.* Cambridge, MA: Harvard University Press.

Zenner, E., Backus, A., & Winter-Froemel, E. (Eds.) (2019). *Cognitive contact linguistics. Placing usage, meaning and mind at the core of contact-induced variation and change.* Berlin: Mouton de Gruyter.

Online dictionaries and corpora

LDOCE = Longman Dictionary of Contemporary English. Compiled by Pearson (Harlow); available online at <https://www.ldoceonline.com/> (last accessed 30 August 2021)

Nexis Uni. Compiled by Lexis Nexis GmbH, Dusseldorf, Germany; available online at <https://www.lexisnexis.de/loesungen/research/akademische-recherche-nexis-uni> (last accessed 30 August 2021)

OALD = Oxford Advanced Learner's Dictionary. Compiled by Oxford University Press; available online at <https://www.oxfordlearnersdictionaries.com/> (last accessed 30 August 2021)

OED = Oxford English Dictionary Online. Murray, J., Bradley, H., Craigie, W., & Onions, Charles T. (Eds.) (1884–1933). *The Oxford English Dictionary; Supplement* (1972–86), ed. by R. Burchfield; Second ed. (1989), ed. by J. Simpson, & E. Weiner; *Additions Series* (1993–1997), ed. by J. Simpson, E. Weiner, & M. Proffitt; Third ed. (in progress) *OED Online* (March 2000), ed. by J. Simpson. Oxford. *OED Online* searchable at: <http://www.oed.com/> (last accessed 30 August 2021).

CHAPTER 6

Cognitive Linguistics and expressing/interpreting proverbs in a second language

Gladys Nyarko Ansah
University of Ghana, Legon

This chapter relies on Cognitive/Cultural Linguistics assumptions to investigate proverb interpretation and expression among Akan-English bilinguals in Ghana. Cognitive linguistic approaches to studying proverbs, e.g., Lakoff and Turner (1989), emphasise the role cognitive models play in human conceptualisation, including proverb interpretation. Using fifty common proverbs in each of their two languages, participants were asked to interpret proverbs in one language and provide their conceptual equivalents in the other language. Findings suggest that while the bilinguals were better able to interpret proverbs whose interpretation needed less cultural competence in both languages, they appeared to rely on L1 cultural models to express/interpret L2 proverbs whose interpretation needed more cultural competence.

Keywords: Akan, English, L2, metaphors, proverbs

1. Introduction

Proverbs may be generally defined as short, pithy sayings that express traditionally held truths or pieces of advice, usually based on common sense or experience. Nevertheless, they have been defined in many different ways across disciplines. From a linguistic perspective, proverbs are formulaic and fixed expressions in language that are often learned en bloc, like idiomatic expressions, as part of language socialisation. From a psychological/cognitive point of view, however, proverbs are often considered as a mirror through which we can see a people's way of thinking (Dzokoto et al. 2018a). From a cultural linguistic perspective, proverbs are described as cultural conceptualisations (Sharifian 2003) because they serve both as a memory bank (for preserving) and as a vehicle for (transmitting) wisdom and knowledge about communities/cultures. In cultural/anthropological studies, proverbs are treated as cultural artefacts that emerge from common/

shared geo-physical, socio-cultural experiences of a given community and tend to reflect the deep knowledge of a people's realities. For this reason, proverbs are often regarded as powerful tools in representing, influencing, or shaping the worldview of a group of people (Dzokoto et al. 2018a; Dzokoto et al. 2018b). As Appiah et al. (2007: iv) put it, proverbs are a "verbal shrine for the soul of a Nation".

Two kinds of proverbs are identified in the literature, namely: Metaphoric and Non-metaphoric proverbs (Bock and Brewer 1980; Nirmala 2013; Belkhir 2022). While non-metaphoric proverbs are said to have literal meanings only, metaphoric proverbs have figurative meanings in addition to their literal meanings. According to Belkhir (2022: 115), processing (translating) proverbs from one language into another requires one's ability to account for both linguistic and cultural dimensions of the proverb because, "languages are used in different physical and sociocultural environments depicting distinct social realities". The cultural dimensions of proverbs, particularly of metaphoric proverbs, make proverb processing (e.g., interpretation/translation) potentially challenging, particularly for non-native speakers of any language, e.g., L2 speakers, especially those whose L1 and L2 contexts are very different.

Akan is a Kwa language that is spoken widely in southern (forest and coastal) Ghana, West Africa, while English is an Indo-European language that is originally native to England, a temperate region, but that is now spoken widely around the World. Psycholinguistic research has shown that the languages that are known and spoken by a bi/multilingual person become part of the same language system, and that the interactions between the two languages have consequences for the bilingual brain, mind and language processing (Kroll et al. 2015: 377). The central question this chapter tries to answer is, considering Akan and English are typologically unrelated languages and are set in different geo-physical and socio-cultural environments, how do native speakers of Akan who have become second language speakers of English, interpret and express proverbs across their two languages?

One way to answer this question is to rely on the traditional cognitive linguistic assumption of embodied cognition that espouses universal human conceptualisation (Lakoff and Johnson 1980) to argue that bilinguals can rely on general embodied cognitive principles to understand and interpret all proverbs in both their L1 and L2. Another way to answer this question is to rely on the notion of cultural embodiment as discussed in Cultural Linguistics research (e.g., Sharifian 2007, 2013) to argue that bilinguals may need a certain level of cultural competence to understand/interpret proverbs that reflect cultural conceptualisations in both languages. A third way is to merge these two assumptions about human conceptualisation, which is what this study does. It combines assumptions from both traditions to explore how Akan-English bilinguals interpret and express proverbs across their two languages.

I argue that while Akan-English bilinguals may rely on general human cognitive principles to understand, express, and interpret both metaphoric and non-metaphorical proverbs, which do not require cultural competence to interpret across their languages, they will need cultural competence, in addition to general human cognitive structures, to understand, express and interpret culture-specific proverbs across their languages. In addition, bilinguals may resort to L1 cultural schemas in expressing/interpreting L2 (metaphoric) proverbs that require cultural competence for understanding/interpretation. In other words, I expect Akan-English bilinguals to understand non-metaphoric proverbs in their two languages more easily than metaphoric ones, especially, from their L2. The main objectives of the chapter therefore are: (i) to ascertain whether or not Akan-English bilinguals would find non-metaphoric proverbs in both languages easier to understand than metaphoric ones and (ii) to identify the potential cultural-cognitive models that guide the bilinguals' interpretation of proverbs across their two languages given that these two languages/cultures are very different.

2. Cognitive/Cultural Linguistics and proverb

Proverbs have been studied widely across disciplines and cultures; e.g., English (Wilson 1994) and Yiddish (Silverman-Weinreich 1981). From ethnolinguistics and cultural anthropology (Lutz 1988; Perry 1988; Mieder and Dundes 1994; Appiah et al. 2007) to philosophy (Gyekye 2011) and rhetorics (Yankah 1989), these studies have often linked the proverbs of particular societies to the life and culture of their people in one way or another such as ethics and belief systems. For instance, Perry (1988) examined the proverbs of Sephardic Jews and linked the proverbs to their philosophy of life.

In the African context, Omoniyi (1995) has discussed proverbs in Song-lashing as a communicative strategy in Yoruba interpersonal conflicts. In addition, while Agyekum (2000, 2005) has discussed proverbs as an aspect of Akan oral literature that is used in mass media communication in contemporary Ghana, Yankah (1986) has examined proverb rhetoric in African judicial process. Again, Yankah (1989) has explored proverbs in the aesthetics of traditional communication among the Akans in Ghana. In recent times, Dzokoto et al. (2018a) have discussed proverbs in relation to Akan romantic relationship rules while Dzokoto et al. (2018b) have examined Akan proverbs to discuss the cultural rules about emotion regulation in Akan. Finally, Ansah and Dzregah (2020) have discussed the role of proverbs in the discursive construction of ethos on female sexual behaviour in contemporary Ghana.

In traditional linguistics, studies on proverbs have tended to focus on lexical and grammatical descriptions (MacCoinnigh 2015), as well as the comprehension/interpretation of proverbial phrases (Andersson 2013; Granbom-Herranen 2011). Even though such studies are useful in their own rights, they may not be adequate in other areas, e.g., in accounting for the meanings of metaphoric proverbs particularly among L2 speakers. This is because proverbs in general and metaphoric proverbs in particular tend to contain cultural references, allusions and nuanced implications that need cultural competence (more than linguistic knowledge) to interpret, especially for non-native speakers (Wolf 2017). Again, Berman and Ravid (2010: 156) assert, "Figurative language involves the ability to adopt a frame of mind that is capable of interpreting particular words or constructions beyond their initially available basic or literal meaning". This is where cognitive linguistic approaches, which use metaphoric (non-literal) language to explore the relationship between the human mind, human language, and socio-physical experience, e.g., Conceptual Metaphor Theory (CMT) become important to the study of proverbs.

Cognitive linguists have employed CMT to study proverbs in different contexts (see this volume). On the one hand, Lakoff and Turner's (1989) Great Chain Metaphor theory attempts to explain common human cognitive principles/structures that are used to understand general human experience. On the other hand, the Extended Theory, posits that proverbs are knots that need to be undone, problems that need to be solved, or mysteries that need unravelling. According to Honeck and Temple (1994: 92), basically, the mind goes through three phases to arrive at understanding proverbs: the literal phase, a figurative-meaning phase, and an instantiation phase. Nevertheless, figurative and literal meanings are mutually dependent as figurative meanings cycle back to include literal meanings. Honeck and Temple (1994) and Temple and Honeck (1999) suggest two situations for the interpretation of proverbs: irrelevant-context situation where a proverb is not used in a context to aid understanding, and a relevant-context situation where a proverb is uttered in a supportive context or in an interaction.

Guided by principles in these theories, Nirmala (2013) has studied the most common concepts that are present in Javanese proverbs and concludes that proverbs are a reflection of human experiences with natural/physical phenomena or environment. His categorisation of proverbs as metaphoric and non-metaphoric was based on the assumptions that whereas a non-metaphoric proverb does not indicate association with any other concept, a metaphoric proverb carries a concept of another experience. In other words, while non-metaphoric proverbs may be understood literally, metaphoric proverbs have figurative meanings that require cross-domain conceptualisations or mappings. He identified the following as the layers of meaning metaphoric proverbs have:

1. literal meaning – the semantic meaning of the words of the proverb,
2. cognitive meaning – the conceptual meaning/representation in the proverbs,
3. literary meaning – the poetic function of the proverb, and
4. cultural meaning – the cultural significance of the proverb.

Similarly, employing cognitive linguistic principles, Paknezhad and Naghizadeh (2016) conducted a study that aimed to ascertain the role image schemas play in the conceptual structure of Arabic and Persian proverbs. The findings of the study corroborate a very important observation about the role of geo-physical and sociocultural environments in proverb formulation, understanding and interpretation. In their own words, image schemas in proverbs are "relatively abstract representations that derive from our everyday interaction with and observation of the whole universe around us" (Paknezhad and Naghizadeh 2016: 282). Mansyur and Said (2019) have also demonstrated how the human body serves as a source domain for metaphoric/metonymic proverbs in Wolio (and across languages/cultures). Their study concludes that while different languages/cultures may employ universal cognitive principles such as metaphorisation and metonymy in proverb construction/interpretation, these metaphors/metonymies are expressed differently across languages because of the influence of (different) cultures and circumstances.

Indeed, in the Cognitive Linguistics tradition, the debate about universal human cognition versus culture-specific cognition has been discussed extensively in the literature (e.g., Lutz 1988; Maalej 1999; Sharifian 2013; Ansah 2013, 2014). This universal vs. culture-specific conceptualisation debate has been extended to the study of proverbs. On the one hand, there are cognitive linguists who believe that proverbs should be analysed along abstract, universal principles of human thought and behaviour. On the other hand, there are those, particularly cognitive/cultural linguists who advocate for analysing proverbs within specific cultural contexts. These notwithstanding, there are cognitive /cultural linguists who take a middle ground (e.g., Buljan and Gradečak-Erdeljić 2013), and suggest an integrative approach, where proverbs may contain both universal human and culture-specific elements. Consequently, the process for proverb interpretation must consider both elements. Buljan and Gradečak-Erdeljić (2013) demonstrate this position in their study of English and Croatian proverbs where they conclude that it is possible for proverbs to share universal/abstract concepts while maintaining their unique culture-specific interpretation.

Moreno's (2005) comparative study of Spanish and English proverbs is another study that subscribes to this position. The study that aimed at determining the universality of proverbs concluded that while the metaphorical propositions behind proverbs may be common across cultures, they are not necessarily universal because they are subject to changes, and that the social and pragmatic contexts of proverbs are important in their interpretation. This is because they are a part, and indicative of their particular social values. Moreno illustrated this with Spanish and English animal proverbs. By comparing the English proverb *Better be the head of a dog than the tail of a lion* and the Spanish proverb, which is translated as 'Better to be a mouse head than a lion's tail', he avers that both languages/cultures use animals to express a common or similar understanding. Nevertheless, it is obvious that the two languages/cultures use different animals in expressing this common/similar understanding. Moreno, thus, concludes that while the way the human mind categorises or structures things may be universal, scripts and the view of reality tend to be culture-specific.

Again, in a study that was designed to produce a semantic comparative analysis of animals in English and Arabic proverbs, Sameer (2016) discovered that the semantic molecules of horses and dogs in Arabic and English are similar and concluded that these proverbs rely on similar mental mechanisms: metaphors and metonymies. For Liu (2013), metaphors in proverbs are representative of the living environments of a people, and a reflection of their experiences. Depending on the similarities and differences in living conditions, beliefs and values, metaphorical proverbs in a language/culture may be different or similar to those in other languages/cultures. It is worthy of note that similar findings about universality vs. language/culture-specificity have been reported in the literature with regard to the conceptualisation of human emotions (e.g., Maalej 1999; Kövecses 2005; Ansah 2010, 2011, 2014).

In spite of the many studies on proverbs from different perspectives and traditions, not much research has been done on proverbs expression and interpretation from Cognitive Linguistics perspectives and among second language speakers particularly from the African/Ghanaian context. This chapter, therefore, attempts to address this situation from Cognitive/Cultural Linguistics perspectives to studying proverbs (e.g., Lakoff and Turner 1989), which underscore the importance of cognitive models, units of non-linguistic knowledge (e.g., cultural schemas) in understanding and interpreting metaphoric proverbs.

3. Methods

The study collected fifty most common proverbs in Akan and English from two online sources for use. The first site, FluentU, (The 50 Most Useful English Proverbs You Should Learn Right Now | FluentU English) is an online blog site that uses natural approaches, e.g., videos of actual/natural language use in context to support the learning of English language and culture. The 50 proverbs are not just listed on the site. Instead, the site provides some visual interpretation as well as a basic explanation to each of the proverbs. Similarly, the Akan proverbs were collected from an online site (The 50 Most Important Akan Proverbs | Adinkra Symbols and Meanings) that is dedicated to providing interpretation and meanings to Akan symbolic language and culture including proverbs and other aphorisms, e.g., adinkra. The 50 proverbs selected are considered as important proverbs in Akan because they are popular, versatile, and demonstrative of Akan philosophy and thought. The site also provides meanings and remarks about these proverbs. The proverbs from Akan and English with their meanings (as provided by the websites) are presented as Appendix 1 and Appendix 2 respectively.

Following Nirmala's (2013) categorisation which may be said to be based on principles similar to those in categorising metaphoric and non-metaphoric language in CMT (e.g., Pragglejaz Group 2007), I categorised the 50 proverbs in each language as metaphoric or non-metaphoric. The categorisation was based on CMT's approach to metaphor identification; e.g., as outlined in the Pragglejaz Group (2007). According to this approach, non-metaphoric language (proverbs) has literal meanings only while metaphoric language (proverbs) has both literal and figurative meanings (Bock and Brewer 1980; Belkhir 2022). Guided by these principles, I assessed the meanings assigned to the proverbs by the online sources to categorise each proverb as either metaphoric or non-metaphoric. Proverbs with only literal meanings were categorised as non-metaphoric while those with both literal and figurative meanings were categorised as metaphoric. In all, 35 of the Akan proverbs were metaphoric and 15 non-metaphoric while 29 and 21 of the English proverbs were metaphorical and non-metaphorical respectively. It is important to note that the applicability of a proverb to wider contexts is not limited by its metaphoricity or non-metaphoricity. Tables 1 and 2 below present my categorisation of the English proverbs as metaphoric or non-metaphoric respectively. For want of space, tables showing metaphoric and non-metaphoric Akan proverbs are attached as Appendix 3.

The (uncategorised) proverbs were put into Google doc forms (without their meanings/explanations) for online distribution. Because understanding proverbs may require some appreciable level of linguistic competence, and because the study focuses on Akan-English bilinguals, participants were purposively selected. They included Akan-English bilinguals who were fluent in both languages and use both languages regularly. These included graduate students, former university students and academics/researchers. The forms were sent through emails or WhatsApp to 40 people. However, only 16 participants responded to (filled and returned) the forms. Participants were asked to explain the meaning of each

Chapter 6. Cognitive Linguistics and expressing/interpreting proverbs in a second language

Table 1. English metaphoric proverbs

Strike while the iron is hot.	*It's no use crying over spilled milk.*
Too many cooks spoil the broth.	*Don't put all your eggs in one basket.*
You can't have your cake and eat it too.	*People in glass houses shouldn't throw stones.*
Many hands make light work.	*A rolling stone gathers no moss.*
Don't cross the bridge before you get to it	*Still waters run deep.*
Where there's a will, there's a way.	*If it ain't broke, don't fix it*
Look before you leap.	*Curiosity killed the cat.*
Don't make a mountain out of an anthill.	*Learn to walk before you run.*
The early bird catches the worm.	*My hands are tied.*
The cat is out of the bag.	*It's the tip of the iceberg.*
Always put your best foot forward.	*Ignorance is bliss.*
The squeaky wheel gets the grease.	*The forbidden fruit is always the sweetest*
You made your bed, now you have to lie in it.	*Close but no cigar.*
Actions speak louder than words.	*It takes two to tango.*

Table 2. English non-metaphoric proverbs

The grass is always greener on the other side of the fence.	*Don't bite the hand that feeds you.*
Don't judge a book by its cover.	*Don't bite off more than you can chew.*
When in Rome, do as the Romans do.	*Don't count your chickens before they hatch.*
Honesty is the best policy.	*First things first.*
Practice makes perfect	*Money does not grow on trees.*
Beggars can't be choosers	*No news is good news.*
An apple a day keeps the doctor away.	*Out of sight, out of mind.*
Better late than never.	*If you scratch my back, I'll scratch yours.*
Two wrongs do not make a right.	*Easy come, easy go.*
Rome was not built in a day.	*Every cloud has a silver lining.*
It's better to be safe than sorry.	*You can't make an omelette without breaking a few eggs.*

Akan proverb in English, and then provide a conceptual equivalent, an English proverb that has the same meaning as the Akan one if they knew one. Similarly, they were asked to provide the meaning of each English proverb as well as its possible conceptual equivalent in Akan. Again, where participants demonstrated understanding of metaphorical proverbs, we wanted to know the cognitive models that aided their understanding, especially of L2 proverbs.

As mentioned, the analysis of the data was based on Cognitive Linguistics assumptions about human cognition (Lakoff and Turner 1989) as well as Cultural Linguistics assumptions about cultural conceptualisations (Sharifian 2007). To illustrate this, here is how (I propose) we may arrive at the interpretation of the English proverb, *You catch more flies with honey than vinegar* generally as 'it is easier to win people to your side with polite/friendly attitudes than with hostile confrontation' by applying principles from Lakoff and Turner's Great Chain Metaphor Theory. This interpretation may be said to be based on our understanding of the nature of flies, honey and vinegar (the *Nature of Things*), our experience of the potential relationship between flies and honey, on the one hand, and flies and vinegar, on the other hand (the Great Chain of Being).

In addition, through a cognitive mechanism of schema transfer (GENERIC IS SPECIFIC), and aided by the context of communication (*Maxim of* Quantity), we are able to map this understanding onto a particular situation; e.g., promising great rewards to get your child to do their school work without a fuss, in order to arrive at the understanding and interpretation given above. From a Cultural Linguistics perspective, we may project that individuals may give culturally salient variations of this interpretation that reflect specific cultural experiences. The results and findings of the data are discussed below.

4. Discussion of results

After six weeks of administering the Google doc forms, 16 out of the 40 participants filled and returned their forms. While 56% of participants were male, 44% were female. Again, whereas 13% of participants were aged above 45 years, 31% were aged between 30 and 45 years old and 56% were aged 18–30 years old. As already indicated, all participants were Akan-English bilinguals who have had a minimum of secondary education.

4.1 Proverb response distribution

Generally, more participants responded to the Akan proverbs than to the English proverbs; i.e., the bilinguals provided responses to the Akan proverbs (providing meanings/interpretations in English and suggesting possible conceptual English equivalent proverbs) more than they did for the English proverbs. Table 3 below shows the response distribution to individual proverbs in English and Akan respectively.

Table 3. Proverb response distribution

English proverb response distribution	
No. of responses	No. of proverbs with this response
5 responses	1 proverb
4 responses	4 proverbs
3 responses	11 proverbs
2 responses	27 proverbs
1 response	7 proverb
Akan proverb response distribution	
No. of responses	No. of proverbs with this response
14 responses	2 proverbs
13 responses	4 proverbs
12 responses	1 proverb
11 responses	1 proverb
10 responses	5 proverbs
9 responses	10 proverbs
8 responses	11 proverbs
7 responses	8 proverbs
6 responses	4 proverbs
5 responses	4 proverbs

From Table 3, we can see that response frequencies for Akan proverbs were generally higher than those for English proverbs. Whereas the highest response frequency for individual Akan proverbs was 14 out of 16 participants, the lowest response frequency was 5 out of 16. The average response frequency for Akan proverbs was 8.6. On the other hand, the highest response frequency for the English proverbs was 5 out of 16 while the lowest response frequency was 1 out of 16. The average response frequency for English proverbs was 2.6. From Table 3 above, we can see that the bilinguals responded more to proverbs in their L1 than in their L2. If we interpret the response frequencies to reflect the bilinguals' ability to understand/interpret these proverbs, we may conclude that the bilinguals showed a stronger/better understanding of the L1 (Akan) proverbs than L2 (English) proverbs. This finding may be corroborating the assertion that non-native speakers may struggle with proverb understanding/interpretation because of the cultural dimensions (Berman and Ravid 2010; Wolf 2017; Belkhir 2022).

4.2 Processing metaphoric and non-metaphoric proverbs

One of the aims of this study was to ascertain whether Akan-English bilinguals would find non-metaphoric proverbs in both languages easier to process (understand/interpret) than metaphoric ones. In order to achieve this aim, I examined the frequencies of responses to the individual proverbs in each language. The data revealed some noteworthy patterns. Tables 4 and 5 below present the frequency distribution for individual proverbs in Akan and English respectively.

Table 4. Response frequencies for Akan proverbs (Average response frequency: 8.6)

Prov.	Response freq.	Prov.	Response freq.	Prov.	Response freq.	Prov.	Response freq.	Prov.	Response freq.
1	14	11	8	21	10	31	8	41	9
2	14	12	9	22	10	32	9	42	5
3	13	13	10	23	9	33	9	43	8
4	13	14	9	24	9	34	8	44	5
5	13	15	8	25	7	35	5	45	9
6	9	16	7	26	8	36	8	46	10
7	12	17	5	27	8	37	7	47	7
8	11	18	9	28	8	38	7	48	6
9	13	19	7	29	7	39	7	49	6
10	10	20	8	30	8	40	6	50	6

Table 5. Response frequencies for English proverbs (Average response frequency: 2.6)

Prov.	Response freq.	Prov.	Response freq.	Prov.	Response freq.	Prov.	Response freq.	Prov.	Response freq.
1	4	11	2	21	3	31	3	41	2
2	5	12	2	22	2	32	3	42	1
3	4	13	2	23	4	33	1	43	2
4	2	14	2	24	2	34	2	44	3
5	1	15	1	25	3	35	1	45	2
6	2	16	2	26	3	36	2	46	3
7	3	17	2	27	2	37	2	47	1
8	2	18	2	28	2	38	2	48	1
9	3	19	3	29	2	39	4	49	2
10	3	20	2	30	2	40	2	50	2

Chapter 6. Cognitive Linguistics and expressing/interpreting proverbs in a second language   143

From Tables 4 and 5 above, the Akan proverbs (1 and 2) with the highest response frequencies (14) were both categorised as metaphoric. However, three of the four Akan proverbs (3, 5, and 9) with the second highest response frequencies (13) were categorised as non-metaphoric; only one (4) was categorised as metaphoric. In other words, 50% of the six Akan proverbs with the highest response frequencies were metaphoric while the remaining 50% were non-metaphoric. Concerning the six Akan proverbs with the least response frequencies (5–6 responses), 50% (35, 45, 50) were categorised as non-metaphoric while the remaining 50% (42, 48, 49) were categorised as metaphorical. Similarly, 60% of the 5 proverbs with both the highest and lowest response frequencies were categorised as non-metaphoric.

It appears that, on the one hand, the bilinguals' understanding of L1 proverbs is not dependent on the metaphoricity but perhaps on proverb currency – proverbs 1, 2 and 4, though metaphoric, are very frequently used in discourses in Ghana while proverbs 35, 44 and 50, though non-metaphoric are not very often used. On the other hand, even though Akan proverbs 1 ('A crab does not give birth to a bird'), 2 ('It is when you climb a good tree that we push you') and 4 ('A child breaks a snail, not a tortoise') are categorised as metaphoric, their processing does not need special Akan cultural competence. One can arrive at their meanings by applying Lakoff and Turner's (1989) theory discussed above. Perhaps, this, together with their high currency, may account for the high response frequencies in spite of their being metaphoric. Thus, this finding supports my initial assumption that bilinguals are likely to rely on general human cognitive structures to process both metaphoric and non-metaphoric proverbs that do not require ample cultural competence for interpretation.

4.3   Identifying cognitive models for interpreting metaphoric proverbs

The second assumption made in this study was that processing proverbs that have cultural undertones, particularly L2 proverbs, might pose a challenge for the bilinguals, and that bilinguals are likely to rely on L1 cultural-cognitive models to process such proverbs. Thus, in trying to achieve the second aim of the study, which is to identify the cognitive models bilinguals use to interpret proverbs from L1 to L2 and L2 to L1, I examined more closely the actual responses they gave for the second task 'provide a conceptual equivalent of L1 proverbs in L2 and vice versa. Here again, a number of patterns emerged from the data.

In the first place, participants generally provided only few conceptual equivalents of proverbs in either language. In many instances, even where potential conceptual equivalents of proverbs in one language existed in the other language, bilinguals either left a blank space or simply said 'no idea'. For instance, the English proverb (45) *Ignorance is bliss*, has a conceptual equivalent in Akan *Ani anhu a ɔnyɛ tan*, lit. 'if the eye does not see something, it is not disgusting'. Nevertheless, while only 2 (out of 16) participants responded to the English proverb, what they provided as conceptual equivalent in Akan was simply a literal translation of the English proverb – 'it is better not to see than to see a thing that will bring trouble to you'. In other words, in the few instances where bilinguals attempted to provide conceptual equivalents for proverbs, they generally provided literal interpretations/meanings of the original proverbs in the other language.

While this finding may be interpreted to indicate the absence of conceptual equivalence of proverbs across the two languages/cultures, we may also argue that the bilinguals in this study are simply not adequately familiar with proverbs and proverbial discourses in their two languages. This is not difficult to explain. On the one hand, the average Akan-English bilingual who lives in the capital city is likely to have been out of touch with traditional Akan geo-physical and practical social culture for a reasonable period. Thus, their apparent unfamiliarity with Akan proverbs may have arisen from lack of exposure/access to communicative contexts where proverbs are often used. On the other hand, their unfamiliarity with English proverbs may be explained from the fact that many Akan-English bilinguals in Ghana have little to no familiarity with English culture beyond what is (re) presented in formal/classroom settings. Relatively young (under 18 years) Akan-English bilinguals in Ghana may be more familiar with English culture due to increasing globalisation through digitisation (e.g., social media, digital/cable TV). This notwithstanding, there were other instances in the data where bilinguals provided actual conceptual equivalents of proverbs across their languages. Tables 6 and 7 below present a replicate of Akan conceptual equivalents given for English proverbs and English conceptual equivalents given for Akan proverbs respectively.

Table 6. Akan conceptual equivalents given for English proverbs

English proverb	Akan equivalent given	Literal translation of Akan equivalent
The early bird catches the worm.	*Sɛ woboro nsuo ntɛm a w'ani yɛ kɔkɔɔ ntɛm.*	If you swim early, your eyes get red quickly.
Two wrongs do not make a right.	*Obi fom kum a wɔnfom nnwa.*	If someone mistakenly kills (a game), we don't mistakenly dissect (dress) it.
Don't bite off more than you can chew.	*Aserewa hwɛ ne ho na wanwene ne buo.*	The sun-bird considers its size to make its nest.

Chapter 6. Cognitive Linguistics and expressing/interpreting proverbs in a second language

Table 6. *(continued)*

English proverb	Akan equivalent given	Literal translation of Akan equivalent
Don't bite the hand that feed you.	Bea a yɛdidi no yɛnsɛe hɔ.	We do not mess up where we eat from.
It takes two to tango.	Twe ma mentwe ma kora bɔ.	Pull, let me pull causes the calabash to break.
People in glass houses shouldn't throw stones.	Sɛ takra tua wo to a yɛnhuri ntra gya.	If a feather is stuck to your bottom, you do not jump over fire.
Learn to walk before you run.	Wofiti prɛko pɔ wo se a, etu mogya.	If you bleach your teeth suddenly, they will bleed.
Money does not grow on trees.	ɛnyɛ apotɔyewa mu na yɛtu mmire.	We do not harvest mushrooms from apotoyewa (an earthen bowl for mashing).
Out of sight, out of mind.	W'ani sa mu a, yɛnni nya wo.	If your eyes are focused on it (food), you get to partake in the eating.
Easy come, easy go.	Hwimhwim adeɛ kɔ soro soro.	That which comes quickly goes up high
You can't make an omelet without breaking a few eggs.	Woannua a wontwa.	If you don't plant, you will not harvest.

Table 7. English conceptual equivalents given for Akan proverbs

Akan proverb	Literal translation	English equivalent given
Ɔkɔtɔ nwo anoma.	A crab does not beget a bird.	A chip of the old block
Tikorɔ nkɔ agyina.	One head does not hold counsel.	Two heads are better than one.
Abɔfra bɔ nwa, ɔmmɔ akyekyedeɛ.	A child breaks snails, S/he does not break a tortoise	Cut your coat according to your cloth.
Oba nyansafoɔ yɛbu no bɛ yɛnka no asɛm.	We speak proverbs not words to a wise child.	A word to the wise is enough
Anoma anntu a obua da.	A bird sleeps hungry if does not fly.	There is no food for the lazy man.
Obi nnim oberempɔn ahyɛase.	Nobody knows the beginning of a great man.	Big things have small beginnings.

Table 7. *(continued)*

Akan proverb	Literal translation	English equivalent given
Kwatrekwa se ɔbɛma wo ntoma a tie ne din.	If nakedness promises you a piece of cloth, listen to its name.	You can't give what you don't have.
Deɛ ɔwɔ aka no suro sonsono.	S(he) who has been bitten by a snake is scared of a worm.	Once bitten twice shy.

From Tables 6 and 7 above, we can see that bilinguals provided conceptual equivalents for both metaphoric and non-metaphoric proverbs in both languages. Nevertheless, they found more Akan conceptual equivalent proverbs for non-metaphoric English proverbs (7 of 11) than they did for metaphoric ones (4 of 11). In providing English conceptual equivalent proverbs for Akan proverbs, the situation was different – there were fewer proverbs (8), 4 of which were metaphoric while the other 4 were non-metaphoric. This finding is consistent with the first finding – that bilinguals appear to rely on general human cognitive structures (as espoused by Lakoff and Turner's (1989) GREAT CHAIN Metaphor) to process proverbs that do not require cultural competence.

However, in selecting a conceptual equivalent in one language for a proverb they understand in another language, the bilinguals appeared to rely on Akan cultural models. For instance, by selecting the Akan equivalent proverb that translates loosely as 'we do not harvest mushrooms from a mashing bowl (made from clay)', for the English proverb *Money does not grow on trees*, the bilinguals needed Akan cultural competence that reflects their knowledge in Akan agrarian economy. Again, in selecting an Akan conceptual equivalent for the English proverb 'you can't make an omelette without breaking an egg', the bilinguals used the farming frame (Planting and Harvesting) in the Akan proverb that loosely translates as 'if you don't plant you will not harvest'. Indeed, the farming frame appears to be very salient in general Akan metaphorical conceptualisations because the traditional Akan cultural context is agrarian (see Ansah 2010, 2014).

Another finding that supports the role culture plays in the conceptualisation of proverb is the revelation that only a few bilinguals were able to provide conceptual equivalents for proverbs that required cultural competence for interpretation. In other words, few bilinguals were able to provide conceptual equivalents to proverbs whose interpretation required intimate knowledge of the geo-physical, social and cultural environments in their two languages. Typically, such proverbs made references to flora and fauna or cultural practices that were peculiar to either Akan or English. I provide below some examples of such culture-specific

Chapter 6. Cognitive Linguistics and expressing/interpreting proverbs in a second language

proverbs in Akan and English that appeared to have posed processing challenges for many bilingual participants:

English
(1) a. *It's the tip of the iceberg.*
    b. *It takes two to tango.*

Only a small amount of an iceberg can be seen above the surface of the water. Most of it lies below. This proverb uses the iceberg to describe a situation where you are only beginning to understand the problem. The little signs that you can see are in fact part of a much larger problem. While iceberg is a common cultural artefact and a potential natural phenomenon from the geographical context (temperate) of English culture, it is alien to Akan language/culture that is situated in a tropical region. For this proverb, only 2 out of 16 participants responded by attempting a literal translation in Akan. Neither of the two participants suggested an Akan conceptual equivalent for this English proverb. Similarly, only two of the 16 participants responded to proverb (1b). Even then, both did not provide any interpretation for this proverb. Nevertheless, one of the two respondents provided an acceptable Akan equivalent proverb that may loosely translate as 'pull and let me pull causes the calabash to break'.

Akan
(2) a. *Agya bi   wu a,   agya bi   te ase.*
       Father some dieCOND father some live
       Lit. 'When one father dies, another father lives'.

This proverb resonates the Akan philosophy of personhood and cultural views on kinship and family relationships where a child is fathered (or mothered) not only biologically but also socioculturally. The raising of children is a communal activity involving the brothers, sisters, cousins, uncles/aunties, and even good neighbours of the child's biological family. In other words, it is normal to have more than one father (or mother) in Akan culture. Under this arrangement, if one's biological father dies or is absent, there are many others to play his role, either individually or collectively. While there were 10 responses to this proverb, only one respondent provided an English equivalent proverb 'if one door closes, another opens'. The remaining nine respondents simply said 'no idea'.

   b. *Obi   akɔnnɔdeɛ ne odompo   nsono*
      Someone delicacy   be odompo (skunk) intestines
      Lit. 'Someone's delicacy is the intestines of an odompo'.

Presumably, the odompo's guts are widely considered undesirable culturally; yet, they are a delicacy to some people. Therefore, we cannot condemn someone for his or her (food) preferences. This is similar to the English proverb *One man's meat is another man's poison* and perhaps *Beauty lies in the eyes of the beholder*. Obviously, this proverb refers to food preferences that are rooted in cultural practices and food options available in their physical environment. While eight participants responded to this proverb, only three provided an English equivalent 'one man's meat is another man's poison'. The remaining five simply said 'no idea'.

Other culture-specific Akan proverbs that yielded few responses with either no or very few given English equivalents are listed in Example (3) below. For each proverb, I provide the literal meaning and the loose meaning, the number of participants that responded to the proverb, and the number of English equivalent proverbs provided. Where such equivalents were provided, I reproduce the given English equivalent.

		Proverb	Resp.	Eng. Equiv.
(3)	a.	*Abaa a yɛdebɔɔ Takyi no yɛde bɛbɔ Baa.* Lit. 'The stick that was used to hit Takyi will be used to 'What is good for the goose is also good for the gander'.	7	0
	b.	*Hu m'ani so ma me nti na atwe mmienu nam.* Lit. 'Two antelopes walk together so they can blow the dust off each other's eyes.' 'No man is an island'.	9	0
	c.	*Wotena dufɔkyeɛ so di bɔɔfrɛ a woto fɔ, w'ano fɔ.* Lit. 'If you sit on rotten wood to eat pawpaw, your bottom gets wet, your mouth also gets wet'. 'Nothing good comes easy'.	6	0
	d.	*Bɔɔfrɛ a ɛyɛ dɛ na abaa da aseɛ.* Lit. 'There is a stick under a sweet pawpaw always'. 'Sweet things always attract fame'.	8	1
	e.	*Abɛ bi rebɛwu a na ɛsɔ.* Lit. 'Some palm trees give best wine in the twilights of their lives' 'Better days ahead'	7	1

Finally, the data also revealed that the bilinguals appeared to have learned the English equivalents of some Akan proverbs as idioms as part of their learning of English vocabulary. In such instances, the bilinguals provided the exact conceptual equivalent proverbs in either English or Akan without resorting to reframing.

For instance, when the bilinguals were asked to provide an English conceptual equivalent to the Akan proverb ɔkɔtɔ nwo anoma (the crab does not beget a bird') they provided the English proverb 'a chip of the old block'. Both of these proverbs refer to a striking resemblance (physical or behavioural) between a parent and their child.

5. Conclusion

This chapter relied on Cognitive Linguistics/Cultural Linguistics assumptions to investigate proverb interpretation and expression among Akan-English bilinguals in Ghana. Using fifty (50) common proverbs in Akan and English that were selected from online sources, 16 participants were asked to offer interpretation to each proverb in one language and then provide a conceptual equivalent of the proverb in the other language. The analysis of responses/data revealed that Akan-English bilinguals were better able to express and interpret proverbs that had little to no cultural undertones in both languages. For both metaphoric and non-metaphoric proverbs with very little cultural content, the bilinguals appeared to rely on universal human cognitive principles, such as are identified in the Great Chain of Being and the *Nature of Things* to express/interpret both L1 and L2 proverbs.

Furthermore, the absence of familiar cultural models in proverbs that referred to language-specific flora and fauna and cultural practices resulted in a lack of understanding and inability of bilinguals to interpret such proverbs, especially metaphoric ones. However, bilinguals appeared to rely on L1 cultural-cognitive models to express/interpret L2 proverbs, both metaphoric and non-metaphoric proverbs that needed cultural competence to process. In other words, while relying on human universal cognition to interpret proverbs that have no deep cultural undertones, the bilinguals appeared to have relied on Akan cultural frames in expressing L2 proverbs through conceptual mappings.

Consequently, we may conclude that as has been argued by cultural linguists (e.g., Kövecses 2005; Sharifian 2007; Ansah 2014, 2017), human conceptualisation appears to be based on both universal and culture-specific cognitive principles. These findings support the position that proverbs are both universal and culture-specific constructions. In other words, the findings speak to the debate put forward by the integrative approach to studying proverbs, e.g., Buljan and Gradečak-Erdeljić (2013), which suggests that proverbs may contain both universal human and culture-specific elements.

References

Agyekum, K. (2005). An Akan oral artist: The use of proverbs in the lyrics of Kwabena Konadu. *Institute of African Studies Research Review*, 21(1), 1–17.

Agyekum, K. (2000). Aspects of Akan oral literature in the media. *Research Review*, 16(2), 1–18.

Andersson, D. (2013). Understanding figurative proverbs: A model based on conceptual blending. *Folklore*, 124(1), 28–44.

Ansah, G. N. (2010). The cultural basis of conceptual metaphors: The case of emotions in Akan and English. *Lancaster University Postgraduate Conference in Linguistics and Language Teaching*, 5, 2–25.

Ansah, G. N. (2011). Emotion language in Akan: The case of anger. *Encoding emotions in African languages*, 119–157.

Ansah, G. N. (2013). Culture in embodiment: Evidence from conceptual metaphors/metonymies of ANGER in Akan and English. *Compendium of Cognitive Linguistics Research*, 2, 63–82.

Ansah, G. N. (2014). Culture in embodied cognition: Metaphorical/metonymic conceptualizations of FEAR in Akan and English. *Metaphor and Symbol*, 29(1), 44–58.

Ansah, G. N. (2017). Cultural conceptualisations of DEMOCRACY and political discourse practices in Ghana. In F. Sharifian (Ed.), *Advances in Cultural Linguistics* (pp. 369–387). Singapore: Springer.

Ansah, G. N., & Dzregah, A. E. (2020). Exploring ethos in contemporary Ghana. *Humanities*, 9(3), 62.

Appiah, P., Appiah, K., & Agyeman-Duah, I. (2007). *'Bu me bɛ': Proverbs of the Akan*. Oxfordshire: Ayebia Clarke Publishing.

Belkhir, S. (2022). Metaphoric proverbs in EFL learners' translation. *Cognitive Linguistic Studies*, 9(1), 110–127.

Berman, R. A., & Ravid, D. (2010). Interpretation and recall of proverbs in three school-age populations. *First Language*, 30(2), 155–173.

Bock, K. J., & Brewer, W. F. (1980). Comprehension and memory of the literal and figurative meaning of proverbs. *Journal of Psycholinguistic Research*, 9(1), 59–72.

Buljan, G., & Gradečak-Erdeljić, T. (2013). Where cognitive linguistics meets paremiology: A cognitive-contrastive view of selected English and Croatian proverbs. *Explorations in English Language and Linguistics*, 1(1), 63–83.

Dzokoto, V. A. A., Schug, J., Adonu, J., & Nguyen, C. (2018a). Marriage is like a groundnut, you must crack it to see what is inside: Examining romantic relationship rules in Akan proverbs. *Interpersona: An International Journal on Personal Relationships*, 12(1), 1–22.

Dzokoto V. A. A., Osei-Tutu A., Kyei J. J., Twum-Asante M., Attah, D. A., & Ahorsu D. K. (2018b). Emotion norms, display rules, and regulation in the Akan society of Ghana: An exploration using proverbs. *Front. Psychol.*, 9(1916).

Granbom-Herranen, L. (2011). How do proverbs get their meanings? The model of interpretation based on a metaphor theory. In B. Nowowiesjski (Ed.), *Bialostockie archiwum jezykowe* (pp. 47–67). Bialystok: Wydawnictwo Uniwersytetu w Bialystok.

Gyekye, K. (2011). African ethics. In E. N. Zalta (Ed.) *Stanford encyclopedia of philosophy*. Stanford: Stanford University. URL: https://plato.stanford.edu/entries/african-ethics/ Accessed October 1, 2021.

Honeck, R. P., & Temple, J. G. (1994). Proverbs: The extended conceptual base and great chain metaphor theories. *Metaphor and Symbol*, 9(2), 85–112.

Kövecses, Z. (2005). *Metaphor in culture: Universality and variation*. Cambridge: Cambridge University Press.

Kroll, J. F., Dussias, P. E., Bice, K., & Perrotti, L. (2015). Bilingualism, mind, and brain. *Annual Reviews of Linguistics*, 1(1), 377–394.

Lakoff, G., & Johnson, M. (1980). *Metaphors we live by*. Chicago: Chicago University Press.

Lakoff, G., & Turner, M. (1989). *More than cool reason: A field guide to poetic metaphor*. Chicago: University of Chicago Press.

Liu, J. (2013). A Comparative study of English and Chinese animal proverbs from the perspective of metaphors. *Theory and Practice in Language Studies* 3(10), 1844–1849.

Lutz, C. A. (1988). *Unnatural emotions: Everyday sentiments on a Micronesian Atoll and their challenge to Western theory*. Chicago: University of Chicago Press.

Maalej, Z. (1999). Metaphoric discourse in the age of cognitive linguistics, with special reference to Tunisian Arabic. *Journal of Literary Semantics*, 28(3), 189–206.

Mac Coinnigh, M. (2015). 5 *structural aspects of proverb*. In H. Hrisztova Gotthardt, & M. A. Varga (Eds.) *Introduction to paremiology* (pp. 112–132). Poland: De Gruyter Open Poland.

Mansyur, F. A., & Said, R. (2019). A cognitive semantics analysis of Wolio proverbs related to the human body. *Advances in Social Science, Education and Humanities Research*, 4(36), 259–262.

Mieder, W., & Dundes, A. (Eds.), (1994). *The wisdom of many: Essays on the proverb*. Wisconsin: University of Wisconsin Press.

Moreno, A. I. (2005). An analysis of the cognitive dimension of proverbs in English and Spanish: The conceptual power of language reflecting popular believes. *SKASE Journal of theoretical linguistics*, 2(1), 42–54.

Nirmala, D. (2013). Local wisdom in Javanese proverbs (a cognitive linguistic approach). In J. S. Nam, & A. S. Nurhayati (Eds.), *Proceedings International Seminar 'Language Maintenance and Shift III'* (pp. 124–128). Semarang: Diponegoro University.

Omoniyi, T. (1995). Song-lashing as a communicative strategy in Yoruba interpersonal conflicts. *Text & Talk*, 15(2), 299–316.

Paknezhad, M., & Naghizadeh, M. (2016). The analysis of the image schemata in Persian and Arabic proverbs with a cognitive semantics approach. *Journal of Applied Linguistics and Language Research*, 3(2), 272–283.

Perry, T. A. (1988). The philosophy of sephardic Jews as seen through their proverbs. *Shofar*, 6(2) 29–35.

Pragglejaz Group. (2007). MIP: A method for identifying metaphorically used words in discourse. *Metaphor and Symbol*, 22(1), 1–39.

Sameer, I. H. (2016). A cognitive study of certain animals in English and Arabic proverbs: A comparative study. *International Journal of Language and Linguistics*, 3(5), 133–143.

Sharifian, F. (2003). On cultural conceptualizations. *Journal of Cognition and Culture*, 3(3), 187–207.

Sharifian, F. (2007). L1 cultural conceptualizations in L2 learning: The case of Persian-speaking learners of English. In F. Sharifian, & G. B. Palmer (Eds.) *Applied Cultural Linguistics: Implications for second language learning and intercultural communication*, (pp. 33–51) Amsterdam & Philadelphia: John Benjamins.

Sharifian, F. (2013). Cultural linguistics and intercultural communication. In F. Sharifian, & M. Jamarani (Eds.), *Language and Intercultural Communication in the New Era* (pp. 60–79). London & New York: Routledge.

Silverman-Weinreich, B. (1981). Towards a structural analysis of Yiddish proverbs. In W. Mieder and A. Dundes. (Eds.). *The wisdom of many: Essays on the proverbs*. New York: Garland.

Temple, J. G., & Honeck, R. P. (1999). Proverb comprehension: The primacy of Literalmeaning. *Journal of Psycholinguistic Research*, 28(1), 41–70.

Wilson, F. P. (1994). The proverbial wisdom of Shakespeare. *The wisdom of many: Essays on the proverb*, 1, 174–189.

Wolf, H. G. (2017). De-escalation – A cultural-linguistic view on military English and militaryconflicts. In F. Sharifian (Ed.), *Advances in cultural linguistics* (pp. 683–702). Singapore: Springer.

Yankah, K. (1986). Proverb rhetoric and African judicial processes: The untold story. *Journal of American Folklore*, 99, 280–303.

Yankah, K. (1989). Proverbs: The aesthetics of traditional communication. *Research in African Literatures*, 20(3), 325–346.

Appendix 1.   50 Common English proverbs

https://www.fluentu.com/blog/english/useful-english-proverbs/

Proverb	Meaning
The grass is always greener on the other side of the fence.	"The grass is always greener" is a proverb that teaches us it's not good to be jealous (to want what other people have). It may seem like everyone around you has "greener grass," meaning nicer cars, better jobs, etc. But your neighbour probably thinks you have greener grass too, which means that your friends and other people think that you have better looks, happier family, etc. So instead of thinking about what everyone else has, this proverb wants you to be thankful for what you have.
Don't judge a book by its cover.	Things are not always what they seem. This proverb teaches you not to make judgments about other people because of how they look or dress. A book with a boring or plain cover could be amazing. The same is true with people. A person might look like an athelete or fool, but there is probably a lot more to them than clothes suggest.

Chapter 6. Cognitive Linguistics and expressing/interpreting proverbs in a second language 153

Appendix 1. *(continued)*

Proverb	Meaning
Strike while the iron is hot.	This old expression comes from the days of blacksmiths (people who work with metal). To shape the metal, the blacksmith would have to beat it with a hammer. Iron is easier to work with when it's hot. This proverb means you should take advantage of the moment. If an opportunity presents itself to you, take it! Take action because the chance may not come again.
Too many cooks spoil the broth.	Or as it's more commonly said, "Too many cooks in the kitchen." This is a well known experience – a lot people all trying to work in a kitchen around a small table or stovetop will make a mess and ruin the food. This proverb talks about the trouble of too many people trying to do the same thing at once.
You can't have your cake and eat it too.	If you eat your cake, you won't have it anymore, will you? So you can't do both. This proverb is about having two opposite desires, and how it's impossible to get both. Its meaning is similar to the proverb, "You can't have the best of both worlds."
Many hands make light work.	If a lot of people carry a heavy object, it does not feel heavy. That is the general meaning of this proverb. If everyone works together to complete something – like cleaning, painting or group projects – then each person has less to do. More importantly, the job will be completed much more quickly.
When in Rome, do as the Romans do.	When you are a visitor somewhere away from home, you should act like everyone else. It is polite to do so, and could keep you from getting into trouble. This proverb is from the ancient days of the Roman Empire when the capital city had visitors from all over the world. Cultures were very different between cities in those times. But while in Rome, one would behave like a Roman, no matter where you came from.
Don't cross the bridge before you get to it	This proverb tells you not to worry so much! Problems will certainly come in the future. But what can be done about that now? It's better to think about what you are doing right now – without worrying about the unknown – and take care of issues when they happen.
Honesty is the best policy.	Lying a lot can be difficult, because you might forget your lies. Soon enough, someone will find out you are lying. Then, you are in trouble. Or even if no one ever finds out, you will feel guilty for not telling the truth. But if you are honest and tell the truth, people will believe you and respect you. You will earn their trust and sleep well at night
Practice makes perfect.	Everything is difficult when you are a beginner. But if you stick with it, if you keep practicing, you can master anything.

Appendix 1. *(continued)*

Proverb	Meaning
Where there's a will, there's a way	This proverb is said to encourage people who want to give up. Sometimes, we face problems that seem impossible. But if you want it bad enough, nothing can stand in your way. That is what this proverb means – if you have the will to meet the problems that are in front of you, there is a way to overcome them.
Look before you leap.	Don't rush into things! Make sure you know what is going to happen next. You would not jump off a cliff without first checking how far the ground is below or what there is to land on. You should wait a few moments and make sure it's a good idea to jump from that cliff. So when making a big "jump" in life, make sure you've looked at the situation and really understand it before you take a big action.
Beggars can't be choosers.	If someone gives you free things or offers to help you do something, you can't ask for a different color or choose the perfect time in your schedule. When you receive free help or goods, you should accept what you're offered – you can't be picky (a "chooser") because you're not paying!
Don't make a mountain out of an anthill.	People sometimes get very upset over small problems. This proverb reminds you to take a moment and see how important (or not important) the issue is. Messing up your laundry or being late for work is not very important when you consider your entire life. So it's important to stay calm and not get angry about tiny problems.
An apple a day keeps the doctor away.	An apple is full of Vitamin C, which keeps you healthy. However, the "apple" in this proverb means eating healthy in general. If you eat well and your diet includes a lot of fruits and vegetables, there will be no need to visit the doctor.
The early bird catches the worm.	This proverb is a lot like the phrase "first come, first served." It simply means that it's usually best to be early. If you arrive earlier – whether it's to a clothing store, restaurant, conference, etc. – you will have the best options to choose from. If you come later, though, the best clothes could have sold out, the restaurant could be full and have a long waiting time, etc.
Better late than never.	While being the early bird is the best, even latecomers may get something for coming. It would be a lot worse if they never came at all. This proverb is said about ending fights with people. It's better to apologize and make up years later, than to never resolve your fight at all.
The cat is out of the bag.	This proverb means that a secret has been told. It comes from the Middle Ages and was common advice given in the market. You may have thought you purchased a tasty pig, but the seller put a simple cat in the bag instead. To "let the cat out of the bag" was to reveal the seller's trick.

Chapter 6. Cognitive Linguistics and expressing/interpreting proverbs in a second language   155

Appendix 1. *(continued)*

Proverb	Meaning
Two wrongs don't make a right.	If somebody insults you or harms you ("a wrong"), doing the same to them ("two wrongs") will not make everything okay. It will most likely cause a back-and-forth fight without end. If somebody is mean to you, don't be mean to them in return because it's not right to do so.
Always put your best foot forward.	When you are starting on a project or a journey, it's best to start with a good attitude and a lot of energy. First impressions (what people think about you when they meet you for the first time) can last for a long time. That's why this proverb is also used when meeting new people or for job interviews. Having a positive attitude – your "best foot" – is the best way to make a good impression.
Rome wasn't built in a day.	Rome is a great city. However, it took many years to be completed. The builders did not rush to complete their work and neither should you. If you wish to create something wonderful and long-lasting, you will have to spend more than a day working on it. You will probably have to spend several days, weeks or even months to do a good job. Take your time and do it right!
It's better to be safe than sorry.	Do everything possible to keep bad things from happening to you. It only takes a second to put on a seatbelt or to check that you locked the door. But if you're not safe, the bad results can last a lifetime. So it's best for you to be careful, otherwise you'll be sorry.
Don't bite the hand that feeds you.	This proverb warns against acting mean to those who provide for you or who do nice things for you. If you were to bite the hand that gave you food, that hand probably won't come back to feed you again. Then what would you eat? So you should be kind and thankful to those who care for you.
The squeaky wheel gets the grease.	If you have a problem but never talk about it, no one will help you. How could they? But if you tell someone, things will get better. This proverb is about someone who complains a lot (the "squeaky wheel") because they get more attention ("the grease"). For example, a child who cries a lot will get more attention from his mother than his silent brothers and sisters.
Don't bite off more than you can chew.	If you take a bite of food that's too big, you won't be able to chew! Plus you could choke on all of that extra food. It's the same if you take on more work or responsibility than you can handle – you will have a difficult time. So it's best not to get involved in too many projects, because you won't be able to focus and get them all done well.

Appendix 1. *(continued)*

Proverb	Meaning
You made your bed, now you have to lie in it.	No one likes sleeping in a poorly made bed. If you make your bed with the sheets all tangled and blankets facing the wrong way, you can't switch with someone else. You have to sleep in that bed. This proverb uses bed-making to describe any bad situation in which you may find yourself. You can't trade places with anyone else. You must live with the results of your actions, so make good choices.
Actions speak louder than words.	The Greek philosopher Plato once said that action is character. People are not defined by what they say because a lot of talk does not mean anything. People are judged by the things they do. Your actions are more important than what you say.
It takes two to tango.	This proverb is often said during a fight in which one person is putting all of the blame on the other person, when both people were actually responsible. Just as one person can't tango (a Spanish dance with two people) alone, two people are responsible for some situations, so you can't just blame one person.
Don't count your chickens before they hatch.	This proverb warns against being too eager. Just because you have five eggs, does not mean you will have five chickens. It is not a good idea to make plans based on expectations (what you think will happen). Wait for all things to come true before building up your dreams. Or worse, your promises. Things may not happen like you thought they would and that could get you in trouble.
It's no use crying over spilled milk.	Milk is easy to get. You may get in trouble for spilling the milk, you shouldn't cry because it isn't a big deal. Also, crying won't solve anything. This proverb advises you to stay calm during such small problems. Don't waste time worrying about little things that cannot be changed. Clean up the mess and go buy some more milk.
Don't put all your eggs in one basket.	Be careful! If you put all your goods in one bag or all your money in one stock, you are taking a big risk. It is smarter to spread your wealth around. That way if one basket should break, you're not left with nothing.
People in glass houses shouldn't throw stones.	"People in glass houses" means anyone who is sensitive about their failures. People like this should not insult others (should not "throw stones") because most likely the other person will turn around and insult you back. And like glass, which is easy to break, your self-esteem (what you think of yourself) will easily break into pieces.

Chapter 6. Cognitive Linguistics and expressing/interpreting proverbs in a second language

Appendix 1. *(continued)*

Proverb	Meaning
A rolling stone gathers no moss.	Only a stone that is in the same place for a long time will have moss growing on it. A stone on the move will remain bare. The same is true with people. If you remain in one place for a long time, the signs of life – friends, family, objects and your local reputation (what people think of you) – will grow on you. But not if you always move from place to place.
First things first.	This proverb advises you to do things in the right order. Do not skip over the more difficult or less enjoyable tasks in order to get to the easier, more fun ones. For example, if you have an exam to study for the same night your friend is having a party, study for the exam first. The party would be more fun, but the exam is more important so it should be done first.
Still waters run deep.	"Still waters run deep" describes people who are quiet and calm. These people often have "deep," interesting personalities. So even if someone doesn't talk a lot, they could still be very thoughtful. The proverb uses water to describe people. When the surface of a body of water is rough and fast, it usually means that it is shallow (not deep) and has rocks close to the surface, like in a river or stream. But water that is calm and still is often very deep, like in a lake.
If it ain't broke, don't fix it.	This phrase is used when someone is trying to change or "improve" a way of doing something that works perfectly well. Why change something that works? You could ruin everything! This proverb goes nicely with the proverb "leave well enough alone."
Curiosity killed the cat.	This proverb is often used to stop someone from asking too many questions. Curiosity (when you're excited and eager to know something) can lead you into dangerous situations. Cats, who are naturally curious, often end up in trouble. They get stuck up in trees or between walls
Learn to walk before you run.	Do things in the right order, from simple to more complicated. For example, do not try to read a difficult English novel when you're just starting to learn English. If you try to jump ahead, you will most likely fail – just like a child who tries to run before learning to walk will fall. All things will come in time, but you must be patient and go through the proper process.
Money doesn't grow on trees.	Things that grow on trees, such as fruit or leaves, are considered plentiful (enough, plenty) because they will grow back. If you eat an apple from a tree, more apples will continue to grow. But money must be earned through hard work, and doesn't "grow back" after you spend it. Once you spend money, it's gone. This proverb is often said to people who waste their money on silly purchases.

Appendix 1. *(continued)*

Proverb	Meaning
My hands are tied.	This phrase should not be taken literally. You say this proverb when you can't do what you would like to do. For example, say you are in charge of an office and everyone (including you) wants to celebrate someone's birthday. But your boss tells you it's against the rules. You could tell your coworkers, "Sorry, my hands are tied." You would like to have a birthday celebration with them, but you can't.
It's the tip of the iceberg.	Only a small amount of an iceberg can be seen above the surface of the water. Most of it lies below. This proverb uses the iceberg to describe a situation where you are only beginning to understand the problem. The little signs that you can see are in fact part of a much larger problem.
No news is good news.	No information about a situation suggests that nothing bad has happened. This phrase is said by families waiting nervously for news of a father or son who has gone to war. To receive news would mean hearing that your loved one has been killed, captured or hurt. Even though it's difficult to know nothing about what's happening, it's still better than hearing bad news.
Out of sight, out of mind.	If you can see something every day, your mind will think about it. This proverb is about the habit of forgetting things that are not nearby. For example, if you want to stop eating chips and junk food, you could move them from the counter top and hide them in a cupboard. If you don't see them, you won't think to eat them. Out of sight, out of mind.
If you scratch my back, I'll scratch yours.	This proverb simply means that if you help me, I'll help you too. Usually, when you do a favor for someone, they do something for you in return. This can be beneficial (helpful) to both people.
Ignorance is bliss.	"Ignorance" is when you don't know or are unaware of something. "Bliss" is pure joy and happiness. So sometimes it feels better and you're more comfortable when you don't know about certain things. For example, if I tell you this fact that from 2000–2012, 2.3 million square kilometres of forests were cut down around the world (which is size of all the states east of the Mississippi River) – you could feel sad and hopeless for the environment. But if I hadn't told you that fact, you would feel happier.
Easy come, easy go.	Money, fame, love or anything that happens easily can be lost just as quickly. If you get a lot of money or suddenly become famous, you could lose that money or fame very quickly – since you didn't work hard to earn it.

Appendix 1. *(continued)*

Proverb	Meaning
The forbidden fruit is always the sweetest.	'Forbidden' means it's not allowed, so this phrase means that if something isn't allowed, you often want it the most (it will 'taste' the sweetest). For example, let's say you're a kid whose parents don't let you drink soda. You go to a friend's house, and her parents ask if you want a soda. You say yes and really enjoy that soda because you never get to drink it at home.
Every cloud has a silver lining.	People say this when things are going badly or when someone is sad. Clouds stand for bad situations. Every bad situation has some good parts to it – you just have to look for them. The proverb is meant to help people feel better and keep going. It's also where the name of the movie "Silver Linings Playbook" came from.
You can't make an omelet without breaking a few eggs.	Sometimes, to get things done, you have to be pushy or break a few rules. You may even have to insult some people. An omelet is a tasty dish and worth the effort to make. However, you must break some eggs to make it. So if you want to get a worthwhile project done or make changes, you can't please everyone. Someone might be offended or hurt, so you have to decide if the price is worth it.
Close but no cigar.	In the old days, fairgrounds would give cigars as prizes for games. The phrase "close but no cigar" means that you were close to succeeding in the game, but you didn't win the cigar. As a proverb it means that even though you did your best or almost had it right, you weren't completely correct.

Appendix 2.   50 Common Akan proverbs

https://www.adinkrasymbols.org/pages/the-50-most-important-akan-proverbs/

Proverb	Meaning
ɔkɔtɔ nwo anoma.	Literally: A crab does not give birth to a bird. This used to acknowledge the resemblance between a child and his parent. The resemblance could be in physical features or character. It is similar to the English saying "the apple does not fall far from the tree."
Woforo dua pa a na yɛpia wo	Literally: It is when you climb a good tree that we push you. We the society and the elders in it can only support a good cause, not a bad one. Hence, if you want our support, you should do good things with which all can publicly identify and support.

Appendix 2. *(continued)*

Proverb	Meaning
Ti kɔrɔ nkɔ agyina	Literally: One head (or person) does not hold council. One person discussing an issue with himself cannot be said to have held a meeting. We need a group of people to hold a meeting. This proverb is similar to the English one that says "two heads are better than one."
Abɔfra bɔ nnwa na ɔmmɔ akyekyedeɛ	Literally: A child breaks a snail, not a tortoise. A child breaks the shell of a snail and not that of a tortoise. The shell of a snail is easier to break than that of a tortoise. Thus, children should do things that pertain to children and not things that pertain to adults. In Akan culture, it is a taboo for a child to challenge adults in any endeavour. Hence, children should take care when engaging with adults lest their actions be misunderstood.
Obanyansofoɔ yɛbu no be, yɛnnka no asɛm.	This proverb is also used to indicate that one is expected to learn from his circumstances and the experiences of others. It is also used to mean that we don't need to belabour a point for the wise to understand. A few words of exhortation should be fine. In that sense, it is similar to the English proverb, "A word to the wise is enough."
Hu m'ani so ma me nti na atwe mmienu nam.	Literally: It is because of "blow the dust off my eyes" that two antelopes walk together. This proverb is also sometimes rendered "Hwɛ me so mma minni bi nti na atwe mmienu nam," which literally means "It is because of 'watch over me while I eat' that two antelopes walk together." It is good to do things in a group. It is good to have a partner. The benefit of having a supporter with you is enough to see you through.
Aboa bi bɛka wo a, ne ofiri wo ntoma mu.	Literally: If an animal will bite you, it will be from your cloth. It is likely that the people who will harm you are those close to you. In fact, it is those who are closest to you who can hurt you the most because they know how best to do it. This proverb can be used to counsel someone who has been hurt by a close associate, even a relative. In that case, the import of the proverb will be that the one who has been hurt should let things go since, after all, it is those who are close to him who could hurt him. However, it could also be used to admonish one to be wary of his close associates because they were the very ones who are likely to hurt him, rather than some supposed enemies.
Anoma anntu a, obua da.	Literally: If a bird does not fly, it goes to bed hungry. You must take action if you want to make a living. It could also be understood as "Nothing ventured, nothing gained" for the bird takes a risk by flying, yet, it needs to do that before it can have any hope of getting food to eat.

Chapter 6. Cognitive Linguistics and expressing/interpreting proverbs in a second language

Appendix 2. *(continued)*

Proverb	Meaning
Obi nnim obrempɔn ahyɛase.	Literally: Nobody knows the beginning of a great man. The beginnings of greatness are unpredictable. Hence, we should not despise small beginnings or condemn people when they are starting and seem to be struggling.
Agya bi wu a, agya bi te ase.	Literally: When one father dies, another father lives. The raising of children is a communal activity in Akan societies. With such an arrangement, a child could have many fathers, where a father is an older male who takes some responsibility for raising the child. In such a situation, if one's biological father dies or is absent, there are many others to individually or collectively play his role. The proverb is used when a substitute is found for something valuable or someone important.
Animguase mfata ɔkanni ba.	Literally: Disgrace does not befit the child of an Akan. It could be interpreted as 'disgrace does not befit an Akan'. Further, it could be interpreted as 'disgrace does not befit man' where 'Okanni ba' is just a substitute for man. Honour is a very important virtue in Akan culture and all must be done to preserve it. Anything that could bring animguasɛ (shame, disgrace) rather than animuonyam (glory, honour) should be avoided like the plague. In fact, there is a proverb, *Ferɛɛ ne animguaseɛ deɛ fanyinam owuo*, that says that it is better to die than to be ashamed and disgraced.
Obi nkyerɛ akwadaa Nyame.	Literally: Nobody teaches a child God. God is everywhere and we can know him through his creation which even children can see. Hence, even children don't need anybody to point out that there is a creator (obɔɔadeɛ) who is the Supreme Being. This is a pervasive Akan world view that is so strongly held that it is the rare Akan who does not believe in God. Saying that even children do not need anybody to tell them that God exists suggests that it is foolish for an adult to claim He doesn't.
Agorɔ bɛsɔ a, efiri anɔpa.	Literally: If the festival (or carnival or party) will be entertaining, it starts from the morning. Just as we can tell how nice a party will be from its very beginning, we can tell how successful a venture will be from its beginning.
Kwaterekwa se ɔbɛma wo ntoma a tie ne din.	Literally: If a naked man promises you a cloth, listen to his name. A man cannot give what he does not have. If the naked man had any clothes, he would wear them first before giving away his extras.

Appendix 2. *(continued)*

Proverb	Meaning
Obi aknnɔdeɛ ne odopo nsono.	Literally: Someone's delicacy is the intestines of an odompo. Presumably, the odompo's guts are widely considered undesirable, yet, that is what somebody enjoys eating. So we can't condemn someone for his preference. This is similar to the English proverb "One man's meat is another man's poison" and perhaps "Beauty lies in the eyes of the beholder."
Wamma wo yɔnko anntwa ankɔ a, wonntwa nnuru.	Literally: If you don't let your friend cross and reach (his destination), you will also not cross and reach yours. You must help your neighbour achieve his goals so you can also achieve yours. This could mean that if you help your friend achieve his goals, he will also help you achieve yours.
Yɛsoma onyansofoɔ, ɛnyɛ anammɔntenten.	Literally: We send a wise person, not one with long legs. The person with long legs may be able to reach his destination faster, but because there is more to communicating a message than just sending the words, it is better to send a wise person who might be slower.
Aboa a onni dua no, Nyame na ɔpra ne ho.	Literally: For the animal who does not have a tail, it is God who sweeps his body. God helps the vulnerable. Even when someone is impoverished, he is not completely dejected because God cares for everybody.
Biribi ankɔka papa a, anka papa annye kyerɛdɛ.	Literally: If something had not touched the papa (dried palm frond?) it wouldn't have made a sound. There is a cause for every effect. You may complain about the dry frond is making noise but it will also complain that you are troubling it. This is similar to "there is no smoke without fire."
Bɔɔfrɛ a ɛyɛ dɛ na abaa da aseɛ.	Literally: It is the pawpaw (papaya) that is sweet that has a stick under it. The sweet papaya has a stick under it because everybody who reaches it wants to pluck a fruit.
Prayɛ, sɛ woyi baako a na ebu: wokabɔmu a emmu.	Literally: When you remove one broomstick it breaks but when you put them together the do not break. This is similar to the English proverb, "In unity lies strength." This principle is so essential for maintaining a stable society when it is vulnerable to attacks from neighbouring tribes. Perhaps, that is where the understanding that it is important to stick together emanated from.
Nsateaa nyinaa nnyɛ pɛ.	Literally: All fingers are not the same. Some fingers are bigger than others. Some fingers are longer than others. In the same way, people are not the same. Some are weak; some are strong. Some are rich; some are poor. Each one is capable of doing things that others cannot do.

Chapter 6. Cognitive Linguistics and expressing/interpreting proverbs in a second language

Appendix 2. *(continued)*

Proverb	Meaning
Obi nnim a obi kyerɛ	Literally: When a child learns how to wash his hands, he eats with adults. Children are immature and need to learn a lot before they can be admitted to the table of men. This idea of knowing how to wash your hands is open to wide interpretation. In particular, it can be used to endorse underhanded practices such as bribery. I have heard the phrase "come and wash your hands" being used to mean come and perform the appropriate unsanctioned rites before even what you may be legitimately entitled to can be given to you or done for you.
Abɔfra hunu ne nsa hohoro a ɔne mpanyinfoɔ didi.	Literally: When a child learns how to wash his hands, he eats with adults. Children are immature and need to learn a lot before they can be admitted to the table of men. This idea of knowing how to wash your hands is open to wide interpretation. In particular, it can be used to endorse underhanded practices such as bribery. I have heard the phrase "come and wash your hands" being used to mean come and perform the appropriate unsanctioned rites before even what you may be legitimately entitled to can be given to you or done for you.
Yɛwo wo to esie so a wonkyere tenten yɛ	Literally: If you are born unto a mound, it does not take you long to grow tall. Early advantages in life tend to persist. For example, one born into a rich family is more likely to be rich even later in life than one born into a small family.
Ayɔnkogorɔ nti na ɔkɔtɔ annya tiri.	Literally: It is because of friend-play that the crab does not have a head. This proverb is sometimes rendered as "Ayɔnkogorɔ nti na ɔkɔtɔ annya tiri". meaning it isbecause of many friends that the crab did not get (or does not have) a head. This proverb speaks to the disadvantages of having many friends. The belief is that a multitude of friends could lead you astray or distract you from worthy pursuits.
Wo nsa akyi bɛyɛ wo dɛ a ɛnte sɛ wo nsa yam.	Literally: If you will find the back of your hand sweet, it is not as sweet at the palm of your hand. You may enjoy life elsewhere but home is home. The palm of your hand is softer than the back of your hand. Hence, it is better to enjoy it than the back of your hand.
Etua wo yɔnko ho a etua dua mu.	Literally: If it is in the body of your neighbour, it is in a tree. Sometimes we are able to empathize with one another. However, it is more common for people not to genuinely care about others because they do not feel what they feel. This proverb is used when something that happened to one person happens to another person. When you experience the same thing another person experienced, you have a better appreciation for it and demand the sympathy you were unable to offer to your neighbour when he was in the same situation.

Appendix 2. *(continued)*

Proverb	Meaning
Obi fom kum a, yɛnfom nnwa.	Literally: If someone kills by mistake, we do not dissect by mistake. In Akan culture, it is a taboo to kill or eat some animals. If that is the case for an animal, then after someone kills it by mistake, we should not worsen the mistake by dissecting or eating that animal. In this sense, this proverb is similar to the English proverb, "Two wrongs do not make a right."
Wohu sɛ wo yɔnko abodwesɛ rehye a na wasa nsuo asi wo deɛ ho.	Literally: If you see your neighbour's beard burning, fetch water by yours. One is supposed to learn from the experiences and circumstances of others.
Tɔɔtɔɔte, tɔɔtɔɔte, yɛrenom nsa na yɛrefa adwen.	Literally: Little by little, little by little, as we drink we make plans. We can transact serious business while relaxing (over drinks). Also, even in a seemingly light moment, we can slowly make progress on other more important issues
Dua a enya wo a ɛbewɔ w'ani no, yɛtu aseɛ; yɛnsensene ano.	Literally: One does not sharpen the stick that would like to pierce his eye. Instead, he uproots it. This speaks to the attitude or practice of getting rid of potential dangers early, rather than encouraging them to grow.
ɔbaa tɔ tuo a ɛtwere barima dan mu.	Literally: When a woman buys a gun, it lies in a man's room. In Akan culture, women usually have a lower status in society than men. Thus, if a woman is married and she acquires property, it is as if she has done it on behalf of her husband. Another (less popular) interpretation of this proverb describes the relationship between the owner of a thing and the user or operator of that thing. Even if you are wealthy enough to buy an equipment or gadget, the one who operates it has more say in how it is used because he has the know-how and you don't.
Baanu so a emmia.	Literally: When two carry, it does not hurt. The load is lighter when two persons carry it – two are better than one.
Nyansapɔ wɔsane no badwemma.	Literally: Wise knots are loosened by wise men. This could also be interpreted as "Knots tied by wise men are loosened by wise men." Not anybody can handle any matter. Delicate matters require the attention of wise men to untangle.

Chapter 6. Cognitive Linguistics and expressing/interpreting proverbs in a second language

Appendix 2. *(continued)*

Proverb	Meaning
Ahunubi pɛn nti na aserewa regyegye ne ba agorɔ a na wayi n'ani ato nkyɛn.	Literally: It is because of "I have seen some before" that when the *aserewa* is entertaining its young it looks away. *Ahunu-bi-pen* is the state of having seen something before. It connotes learning by first-hand experience. This proverb says that the *aserewa* (a small bird) has had a bad experience by looking on while entertaining its young so it has decided not to do that again. It has decided to look away because of that experience.
Abaa a yɛde bɔ Takyi no yɛde bɛbɔBaa.	Literally: The stick that is used to hit Takyi is also used to hit Baa
Yɛtu wo fo na wanntie a, wokɔ Anteade.	Literally: If you do not heed advice, you go to Anteade (the town for those who don't heed advice)
Abɛ bi rebewu a na ɛsɔ.	Literally: It is when some palm trees are about to die that they give good wine.
Hwimhwim adeɛ kɔ srosro.	Literally: What comes easily goes easily.
Abɔfra a ɔmma ne maame nna no, bɛntoa mpa ne to da.	Literally: For the child who does not let his mother sleep, the enema will never depart from his bottom.
Nwansena nni hwee koraa ɔposa ne nsam.	Literally: Even if the housefly does not have anything, it rubs its hands together.
Nea ɔwɔ aka no pɛn no suro sonsono.	Literally: The one who has been bitten by a snake before is afraid of a worm. Though the worm is small and harmless compared with the large and harmful snake, the bitter experience one learns from a snake bite is enough to instill such caution that anything that looks like a snake is feared. This proverb is used when one takes extra precaution because of a previous experience and is similar to the Engish proverb "Once bitten, twice shy."
Funtumfunafune dɛnkyɛmfunafu, wɔn afuru bom nanso worediedi a na wɔreko efiri sɛ aduane dɛ yɛte no wɔ menetwitwie mu.	Literally: *Funtumfunafu* and *dɛnkyemfunafu* (two conjoined crocodiles) have their stomachs joined together yet when they are eating they fight because the sweetness of the food is felt as it passes through the throat.
Owuo atwedeɛ, baakofoɔ mforo.	Literally: Death's ladder: It is not climbed by one person. This proverb expresses the inevitability of death for everyone. The implication is for everyone to be humble and live life so as to be considered worthy in the afterlife.

Appendix 2. *(continued)*

Proverb	Meaning
Efie biara mmaninsɛm wɔ mu.	Literally: In every house, there are those who cause trouble.
Obi abawuo tuatua obi aso.	Literally: The death of someone's child annoys another. While a bereaved parent may wail loudly to mourn his or her loss, an unconcerned observer who does not feel the loss may dismiss their wailing as mere noise-making. This proverb captures the spirit of "He who feels it knows it" in that try as one may to sympathize with another's bereavement, he may never truly appreciate the depth of grief of those closest to the tragedy. This proverb is also used even in situations which don't involve loss or bereavement. When there is a serious issue at stake but it is hard to convince others who might not feel directly threatened or affected by it to take action, a patron may invoke the proverb to express his despair at their indifference, though expected.
Nsuo a edɔ wo na ɛkɔ w'ahina mu.	Literally: It is the water (river) that loves you that enters your pot. This may refer to water entering into a pot when one uses it to fetch water from a river or stream. Presumably, if the water does not love you it will not enter your pot. In reference to lovers, this could mean that if someone loves you he would propose to you or that if someone loves you he will come to you or be involved in your affairs.
Wotena dufɔkyeɛ so di bɔɔfrɛ a wo to fɔ, w'ano nso fɔ.	Literally: If you sit on rotten wood to eat pawpaw (papaya), your bottom gets wet and your mouth also gets wet. The rotten wood is a comfortable place to sit and the pawpaw is a nice fruit to eat. Hence, this proverb describes two activities that are pleasant to do but it reminds us that they still come at a cost – your bottom gets wet and your mouth also gets wet – so we can't always have all things being rosy.
Dua kontonkyikuronkyi na ɛma yɛhunu odwomfoɔ.	Literally: It is the crooked wood (or stick) that reveals who the true sculptor is. Any sculptor may be able to work with good wood. But it would take a great sculptor to make something out of crooked and unworkable wood. This proverb could be used to someone in explaining the extent of his accomplishments, especially if he feels he began from a difficult place and had to overcome many setbacks and disadvantages that may not be obvious to others.

Appendix 3. Metaphoric Akan proverbs

Proverb	Meaning
ɔkɔtɔ nwo anoma.	Literally: A crab does not give birth to a bird. This used to acknowledge the resemblance between a child and his parent. The resemblance could be in physical features or character. It is similar to the English saying "the apple does not fall far from the tree."
Woforo dua pa a na yɛpia wo	Literally: It is when you climb a good tree that we push you. We the society and the elders in it can only support a good cause, not a bad one. Hence, if you want our support, you should do good things with which all can publicly identify and support.
Abɔfra bɔ nnwa na ɔmmɔ akyekyedeɛ	Literally: A child breaks a snail, not a tortoise. A child breaks the shell of a snail and not that of a tortoise. The shell of a snail is easier to break than that of a tortoise. Thus, children should do things that pertain to children and not things that pertain to adults. In Akan culture, it is a taboo for a child to challenge adults in any endeavour. Hence, children should take care when engaging with adults lest their actions be misunderstood.
Hu m'ani so ma me nti na atwe mmienu nam.	Literally: It is because of "blow the dust off my eyes" that two antelopes walk together. This proverb is also sometimes rendered "Hwɛ me so mma minni bi nti na atwe mmienu nam," which literally means "It is because of 'watch over me while I eat' that two antelopes walk together." It is good to do things in a group. It is good to have a partner. The benefit of having a supporter with you is enough to see you through.
Aboa bi bɛka wo a, ne ofiri wo ntoma mu.	Literally: If an animal will bite you, it will be from your cloth. It is likely that the people who will harm you are those close to you. In fact, it is those who are closest to you who can hurt you the most because they know how best to do it. This proverb can be used to counsel someone who has been hurt by a close associate, even a relative. In that case, the import of the proverb will be that the one who has been hurt should let things go since, after all, it is those who are close to him who could hurt him. However, it could also be used to admonish one to be wary of his close associates because they wre the very ones who are likely to hurt him, rather than some supposed enemies.

Appendix 3. *(continued)*

Proverb	Meaning
Agya bi wu a, agya bi te ase.	Literally: When one father dies, another father lives. The raising of children is a communal activity in Akan societies. With such an arrangement, a child could have many fathers, where a father is an older male who takes some responsibility for raising the child. In such a situation, if one's biological father dies or is absent, there are many others to individually or collectively play his role. The proverb is used when a substitute is found for something valuable or someone important.
Agorɔ bɛsɔ a, efiri anɔpa.	Literally: If the festival (or carnival or party) will be entertaining, it starts from the morning. Just as we can tell how nice a party will be from its very beginning, we can tell how successful a venture will be from its beginning.
Obi akɔnnɔdeɛ ne odopo nsono..	Literally: Someone's delicacy is the intestines of an odompo. Presumably, the odompo's guts are widely considered undesirable, yet, that is what somebody enjoys eating. So we can't condemn someone for his preference. This is similar to the English proverb "One man's meat is another man's poison" and perhaps "Beauty lies in the eyes of the beholder."
Wamma wo yɔnko anntwa ankɔ a, wonntwa nnuru.	Literally: If you don't let your friend cross and reach (his destination), you will also not cross and reach yours. You must help your neighbour achieve his goals so you can also achieve yours. This could mean that if you help your friend achieve his goals, he will also help you achieve yours.
Bɔɔfrɛ a ɛyɛ dɛ na abaa da aseɛ.	Literally: It is the pawpaw (papaya) that is sweet that has a stick under it. The sweet papaya has a stick under it because everybody who reaches it wants to pluck a fruit.
Abɔfra hunu ne nsa hohoro a ɔne mpanyinfoɔ didi.	Literally: When a child learns how to wash his hands, he eats with adults. Children are immature and need to learn a lot before they can beadmitted to the table of men. This idea of knowing how to wash your hands is open to wide interpretation. In particular, it can be used to endorse underhanded practices such as bribery. I have heard the phrase "come and wash your hands" being used to mean come and perform the appropriate unsanctioned rites before even what you may be legitimately entitled to can be given to you or done for you.
Yɛwo wo to esie so a wonkyere tenten yɛ	Literally: If you are born unto a mound, it does not take you long to grow tall. Early advantages in life tend to persist. For example, one born into a rich family is more likely to be rich even later in life than one born into a small family.

Chapter 6. Cognitive Linguistics and expressing/interpreting proverbs in a second language   169

Appendix 3. *(continued)*

Proverb	Meaning
Ayɔnkogorɔ nti na ɔkɔtɔ annya tiri.	Literally: It is because of friend-play that the crab does not have a head. This proverb is sometimes rendered as "Ayɔnkogorɔ nti na ɔkɔtɔ annya tiri" meaning it is because of many friends that the crab did not get (or does not have) a head. This proverb speaks to the disadvantages of having many friends. The belief is that a multitude of friends could lead you astray or distract you from worthy pursuits.
Wo nsa akyi bɛyɛ wo dɛ a ɛnte sɛ wo nsa yam.	Literally: If you will find the back of your hand sweet, it is not as sweet at the palm of your hand. You may enjoy life elsewhere but home is home. The palm of your hand is softer than the back of your hand. Hence, it is better to enjoy it than the back of your hand.
Etua wo yɔnko ho a etua dua mu.	Literally: If it is in the body of your neighbour, it is in a tree. Sometimes we are able to empathize with one another. However, it is more common for people not to genuinely care about others because they do not feel what they feel. This proverb is used when something that happened to one person happens to another person. When you experience the same thing another person experienced, you have a better appreciation for it and demand the sympathy you were unable to offer to your neighbour when he was in the same situation.
Obi fom kum a, yɛnfom nnwa.	Literally: If someone kills by mistake, we do not dissect by mistake. In Akan culture, it is a taboo to kill or eat some animals. If that is the case for an animal, then after someone kills it by mistake, we should not worsen the mistake by dissecting or eating that animal. In this sense, this proverb is similar to the English proverb, "Two wrongs do not make a right."
Wohu sɛ wo yɔnko abodwesɛ rehye a na wasa nsuo asi wo deɛ ho.	Literally: If you see your neighbour's beard burning, fetch water by yours. One is supposed to learn from the experiences and circumstances of others.
Dua a enya wo a ɛbewɔ w'ani no, yɛtu aseɛ; yɛnsensene ano.	Literally: One does not sharpen the stick that would like to pierce his eye. Instead, he uproots it. This speaks to the attitude or practice of getting rid of potential dangers early, rather than encouraging them to grow.
Baanu so a emmia.	Literally: When two carry, it does not hurt. The load is lighter when two persons carry it – two are better than one.

Appendix 3. *(continued)*

Proverb	Meaning
Ahunubi pɛn nti na aserewa regyegye ne ba agorɔ a na wayi n'ani ato nkyɛn.	Literally: It is because of "I have seen some before" that when the aserewa is entertaining its young it looks away. Ahunu-bi-pen is the state of having seen something before. It connotes learning by first-hand experience. This proverb says that the aserewa (a small bird) has had a bad experience by looking on while entertaining its young so it has decided not to do that again. It has decided to look away because of that experience.
Abaa a yɛde bɔ Takyi no yɛde bɛbɔ Baa.	Literally: The stick that is used to hit Takyi is also used to hit Baa
Yɛtu wo fo na wanntie a, wokɔ Anteade.	Literally: If you do not heed advice, you go to Anteade (the town for those who don't heed advice)
Abɔfra a ɔmma ne maame nna no, bɛntoa mpa ne to da.	Literally: For the child who does not let his mother sleep, the enema will never depart from his bottom.
Nwansena nni hwee koraa ɔposa ne nsam.	Literally: Even if the housefly does not have anything, it rubs its hands together.
Nea ɔwɔ aka no pɛn no suro sonsono.	Literally: The one who has been bitten by a snake before is afraid of a worm. Though the worm is small and harmless compared with the large and harmful snake, the bitter experience one learns from a snake bite is enough to instill such caution that anything that looks like a snake is feared. This proverb is used when one takes extra precaution because of a previous experience and is similar to the English proverb "Once bitten, twice shy."
Owuo atwedeɛ, baakofoɔ mforo.	Literally: Death's ladder, it is not climbed by one person. This proverb expresses the inevitability of death for everyone. The implication is for everyone to be humble and live life so as to be considered worthy in the afterlife.
Obi abawuo tuatua obi aso.	Literally: The death of someone's child annoys another. While a bereaved parent may wail loudly to mourn his or her loss, an unconcerned observer who does not feel the loss may dismiss their wailing as mere noise-making. This proverb captures the spirit of "He who feels it knows it" in that try as one may to sympathize with another's bereavement, he may never truly appreciate the depth of grief of those closest to the tragedy. This proverb is also used even in situations which don't involve loss or bereavement. When there is a serious issue at stake but it is hard to convince others who might not feel directly threatened or affected by it to take action, a patron may invoke the proverb to express his despair at their indifference, though expected.

Chapter 6. Cognitive Linguistics and expressing/interpreting proverbs in a second language

Appendix 3. *(continued)*

Proverb	Meaning
Nsuo a ɛdɔ wo na ɛkɔ w'ahina mu.	Literally: It is the water (river) that loves you that enters your pot. This may refer to water entering into a pot when one uses it to fetch water from a river or stream. Presumably, if the water does not love you it will not enter your pot. In reference to lovers, this could mean that if someone loves you he would propose to you or that if someone loves you he will come to you or be involved in your affairs.
Wotena duʃɔkyeɛ so di bɔɔfrW a wo to fɔ, w'ano nso fɔ	Literally: If you sit on rotten wood to eat pawpaw (papaya), your bottom gets wet and your mouth also gets wet. The rotten wood is a comfortable place to sit and the pawpaw is a nice fruit to eat. Hence, this proverbs describes two activities that are pleasant to do but it reminds us that they still come at a cost – your bottom gets wet and your mouth also gets wet – so we can't always have all things being rosy.

PART III

Cognitive categories in the proverbs of individual languages and cultures

CHAPTER 7

Emotion in Greek proverbs
The case of (romantic) love

Maria Theodoropoulou
Aristotle University of Thessaloniki, Greece

This is a study 'inside the proverb'. It draws its data from proverb collections and examines Greek proverbs both on romantic love and on love, both figurative and nonfigurative. The study aims at comparing the conceptualisation of these emotions in proverbs with the one in conventionalised expressions of everyday speech as captured in cognitive models approach (e.g., Kövecses 1990). The proverbs are examined with respect to the cognitive mechanisms they employ, the functions they perform, as well as the linguistic means (verb vs. noun) by which they are expressed. The results show that the two emotions are distinguished quantitatively and qualitatively regarding the aforementioned dimensions. The analysis shows that the conceptualisation of romantic love in cognitive models approach pertains to the subjective experience, while proverbs on both romantic love and love foreground the relationships within the community. In this sense, the cognitive models perspective is a 'look inside the subject' while that of proverbs is a 'look from above onto the community'. Finally, the 'Cause and Effect figurative pattern' is highlighted as probably genre specific due to its great evidential power.

Keywords: (romantic) love, figurativity, Cause and Effect figurative pattern

1. Introduction

I   agap-i   pirg-ous   katal-ei   kai kastr-a
DEF.NOM.SG love-NOM.SG tower-ACC.PL dissolve.IPFV-3SG.PRS and castle-ACC.PL
rihn-ei   kato.
throw.IPFV-3SG.PRS down.ADV
Lit. 'Love dissolves towers and tears down castles'.

In the form above, this proverb is mentioned on many sites that record Greek proverbs and is considered to extol the power of love. However, in the collection of proverbs by the leading Greek folklorist, Nikolaos Politis (1899), the proverb continues as follows:

> kai palikar-ia tou   spath-iou   ta   rihn-ei
> and lad-ACC.PL DEF.GEN.SG sword-GEN.SG PRO.ACC.PL throw.IPFV-3SG.PRS
> tou   thanat-ou.
> DEF.GEN.SG death-GEN.SG
> Lit. 'and propels sword-yielding lads to their deaths'.

Because of the garden path effect (e.g., Milne 1982) that is due to the Greek noun *agapi* having a double meaning, 'love' and 'romantic love', the continuation of the proverb leads us to understand that it refers to the power of romantic love: *eros* as a driving force that can overturn what is most difficult to overturn. After all, EMOTION IS FORCE is the master metaphor of emotion according to Kövecses (2000). However, *eros* is also a force that can kill; this is another metaphor denoting the supreme pain that can be caused by romantic rejection or frustration. Why is this psychological pain metaphorised as death, that is, as the cessation, the end, of biological existence? Because, as Lieberman (2013: 40) argues, "when human beings experience threats or damage to their social bonds, the brain responds in much the same way it responds to physical pain". It is the price paid by the human beings for their sociality that is deeply rooted in their body, in their brain (see Lieberman's 2013: 15 default network).

This proverb cannot be considered as familiar today, at least not for the younger generation of Greek speakers. A relevant Google search does not yield any results to suggest evidence of its use, but only its listing in proverb collections. Apparently, sword-wielding lads, castles and towers are not images that are familiar to today's modern culture. Could this also mean the 'diminishing' of belief in the power of love and romantic love? "We have an intense need for social connection throughout our entire lives", as Lieberman (2013: 48) points out – and this need is grounded in the infant's innate connection to a caregiver. "The price for our species' success at connecting to a caregiver is a lifelong need to be *liked and loved*,[1] and all the social pains that we experience go along with this need" (op. cit.). In this sense, love and, by extension, romantic love, seem to be the emotions through which the connection with the other is predominantly realised; i.e., the social nature of human being. Moreover, they are also what ensures the survival and reproduction of the species (Lieberman 2013: 39; Fisher, Aron, Strong, Mashek, Li, and Brown 2005: 60).

This study seeks to examine how these emotions, which constitute the fabric of a human being's social existence, are represented in Greek proverbs; i.e., in a

---

1. The emphasis is mine.

place of predominantly collective expression of a cultural community. Proverbs are the repository of collective "wit and wisdom" (Honeck [1997] 2016) in relation to various aspects of people's lives and the environment in which they live, carrying an imperative tone "often adding a level of advocation, extollation, or advisement" (Colston 2019: 96). In this sense, proverbs could be conceived as a collective subject's discourse addressing the members of an imagined community (Anderson 1983) – this collective subject engaging in social cognition; i.e., "thinking about other people, oneself, and the relation of oneself to other people" (Lieberman 2013: 18). Love and romantic love are, of course, the driving basis of this kind of thinking as well as its object in itself.

2. Figurativity and proverbs

Metaphor is the key point on which the two most hotly debated approaches to proverb comprehension have been formulated: Extended Conceptual Base Theory (ECBT, Honeck [1997] 2016; see also Honeck and Temple 1994) and Great Chain Metaphor Theory (GCMT, Lakoff and Turner 1989). The first one is part of the approaches that traditionally link the figurative meaning of proverbs to the ability to think abstractly.[2] Honeck ([1997] 2016: 36) postulates that proverbs can be treated as abstract theoretical mental entities, detached from the cultural context in which they are produced and understood. It therefore comes as no surprise that the *conceptual base*, the key notion of Honeck's six-stage serial model as the medium of proverb understanding, is considered abstract and general. As Honeck (op. cit.: 130) argues, "proverbs use familiar concepts to engender a more abstract meaning." He adopts a universalist perspective claiming that proverb production, its understanding and use can be explained by general cognitive principles that exceed the cultural specificities (op. cit.). In the same vein, Honeck (op. cit.: 137) introduces the cognitive ideals hypothesis: i.e., society's and the individual's ideals, norms, standards of perfection that form a 'generic ideal' instantiated by the 'specific' ideals underlying in proverbs. Based on this, he also proposes a typology of proverbs distinguishing between proverbs that confirm or disconfirm the generic ideal.

Honeck's model, despite its empirical support, has been strongly criticised, among others, because it does not accept – and therefore does not take into

---

2. See the use of psychological tests to evaluate the ability for abstract thinking in schizophrenia, intelligence psychopathology and brain dysfunctions, as well as critique of this stance in Gibbs and Beitel 1995. An alternative approach is suggested in Gibbs and Colston (2012: 181) for a possible dependence of proverb understanding on people's theory of mind.

consideration – the influence of cultural experience on the understanding and use of metaphor (Gibbs and Beitel 1995; Gibbs, Johnson and Colston 1996). It also ignores the sociocultural discursive dimension of proverbs (Ben Salamh and Maalej 2018: 22). Furthermore, the serial model of the processing of proverbial meaning has shown to be psychologically invalid (Gibbs 1994; Colston 1995; Colston 2000) – more general criticism has also been made about the experimental methods used to confirm the theory (Gibbs and Colston 2012: 177–178; see also Colston 1995). Finally, Gibbs and Beitel (1995: 144) object to Honeck's key argument concerning the abstractness of proverbial meaning. They argue that what the proverb refers to is abstract; proverb understanding, though, "includes specific and detailed knowledge that is neither general nor abstract." More specifically, they argue that the mental representations used in proverb understanding "are not abstract but concrete and metaphorical" (op. cit.).

According to Lakoff and Turner (1989: 162), proverbs instantiate the GENERIC IS SPECIFIC metaphor. This metaphor maps a specific-level schema (evoked by the proverb) to a large number of other specific-level schemas that share the same generic-level structure. In this sense, "GENERIC IS SPECIFIC maps specific levels schemas onto the generic-level schema they contain" (op. cit.: 163), provided that the mapping preserves the generic structure of the source domain (op. cit.; see *Invariance* principle; Lakoff 1990). In this way, the understanding of a whole category of situations in terms of one particular situation is possible. As Lakoff and Turner (op. cit.: 162–163) note, GENERIC IS SPECIFIC can be thought of "as a variable template that can be filled in in many ways". The power of the GENERIC IS SPECIFIC metaphor is that it combines the generality offered by the generic-level schema with the richness offered by the specific-level one: not only the vast array of knowledge but also vivid images that are grounded on the everyday experience.

The GENERIC IS SPECIFIC metaphor is one of the four components of GCMT proposed by Lakoff and Turner (1989). The second one is the *Great Chain of Being* (a notion taken from Lovejoy 1936), a cultural model based on which the beings and their properties are organised in a hierarchy, reflecting thus the relation of human beings either "to 'lower' forms of existence" (Basic Great Chain) or "to society, God and the Universe" (The Extended Great Chain) (op. cit.: 167). The third component is *the Nature of things*, "a largely unconscious, automatic, commonplace theory about the nature of things, that is, the relationship between what things are like and how they behave" (op. cit.: 170). The linking of these components to the GENERIC IS SPECIFIC metaphor allows the understanding of human attributes in terms of non-human ones (and conversely). This is a crucial point because according to Lakoff and Turner (op. cit.: 166) proverbs offer "ways of understanding the complex faculties of human beings in terms of other things". Finally, they endorse the *Maxim of Quantity* (Grice 1975) as the fourth component of GCMT, a "pragmatic principle of communication" (op. cit.: 171–172), through which the flow of knowledge between the four components is regulated.

GCMT differs radically from ECBT for two reasons: Firstly, because – metaphorical – proverbs are considered as instantiations of the metaphorical mind (Gibbs, Colston and Johnson 1996) and not the outcome of the failure of processing of the so-called 'literal' meaning; this is the reason why Gibbs and Beitel (1995) view proverbs as evidence of the way people think. Secondly, in contrast to the universalist perspective that is endorsed by ECBT, culture is conceived as an inherent component of GCMT, since the Great Chain of Being is fundamentally a cultural construal. As Gibbs (2001: 185) points out, "proverbs express enduring cultural themes in people's life", and a number of studies have highlighted the important socio-cultural differences in the conceptualisation of different themes (e.g., animals) in different languages (e.g., Belkhir 2014, 2019; Dabbagh and Noshadi 2015; Fahmi 2017; Ben Salamh and Maalej 2018; Saragih and Mulyadi 2020).

Based on the above, it seems that most of the literature has dealt either with the metaphorical interpretation of the proverb or with its cultural determinants. There has been some research on the functions of proverbs (Gibbs 2001; see Gavriilidou 2002 for Greek) as well as their characteristics (Gibbs and Beitel 1995). Although it is acknowledged that "proverbs can also contain other kinds of figures" (Colston 2019: 109), "as well as non-figurative terms … the combination of these various types of speech within proverbs can result in unique challenges to language processing" (Colston 2000: 628), to the best of our knowledge this issue has not been thoroughly explored. For example, Gibbs and Beitel (1995: 134; see also Gibbs 2001) mention hyperbole, paradox and personification as kinds of figurativity that are contained in the proverbs – Colston (op. cit.) adds irony to these. However, personification and paradox are also cited by them as part of the linguistic, 'poetic' characteristics of proverbs, together with meter, rhyme, slant rhyme, alliteration and assonance (op. cit.). Although the study of figurativity has come a long way within Cognitive Linguistics, the exploration of the full range of figurativity as it is instantiated in proverbs remains an issue.

3. Research questions and method

A research on the collections of Greek proverbs in relation to emotions shows love and romantic love to be the most proverbialised emotions. Politis (1899) counts 43 proverbs with the noun *agapi* 'love', 3 proverbs with the word *agapitikia* 'lover', and 70 proverbs with the verb *agapo* 'to love', including their variations. The high proverbialisation of these emotions is not surprising if one takes into account their importance in maintaining relationships within the community and for reproduction (see Section 1).

The aim of the present study is to examine the particular proverbs in Greek. We adopt an approach similar to the one with which emotions have been examined in the framework of Cognitive Linguistics: cognitive models have been used as the theoretical tool by which the knowledge about a concept is represented (Kövecses 1990; see also Lakoff and Kövecses 1987 about anger). Cognitive models of emotions are considered to be produced out of metaphors, metonymies (i.e., physiological and behavioural reactions aroused by the emotion) and related concepts that are instantiated in the conventionalised language used in everyday speech – including idioms, cliché and proverbs (e.g., Kövecses 1990). The basic premise guiding this approach is that emotions "are not clearly delineated in terms of the naturally emergent dimensions of our experience. Though [they] can be *experienced* directly, [they] can[not] be fully comprehended on their own terms" (Lakoff and Johnson 1980: 177). Thus, metaphor assumes the role of structuring "partly the emotion concepts ... enriching their content with varying amounts of information" (Kövecses 1990: 204). Further research on the language of emotions highlighted not only the role of metaphor and metonymy in conceptualising and expressing emotions but also instances of interaction of these mechanisms: e.g., metaphor within metonymy regarding the idiomatic expressions of emotions (Theodoropoulou 2012a); the pattern 'Cause (personification of the emotion) and Effect plus metaphor' spotted in the discourse elicited from responses to questionnaires on fear and romantic love (Theodoropoulou and Xioufis 2018).

Subsequent research has questioned both the approach as a whole and its individual points (e.g., Theodoropoulou 2004; Barsalou and Wiemer-Hastings 2005; Crawford 2009; Foolen 2012; Theodoropoulou 2012b; Sauciuc 2013). However, we consider that the basic question posed by the cognitive models approach, i.e., the knowledge about an emotion, can be asked in the same way in relation to proverbs, insofar as they are seen as carriers of the collective knowledge and experience. Consequently, the basic question of this research is what kind of knowledge in relation to love and romantic love, i.e., which aspects of these concepts, is highlighted by Greek proverbs. A further question follows as to whether this knowledge is different from the knowledge represented in the cognitive model(s) of these emotions. Kövecses (1986) argues that there are two cognitive models of romantic love in English: an ideal and a typical one: "the typical model can be said to have more social reality than the ideal. The language-based typical model is likely to be closer to the model people actually use in the course of their everyday lives. In contrast, the language-based ideal model is one, I surmise, which, in all probability, we reserve for our 'romantic moments'" (Kövecses 1986: 97).

Although he acknowledges that the two models share most features, there are points of divergence: the typical model involves the Stage "Attempt at control" of the romantic love, "love's culminating in marriage" as well as the active search for it (op. cit.: 104). Consequently, both cognitive models proposed by Kövecses' (1986) can offer a basis for the comparison we attempt here.[3]

Further questions that are explored in this study are: as the 'Cause and Effect plus metaphor' pattern has been spotted in data that differ from the conventionalised language from which Kövecses draws his research data, can we identify additional figurative patterns used by Greek proverbs? In addition, do the two emotions, love and romantic love, differ as to the linguistic forms and the figurative mechanisms they use? In this sense, this study is a 'look inside the proverb'.

The data of this research has been drawn from Politis' (1899) and Stratis' (2006) collections of proverbs. In this sense, this study is not a corpus-based one. This methodological choice was necessary as, it aligns with Kövecses' (1990) lexical approach, ensuring the feasibility of the attempted comparison. Due to the large number of proverbs recorded in these collections, only those cited on corresponding sites are examined here; that is, a total of 34 proverbs.[4] The data includes proverbs that contain the words *agapi, agapo* and *agapitikia* ('love', 'to love', 'lover').[5]

Furthermore, not only proverbs that contain some kind of figurativity are included but also 'literal' ones, known as 'aphorisms' (Gibbs and Beitel 1995; Gibbs 2001) or 'free-mapping proverbs' (Maalej 2009). The reason for this choice is, firstly, that nonfigurativity conveys knowledge as well; secondly, that we seek to examine whether there is a difference as to the knowledge conveyed by metaphor compared to what is conveyed by nonfigurativity. The proverbs were analysed quantitatively and qualitatively on the basis of the emotion (romantic love, love), the cognitive mechanisms and the linguistic means (verb vs. noun) that are used, as well as the functions they perform.[6]

---

3. Although there are studies on romantic love in Greek (e.g., Xioufis 2015; Xioufis in progress; Theodoropoulou and Xioufis 2018; Theodoropoulou and Xioufis 2021) adopting Conceptual Metaphor Theory (Lakoff and Johnson 1980), these do not endorse the cognitive models approach.

4. It should be noted that some of the proverbs analysed here were unknown to me personally, but were known to others (of different local origins). This could indicate the existence of local differences in the use of proverbs, which the corpora probably cannot capture.

5. Proverbs that contain the verb *agapo* meaning 'to like' have been excluded from this analysis.

6. Although the literature does report characteristics of proverbs, this does not mean that all proverbs should display them; it is possible that proverbs exhibit a prototypical structure, with some being best examples and others peripheral ones. It would be worth exploring whether what constitutes a proverb is culturally determined.

Before proceeding to the analysis of these proverbs, we would like to clarify a point regarding romantic love that we consider as important for the following analysis: the fact that this emotion is metaphorised by opposite metaphors has been pointed out in the literature (Ungerer and Schmidt 1996) as an idiosyncrasy of romantic love. This has also been confirmed in Theodoropoulou's and Xioufis' (2021) study mentioned above. For example, the questions "Have you ever fallen in love? Can you tell how you felt?" have received metaphors such as "Heaven and Hell" or "In the beginning it was like massage and then like depilation" as answers. We consider these answers as evidence of what we call the *dual nature* of romantic love: romantic love involves a person as the object of the subject's desire. Its duality is determined by the fulfilment or not of this desire: i.e., fulfilment of the desire leads to satisfaction and happiness; rejection or loss of the object of love/the romantic relationship leads to great sadness and psychological pain (Theodoropoulou and Xioufis 2021; see also Lieberman 2013).

4. Analysis

4.1 Romantic love

4.1.1 *The 'Cause and Effect figurative pattern'*

A significant number of proverbs instantiates the Cause and Effect pattern, in which both Cause and Effect are stated explicitly (see also Theodoropoulou and Xioufis 2018) and there is some kind of figurativity either in the CAUSE or in the EFFECT part of the proverb. For example, in

(1) Opou   d-eis   poll-i   agap-i,   dek-s-ou   kai
    ADV.LOC.ANAPH see.PFV-2SG a lot-ACC.SG love-ACC.SG accept-PFV-2SG.IMP and
    poll-i   amah-i.
    a lot-ACC.SG fight-ACC.SG
    Lit. 'Where you see a lot of love, accept a lot of fighting', 'Where there is a lot of love there is also a lot of fighting'.

the Cause is *a lot of love*, that is an instance of objectification, and the Effect is *a lot of fighting*, that is a metonymy for SQUABBLING or AGGRESSIVITY. What the proverb highlights is an unavoidable connection between the intensity of the emotion and the degree of the conflict between those involved in a romantic relationship. We do not consider this proverb as an instantiation of the LOVE IS WAR metaphor, for example *He conquered her* (Kövecses 1990:41), which Kövecses (1986:105) considers to pertain to the "Attempt at control" stage of the typical model. This is because the proverb does not refer to the relationship of the one lover to the other, i.e., one's efforts to make a person fall in love with him/her, but to the relationship between two lovers itself. Arguably, this proverb brings to light the dual nature of romantic love, which involves opposite experiences, as discussed above. Finally, there is the 'secondary' metaphor KNOWING IS SEEING (Where you *see* a lot of love...) in the CAUSE part of the sentence. We consider it as secondary because it does not exist in some variations of this proverb. This proverb describes a state of affair and – depending on the context – could function as a warning or reassurance (these things happen or you quarrel because you love each other a lot).

(2) *Agap-i   dihos   peism-ata   den eh-ei*
love-NOM.SG without stubbornness-ACC.PL NEG have.IPFV-3SG.PRS
nostimad-a.
tastiness-ACC.SG
Lit. '(Romantic) love without stubbornness has no flavour'.

(3) *Agap-i   tis   Apokri-as,   staht-i   tis*
love-NOM.SG DEF-GEN.SG Carnival-GEN.SG ash- NOM.SG DEF-GEN.SG
panostri-as
hearth- GEN.SG
Lit. '(Romantic) Love of the Carnival, ashes of the hearth'.

(4) *Horis   psom-i   horis   kras-i,   pagon-ei   ki*
without bread-ACC.SG without wine-ACC.SG freeze.IPFV-3SG.PRS and
i   agap-i.
DEF-NOM.SG love-NOM.SG
Lit. 'Without bread without wine, even romantic love freezes'.

The same pattern is met in these cases as well but there is a metaphor in the EFFECT part of the sentence. In (2), this is ROMANTIC LOVE IS APPETISING FOOD, which is also met in the conventionalised expressions of this emotion both in English (Kövecses 1986: 67, 1990: 128) and Greek (Xioufis 2015: 81; Theodoropoulou and Xioufis 2021). However, there is a difference: in the conventionalised expressions, it is the object of love that is metaphorised as Appetising Food; in the proverb, it is the romantic relationship. In this sense, *agapi* '(romantic) love' could be considered a WHOLE FOR PART metonymy: ROMANTIC LOVE FOR ROMANTIC RELATIONSHIP. Kövecses (1990: 129) states that this metaphor indicates that love is a need and links it with liking and sexual desire. This proverb also reassures because it profiles a negative behaviour as a positive one; i.e., as an inevitable component of a romantic relationship. In (3), the metaphor in the EFFECT part of the sentence is ROMANTIC LOVE IS AN OBJECT THAT CAN BE BURNED. What the proverb highlights is the ephemeral nature of a romantic relationship when it starts during a state of fun and relaxation. In this sense, this proverb is a warning.[7] Here too, the word *agapi* 'romantic love' refers to a romantic relationship and could be considered a WHOLE FOR PART metonymy. Furthermore, in the CAUSE part of the proverb *psomi* 'bread' and *krasi* 'wine' are metonymies for FOOD (PART FOR WHOLE metonymies). In (4), the metaphor is ROMANTIC LOVE IS A LIQUID but, in this case, the word *agapi* 'romantic love' refers to the emotion itself. Arguably, this is the opposite of the metaphor LOVE IS FIRE, which highlights the intensity of the emotion and is evidenced in English (Kövecses 1986: 84, 1990: 46) and Greek (Theodoropoulou and Xioufis 2021), as is shown in one of its variations:

(5) Erot-as   horis   psom-i   grigora   tha
romantic love- NOM.SG without bread- ACC.SG quickly.ADV FUT
svi-s-ei.
blow out-PFV-3SG
Lit. 'Love without bread will soon be over'.

(4) could also be considered as an instance of the metaphor ROMANTIC LOVE IS A LIQUID IN A CONTAINER[8] which – should the container overflows – highlights the intensity of the emotion (Kövecses 1991: 83): by not inferring a kind of container there is no possibility of overflowing; i.e., no possibility to highlight an intense emotion. This is because what the proverb highlights is the end of romantic love when other, more vital needs are not fulfilled. In this sense, (4) is also a warning.

(6) Opoi-os   agap-a   stravon-etai.
whoever-NOM.SG love.IPFV-3SG.PRS blind.IPFV-3SG.PRS.PASS
Lit. 'Whoever falls in love gets blinded'.

This proverb follows the same pattern as the former ones. There is also the metaphor INABILITY TO PERCEIVE REALITY IS INABILITY TO SEE, a version of the KNOWING IS SEEING metaphor, in the EFFECT part of the sentence. This metaphor has been identified in literature as the metonymy INTERFERENCE WITH ACCURATE PERCEPTION (Kövecses 1986: 87, 1990: 36). Arguably, this is a metaphor because s/he who falls in love does not really get blinded. Actually this is a metaphor experientially grounded (Xioufis 2015: 39–40), as neuro-biological research suggests. As Bartels and Zeki (2004: 1164) point out, "… both romantic and maternal love activate specific regions in the reward system and lead to suppression of activity in the neural machineries associated with the *critical social assessment of*

---

7. The fact that the CAUSE part of the proverbs (2)–(5) could be paraphrased with a temporal or hypothetical sentence (e.g., *when/if a love affair starts during Carnival, it will turn to ashes* or *when/if there is no bread and wine, love will freeze*) does not negate the fact that there is CAUSE-EFFECT reasoning – that is embedded in a temporal or a hypothetical sentence.

8. This can be inferred by the use of the verb *pagonei* 'freezes', since its basic meaning refers to liquids. It is hard to imagine liquids freezing outside of a container.

other people[9] and with negative emotions". Furthermore, Zeki (2007: 2577) clarifies, "…if those in love suspend judgment about their lovers, they do not necessarily as well suspended judgment about other things… The suspension of judgment is selective, and argues for a very specific set of connections and brain operations when it comes to love". It is difficult to decide whether this proverb is also a warning or if it expresses a general truth. (See also LOVE IS BLIND).

(7) Mati-a   pou den   vlepont-ai   grigora
    Eye-NOM.SG that NEG see.IPFV-3PL.PRS.PASS quickly.ADV
    lismon-iountai.
    forget.IPFV-3PL.PRS.PASS
    Lit. 'Eyes that are not seen are quickly forgotten'.

This is also the same pattern. It differs from the former ones in that there is the metonymy EYES FOR THE ONE IN LOVE in the CAUSE part of the sentence. Eyes are considered as the salient part of the human face and eye contact is a typical behaviour of lovers. Furthermore, vision is also the principal sense – and the primary one – by which the presence of the other is perceived in the first place. Thus, we could argue that there is an underlying PART FOR WHOLE metonymy: SEEING FOR GETTING TOGETHER. The proverb highlights the need for lovers to get together frequently in order to keep their love alive. In this sense, this proverb is also a warning.

(8) I   agap-i   pirg-ous   katal-ei   kai
    DEF.NOM.SG love-NOM.SG tower-ACC.PL dissolve.IPFV-3SG.PRS and
    kastr-a   rihn-ei   kato   kai palikar-ia tou
    castle-ACC.PL throw.IPFV-3SG.PRS down.ADV and lad-ACC.PL DEF.GEN.SG
    spath-iou   ta   rihn-ei   tou   thanat-ou.
    sword-GEN.SG PRO.ACC.PL throw.IPFV-3SG.PRS DEF.GEN.SG death-GEN.SG
    Lit. 'Love dissolves towers and tears down castles and propels sword-yielding lads to their deaths'.

The basic pattern is the same here: romantic love as the CAUSE and the tearing down of towers and castles as well as the desire for sword-wielding lads to die, as the EFFECT. More importantly, the verbs used in this proverb personify the Cause. Personification is an ontological metaphor (Lakoff and Johnson 1980; Kövecses 2010) and as Dancygier and Sweetser (2014: 62–65) state,

> allows speakers to attribute volitional behaviour to abstractions, and also to represent the ways in which the speaker is affected by them… the crucial effect is to allow us to talk about how humans are affected by events, emotions, and the

---

9. The emphasis is mine.

behaviours associated with them... Giving *this idea,* the power to have an effect (for example on one's mood) is primarily useful in describing that effect, rather than conveying any details of how the effect is achieved. As a result, personifications of this kind are frequently used with verbs of causation and other transitive verbs attribute agenthood to the subject.

The combination of the personification of this emotion as a volitional agent with the profiling of its actions – "personification is useful in describing the effect" (Dancygier and Sweetser 2014: 65) – contributes to the metaphorisation of romantic love as FORCE. This metaphorisation is accentuated by the strong images that are evoked: not only is the image of a powerful – external – natural force such as an earthquake or a hurricane evoked through the effects – hence: ROMANTIC LOVE IS A NATURAL FORCE (see also Kövecses 1986: 83). It is also an equally powerful internal force that is inferred which makes lads holding swords, i.e., fighting for life, want to die: ROMANTIC LOVE IS A PSYCHOLOGICAL FORCE.

Apart from the strong contrast that is used (life vs. death), the highlighting of this kind of force of emotion is reinforced by two other orientational metaphors (Lakoff and Johnson 1980): HAVING CONTROL IS UP and DEATH IS DOWN. The verb *rihno kato* 'throw down', with the element of downward movement it contains, contributes to this effect as well. Overall, this proverb profiles also the dual nature of romantic love by highlighting both its constructive and destructive power. The excess of the expressive means used in this proverb makes it the most 'expressive' proverb of romantic love. In this sense, these means are put to service for the purpose of this proverb, which, is to extol romantic love.

4.1.2 *Metaphors and metonymies*

In this section, we examine proverbs that do not fall in the previously explored pattern. They just contain either metaphor(s) or metonymies highlighting different aspects of romantic love.

(9) Apo   ta   mati-a   pian-etai   i   agap-i.
    From DEF-ACC.PL eye-ACC.PL catch.IPFV-3SG.PRS.PASS DEF-NOM.SG love-ACC.SG
    Lit. 'Love is caught by the eyes'.

Proverb (9) highlights the eyes as the factor that triggers romantic love. In this sense, it could be seen as being transitive between the previous ones that explicitly express the cause and those that are only instantiations of metaphor. The proverb does not clarify whether the eyes are a metonymy for the gaze, that is, if love starts when the gaze of two people meet; or whether it is the erotic attraction caused when seeing the object of love:[10] in this case, eyes could be considered as a metonymy for VISION. Interestingly, love is metaphorised as something tangible in this proverb: ROMANTIC LOVE IS A TANGIBLE ENTITY (see also below). Equally interesting is the linguistic instantiation *pianetai* 'is caught' because the connotations of the verb indicate the instantaneous, abrupt movement we make when we catch something; hence the onset of the emotion is highlighted as something instantaneous, as every onset is, but also as something sudden and passive as well, i.e., as something that just happens. An inference is at work here also: I caught it, so I have it – at least at this moment: in this way, the emergence of the emotion is highlighted.

The same observations regarding the use of the verb *piano* 'to catch' can be made in proverbs (10), (11), and (12) hereafter.

(10) *Kainourgi-a agap-i   pian-etai,   pali-a   den*
new-NOM.SG love-NOM.SG catch.IPFV-3SG.PRS.PASS old-NOM.SG NEG
lismon-ietai.
forget.IPFV-3SG.PRS.PASS
Lit. 'Although there is a new lover, the old one is not forgotten'.

(11) *Kainourgi-a agap-i   e-pia-s-a,   pali-a   mou,*
new-ACC.SG love-ACC.SG PST-catch-PFV-1SG.PST old-VOC.SG POSS.GEN.SG
sta-s-ou   piso.
stand-PFV-2SG.IMP back.ADV
Lit. 'I have got a new lover, my old lover, stand back'.

(12) *Kainourgi-a agap-i   e-pia-s-es,   pali-a   mi*
new-ACC.SG love-ACC.SG PST-catch-PFV-2SG.PST old-ACC.SG NEG
lismon-is-is   giati   tha erth-ei   o   kair-os   pou
forget-PFV-2SG.IMP because FUT come.PFV-3SG DEF.NOM.SG time-NOM.SG that
tha metano-is-is.
FUT regret-PFV-2SG
Lit. 'You've caught a new love, don't forget the old one, For the time will come when you will regret it'.

Furthermore, in (10), (11) and (12) *love* is a WHOLE FOR PART metonymy: LOVE FOR LOVER. These proverbs seem at first glance to communicate contradictory messages: in (10) why does the old love persist in existing – even in memory – although there is a new one? The safest explanation that could be given is that the proverb describes a situation where the old love has not been overcome and the

---

10. See Kövecses (1990: 130): BEAUTY IS A FORCE (PHYSICAL OR PHYSIOLOGICAL); LIKING IS THE REACTION TO THAT FORCE.

new love is one of the ways the subject chooses to overcome it.[11] It is precisely this overcoming that (11) captures with the triumph that is expressed by this proverb. Furthermore, the change of the verb *piano* 'to catch' from passive to active voice on the one hand suggests an active attitude in the search of romantic love (see Kövecses' 1986 typical model), justifying thus the triumph being expressed; on the other hand, it metaphorises the object of love as PREY (see *I caught a fish*). However, (12) outlines another aspect of love relationships: the proverb urges the maintenance of the relationship with the old lover in order to have a 'saviour' in case the new relationship does not go well. Taking into consideration Honeck's (2016: 137) generic ideals, if ensuring love, i.e., the existence of love relationships, is a generic ideal because of its importance in a community, this proverb seems to be concerned with ensuring the recipient's psychological integrity. The collective subject appears to be aware of the effects of the dual nature of love and tries to protect the recipient from its destructive ones.

(13) O   ero-s   hron-ia   den koit-a.
      DEF.NOM.SG romantic love-NOM.SG year-ACC.PL NEG look at.IPFV-3SG.PRS
      Lit. 'Romantic love does not take into consideration the age of the object of love'.

Proverb (13) that is broadly used to refer to relationships in which those involved have a great difference regarding their age, personifies romantic love: it renders love a volitional agent that sets its own terms by defying social stereotypes. It can be viewed as an instance where the emotion predominates over a supposed social 'rationality'. It is no accident that a Google search shows that this proverb is used in texts that offer evidence in order to prove the truth it expresses. There is also the metaphor TAKING INTO CONSIDERATION IS SEEING (an instance of COGNITION IS VISION metaphor; Dancygier and Swetser 2014: 20) in this proverb that objectifies or personifies the age of the lover.

(14) O   erot-as   kai o   vih-as   den
      DEF.NOM.SG romantic love-NOM.SG and DEF.NOM.SG cough.NOM.SG   NEG
      kriv-ontai   / o   vih-as   kai o
      hide.IPFV-3PL.PRS.PASS   DEF.NOM.SG cough.NOM.SG   and DEF.NOM.SG
      erot-as   den kriv-ontai.
      romantic love-NOM.SG   NEG hide.IPFV-3PL.PRS.PASS
      Lit. 'Love and cough can't be hidden/ Cough and love can't be hidden'.

---

11. Kövecses (1991: 91) considers such cases as divergences from the prototypical cognitive model. More specifically, it is an instance of the 'love on the rebound' cognitive model pertaining to situations where one falls in love in the wake of an unsuccessful relationship with another person.

Proverb (14) objectifies romantic love in order to show that others easily perceive one who is in love. This message is accentuated by the equation of love, an emotion whose manifestations can be controlled – even through effort – with a cough, that is a reflexive physical reaction and cannot be controlled.

(15) *I   agap-i   ei-nai   daneik-ia.*
DEF.NOM.SG love-NOM.SG COP.IPFV-3SG.PRS borrowed-NOM.SG
Lit. 'Love is borrowed'.

Proverb (15) objectifies romantic love by metaphorising it as a GIVE-AND-TAKE OBJECT. It highlights the necessity of the reciprocity in romantic relationships profiling it as something vital for the relationship to continue to exist. It could therefore be considered as prompting reciprocity. It is no accident that Kövecses (1991: 91) considers "unrequited love" as divergence from the prototypical cognitive model (see also (21) below).

(16) *Mite niht-a   dihos   mer-a,   mite ni-os   dihos*
NEG night-NOM.SG without day-ACC.SG NEG young man-NOM.SG without
agapitik-ia.
lover-ACC.SG
Lit. 'No night without day, no young man without a lover'.

Proverb (16) exhibits a typical proverbial structure: No X without Y (Gibbs 2001: 168). It is very interesting from the point of view of the cognitive mechanisms that are involved. At first glance, this proverb seems to be an analogy that connects the two domains, the 24-hour period, and the romantic relationship: as there is no night without day, so there is no young man without a lover. However, given that analogy is bi-directional, if one reverses the parts of the proverb one does not get the same meaning: "as there is no young man without a lover, so there is no night without day" is not the same and sounds strange. Consequently, there seems to be uni-directionality in the mapping. Therefore, this is definitely a metaphor that can be labelled THE TWO PARTNERS OF THE ROMANTIC RELATIONSHIP IS THE TWO HALVES OF A 24-HOUR PERIOD.

The question that arises, of course, is which element from the source domain is used to structure the target domain. To answer this question, one should take into consideration that day and night are complementary: the night needs the day to form the whole; i.e., the 24-hour period. This is a natural law: the two parts invariably go together, because the lack of one leaves the whole be incomplete. This natural necessity is brought about in the proverb; this is the structural element that is mapped in the dipole of the young man and his lover. While in reality a young man can exist without a lover, the proverb profiles this as something unnatural. What it highlights instead as naturally inevitable and necessary is that one part needs the other – they are naturally complementary: the parts of a whole become *halves* (see *S/he is my other half*) – for the whole to exist; that is, the completion of one by the other. This metaphor could be viewed as an instantiation of the LOVE IS UNITY OF TWO COMPLEMENTARY PARTS metaphor, the central metaphor of romantic love according to Kövecses (1986: 62). This metaphor construes the relationship between the two lovers as "being in harmony", the "perfect match", the partner being irreplaceable, etc. In other words, the UNITY metaphor is set on psychological terms, on the basis of subjective feelings. This construal is completely different from that made by the proverb, as the proverb sets the UNITY metaphor on natural terms. It profiles it as completely objective: this is what happens – and must happen – in nature and society. In this sense, the erotic unity of two people is profiled as a natural phenomenon.

(17) *Opoi-os han-ei s-ta harti-a*
whoever-NOM.SG loose.IPFV-3SG.PRS to-DEF.ACC.PL card-ACC.PL
kerdiz-ei s-tin agap-i.
win.IPFV-3SG.PRS to-DEF.ACC.SG love-NOM.ACC
Lit. 'Whoever loses at cards wins in love'.

In proverb (17), romantic love is metaphorised as a gambling game and is structured following an opposition (win vs. lose). It seems that it is playing cards, i.e., a real gambling game, that motivates this kind of metaphorisation. This is because the proverb profiles winning in love as compensation for losing at cards. The proverb offers comfort because what it is acquired in return is far more valuable than what is gained at cards (e.g., money, satisfaction of winning). In this sense, the proverb implicitly involves an evaluation of the emotion.

The evaluation of romantic love on another level is what highlights the proverb

(18) *I orfani-a kai i ksenit-ia*
DEF.NOM.SG orpahnhood-NOM.SG and DEF.NOM.SG emigration- NOM.SG
i pikr-a ki i agap-i, ol-a
DEF.NOM.SG bitterness-NOM.SG and DEF.NOM.SG love-NOM.SG all-NOM.SG
e-zigi-s-tikane, variter-i ei-n' i
PST-weigh-PFV-3PL.PST.PASS heavier-NOM.SG COP.IPFV-3SG.PRS DEF.NOM.SG
agap-i.
love-NOM.SG
Lit. 'Orphanhood and emigration, bitterness and love, all weighed together, love proves heavier'.

Proverb (18) compares (COMPARING IS WEIGHING) by objectification some of the most painful experiences: orphanhood (deprivation of a parent), emigration (deprivation of home and family), bitterness (which is a metaphor: GREAT SADNESS

IS BITTERNESS) and romantic love. It highlights romantic love as the most painful experience through the metaphor PAIN IS WEIGHT. Given the dual nature of romantic love, maybe romantic love here could be considered a PART FOR WHOLE metonymy, as it is one of the effects of this emotion that is highlighted.

4.1.3 Non figurativity

Interestingly, all 'literal' proverbs, i.e, proverbs that do not contain any kind of figurativity, use the verb *agapo* 'to love'. A number of them are direct or indirect summonses in order to avoid something: e.g., the loss of love interest by the other person (19) or love towards a forbidden person (20); more specifically, this is achieved by expressing repulsion through a culturally determined gesture (faskela). Other proverbs aim at indicating the right attitude towards love or lover, such as reciprocity in (21; see also (15)), the absence of fear in (22) as well as the seriousness and the respect for one's emotions in (23). Interestingly, (21) and (22) as well as (24) below make use of the CAUSE and EFFECT pattern.

(19) *Ekei opou poth-eis mi daneiz-eis, kai*
there.LOC that.LOC.ANAPH. desire.IPFV-2SG.PRS NEG lend.IPFV-2SG.IMP and
ekei pou agap-as mi sihnop-as
there.LOC that.LOC.ANAPH love.IPFV-2SG.PRS NEG go often.IPFV-2SG.IMP
Lit. 'Where the one you desire is, do not lend, and where the one you love is, do not go often'.

(20) *Faskel-a tis pou agap-a*
[gesture]-ACC.SG PRO.GEN.SG that.ANAPH love.IPFV-3SG.PRS
pantremen-o i pap-a.
married man-ACC.SG or priest- ACC.SG
Lit. 'Show a demeaning hand gesture to her who loves a married man or a priest'.

(21) *Agap-a me na s' agap-o,*
love.IPFV-2SG.IMP PRO.1SG.ACC to PRO.2SG.ACC love.IPFV-1SG
thel-e me na se thel-o.
want.IPFV-2SG.IMP PRO.1SG.ACC to PRO.2SG.ACC want. IPFV-1SG
Lit. 'Love me to love you back; want me to want you back'.

(22) *Opou agap-a den ntrep-etai, mide*
ADV.LOC.ANAPH love.IPFV-3SG.PRS NEG be ashamed.IPFV-3SG.PRS.PASS NEG
kai de fov-atai.
and NEG be afraid.IPFV-3SG.PRS.PASS
Lit. 'He who loves is not ashamed, nor is he afraid'.

(23) *Agap-o   tha p-ei   agap-o   ki   ohi*
    love.IPFV-1SG.PRS FUT say.IPFV-3SG.PRS love.IPFV-1SG.PRS and NEG
    paiz-o   kai gel-o.
    play.IPFV-1SG.PRS and laugh.IPFV-1SG.PRS
    Lit. 'To love is to love, not to play and laugh.'

Furthermore, through this kind of proverb, a negative attitude towards this emotion is expressed (it is a waste of time; falling in love requires spending money on the lover), as for example in

(24) *Opoi-os   thel-ei   n' agap-is-ei,   thel-ei   na*
    whoever-NOM.SG want.IPFV-3SG.PRS to love-PFV-3SG want.IPFV-3SG.PRS to
    hasomer-is-ei   thel-ei   aspr-a   na ksodia-s-ei   kai na
    waste-PFV-3SG time want.IPFV-3SG.PRS white-ACC.PL to spend-PFV-3SG and to
    min ta   logaria-s-ei.
    NEG PRO.ACC.PL count-PFV-3SG
    Lit. 'Whoever wants to fall in love wants to waste their time,[12] they want to spend money without counting it.'

(25) *Agap-a   me   ma min to   le-s,   gia na*
    love.IPFV-2SG.IMP PRO.ACC.SG but NEG pro.ACC.SG say.PFV-2SG.IMP for to
    teleion-oun   i   doulei-es.
    end.IPFV-3PL.PRS DEF.NOM.PL work-NOM.PL
    Lit. 'Love me but don't say it to get the job done.'

Finally, marital love is acknowledged as good luck but causing erotic attraction causes 'secret pride' – it enhances self-confidence:

(26) *An me   agap-aei   o   andr-as   mou,*
    if PRO.ACC.SG love.IPFV-3SG.PRS DEF.NOM.SG man-NOM.SG POSS.GEN.SG
    s-tin   tih-i   to   'h-o   har-i,   an
    to-DEF.ACC.SG luck-ACC.SG PRO.ACC.SG have.IPFV-1SG.PRS debt-ACC.SG if
    me   agap-aei   ki   all-os   kan-eis,   to
    PRO.ACC.SG love.IPFV-3SG.PRS and other-NOM.SG anyone-NOM.SG PRO.ACC.SG
    'h-o   krif-o   kamar-i.
    have.IPFV-1SG.PRS secret-ACC.SG proud-ACC.SG
    Lit. 'If my husband loves me, I'm grateful to be lucky, if someone else loves me, I have a secret pride.'[13]

---

12. There is an objectification of time in this proverb; since the metaphor pertains to time and not romantic love, this proverb has not been included in the figurative ones.
13. There is an objectification of pride in this proverb; this proverb has not been included in the figurative ones because the metaphor in this case refers to pride and not romantic love.

4.2 Love

All the proverbs in this corpus that refer to love use the verb *agapo* 'to love' and its participle and not the noun *love*. They are either direct or indirect summonses (28)–(30) – the use of imperative is indicative – or they express general truths (32)–(33). All are nonfigurative except (27) that instantiates the metaphor BROTHERLY LOVE IS AN IMPREGNABLE CASTLE, thus extoling brotherly love.

(27) *Adelf-ia   agap-imen-a,   kastr-a   pou den*
sibling-NOM.PL love.PFV-PTCP.PRF-NOM.PL castle-NOM.PL that NEG
pairn-ontai.
take.IPFV-3PL.PRS.PASS
Lit. 'Siblings who love each other, castles that can't be conquered'.

Nevertheless, extolling brotherly love could be seen as encouraging it, if one takes into account the proverb in

(28) *Ton   adelf-o   sou   agap-age   ki   ohi*
DEF.ACC.SG brother-ACC.SG POSS.GEN.SG love.IPFV-2SG.IMP and NEG
to   mertik-o   tou.
DEF.ACC.SG share-ACC.SG POSS.GEN.SG
Lit. 'Love your brother and not his fortune'.

Furthermore, there is the metaphor KEEPING DISTANCE/BOUNDARIES IN A RELATIONSHIP IS NOT TEARING DOWN THE FENCE in:

(29) *Agap-a   to   geiton-a   sou,   alla mi*
love.IPFV-2SG.IMP DEF.ACC.SG neighbour-ACC.SG POSS.GEN.SG but NEG
gkremiz-eis   to   fraht-i.
tear.IPFV-2SG.IMP down DEF.ACC.SG fence-ACC.SG
Lit. 'Love your neighbour, but don't tear down the fence'.

The same idea is expressed non-figuratively, but using the CAUSE and EFFECT pattern, generally regarding the relationships within a community in:

(30) *Kalitera   makria ki   agap-imen-oi   para apo konta   kai*
better.ADV far.ADV and love.PFV-PTCP.PRF-NOM.PL than from close.ADV and
malo-men-oi.
quarell.PFV-PTCP.PRF-NOM.PL
Lit. 'Better to be far apart and loved than close and at each other's throats'.

Moreover, although (31) is an explicit summons, (32) is a warning; (33) conveys a general truth.

(31) *Agap-age   ton   fil-o   sou   me   ta*
love.IPFV-2SG.IMP DEF.ACC.SG friend-ACC.SG POSS.GEN.SG with DEF.ACC.PL
elattoma-ta tou.
fault-ACC.PL POSS.GEN.SG
Lit. 'Love your friend with his faults'.

(32) *O   The-os   agap-aei   ton   kleft-i,*
DEF.NOM.SG God-NOM.SG love.IPFV-3SG.PRS DEF.ACC.SG thief-ACC.SG
agap-aei   kai ton   noikokir-i.
love.IPFV-3SG.PRS and DEF.ACC.SG landlord-ACC.SG
Lit. 'God loves the thief but He also loves the landlord'.

(33) *Omoi-os   ton   omoi-o   agap-a   ki*
similar-NOM.SG DEF.ACC.SG similar-ACC.SG love.IPFV-3SG.PRS and
omoi-os   ton   omoi-o   thel-ei.
similar-NOM.SG DEF.ACC.SG similar-ACC.SG want.IPFV-3SG.PRS
Lit. 'Persons of a kind love and want people of the same kind'.

Finally, (34) is a GENERIC IS SPECIFIC metaphor, expressing the idea that "What interests me is to be loved by some person who has authority; all the others are indifferent".

(34) *As m'   agap-a   o   episkop-os   ki   as*
let PRO.ACC.SG love.IPFV-3SG.PRS DEF.NOM.SG bishop-NOM.SG and let
me   mis-oun   oi   diak-oi.
PRO.ACC.SG hate.IPFV-3PL.PRS DEF.NOM.PL deacon-NOM.PL
Lit. 'Let the bishop love me and the deacons hate me'.

To sum up, it seems that most love proverbs aim at regulating the relationships among the members of a community. It is noteworthy to note that no proverb uses the noun *love* or the verb *to love* referring to the relationship between parents and children that forms the core of a community, at least in Western cultures.

5. Discussion

In relation to the above analysis, we should point out that the proverbs on romantic love and love are differentiated at multiple levels:

a. quantitatively: 26 proverbs on romantic love versus 8 proverbs on love (76.47% vs. 23.52%);
b. regarding the use of figurativity: 69.23% romantic love-proverbs use some kind of figurativity, whereas in the case of love only 37.5% proverbs do so;

c. regarding the functions they perform: proverbs on romantic love are warnings or reassurance when they instantiate the 'Cause and Effect figurative pattern'; when they contain metaphor and metonymies they express general truths, they are advocative, they are expressive and they prompt to particular behaviours. Love-proverbs as well as nonfigurative proverbs on romantic love are mostly direct or indirect summonses; and
d. regarding the linguistic forms that are used: the noun *agapi* 'love' is mostly used in romantic-love proverbs – *agapitikia* 'lover' is used twice[14] and the verb *agapo* 'to love' once. Both nonfigurative proverbs on romantic love and love use the verb.

The quantitative predominance of proverbs referring to romantic love over the ones referring to love shows clearly the priority given to this emotion in Greek culture and should be examined in relation to the increased figurativity these proverbs show. This, once again, could be explained on the basis that romantic love is the emotion that motivates a man and a woman to become a couple, contributing to the maintenance and reproduction of the species. As has been mentioned, proverbs on love are mostly nonfigurative and aim mainly at regulating the broader relationships within a community: they are direct or indirect summonses; that is why they use the verb – very often in the imperative or embedded in Cause and Effect reasoning. These relationships are relationships between friends, neighbours, adult siblings – not siblings who are children – and even between the community and a potential thief. Even when proverbs express a general truth they state that this is the way things are in the world – and this is indisputable: this is the order of this 'world'. That is why they often function as warnings (and/or reassurance in the case of romantic love). Nonfigurative proverbs on romantic love are also direct or indirect summonses and they, too, use the verb. However, their aim is to ensure the 'proper' development of the romantic relationship, its preservation. There is, of course, room for expressing a negative attitude towards romantic love – which is the result, quite possibly, of some negative experience. This indicates that the collective subject acknowledges the dual nature of love as proverbs (8) and (16), even (10), demonstrate.

That is the big difference from the cognitive models approach; i.e., the knowledge captured by the conventionalised expressions used in everyday speech. Kövecses' (1986) models do not incorporate the painful aspect of romantic love in their content. Romantic frustration, disappointment, and unrequited love are considered divergences from the prototypical cognitive models. In other words, the inherent duality of romantic love is not acknowledged by this approach. The

---

14. The one use is a metonymy FOR LOVER; see (7).

other major difference one detects is the absence of the body in the proverbs; i.e., the absence either of THE PHYSIOLOGICAL OR BEHAVIOURAL REACTION FOR THE EMOTION metonymies (e.g., Kövecses 1990), or the metaphor within metonymy interactional pattern (Theodoropoulou 2012a). Cognitive models are 3-stage (ideal love) or 5-stage (typical love) scenarios that describe all the phases a subject goes through when in love: from the onset of emotion until its culmination or its elimination. They focus on the feelings and emotions the subject experiences in relation to the object of love. In this sense, the human body is foregrounded, either itself or as behaviour. Therefore, the information provided by the cognitive models concerns the subjective experience.

On the contrary, proverbs focus on relationships. More specifically, proverbs on romantic love focus on the romantic relationship itself, not on the subjective experience. They do not provide detailed descriptions of the emotional experience. The proverbial eye catches the onset of the emotion, profiles love as a high value and describes what happens in general in romantic relationships as a state of affairs. That is why it recognises the painful aspect of love; because it actually happens. We could say that the cognitive models approach is a 'look inside the subject'. Proverbs, on the other hand, are a 'look from above onto the community', a look that falls on the community and cares about relationships; it is a collective gaze that tries to preserve the integrity of the community through the integrity of its members.

Regarding the use of figurativity, one of the most interesting findings of this study is the identification of the 'Cause and Effect figurative pattern'. It shows a high frequency (44.44%) and its main characteristics are that it is based on Cause-Effect reasoning and that its main functions are warning or reassurance. In other words, proverbs using this pattern aim at persuading. Even (8) that extols the power of love does not do so in an arbitrary way, but extollation is justified by using this particular pattern. This is because this kind of reasoning has evidential power. That is why it is also used in nonfigurative proverbs (see 21, 22, 24). This way, by which the collective subject addresses the recipient, is different from the direct or indirect summonses used in the nonfigurative proverbs, where the summons is based on the authority of the collective experience. What is interesting in this pattern is the use of metaphor in the EFFECT part of the proverb, the CAUSE part being nonfigurative. Arguably, the fact that the reasoning begins nonfiguratively and ends up with a metaphor creates a kind of garden-path effect. This forces the recipient to reconsider romantic love in metaphorical (or metonymic) terms. In other words, it forces the recipient to construe romantic love as something else, which is concrete and can evoke particular feelings. When the outcome of a romantic relationship is construed as ashes of the hearth (in 3), this not only evokes a vivid and concrete image; this image also expresses the frustration which is the result of the failure of a romantic relationship and the emotional investments that it carried. Construing romantic love as appetising food (in 2), not only does it force one to change one's perspective; it also eliminates the irritation or the potential disappointment that stubbornness brings to a relationship. Construing the end of romantic love as a frozen liquid (in 4) not only evokes the sensation of cold; it also brings to mind connotations of death and an irreversible end. In this sense, the strong images that are mentioned in literature as a characteristic of proverbs *compensate* the abstract referent of the proverb with experience. Precisely, this evocation of the experience *reinforces* the evidential power of Cause and Effect reasoning. Finally, the occurrence in several cases of the ROMANTIC LOVE FOR ROMANTIC RELATIONSHIP metonymy can be explained on the basis that in this way the emotion, that is, the cause, i.e., the *primum movens*, of the relationship, is highlighted.

The same could be said about metaphor in relation to the second category of the proverbs examined. This category displays a wide range of functions; i.e., description of a general truth (9, 10, 13, 14), expression of emotion (18 but also 11), offering comfort (17), giving a piece of advice (12), and prompting. What is being prompted is that which is considered highly valued in the community because it contributes to its maintenance and reproduction: reciprocity (15), the pairing of a young man with his lover (16). What is the power of metaphor in these proverbs? The way metaphor contributes to offering comfort (17), as well as the role of personification and/or objectification – hence the increased use of the noun *agapi* – have already been analysed, highlighting the flexibility and the malleability these mechanisms offer. Importantly, in the case of emotions metaphor is put in the service of expressivity (Foolen 2012; Theodoropoulou 2004); i.e., metaphors of emotions serve the – inherent – need of emotion to be expressed (Theodoropoulou 2012a, b). However, why is the same idea, the same message, expressed figuratively and nonfiguratively in proverbs? In other words: what is the difference between the figurative *Love is borrowed* (in 15) and the nonfigurative *Love me and I love you back; want me and I want you back* (in 24), both prompting the reciprocity in a romantic relationship? The nonfigurative presupposes the love and desire of the other in order for the subject's love and desire to exist and continue to exist. The figurative one, though, by metaphorising the romantic love as something borrowed on the one hand attributes equality to both involved in the relationship; on the other hand, and this is the most important, it focuses on another aspect – and possibly the very aspect of reciprocity: the obligation to give back what you have borrowed. Metaphor carries the moral weight that is not carried by the nonfigurative proverb. In this case, too, there is a feeling that is evoked through the concrete, i.e., love as object. These arguments about the power of metaphor, made on a theoretical level, are in accordance with Colston's (2019: 103) view, who attributes the advocative strength of metaphorical proverbs, compared to the non-metaphorical ones, to the running of embodied simulations (Bergen 2012).

Finally, why do romantic-love proverbs show higher figurativity compared to proverbs on love? In any case, romantic love is considered the most metaphorised emotion (Ungerer and Schmidt 1996; Kövecses 2000).[15] It can be argued, once again (Theodoropoulou and Xioufis 2021), that it is the high value attributed by the community to this emotion, as well as the complexity of romantic love, i.e., its dual nature, that motivates its increased figurativity. It is because figurativity can handle this complexity.

6. Conclusion

Do the proverbs that highlight the painful aspect of romantic love disconfirm the generic ideal, postulated by Honeck (2016)? If this could be true of the proverbs on love, is it true of the proverbs on romantic love? The proverbs oppose to Honeck's Manichaean point of view, a perspective, which accepts the human being in its entirety: the proverbs on romantic love are the collective gaze that embraces human nature in its heights and in its depths. Of course, this gaze is also motivated by the biological imperative of the preservation of the species. However, at the same time it takes into account and encompasses human fragility. In this respect, the proverbs on romantic love show an admirable flexibility because they, as a whole, reconcile the contradictions of the human being.

"There may be a reason why proverbs are generally stated in concrete terms. Concrete statements are not only a rich source of information, but the real world that they refer to has a more transparent and specifiable logic than abstractly stated words and ideas. That is, the physical constraints inherent in the environment yield a more lucid and compelling intrinsic logic", as Honeck (2016: 180) points out. This statement is valid – but only to a certain extent: it conceals the fact that apart from providing information, the concrete thing is a source of sensations, feelings, and emotions that are the result of the human being's interaction with its environment. The power of the proverb to persuade, to comfort, to extol is based on the power of metaphor, and figurativity in general, to imbue information with vivid experience: this is the function of the concrete images contained in the proverb – which the subjects use to understand it (Gibbs and Beitel 1995). The 'Cause and Effect figurative pattern' spotted in the data, possibly being genre specific, demonstrates that logic is not enough to secure the goal, i.e. persuasion;

---

15. The results in Theodoropoulou's and Xioufis' (2021) study suggest that romantic love is the emotion most figuratively conceptualised and expressed (i.e., metaphors *and* metonymies).

it needs to be reinforced by experience. The present study attempted to show that in this interweaving of cognition and emotion, which uses a wide range of figurative means, the collective need with the subjective experience are intertwined.

Acknowledgements

I would like to express my warmest thanks to Shampy Eager for editing the English version of this text.

References

Anderson, B. (1983). *Imagined communities: Reflections on the origin and spread of Nationalism*. London: Verso.

Barsalou, L. W., & Wiemer-Hastings, K. (2005). Situating abstract concepts. In D. Pecher, & R. Zwaan (Eds.), *Grounding cognition: The role of perception and action in memory, language, and thought* (pp. 129–163). Cambridge: Cambridge University Press.

Bartels, A., & Zeki, S. (2004). The neural correlates of maternal and romantic love. *Neuro Image* 21, 1155–1166.

Belkhir, S. (2014). Cultural influence on the use of DOG concepts in English and Kabyle proverbs. In A. Musolff, F. MacArthur, & G. Pagani (Eds.), *Metaphor and intercultural communication* (pp. 131–146). London: Bloomsbury.

Belkhir, S. (2019). Animal related concepts across languages and cultures from a cognitive linguistic perspective. *Cognitive Linguistic Studies*, 6(2), 295–324.

Ben Salamh, S. B., & Maalej, Z. (2018). A cultural linguistics perspective on animal proverbs, with special reference to two dialects of Arabic. *Arab World English Journal for Translation and Literary Studies*, 2(4), 21–40.

Bergen, B. K. (2012). *Louder than words: The new science of how the mind makes meaning*. New York: Basic Books.

Colston, H. (1995). Actions speak louder than words: Understanding figurative proverbs. *Dissertation Abstracts International Section B The Sciences and Engineering*, 56, (7B), 4040.

Colston, H. (2000). Book review: Richard Honeck, A proverb in mind: The cognitive science of proverbial wit and wisdom. *Journal of Pragmatics*, 32, 627–638.

Colston, H. (2019). *How language makes meaning: Embodiment and conjoined antonymy*. Cambridge: Cambridge University Press.

Crawford, E. (2009). Conceptual metaphors of affect. *Emotion Review*, 1(2), 129–139.

Dabbagh, A., & Noshadi, M. (2015). An interpretation of the significance of 'time': The case of English and Persian proverbs. *Theory and Practice in Language Studies*, 5(12), 2581–2590.

Dancygier, B., & Sweetser, E. (2014). *Figurative language*. Cambridge: Cambridge University Press.

Fahmi, M. E. E. (2017). A cross-cultural study of some selected Arabic proverbs and their English translation equivalents: A contrastive approach. *International Journal of Comparative Literature & Translation Studies*, 4(2), 51–57.

Fisher, H., Aron, A., Mashek, D., Strong, G., Li, H., & L. L. Brown. (2005). Motivation and emotion systems associated with romantic love following rejection: An fMRI study. Program No. 660.7. 2005. Abstract Viewer/Itinerary Planner. Washington, DC: Society for Neuroscience.

Foolen, A. (2012). The relevance of emotion for language and linguistics. In A. Foolen, J. Zlatev, U. Lüdtke & T. Racine (Eds.), *Moving ourselves, moving others: Motion and emotion in consciousness, intersubjectivity and language* (pp. 347–368). Amsterdam & Philadelphia: John Benjamins.

Gavriilidou, Z. (2002). I paroimia ston elliniko tipo [Proverbs in Greek press]. *Proceedings of the 5th International Conference on Greek Linguistics* (pp. 207–210). Paris: L'Harmattan.

Gibbs, R. (1994). *The poetics of mind: Figurative thought, language, and understanding*. New York: Cambridge University Press.

Gibbs, R. W. (2001). Proverbial themes we live by. *Poetics*, 29, 167–188.

Gibbs, R. W., & Beitel, D. (1995). What proverb understanding reveals about how people think. *Psychological Bulletin*, 118(1), 133–154.

Gibbs, R. W., & Colston, H. (2012). *Interpreting figurative meaning*. Cambridge: Cambridge University Press.

Gibbs, R. W. Jr., Colston, H. L., & Johnson, M. D. (1996). Proverbs and the metaphorical mind. *Metaphor and Symbolic Activity*, 11(3), 207–216.

Gibbs, R. W. Jr., Johnson, M. D., & Colston, H. (1996). How to study proverb understanding. *Metaphor and Symbolic Activity*, 11(3), 233–239.

Grice, H. P. (1975). Logic and conversation. In P. Cole & J. Morgan (Eds.), *Syntax and semantics, Vol.3: Speech acts* (pp. 41–58). New York: Academic Press.

Honeck, R. P. ([1997] 2016). *A proverb in the mind: The cognitive science of proverbial wit and wisdom*. Second edition. London & New York: Routledge.

Honeck, R., & Temple, J. (1994). Proverbs: The Extended Conceptual Base and Great Chain metaphor theories. *Metaphor and Symbolic Activity*, 9, 85–112.

Kövecses, Z. (1986). *Metaphors of anger, pride and love: A lexical approach to the structure of concepts*. Amsterdam & Philadelphia: John Benjamins.

Kövecses, Z. (1990). *Emotion concepts*. New York: Springer/ Verlag.

Kövecses, Z. (1991). A linguist's quest for love. *Journal of Social and Personal Relationships*, 8(1), 77–97.

Kövecses, Z. (2000). *Metaphor and emotion*. Cambridge: Cambridge University Press.

Kövecses, Z. (2010). *Metaphor: A practical introduction*. Oxford: Oxford University Press.

Lakoff, G. (1990). The Invariance hypothesis: Is abstract reason based on image-schemas? *Cognitive Linguistics*, 1(1), 39–74.

Lakoff, G., & Kövecses, Z. (1987). Anger. In G. Lakoff, *Women, fire and other dangerous things. What categories reveal about the mind* (pp. 380–415). Chicago & London: The University of Chicago Press.

Lakoff, G, & Johnson. M. (1980). *Metaphors we live by*. Chicago: University of Chicago Press.

Lakoff, G., & Turner, M. (1989). *More than a cool reason: A field guide to poetic metaphor.* Chicago: University of Chicago Press.

Lieberman, M. D. (2013). *Social: Why our brains are wired to connect.* New York: Broadway Books.

Lovejoy, A. (1936). *The Great chain of being: A study of the history of an idea.* Cambridge, Massachussets & London: Harvard University Press.

Maalej, Z. (2009). A cognitive-pragmatic perspective on proverbs and its implications for translation. *International Journal of Arabic-English Studies,* 3(10), 1844–1849.

Milne, R. W. (1982). Predicting garden path sentences. *Cognitive Science,* 6, 349–373.

Politis, N. (1899). *Meletai peri tou viou kai tis glossis tou Ellinikou laou.* Vol. 1: *Paroimiai* [*Studies on the life and language of the Greek people.* Vol. 1: *Proverbs*]. Athens: Bivliothiki Marasli.

Saragih, E. L. L., & Mulyadi, M. (2020). Cognitive semantic analysis of animal proverbs in Toba language. *Retorika,* 13(2), 217–224.

Sauciuc, G.-A. (2013). The role of metaphor in the structuring of emotion concepts. *Cognitive Semiotics,* V(1–2), 244–267.

Stratis, M. (2006). *Paroimies: Arhaies ellinikes, romaikes, neoellinikes, alvanikes* [*Proverbs: Ancient Greek, Roman, Modern Greek, Albanian*]. Thessaloniki: Ianos.

Theodoropoulou, M. (2004). *Sta glossika monopatia tou fovou* [*Treading the linguistic paths of fear*]. Athens: Nissos.

Theodoropoulou, M. (2012a). Metaphor-metonymies of joy and happiness in Greek: Towards an interdisciplinary perspective. *Review of Cognitive Linguistics,* 10(1), 156–183.

Theodoropoulou, M. (2012b). The emotion seeks to be expressed: Thoughts from a linguist's point of view. In A. Chaniotis (Ed.), *Unveiling emotions: Sources and methods for the study of emotions in the Greek world* (pp. 433–468). Stuttgart: Steiner.

Theodoropoulou, M., & Xioufis, T. (2018). The interplay of metaphor and metonymy in the Greek language of fear and romantic love: The role of personification. Paper presented at the 4th International Conference on Figurative Thought and Language, Braga, Portugal, October 23–28.

Theodoropoulou, M., & Xioufis, T. (2021). Comparing the Greek metaphors for fear and romantic love. In T. Markopoulos, C. Vlachos, A. Archakis, D. Papazachariou, A. Roussou & G. Xydopoulos (Eds.), *Proceedings of the 14th International Conference on Greek Linguistics,* 1278–1288. Patras: University of Patras.

Ungerer, F., & Schmidt, H.-G. (1996). *An introduction to cognitive linguistics.* Addison-Wesley: Boston.

Xioufis, T. (2015). *Mia proti dierevnisi tis mi kiriolektikis glossas tou erota* [*A first approach to the figurative language of romantic love*]. MA dissertation, Linguistics Department, School of Philology, Aristotle University of Thessaloniki.

Xioufis, T. (in progress). *O erotas sto Twitter: Kiriolektiki kai mi kiriolektiki glossa* [*Romantic love on Twitter: Figurative and nonfigurative language*]. Ph.D. diss., Aristotle University of Thessaloniki, Greece.

Zeki, S. (2007). The neuro-biology of love. *FEBS Letters* 581, 2575–2579.

Web sites on proverbs

https://www.gnomikologikon.gr/greek-proverbs.php?page=1

https://perivoliderelidomokou.gr/parimies

https://memtfi.webnode.gr/%cf%80%ce%b1%cf%81%ce%bf%ce%b9%ce%bc%ce%af%ce%b5%cf%82-%ce%ba%ce%b1%ce%b9-%ce%b1%ce%b9%ce%bd%ce%af%ce%b3%ce%bc%ce%b1%cf%84%ce%b1-/

https://www.hallofpeople.com/gr/paroimies-main.php

CHAPTER 8

LIVING IS MOVEMENT
A cognitive analysis of some Akan proverbs

Yaw Sekyi-Baidoo
University of Education, Winneba, Ghana

Proverbs, sayings, metaphors, and symbolism represent connections between physical experiences, their cognitive engagements and language, which becomes both a storage place and a promoter of this symbiosis. Departing from the universal LIFE IS A JOURNEY conventional metaphor, the study examines the representation of the connection between movement and living and how they are reflected in Akan philosophical values. Guided by Johnson's schema theory, Lakoff and Johnson's Conceptual Metaphor theory, and Lakoff and Turner's (1989) Great Chain Metaphor Theory, the study discusses the LIVING IS MOVEMENT schema and component conceptual metaphors in Akan proverbs. It also examines related orientational metaphors including 'SUCCESS IS UP/AWAY' and SECURITY IS IN/WITHIN in the proverbs, linking all these cognitive representations of *movement* to the Akan philosophy of 'life and its living'.

Keywords: living, movement, metaphor, schema, conceptual

1. Introduction

The proverb has eluded a conclusive definition, and this is as result of the wide variety of items that are often admitted into the proverb classification, the various ways in which different cultures have approached the concept of proverb and established wise sayings, and the variety of structural forms that have been classified as such. Norrick (2014: 7) makes this conclusive remark:

> There is no a priori reason to expect the proverbs of a community to constitute a coherent syntactic type or to express a consistent set of propositions. We should not expect to discover a single characteristic *proverbiality* or a single inclusive definition of the proverb, and we should not be surprised when isolated proverbs contradict each other.

Yet, in spite of this difficulty to define, it is possible to identify a group of entries that are marked not just by their universal truth, wisdom and philosophy and their syntactic or discourse form but also, and primarily so, by their relying on indirect representations. They also present general truths using specific representations, human philosophies through non-human images possibly; and their interpretation demands a deeper, indirect sense making that appreciates the cognitive connectivity between the multiplicity of human experience and objects.

It is the recognition of differences within the category of proverbs that leads Nirmala (2013:125) to distinguish between *metaphorical* and *non-metaphorical* proverbs. For her, the consideration is simple: a proverb can be classified as non-metaphorical "since in the proverb there is no expression conveying a concept which can be conceptualized with or from another concept". However, one such as 'don't change the harvest season' is metaphorical, because one would be applying the embodied experience of planting, budding, fruiting, maturing and harvesting, as experience with the plant or crop, to a different context of application or interpretation – courtship, entrepreneurship, education, or even cooking. A similar distinction, between *literal* and *figurative* proverbs, is made by Norrick (1985:1) and (Dobrovol'skij et al. 2005:27). Focusing on the second category of proverbs, we could assert that proverbs are metaphors, and that the cognitive principles and strategies underlying the creation, interpretation, and analysis of metaphors could be applied in one way or another to the study of these proverbs. This goes in line with Lakoff and Johnson's (1980:5) simple and definitive statement: "the essence of metaphor is understanding and experiencing one kind of thing in terms of another".

The connection between the proverb and metaphor has been made much clearer with the advent of Conceptual Metaphor Theory, which sought to release metaphor from the hitherto strangleholds of literary and specialised language to our everyday conceptualisation. With conceptual metaphor theory, we observe that the distinction we find between the different aspects of our experience might only be physical or overt. At the level of mental processing, there is a wide possibility of similarity or compatibility between items that could be materially incompatible, as, for instance, between *human life* and *candlelight*. Cognitively, there would be several similarities between them – birth vs. lighting, illness and dangers vs. flickering winds, premature death vs. premature loss of flame, and finally, the old age deaths vs. full consumption of the candle stalk, and the general fact that for each of them the light or life would commence one moment and come to a sure end. Lakoff and Johnson (1980:3–4) have this to say about the prevalence of metaphor in human life:

> Our conceptual system thus plays a central role in defining our everyday realities. If we are right in suggesting that our conceptual system is largely metaphorical, then the way we think, what we experience, and what we do every day is very much a matter of metaphor.
>
> But our conceptual system is not something we are normally aware of. In most of the little things we do every day, we simply think and act more or less automatically along certain lines. Just what these lines are is by no means obvious. One way to find out is by looking at language. Since communication is based on the same conceptual system that we use in thinking and acting, language is an important source of evidence for what that system is like.

Fortunately, metaphorical proverbs employ the very strategies and principles of regular metaphors in their construction as well as in their study. What metaphor affords is the opportunity to perceive one experience using the conceptualisation of another i.e., though things may be physically or ontologically distinct, the mind is able to draw similarities or parallels between them.

The most influential contestation in the study of the proverb has been whether the focus should be on the use of the proverb in its cultural setting, generating meanings, thoughts and emotions, reflecting the way cultures have perceived life and the things around them, influencing behaviour and being a source of art, as pursued by people in ethnography; or whether we should focus on the cognitive perspectives of explaining how the proverb was put together or how it could be interpreted, with, sometimes, a mind to finding universal cognitive patterns. This contestation of focus is captured by Buljan and Gradečak-Erdeljić (2013: 63):

> One question that has been hotly debated in paremiology is whether proverbs should be accounted for by mental theories of proverb comprehension or they should be considered a social phenomenon that can only be studied within its cultural matrix.

Gladly, over the past few decades, the realms of Cognitive Linguistics have seen a growing attention to the cultural specifics even in the mentalistic approach to meaning comprehension. There have been countless papers and chapters from different parts of the world that apply cognitive perspectives of the Conceptual Metaphor Theory (CMT) of Lakoff and Johnson (1980), the Conceptual Blending Theory of Fauconnier and Turner (2002) and related perspectives to different cultures. Such studies report how the employment of cognitive perspectives help for a deeper understanding of the thought processes that underlie the creation of proverbs and how the proverbs reflect the people's conceptualisation of the world and its connection to cultural values.

The Akan proverb has received considerable attention from different perspectives, but these have generally come from a discourse, pragmatic or ethnographic point of view, with little known attention to cognitive and philosophical considerations. Studies such as Yankah (1989) and Agyekum (2021) have looked at the proverb from ethnographic, pragmatic, and literary points of view. Beyond the Akan, Aku-Sika (2016) and Ogwudile (2016) among several others have studied the Ewe, Igbo, and Yoruba proverbs from the perspectives of discourse, power, and socio-cultural identity.

The philosophical and cognitive perspectives to the proverb have not received much attention in Akan and other West African contexts. Among the few of such attention are Oluyemisi (2017) and Kazeem (2010) who study the Yoruba proverb from the point of view of philosophical considerations and logic. In Ghana, Diabah and Amfo (2015, 2018) have looked at gender representation in Akan proverbs, but do not employ clearly cognitive perspectives. With respect to the employment of cognitive perspectives, Andersson (2013) used conceptual blending to study figurative proverbs, and Lemghari (2017) investigated the place of conceptual metaphors in constructing lexical polysemy. The general focus in cognitive perspectives in the study of the proverb has been on the representation of humans and human qualities (target) using animal and objects (sources), and studies here include Mansyur and Said (2020), Olateju (2005), Rodríguez (2009), and Kobia (2016) across different cultural contexts, English-Spanish, Swahili, and Wolio. In addition, attention seems to be given to target-source representations rather than schemas.

It is evident from the review above that the Akan proverb has not received any known real cognitive attention. It follows therefore that the relationship between the proverb, on the one hand, and the Akan cognitive system and the philosophy and values of the communities, on the other, has not been given any known direct attention.

This study proceeds with the understanding that beyond target and source concepts, the Akan proverb exploits an overriding conceptualisation that connects *living* to *movement*, and that within the broad image schema of LIVING IS MOVEMENT, conceptual and orientational metaphors are intricately exploited to reflect the Akan philosophy of life and its living. The purpose of the chapter is to discuss the representation of the LIVING IS MOVEMENT image schema in Akan proverbs, and the conceptual and orientational metaphors that reflect the Akan conceptualisation of movement and the philosophy of life and its living.

The work is guided by the following questions:

1. In what conceptual metaphors is the LIVING IS MOVEMENT schema revealed in Akan proverbs?

2. How is the connection between LIVING and MOVEMENT expressed in orientational metaphors conceptualising relations to *space*?
3. In what ways do the various proverbs and their conventional metaphors and schemas reflect the Akan philosophy of *living*?

The discussion begins with an attempt to distinguish the LIVING IS MOVEMENT schema from the universal LIFE IS A JOURNEY metaphor and to establish the meaning of the concept *movement* as used in the chapter. It then examines the Akan philosophy of life and living as a preparation of the discussions that follow. The discussion proper focuses, first, on the conceptual metaphors in the schema, including SUSTENANCE IS MOVEMENT, PROGRESS IS MOVEMENT, UNSAFETY IS OUTSIDENESS/SAFETY IS INSIDENESS; SAFETY/HONOUR IS MOVEMENT, SAFETY/PROSPERITY IS JUDICIOUS MOVEMENT IN SPACE AND TIME, and orientational considerations involving IN/INSIDENESS and OUT/OUTSIDENESS. The second part of the chapter looks at the orientational metaphors as expressed in the proverbs. Spicing all these discussions would be the Akan philosophical underpinnings, which would be taken up as necessary.

2. Theoretical framework

The study is set in cognitive semantics, which is concerned with conceptual content and its organisation in language (Talmy 2000). Its underlying principles include the relationship between the organisation of the cognitive mind and physical, human experience (embodied) and the fact that the experience of the world creates a conceptual structure, or structure of meaning, which becomes the basis for the conceptualisation, inference, and expression of human experience (Evans and Greene 2006: 160–62). Within this general idea of cognitive semantics, the chapter set out to investigate the conceptual representation of movement in Akan proverbs as an embodiment and expression of living as a human experience.

The study falls within the broad cognitive semantic framework, and is guided by Lakoff and Johnson's (1980) CMT, which is concerned with the establishment of the systematic correspondence, in the conceptual system, between the target and source domains. In this regard, the study looks at the concepts within the proverbs with the ultimate aim of discovering how the aspects of the source domains revolving around movement reflect ideas about the human being, who is the target. Again, the chapter exploits Lakoff and Turner's (1989) the GREAT CHAIN metaphor theory and its extended form (Krzeszowski 1997: 68), which explain the correspondence between items on different levels of the hierarchy of beings and their use in the interpretation of metaphors and proverbs. Finally, the chapter employs the cognitive concept of schema, originally expressed by Lakoff and Johnson (1980) and developed in Johnson (1987) as orientational metaphors, to help account for the recurrent spatial representations of IN, UP, OUT and AWAY in the conceptualisation of movement, position and posture as a representation of *living* in the Akan proverb.

3. Research methodology

The study seeks to investigate Akan people's understanding and expression of their experiences, and it involves some content analysis. It relies on proverbs collected across different sources including book collection of Akan proverbs (Rattray 1916; Akrofi 1962; Agyeman-Duah et al. 2017). I also obtained some from online sites including especially www.adinkrasymbols.org and gh.opera.news/gh/en, and from my relevant online social media pages where I requested for suggestions for sayings and proverbs about movement and life; and on some of these pages, I also had discussions on the interpretation of some of the sayings and proverbs. Finally, I relied on my knowledge and intuition as a native speaker of the Akan language.

The procedure involves, first, an identification of the 'movement and living/life' ethos of each proverb, then each problem is broken down using the conceptual metaphor framework to identify their sources and targets and their philosophies. These are used to group the proverbs into their different perspectives in relation to movement and philosophical values. Finally, proverbs are taken through spatial analysis in order to discover the relevant cognitive representations that are used for the discussion of the orientational metaphors.

4. Conceptual representation, metaphor, and philosophy

4.1 From LIFE IS A JOURNEY to LIVING IS MOVEMENT

Life has often been represented as a journey, a movement from place A to B, with metaphors representing various aspects of this movement. Lakoff and Turner (1989: 60–61) express the pervasiveness of the journey metaphor as follows:

> Our understanding of life as a journey uses our knowledge about journeys. All journeys involve travellers, paths travelled, places where we start, and places where we have been. Some journeys are purposeful and have destinations that we set out for, while others may involve wandering without any destination in mind,

consciously or more likely unconsciously, a correspondence between a traveller and person living life, the road travelled and the 'course' of a lifetime, a starting point and a time of birth, and so on.

They identify the following conceptual correspondences between the two conceptual domains of JOURNEY (as source) and LIFE (as target):

- The person leading a life is a traveller
- His purposes are destinations
- The means for achieving purposes are routes
- Difficulties in life are impediments to travel
- Counsellors are guides
- Progress is the distance travelled
- Things you gauge your progress by are landmarks
- Choices in life are crossroads
- Material resources and talents are provisions

Kövecses (2005) presents the following mappings between LIFE and JOURNEY:

- travellers → people leading a life
- motion along the way → leading a life
- destination(s) → purpose(s) of life
- different paths to one's destination(s) → different means of achieving one's purpose(s)
- distance covered along the way → progress made in life
- locations along the way → stages in life
- guides along the way → helpers or counsellors in life

LIFE IS A JOURNEY conceptual metaphor is similarly discussed by Katz and Taylor (2008) who focus on the conceptualised events up to one's old age and the cognitive reactions to these experiences as a part of the journey of life. Abdulmoneim (2006) looks at the metaphor of LIFE IS A JOURNEY from the point of view of the representations in the Holy Quran. Since the journey here is associated with one's religious journey, it includes the related concepts of THESTRAIGHTWAY and THE WAY OF HELL.

Life is experienced to mean movement of things within persons, animals and other living things. Out-body movements are dependent on in-body movements or functions, so a when one makes a step of even an inch, we know that it is because there is a movement of heart, veins and limbs within. LIFE IS A JOURNEY is a representation of existence from its beginning to the end, reflecting the different situations, roles, decisions etc. which all end ultimately with death or salvation. With its focus on life and death then, the LIFE IS A JOURNEY metaphor could be seen generally as in-body or existential, since the ultimate consideration is the spots and experience and roles between the onset of physical existence and the end of it.

Departing from this is a schematic focus, not on the movements between the polarities of life, but on the movements while life goes on. It is based not on the primary focus on the in-body movements on which life is premised. LIVING IS MOVEMENT takes off from this schema but departs in the sense that the representations in LIFE IS A JOURNEY are about the transitions in life; living is concerned not about this movement from the beginning to the end, but about movements *within* life. These movements do not signify the transience of life with its other implications, but about the fact that *living* itself involves movements of things, such that *not moving* could be seen as *having life* anyway, but *not living*. Thus, within a broad consideration of existence is the manner or nature of the experience of existence, and this is where the LIVING IS MOVEMENT SCHEMA and philosophy features.

This schema could be precedent on the idea that all things that have life exhibit some movement, bodily or mentally, to indicate their existence. However, since the body is what is observable, it becomes the basis for the cognitive schemas of embodied metaphor. Basson (2011: 19–20) presents the relationship between *living* and *movement* thus:

> Although daily movement from one point to the next is considered a rather mundane motor activity, it is crucial for our everyday functioning and interaction in the world. In fact, to be alive is to be in motion. As we go about our daily activities, we perceive our own bodies and other objects as being in motion.
> Motion plays an important role in both our perceptual organisation and in our linguistic conceptualisation of reality. As one of our most basic motor activities, movement lies at the core of our functioning in the world. Not surprisingly, motion features prominently in our conceptual system.

MOVEMENT or MOTION is understood to cover all conscious displacement associated with a protagonist – a human being or any of its lower rank representation, and these include in-body or out-body movements. IN-BODY movements are movements of the parts of the body within the body itself, i.e., sitting, rising, and even the movement of deep inner organs as the eyes and the tongue, whilst BODY-OUT movements are those that, by oneself or by another, go beyond one's own position area. Thus, running, flying, climbing, and throwing of objects could be said to be body-out. Another consideration of movement is the circumstantiality – way or direction of movement, duration or time, speed, path of movement as well as the frequency of movement. In this respect, the chapter seeks to investigate how far the cognitive representations of in-body and body-out movements reflect the Akan philosophy of living – the way in which life is lived for an optimal experience.

4.2   The Akan philosophy of life and its living

It would be useful, at this juncture, to discuss the Akan philosophy of life/living, drawing attention to the distinction between 'life' and 'living', and the major philosophical concepts or values that underlie these notions. Akan is a Kwa language spoken predominantly in Southern Ghana, its major sub-dialects including Agona, Akwapim, Akyem, Asante, Bono, Breman, Denkyira, Fante, and Wassa. In addition to these sub-dialects, there are other historical Akan dialects in Ghana including, Ahanta, Sefwi, Nzema, Aowin and the Baule and Anyi in neighbouring Cote D'Ivoire as well as the Abono ethnic group, which is the other half of the Bono group in Ghana. This chapter, however, focuses on the Modern Akan language as spoken in Ghana. These dialects have a very high mutual intelligibility, and unlike their phonological and grammatical variations, their vocabulary, and even more so, their idioms, proverbs, and cognitive representations are common.

The Akan tries to make a rather subtle distinction between *life* (existence) and *living*; and as in the mappings of Lakoff and Turner (1989) and Kövecses (2005), the aspects of existence and livelihood seem to have been fused. The difficulty of a strict distinction of the two comes from the understanding that there is no way one sees or speaks of existence without bringing in the issue of how life itself is lived. This notwithstanding, the Akan makes a conceptual distinction between *nkwa* (life) and *owu* (death), on the one hand, which are related directly to the existential, and expressions such as *ɔbra* 'life', *abrabɔ* 'living', and *asetena* 'life', on the other, which are connected to the nature of the experience of existence. Christaller (1881: 46) sees *ɔbra* as "the coming into this world, the state of existence or life in this world", adding "manner of life…conduct". The other issues of existentialism relating to destiny are also associated with *ɔbra*. When the verb *bɔ* 'create' is added, the meaning shift to the efforts and decisions in the way of life; i.e., *living*. Christaller's (1881) entry for *abrabɔ* focuses on the idea of *living*, but also mentions the 'life in this world'. Thus, it seems that whilst the concept ɔBRA may in its deepest sense refer to 'existence' and ABRABƆ to 'way of living', the two are connected since, as explained earlier, living reveals existence, and existence is the basis and the culmination of living. In this connection, the Akan concepts of LIFE and LIVING could be constructed using either of the two expressions, *ɔbra* 'life' and *abrabɔ* 'living'.

Our attention in the discussion of the Akan concept of life would depend, thus, on the actual sense as carried in the saying or proverb. The following sayings reflect the Akan philosophy of life and living:

Chapter 8. LIVING IS MOVEMENT   211

- *Ɔbra yɛ ko.*
  life   BE war
  Lit. 'Life is war'.
- *Abrabɔ yɛ animia.*
  living   BE endurance
  Lit. 'Life is endurance'.
- *Ɔbra yedi   no   adane-adane.*
  life 1PL experience DEF changes-changes
  Lit. 'Life involves changing experiences'.
- *Ɔbra yɛ aforosiane.*
  life   BE ascending-descending
  Lit. 'Life is ascending and descending'.
- *Ɔbra te sɛ   bɔɔdedwo: w'ankisa a   ɛbɛhye.*
  life   BE like plantain-roast: 2SG tend CONJ 3SIG-INGR-burn.
  Lit. 'Life is like roasting plantain: if you don't attend to it, it will burn.'
- *Ɔbra ne woara   bɔ.*
  life   BE 2SG-REFLEX create
  Lit. 'Life is by personal effort and experience'.
- *Ɔbra twa wu.*
  life   cuts death
  Lit. 'Life moves inevitably to death'.

It would be noticed that apart from the last saying, which could be said to be concerned with the existentiality of life, the others, in spite of the alternative use of *ɔbra* 'life' or *abrabɔ* 'living' are all focused on the experience of life, how is it that life is lived. The concepts of WAR, FIRE, and constant ASCENDING AND DESCENDING in the expressions of *ko* 'war', and *hye* in *ɛbɛhye* 'burn' *aforosiane* 'ascending-descending' reflectthe challenging nature of the experience of life. To these challenges, the sayings also reflect the nature of posturing, understanding and effort that one needs in order to thrive in success: *animia* 'endurance', *kisa* 'turn with care' and *woara bɔ* 'by oneself'. Within the considerations of *ko* 'war', and *hye* 'burn', one can identify the concepts OPPOSITION, ADVERSITY, and FAILURE; and it is against the background of these notions that the attitudes of personal effort, perseverance and vigilance or alertness are recommended as effective response to the fighting, fire, and unpredictability that characterise life.

5. Discussions

The examination of the cognitive representation of movement in Akan proverbs about 'living' is undertaken with three main considerations. First is a discussion of the MOVEMENT IS LIVING conceptual metaphor, which is undertaken under its different conceptual themes. The next section, from a schema point of view, examines the relationship between the Akan conceptualisation of LIVING and spatial orientations in is called orientational metaphors. Within all these is the discussion of the Akan philosophy of *life and living*, which is fused in the analysis.

5.1 The LIVING IS MOVEMENT schema

Conceptual metaphors in this schema include SUSTENANCE IS MOVEMENT, PROGRESS IS MOVEMENT, and SAFETY IS MOVEMENT.

5.1.1 *The SUSTENANCE IS MOVEMENT metaphor*

Sustenance is about the maintenance of breath: that one remains alive; and it includes sickness, which challenges one's experience of existence, as well as other bodily needs, especially food and water. Some Akan proverbs reflect the Akan philosophy of the centrality of movement in the maintenance of existence, and in this sense, living becomes connected to life itself:

(1) *Anoma anntu a obuada.*
 bird NEG-fly CONJ 3SG-hungers-sleeps
 Lit. 'If the bird fails to fly it lies famishing'.

(2) *Wote faako a wote w'adeɛ so.*
 2SG-sit place-one CONJ 2SG-sit 2SG-POSS-things on
 Lit. 'When you sit immobile, you sit on the progress of your things'.

Table 1. Conceptual representation of LIVING IS MOVEMENT

	Source domain	Target domain	Movement concepts
Anoma anntu a obua da. 'The bird that doesn't fly lies down famishing'.	Bird not flying: Bird famishing	Lazy, effortless person who famishes and suffers	*anntu: bua da* 'not flying: lying hungry'
Wote faako a wote w'adeɛ so. 'If you sit at one place you sit on you progress'.	Sitting immobile: thwarting progress	Effortless, gutless person, who destroys one's own progress	*te faako – te…so* 'sitting – thwarting'

The idea of LIVING or LIFE is evident in the related concepts of 'the bird' and 'flying'. The bird is associated with or defined first by its features and wings, which are for flying, which is believed to be its main source of life and sustenance. The philosophy is 'moving out ensures that life goes on, and moving out brings nourishment'.

Using the *bird* imagery makes *flying* a natural, unavoidable behaviour; and that is why its absence is linked to the existential – *famishing*, which is associated with emaciation, weakness, and eventual death. MOVEMENT, thus, is presented as an existential need for general livelihood and prosperity. In this context, movement brings 'nourishment'. The concept of NOURISHMENT, primarily associated with *food*, is a metaphor representing all aspects of satisfaction or maintenance of the BIRD (source) and the HUMAN BEING (target) physically, mentally, emotionally, spiritually, etc.

5.1.2 The PROGRESS IS MOVEMENT metaphor

The cognitive representation of *movement* and *progress* is best understood when put side-by-side the SUSTENANCE IS MOVEMENT metaphor as presented above. The FAMISHING IS ZERO MOVEMENT image is distinguished in terms of cognitive value from NO SOLUTION/NO PROGRESS IS ZERO MOVEMENT in the sense that the two represent a shift from MOVEMENT FOR EXISTENCE to MOVEMENT FOR PROGRESS/ UPLIFTMENT. The major difference is evident in the resultant images of ZERO MOVEMENT – *bua da* 'sleeping in hunger' and *...te wʹadeɛ so* 'sitting on something', which is itself a metaphorical expression meaning 'prevention of growth', or 'repression', or 'clampdown'. This is supported by the idea that the actions in the two clauses of the proverb are the same, i.e., 'sitting', and performed by the same actor. In this sense, one becomes the architect of one's own retrogression.

Another cognitive fact worth noting is the differential presentation of the lower order being 'the bird' and the higher order 'the human being'. The animal (lower order) is generally associated with naturalness, and its activities are generally tied to its natural needs. The human being is, conversely, a combination of the natural and the optional, i.e., artificial aspects of life. Therefore, 'being a bird' implies 'flying', or 'keeping one's existence' since the bird needs to fly in order to obtain food and other bodily needs to live on. However, 'being a human being' does not necessarily mean moving or that a human being does not need to move out to obtain natural bodily needs. Thus, movement brings sustenance to the bird, but it brings prosperity, which is an option, to a human being; hence, PROSPERITY IS MOVEMENT. It is evident that the lower order concept of BIRD is needed to construct the EXISTENCE IS MOVEMENT metaphor to reflect the Akan philosophy of movement as an existential need. Yet, the higher order concept HUMAN BEING is needed for the PROGRESSING IS MOVEMENT metaphor, which points to the Akan philosophy that prosperity is a choice for every human being.

Alongside the discussions of the movements is the identification of two major spatial orientations – IN (the space originally or naturally associated with the experiencer) and OUT (the space outside of the experiencer's natural space). The two conceptual descriptions discussed above point to the cognitive situation:

- EMPTINESS/STAGNATION IS IN
- PLENITUDE/PROGRESS IS OUT

'Not flying' and 'sitting at one place', thus, represent a concentration on IN with the result of lack of nourishment and lack of progress, which together represent emptiness and stagnation. The converse, 'flying' or 'stepping out' represent nourishment or fullness and prosperity. I return to the idea of spatial orientations in forthcoming sections.

5.1.3 The SAFETY/HONOUR IS MOVEMENT metaphor

OUT may be associated with plenitude and progress, as indicated above, but it is with this same spatial orientation that we find threat to peace, introducing a cognitive concept, DANGER IS OUT. This is based on the understanding that there could be competing interests for plenitude and progress outside, bringing contestation, adversity, and threat, which would associate both prosperity and danger to the same spatial orientation. Thus, PROGRESS IS OUT: DANGER IS OUT becomes the complex cognitive and philosophical consideration as expressed in proverbs (3), (4), and (5) below:

(3) Ɔkɔtɔ dwane kɔ po mu.
     crab   escapes go sea inside
     Lit. 'The crab escapes into the sea'.

(4) Ɔtwe ne ɔtwe ko na wohun gyahene a wodwane bɔmu.
     duyker and duyker fight and 3PL-see fire-king CONJ 3PL-escape together
     Lit. 'When two duykers are fighting and they see a lion, they escape together'.

(5) Nkuro dɔɔso a yɛntena faako nnye   animguaseɛ.
     towns plenty CONJ 1PL-stay one-place NEG-take face-pour-down
     Lit: 'With several towns, we don't stay at one place to face disgrace'.

The underlying conceptual metaphor in the proverbs above is SAFETY IS MOVEMENT. In proverb (3), the central idea *dwane* 'escaping' is defined as 'to slip away from pursuit or peril; avoid capture, punishment, or any threatened evil'; and two things are central to the pragmatics of *escaping*:

- What one is escaping from
- Where one is escaping to

The proverb seems not interested in 'from what?' and this makes the idea of 'escape' generic and an unavoidable part of life. To the issue of 'to what'/'where', we have *po mu* 'into the sea', and this is crucial in arriving at the cognitive import of the proverb and its place in Akan philosophy:

- The sea is a natural habitat for the crab and other aquatic creatures,
- The sea is wide and easily covers the crab and shields it from its pursuers,
- The land, on the contrary, restricts the crab to holes, which makes it easily pursuable,
- The crab generally settles at the bottom of the sea, which gives it maximum security.

Associated with the proverb is the metaphor SAFETY IS WITHIN, or BEING SAFE IS BEING WITHIN/INSIDE. The 'sea' (source) maps onto 'one's own territory'. That is to say,

- place of one's knowledge
- place of one's own kind
- place of adequate space
- place of adequate shelter

However, surely, the cognitive concept SAFETY IS WITHIN does not contradict the earlier ones that associate sustenance and prosperity with MOVING OUT, but complements it in the expression of the Akan philosophy of life. SAFETY as presented in the proverb is 'a response to threat in movements towards sustenance and prosperity'. In that sense, in terms of sequencing, the call for MOVEMENT FOR SAFETY comes after the call to MOVEMENT FOR PROSPERITY. In a composite philosophy then, 'we move out for sustenance and prosperity, but we escape within when we come under threat', as illustrated by abovementioned proverb (4).

The central philosophy of safety is expressed in the *dwane* 'escape', but three other things come out here:

- The situation before the escape – internal conflict/fighting
- What they are escaping from – the lion (external force)
- Manner of escape – antelopes together

By connecting the situation before the escape and the manner of escape around the antelopes themselves – in the presentation of disjunction (fighting) and conjunction (together) – the proverb connects 'safety' not to 'space' (as in the case of the crab), but to 'human relationship', with the cognitive principle: SAFETY IS HUMAN RELATIONSHIP. Thus, the fallout philosophies are:

- Togetherness is safety
- Safety is more important than interest
- Safety is natural, interest is artificial and selfish
- Existential safety is more important than optional, self-centred interest

Whilst *dwane* 'escape' seems to be the overt central concept of MOVEMENT, the philosophy rests on the movement as expressed in *ko* 'fight' and *bɔ mu* (lit. 'hit together' – unite). *Dwane* 'escape' focuses on movement from an external force, whilst *ko* and *bɔ mu* are conflictual and harmonising movements within. This is further discussed below. In 'fighting', we see power in opposite directions, but against a single identity of 'the antelope', since the two in the fight together represent the natural phenomenon of the 'antelope'. Therefore, *ko* 'fighting' becomes MOVEMENT WITHIN FOR MUTUAL DESTRUCTION. *Bɔ mu*, conversely, gives the image of 'joining together – from different positions). In the two, then, we see MOVEMENTS IN SEPARATION and MOVEMENTS IN UNITY.

The philosophy of 'safety' and 'movement' does not rest on the concept of 'escaping from the lion', but in 'escaping together', endorsing the cognitive principle, SAFETY IS RELATIONSHIP or SAFETY IS TOGETHERNESS. Thus, safety may not just be in the fact of the movement away from an external force, but that this movement is done together in unity. Here, the source *dwane bɔ mu* 'escape together' maps onto human concepts such as, 'looking together', 'thinking together', 'deciding together', 'moving together', etc. as the target concepts. Connecting to the conceptualisation of movement and safety, IN-MOVEMENT for unity, *bɔ mu* becomes the strength for a successful OUT-MOVEMENT from the enemy,

Proverb (5) instantiating the SAFETY IS MOVEMENT metaphor captures the central issue of movement or escape indirectly as *yɛntena faako* 'We don't remain at a place', and the cause of escape is *animguaseɛ* 'dishonour', which, as a source, maps onto all human experiences that negate well-being, peace, progress, safety, honour, health, etc., as its target. In this proverb, we see a shift from the representation of lower beings (the crab and the antelope), in proverbs (3 and 4), to the use of the higher being (human being). Again, we see a change from the direct representation of *wodwane* 'escaping' to the indirect representation of *yɛntena faako* 'not remaining at a place'. Finally, there is a cognitive change from the representation of the existential, mandatory situations of animals running away from their assailants for basic safety, to a more discretionary situation of one possibly enduring dishonour, curtailing it after sometime, or avoiding it altogether.

One important reflection here is the presentation of the conceptual principle: UNSAFETY IS OUTSIDE/ SAFETY IS INSIDE and the way this is represented across the three proverbs. The concept OUTSIDE/INSIDE is captured with different cognitive considerations in proverb (3). OUTSIDE could be seen as external to one's most natural or bona fide space. In the sea (INSIDE), all natural dwellers are animals, who are all secure. Outside of the sea, the width of space is reduced and there is a greater tendency of the threat from other beings and conditions. Conversely, in proverb (4), the concept of OUTSIDE/INSIDE is expressed in terms of not only space, where bona fide space is INSIDE AND SAFE, and non-bona fide space where aliens could be as OUTSIDE AND UNSAFE. There is also the concept of INSIDE with respect to 'bond in kind' or 'unity', where lack of bonding or unity is seen as 'outside of oneself'. In that sense, the onset of *unsafety* or OUTSIDENESS is not the appearance of the lion, but the fight between the antelopes; for, perhaps, if they were united together, their departure from the location of the lion or their mutual vigilance may have made them avoid the imminent danger posed by the lion, in the first place. In the same sense, then, though still OUT in the same space as the lion, their 'escaping together' is INSIDE and points to safety.

Finally, in proverb (5), the concept of INSIDE/OUTSIDE is seen in terms of oneness or cohesion in a community, as with the situation of the antelopes. However, in the case of the antelopes, there is a natural external threat in the form of *the lion*. In this proverb, the internal and external are both posturing within human community. *Nkuro* refers to 'community', a people bonded and united in trust and mutual support, which cognitively points to INSIDENESS, and any situation of absence of bonding, trust, or support points to OUTSIDENESS. It is in this context that it would be advised that one looks for another community of trust and support, which becomes a new 'inside'. Proverb (6) below reinforces the metaphor of COHESION IS INSIDENESS through the picture of the alternation of eating and keeping watch between a pair of antelopes for common safety and nourishment.

(6) *Hwɛso-ma-mennidi-bi   nti   na   atwe   mmienu nam.*
    look-on let-me-eat-some reason that duykers two   move
    Lit. 'Look-on-as-I-also-eat is why antelopes move in pairs'.

The idea of the external threat is not mentioned, but the cognitive principle is that two basic things are needed simultaneously – *nourishment* and *security*. *Nourishment* is presented in the conceptual metaphor GETTING NOURISHMENT IS MOVEMENT OUT as discussed, and *security* is based on the principle and metaphor SAFETY IS KEEPING WITHIN. Since nourishment/sustenance and security/safety are concurrent needs, the antelopes, whilst *outside* to seek nourishment for sustenance, take turns to nourish and watch out for possible threats to their safety. SAFETY being cognitively connected to INSIDENESS, it is necessary to explain how the idea of *the inside* is conceptualised in the proverb. Here, we see INSIDENESS not as spatially construed, but in terms of the 'bonding of communality', and OUTSIDENESS in terms of all this that defy or challenge the bonding. It is important to observe that, here, 'communality' is distinguished from 'nature' or typology;

thus, the animals do not exhibit communality just because they of the same animal species (as antelopes), but that they exhibit bonding in their activities, which is only enhanced by their natural typology as antelopes. INSIDENESS is, thus, evident in

- moving out in pairs
- finding food together
- being together in consciousness about the adversary
- arranging and practising the alternation of eating and keeping watch
- maintaining to be each other's keeper and common keepers of unity

The concentration on bonding in the determination of INSIDENESS is reinforced by other proverbs, in Akan, which also project bonding and service above the naturalness of family relations:

(7) a. *Nnyɛ obi biribi ne ne bi; obi biribi ne nea w'ayɛ no yie*
NEG 3SG relation BE 3SG-POSS kin 3SG relation BE REL do-PERF 3SG good
Lit. 'It isn't one's kin who are his relations; one's true kin are those who do one good'.
b. *Anoma nua ne nea ɔne no da dua korɔ.*
bird sibling be REL with 3SG roost-on tree same
Lit. 'A bird's relative is the one with which it roosts on the same tree'.

5.1.4 *Inside may not be entirely safe*

Whilst going by the conceptual representation of SAFETY IS INSIDE, the Akan proverb, as seen in (12), further carries the idea that the cohesive principle of INSIDENESS could be more social than physical. Akan philosophy explores the caution that within the INSIDE, which is safety, could be hidden adversaries who are different from those OUTSIDE. The difference between the INSIDE-ADVERSARY and the OUTSIDE-ADVERSARY conceptualisation is that whereas the outside is anticipated, known, and could be avoided or challenged and defeated, the inside-adversary is often unanticipated, and cannot easily be identified; since it has the identity of an *insider*, but, in reality, operates from perspective of OUTSIDE. The fusion or confusion of SECURITY/INSECURITY and INSIDENESS/OUTSIDENESS gives the following cognitive situation:

- OUTSIDE IS INSIDE
- INSIDE IS OUTSIDE

The corresponding philosophy is:

- To be safe is to be among your own,
- but within those you see as your own,
- might be others who are not your own,

which is expressed in proverb (8):

(8) *Aboa   bi   bɛka   wo   a   ofiri   wo ntoma mu.*
    animal some ING-bite 2SG CONJ 3SG-come-from 2SG clothes inside
    Lit. 'The animal that bites you comes from inside your own clothes'.

The FUSION/CONFUSION is explained thus:

- *bɛka wo* 'bite you' – behaviour associated with OUTSIDE
- *aboa* 'animal' – not human, and therefore OUTSIDE
- *ntoma mu* 'your clothing' – state of INSIDENESS
- *firi wo ntoma mu* 'comes from inside your own clothes'– change of posture – from INSIDE to OUTSIDE

The philosophy is to attempt to keep the inside safe from OUTSIDE elements (enemies), to be watchful of elements INSIDE (monitoring their loyalty), or to ensure that OUTSIDE elements, even if they are able to hide successfully INSIDE, would not be able to launch an attack (ensuring constant vigilance and safety).

5.1.5 *SAFETY/PROSPERITY IS JUDICIOUS MOVEMENT metaphor*

As seen in the discussions above, the Akan philosophy of life cognitively associates both SUSTENANCE/PROSPERITY and INSECURITY with OUTSIDENESS. This presents a rather paradoxical situation since both *sustenance* and *security* are basic necessities of existence; for how could one be advised to step out in order to sustain and progress oneself, and at the same time be advised that stepping out is dangerous? Akan proverbs respond to this by drawing attention to relevant considerations and choices relating to OUTSIDENESS, in order that though one steps out, one would be able to avoid the insecurity of the OUTSIDE, and return INSIDE safe.

5.1.5.1 *Negotiating space with time*

A remarkable aspect of the proverbs of the Akan philosophy of life and its cognitive representation is the connection between MOVEMENT, on the one hand, and TEMPORALITY and SPATIALITY, on the other hand. The philosophy is that success (and security) in living depends not on the simple, primary consideration of MOBILITY against IMMOBILITY, but on the choices in mobility in relation to time/duration and spaces/routes. The close connection between spatiality and temporality is as a result of the fact that they are both underlying natural aspects of reality; i.e., that all things happen in space and in time, featuring simultaneously, making one's ability to negotiate their interplay a crucial aspect of life. The proverbs under consideration here are

(9) *Akokɔ da   ntɛm a   onnya   amanne.*
     fowl sleep early CONJ 3SG-NEG-get trouble
     Lit. 'If a fowl roosts early, it avoids trouble'.

(10) *Nwansana kyɛ   funu   ho a   wosie   no.*
     housefly delays corpse side CONJ 3PL-bury 3SG
     Lit. 'If the housefly stays too long around the corpse it gets buried also', or, 'The housefly that stays too long around the corpse gets buried too'.

(11) *Anoma kyɛ   dua so a   ɔgye   boɔ.*
     bird delays tree on CONJ 3SG-collects stone
     Lit. 'If a bird perches too long on a tree, it gets stoned'.

(12) *Wo twa mu twa mu a   wobisa w'ase.*
     2SG pass pass   CONJ 3PL-ask 2SG-POSS-source
     Lit. 'If you draw unnecessary attention, you expose yourself/put yourself at a risk'.

The TIME schema is expressed in such concepts as, *ntɛm* 'early' in (9), *kyɛ* 'for a long time' in (10, 11), and *twa mu twa mu* 'passing and passing' in (12), which points to stretching out time-duration. As discussed above, space is categorised into IN-SPACE and OUT-SPACE, where *in-space*, a territory identified as one's own regular space associated is with safety, and, OUT-SPACE isa territory outside one's space, which is psychologically identified as 'belonging to others'. The OUT-SPACE is associated with insecurity, and this represented directly or in the reverse in the proverbs as shown in proverb (9) wherein *da* 'roost/be home' is spatially interpreted as:

- In one's own territory – safety
- Outside of the danger territory – safety

In proverb (10), *funu ho* 'by the corpse' is interpreted as:

- Outside of the fly's space – unsafety
- In the space of humans (mourners) – unsafety

The underlying philosophy is:

- Staying out for long is unsafe
- Coming in early is safe

In proverbs (9)–(12) then, the fowl goes out, in keeping with the philosophical and cognitive conceptualisation that PROSPERITY/SUSTENANCE IS OUT, but comes roosting (IN) early enough (TIME) to avoid trouble. The case of the housefly is worth a more extensive explanation. The insect is generally associated with decomposition, putrid smells, incinerators and human habitation or congregation – including the where a corpse is laid in state, which combines human congregation and decomposition. To go these places is to 'move out'; and in such places, the housefly would be able to get nourishment. However, since these places are the natural environments for the housefly, it could also be seen as 'staying/moving in'.

In the context, the area around the corpse is IN, because it has the decomposition, which is the natural environment of the fly. Yet, it is also OUT, because it is a space shared with humans, for whose sake there is a corpse; and more importantly, it is under the power of humans, who control the environment and its activities, including the burial and its organisation. With this combination of INSIDENESS and OUTSIDENESS, the compromise behaviour for the housefly is to stay, for as long as the corpse is in state, but not up to the burial, when human's take full control of the space and turn the space SHARED to OUTSIDE space for the housefly. *Funu ho* 'by the corpse' maps onto all situations of both exposure and risk in the life of a human being, some of them might appear most comfortable; and the resultant *wosie no* 'is buried with the corpse' maps onto all adversities that befall one for overstaying one's peace within the arena of risk.

A similar situation is captured in proverb (11). *Dua so* 'on a tree' is both an OUT-SPACE and IN-SPACE for the bird, whose natural territory is the sky, which is therefore the bird's IN-SPACE. Yet, the bird perches on a tree, where it could also have food, satisfying the need to *move out* for prosperity and sustenance. However, it is the same place where the bird encounters the human being. Human beings work in and exploit the land where trees can be found. The tree, rather than the high altitude of the skies, is within the reach of human missiles. Perching on the tree, the bird has a stability of posture, which gives the human pursuer the stability of aiming, rendering it vulnerable for attacking. In this context, *dua so* 'on a tree' could be conceptualised as OUT space. However, here, again, the insecurity is not in the perching itself (OUT-SPACE), but in the extensive perching time, which allows humans to take note, aim, and fire missiles at it.

Exposure or insecurity may not just be associated with delaying but with overexposure, or in drawing needless attention, and this is expressed in proverb (12). *Twa mu twa mu* 'passing by repeatedly' is basically a spatial consideration, but its repeated nature gives it an extensive time coverage, and it could be explained as 'a long time' of self-exposure or 'a delay outside'. The cognitive distinction between *twa mu* and *twa mu twa mu* is in the difference between a 'regular passing through' to one's destination and 'keep passing and passing' where some people are to draw their attention. Possible reactions or interpretations for *twa mu twa mu* 'keep passing and passing' include the following:

- For passing in and out repeatedly, one could be looking for something in the area – drawing curiosity,
- One could be spying on the activities of people gathered in the arena – drawing suspicion,
- One could be a stranger who may have lost direction or who could be looking for somebody – drawing attention,
- One could be seeking to draw attention to oneself – drawing curiosity or scorn.

The resultant concept *wobisa w'ase*, lit. 'they enquire about your source or beginning' can be best understood when interpreted from the point of view of the response to the enquiry, i.e., *kyerɛ NP ase* 'reveal NP's sources'. The regular risk in 'getting one's sources revealed' it is that the negatives around one's ancestry, parentage, siblings and one's own life are included, making it not just an explanation one's identity, but an exposition of the negatives about one's life. *Wobisa w'ase* maps therefore onto the general idea of vulnerability, based on the philosophy:

> 'Go out for the necessities of life, but don't stay too much out that you would put yourself at risk', or, 'Do not overexpose yourself or you would become vulnerable'.

5.1.5.2 SAFETY IS CHANGE OF DIRECTION/OUT-SPACE *metaphor*

Safety, as seen above, is associated with the judicious control of exposure to danger or attack. However, attacks may still come; and in such cases, safety may not come by one avoiding danger through the judicious use of time in the OUT-SPACE, but through the exploitation of alternative spaces within the OUTSPACE, as revealed in proverbs (13), (14), and (15).

(13) Ɔpɔnkɔ mman   kwa.
     horse NEG-change-path nothing
     Lit. 'The horse does not branch for nothing'.

(14) Ɔkɔtɔ pem bo   a   ɔsan   n'akyi.
     crab hits rock CONJ 3SG-turn 3SG-POSS-back
     Lit. 'The crab retreats when it hits a rock'.

(15) Obi nnyina   nkran   mu   ntutu   nkran.
     INDEF NEG-stand driver-ants inside NEG-pluck driver-ants
     Lit. 'One does not stand pluck driver-ants from oneself whilst still standing in their colonies'.

In proverbs (13)–(15), this is conceptually represented as SAFETY IS CHANGE OF DIRECTION/POSITION. The conceptual metaphor is presented in a cognitive structure involving: THE PHENOMENON MOVING – THE OBSTACLE – THE AVOIDANCE RESPONSE – RESULTANT SAFETY.

The phenomenon 'moves' in recognition of the schema LIVING IS MOVEMENT and the conceptual metaphors, PROSPERITY/SUSTENANCE IS MOVEMENT/OUT and UNSAFETY IS OUTSIDE as discussed above, which points simultaneously to the need for security and prosperity associated with OUTSIDENESS. However, if 'living' must go on in spite of obstacles and dangers, which makes it necessary for one to stay OUT for sustenance and prosperity, then one only needs to change the direction or location. This is captured in the conceptualisation of 'avoidance' or 'the exploitation of alternative spaces or routes' in:

- Diversion – *mman* – for another route to the same objective of movement (13)
- Retreat – *san akyi* – first an abandonment of a current move, and a second, for a possible adoption of other moves (14)
- Repositioning – *yennyina nkran mu* – for space to deal with problems of current movement (15)

These different *directions of movements and spaces* map out to all situations of change of plans, activities, job, decisions, and relationship in the face of unsurmountable barriers to meaningfulness in life. The philosophy is:

> 'Step out or work towards for sustenance and prosperity, but do not hesitate to change your plans and ways when your current moves appear unhelpful and intractable'.

5.2 LIVING IS MOVEMENT orientational metaphor – SUCCESS IS UP/AWAY; SECURITY IS/WITHIN

This section of the chapter attempts to see the proverbs as involving orientational metaphors that connect two crucial aspects of *living* – security and success – to spatial orientations. The discussions on 'security/safety in movement' earlier drew attention to the connection between space and philosophical concept. The identification and discussion of the cognitive concepts – SUCCESS IS UP/AWAY and SECURITY IS WITHIN – is based on the concept of orientational metaphors (Lakoff and Johnson 1980). Wilcox (2000: 97) expresses the orientational relationship between UPNESS and *goodness* thus:

> In the up-down category, the metaphorical mapping of 'upness' – or more specifically, and orientational metaphor GOOD IS UP – occurs in signs such as, HAPPY, RICH, IMPROVE, POSITIVE, SUCCESS, INVENT, WIN, EXCITE, PROMOTION, and SMILE, as well as many others.

5.2.1 Akan spatial conceptualisation

The Akan spatial conceptualisation of success (and failure) and the related senses of 'activity'and 'progress'is clearly seen in several expressions and sayings and in adposition elements. The saying points to an altitudinal conceptualisation of progress or success. *Aforosane* is literally interpreted as *foro* 'to climb' and *sane* 'to descend', making *aforosane*, lit. 'ascending and descending', which, in terms of orientation, is represented as UP and DOWN, or HIGH and LOW. Since in descending a hill, for instance, one expends less energy and effort than ascending, which demands energy (for the human being as well as even for the automobile), it is possible to argue that DESCENDING, with its sense of relief, rather inclines cognitively to PROGRESS.

(16) Ɔbra yɛ aforosiane.
      life BE climbing-descending
      Lit. 'Life is ascending and descending'.

The idea of *aforosane* (or *aforosiane*) is, for our discussions, seen in terms of *altitude* rather than *force*, where high altitude (*foro*) means 'high or up in the game' meaning 'progress' or 'success', and *siane* 'low' meaning 'down in the game' or 'failure', and this is where one can see the cognitive orientation of UP/HIGH to success. This is further clarified in the use of the term *asiane*. Christaller (1881: 436) defines *asiane* to include "impending danger, peril, adventure". With that definition, one observes that the concept was itself formed as a metaphor which links the source concept of 'descending' or 'going down a slope' to the target idea of 'negative happenings or experiences in life'. This, thus, points to the metaphorical orientation of success to UP and failure to DOWN.

One manifestation of the UP orientation to success, achievement or accomplishment in Akan is the use of the adposition element *so*, which is generally interpreted literally or metaphorically as ON/UP as against IN or BELOW. The expressions *nkɔsoɔ*, lit. 'going up' for progress and *di NP so*, lit. 'situate up of NP' for overcoming or victory point to a high altitudinal orientation (progress, triumph, and victory), as expressed in *so*. On the contrary, we conceptualise decline and disgrace, which could be seen as negative, in low altitudinal orientation, as in: *brɛ ase*, lit. 'press down' for decline, and *animguase*, lit. 'face pours down' for disgrace.

The use of *so* 'on' to refer to endeavour, or work, also speaks the UP orientation. We speak of *adwuma so*'on the job', in terms of the activities, goings-on in respect of the attainment of the goals of the organisation, as against *adwuma mu*, lit. 'in the workplace', where the emphasis is on the context of work, rather than the activities that lead to attainment or achievement. In the same way, *abɛ so*, lit.

'on the palm or palm tree' is used for activities involving the palm tree, especially in tapping and brewing of palm wine or related alcoholic beverages.

5.2.2 SUCCESS IS UP

In proverbs (17) and (18), the idea of *foro* 'climb' or 'mount' and *tu*, as in *anntu* 'not fly' are associated with UP, as one only climbs up and birds fly UP:

(17) Woforo   duapa   a   na   yepia   wo.
    2SG-climb tree-good CONJ then 1PL-push 2SG
    Lit. 'It is when you climb good trees that people would push you.'

(18) Anoma anntu   a obuada.
    bird   NEG-fly CONJ3SG-hungers-sleeps
    Lit. 'If the bird fails to fly it famishes.'

Moreover, it is to these activities that the idea of effort, activity, and eventual achievement, or success is associated. Thus, 'climbing' is progressive and UP. Again, in the idea of UP or HIGH is reflected in the concepts of *esie so* 'anthill' and *tenten* 'tall', and these all refer to situations of goodness or success.

(19) Yɛwo   wo to esie   so   a   wonkyere   tenten yɛ.
    3PL-born 2SG put anthill top CONJ 2SG-NEG-delay tall   be
    Lit. 'If you're born on an anthill, it doesn't take you long to become all.'

5.2.3 FAILURE IS LOW/STATIC

In the concepts *ahweasee*, lit. 'falling down', expressing 'failure', or 'flop', *animguasee*, lit. 'face pouring down' meaning 'disgrace', and *nkoguo*, lit. 'fight down' denoting 'defeat', or 'loss', the LOW/DOWN orientation is projected as follows: *Hwe* 'fall' or 'crush' and *gu* 'fall' or 'pour' are all connected in their senses to 'fall'. *Hwe* may refer to solids with *gu* to liquid, or things in their quantities, or with mass concepts. In both concepts, is the cognitive orientation of DOWN, because naturally nothing really falls or crushes 'up' or 'high'. Added to this inherent DOWNNESS is the use of *ase*. In addition, worthy of consideration is the term *asiane*, which as seen above, is a metaphorical representation of 'failure' or 'loss'.

In proverbs (20) and (21), the concepts *da fam*, lit. 'lie on the ground' and *hwe ase*, lit. 'crash down' signify 'failure', 'defeat', or 'destruction', whichpoint cognitively to LOW:

(20) Woda fam'   resu,   wose 'mesɔre a   w'awu'.
    2SG-lie ground cry-PROG, 2SG 1SG-rise COND 2SG-die
    Lit. 'You're lying down crying; you say: you're dead if I rise up.'

(21) *Woforo   dua a,   foro   dua tenten, na   wohwe ase   a   atumpan*
2SG-climb tree CONJ climb tree tall   CONJ 2SG-fall down CONJ talking
ama   wo   dammirifa.
drums give.FUT2SG condolences
Lit. 'When climbing a tree, climb the tall tree, so that when you fall, talking drums would give you condolences'.

The concept LOW in proverb (21) is underscored by the associated concepts *dammirifa* 'condolences' and *resu* 'crying', which also signify 'failure', 'pain', and 'regret'.

5.2.4 SUCCESS IS AWAY/FAILURE IS HERE

Associated with the concept of UP in relation to SUCCESS IS AWAYNESS. In fact, UP is a manifestation of AWAYNESS, and thus the orientational principle is AWAYNESS/UP IS SUCCESS, whilst IMMOBILITY/DOWN IS FAILURE. In proverb (22), *faako*, lit. 'same place' points to immobility, and the proverb denotes the absence of solutions to our drawbacks, which is failure.

(22) *Wote   faako   a   wote   w'adeɛ   so.*
2SG-sit place-one COND 2SG-sit 2SG-POSS-things on
Lit. 'When you sit immobile, you sit on your own progress'.

Similarly, proverb (23) sees success or achievement in terms of AWAYNESS, as represented in the concepts *kɔ* 'go' and *du* 'arrive'.

(23) *Wamma   wo yɔnko   antwa   ankɔ   a   wontwa   nnu.*
2SG-NEG-let 2SG neighbour NEG-cut NEG-go CONJ 2SG-NEG-cut NEG-reach
Lit. 'If you don't allow your neighbour to make progress you would not reach your goal'.

In the representation, we see comparative AWAYNESS *kɔ* 'go', which is associated with a departure from setback or a movement towards success or accomplishment, and *du* 'arrive' as a farther departure from setback and the attainment of success.

6. Conclusion

Philosophies and values could be said to be as much embodied as metaphors, because they arise from our experience of the world. Whilst philosophies are thought embodiments of experience, metaphors and proverbs are representational embodiments as we utilise the established cognitive principles to relate concepts to one another. It is therefore to be expected as in the discussions that the

Akan metaphorical proverbs and the cognitive orientations have so much in connection with the philosophies, and indeed, the proverbs could simply be seen as metaphorical representation of philosophical statements, which could be presented in non-metaphorical or metaphorical renditions.

In response to the objectives, the study found that Akan has a number of proverbs about life and living, which are constructed around the cognitive concept of movement. The study discovered, that operating with the general schema LIVING IS MOVEMENT, the proverbs have conceptual metaphors reflecting the issues of sustenance, progress, and security, with varied philosophical positions about the place of MOVEMENT in the attainment of these crucial concepts in the experience of life. The study observed that controlling the overall cognitive space is the concept of OUTSIDE and INSIDE or OUTSIDENESS and INSIDENESS, expressed in the conceptual metaphors and in the orientational metaphors SUCCESS IS UP/AWAY, SECURITY IS IN, and FAILURE IS IN. Since cognitive orientations, conceptual metaphors and philosophical values are all derived from the people's experiences, the proverbs, which are also based on the experiences, do reflect Akan philosophy. It would be necessary, going forward, to look at the place of causation in the conceptualisation of movement or motion in the enactment of the Akan philosophy of life and its living.

References

Abdulmoneim, B.M.S. (2006). The metaphorical concept "life is a journey" in the Qur'an: A cognitive-semantic analysis. *Metaphorik. de*, 10, 94–32.

Agyekum, K. (2021). Proverbs in Akan highlife lyrics: A case of Alex Konadu's lyrics. *Journal of Pragmatics*, 174, 1–13.

Agyeman-Duah, I., Appiah, K.A., & Appiah, P. (2017). *Proverbs of the Akans*. Banbury: Ayebia Clarke Publishing.

Akrofi, C.A. (1962). *Twi mmebusem: Twi proverbs, with English translations and comments*. London: Macmillan.

Aku-Sika, C.M. (2016). Gendered power relations as expressed in selected Ewe proverbs. MA Diss., University of Ghana, Legon.

Andersson, D. (2013). Understanding figurative proverbs: A model based on conceptual blending. *Folklore* 124(1), 28–44.

Basson, A. (2011). The path image schema as underlying structure for the metaphor moral life is a journey in Psalm 25. *OTE* 24(1), 19–29.

Buljan, G., & Gradečak-Erdeljić, T. (2013). Where Cognitive linguistics meets paremiology: A cognitive-contrastive view of selected English and Croatian proverbs. *Explorations in English Language and Linguistics* 1(1), 63–83.

Christaller, J. G. (1881). *A Dictionary of the Asante and Fante language called Tshi (Chwee, Twi): With a Grammatical Introduction and Appendices on the Geography of the Gold Coast and other subjects.* Basel: Evangelical Missionary Society.

Diabah, G., & Amfo, N. A. A. (2015). Caring supporters or daring usurpers? The representation of women in Akan proverbs. *Discourse & Society*, 26, 3–28.

Diabah, G., & Amfo, N. A. A. (2018). To dance or not to dance: Masculinities in Akan proverbs and their implications for contemporary societies. *Ghana Journal of Linguistics*, 7(2), 179–198.

Dobrovol'skij, D., Dobrovol'skiĭ, D. O, & Piirainen, E. (2005) *Figurative language: Cross-cultural and cross-linguistic perspectives.* Amsterdam: Elsevier.

Evans, V., & Green, M. (2006). *Cognitive linguistics: An introduction.* Mahwah: Lawrence Erlbaum Associates Publishers.

Fauconnier, G., & Turner, M. (2002). *The way we think: Conceptual blending and the mind's hidden complexities.* New York: Basic Books.

Johnson, M. (1987). *The body in the mind: The bodily basis of meaning, imagination, and reason.* Chicago: University of Chicago Press.

Katz, A. N., & Taylor, T. E. (2008). The Journeys of life: Examining a conceptual metaphor with semantic and episodic memory recall. *Metaphor and Symbol*, 23, 148–173.

Kazeem, F. A. (2010). Logic in Yoruba proverbs. Itupale: *Online Journal of African Studies*, 2, 1–14.

Kobia, J. M. (2016). A conceptual metaphorical analysis of Swahili proverbs with reference to chicken metaphor. *International Journal of Education and Research;* 4(2), 217–228.

Kövecses, Z. (2005). *Metaphor in culture: Universality and variation.* Cambridge: Cambridge University Press.

Krzeszowski, T. P. (1997). *Angels and devils in hell: Elements of axiology in semantics.* Warszawa: Wydawnictwo Energeia.

Lakoff, G., & Johnson, M. (1980). *Metaphors we live by.* Chicago: Chicago University Press.

Lakoff, G., & Turner, M. (1989). *More than cool reason: A field guide to poetic metaphor.* Chicago: University of Chicago Press.

Lemghari, E. (2017). Conceptual metaphors as motivation for proverbs lexical polysemy. *International Journal of Language and Linguistics*, 5(3), 57–70.

Mansyur, F. A., & Said, R. (2020). A cognitive semantics analysis of Wolio proverbs related to the human body. *Advances in Social Science, Education and Humanities Research*, 436 [1st Borobudur International Symposium on Humanities, Economics and Social Sciences], 259–262.

Nirmala, D. (2013). Local wisdom in Javanese proverbs (a cognitive linguistic approach). In J. S. Nam, & A. S. Nurhayati (Eds.), *Proceedings International Seminar 'Language Maintenance and Shift III'* (pp. 124–128). Semarang: Diponegoro University.

Norrick, N. R. (1985). *How proverbs mean. Semantic studies in English proverbs.* Berlin: Mouton.

Norrick, N. R. (2014). Subject area, terminology, proverb definitions, proverb features. In H. Hrisztova-Gotthardt, & M. A. Varga. *Introduction to paremiology: A comprehensive guide to proverb studies* (pp. 7–25). Berlin: De Gruyter Open.

Ogwudile, C.E.C. (2016) Encouragement proverbs and their discourse relevance: A case study of Oghe dialect of Igbo. *Mgbakoigba, Journal of African Studies*, 6(1), 1–10.

Olateju, A. (2005). The Yoruba animal metaphor: Analysis and interpretation. *Nordic Journal of African Studies* 14(3), 368–383.

Oluyemisi, A.O. (2017). Philosophical issues in Yoruba proverbs. *International Journal of African Society, Cultures and Traditions* 5(2), 21–30.

Rattray, R.S. (1916). *Ashanti proverbs*. Oxford: Clarendon.

Rodríguez, I.L. (2009). Of women, bitches, chickens and vixens: Animal metaphors for women in English and Spanish. *Culture, Language and Representation*, 7, 77–100.

Talmy, L. (2000). *Toward a cognitive semantics*. Cambridge, MA: MIT Press.

Wilcox, P.P. (2000). *Metaphor in American Sign Language*. Washington, DC: Gallaudet University Press.

Yankah, K. (1989). *The proverb in the content of Akan rhetoric: A theory proverb praxis*. Bern, Frankfurt au Main: Peter Lang.

CHAPTER 9

The role of Persian proverbs in framing Iran's nuclear program
A cognitive linguistic approach

Mohsen Bakhtiar
Ferdowsi University of Mashhad, Iran

This chapter explores how Persian proverbial metaphors are used in discourse to frame Iran's nuclear program. To that end, contextual uses of a sample of Persian proverbs were analysed in terms of Conceptual Metaphor Theory. The results demonstrate that proverbs' scope of operation goes way beyond their conventional functions. They are used to propagate pessimism, express sarcasm, make accusations, threaten and humiliate the rival camp, fabricate a new political reality, and manipulate the content and courses of action. The research also finds that proverbs are apt tools for framing complex socio-political issues, as they encapsulate a bundle of integrated figurative conceptualisations, providing users with ready-to-use conceptual slots to apply to complex scenarios with multiple roles and relations. Finally yet importantly, the research shows that the analysis of proverbs in discourse context provides a more comprehensive view of proverbs by completing the chain of association between the specific-level schema, generic-level schema and the immediate context of use.

Keywords: Iranian culture, Persian proverbs, Iran's nuclear deal, Iran's nuclear program, metaphor, metonymy, framing

1. Introduction

Iran's nuclear program has been one of the most controversial issues of international relations and has had impacts on the political situations in the Middle East as well as the economic status of millions of Iranians. Briefly, the crisis began in 2003 when information leaked that Iran had been covertly developing and planning its nuclear projects, which provoked alarm in the West and hot debates inside Iran between conservatives and reformists whether to suspend the nuclear project and cooperate with the international community (Mousavian 2012). Iran entered into negotiations with the EU-3 (France, Germany, and the United Kingdom) and agreed in October 2003 to suspend the enrichment activities, sign the Additional Protocol, and cooperate with the IAEA.

In 2005, the new president, Mahmoud Ahmadinejad, sharply criticised the preceding concessions and adopted a confrontational policy towards the West. The enrichment activities restarted and Iran ended its voluntary implementation of the Additional Protocol. In response, the IAEA reported Iran to the UN Security Council and several resolutions were passed against the country. During the presidency of Ahmadinejad, tensions with the international community further increased, as Iran boosted its nuclear activities by constructing more enrichment facilities. In return, the UN Security Council, the U.S. and the EU reacted by imposing heavier sanctions on Iran. The sanctions targeted the Central Bank of Iran and prohibited the import, financing, insurance, and brokering of Iran's natural gas and oil (Gaietta 2015; Joyner 2016).

In July 2015 after several rounds of failed negotiations over the years, Iran eventually signed an accord with the P5+1 formally known as the Joint Comprehensive Plan of Action (JCPOA). Under its terms, Iran agreed to reduce its stockpile of uranium and operational centrifuges, and open its nuclear facilities to more extensive inspections in exchange for sanction reliefs (www.theguardian.com, 14 July 2015). Despite the fact that Iran had abided by the terms of the deal in accordance with UNSCR 2231 (www.iaea.org/newscenter/focus/iran/iaea-and-iran-iaea-reports), in May 2018, then-U.S. president Donald Trump withdrew from the accord. He called it a flawed agreement, citing Iran's support for terrorism as well as pursuit of ballistic missiles as justifications for the U.S. withdrawal (www.nytimes.com, 08 May 2018). The economic sanctions were reactivated and new sanctions were imposed. The U.S. adopted the maximum pressure strategy to force Iran to negotiate over its ballistic missiles program and regional presence. During Trump's presidency, Iran never accepted to negotiate under sanctions and announced that it would not negotiate a new deal (www.middleeasteye.net, 25 September 2019). With Joe Biden becoming president in January 2021, hopes have risen for a revival of the JCPOA.

This research seeks to find out how Persian proverbs are employed in discourse to frame Iran's nuclear program. Moreover, it explores the figurative structure of the proverbs in order to present the specific ways in which Persian proverbial metaphors address various aspects of Iran's nuclear program. There has been a large number of research investigating proverbs and proverbial metaphors across languages and cultures (Mieder 1993; Gibbs and Beitel 1995; Moreno 2005; Maalej 2009; Belkhir 2012, 2021; Ben Salamh and Maalej 2018; Lemghari 2019). However, in many studies, proverbs have been researched as static metaphorical structures outside context. A large body of research has explored domain-specific proverbs (e.g., animal or food proverbs) or have focused on the metaphorical source domains and image schemas underlying the source domains, but there are not many studies with a focus on the dynamicity of the meaning of proverbs across discourse contexts (Orwenjo 2009; Barajas 2010). The versatile nature of proverbs should be examined in context, as "proverbs' semantic load is derived from the context and circumstances of use" (Orwenjo 2009: 125) and studying them outside linguistic context may not fully show their conceptual and pragmatic affordances. Therefore, a cognitive linguistic investigation of proverbs as dynamic figurative structures in discourse may reveal the various ways in which they fulfil communicative functions. The topic of the present study is a complex ongoing issue with ideological, social, political, and economic dimensions. The study of the selected Persian proverbs may explain why these pieces of conventional wisdom are deemed appropriate tools for the evaluation of the nuclear program. The other goal of the research is to discover which proverbs are specifically used to support the nuclear deal and which ones are used to oppose the deal. In addition, it would be interesting to see whether any of the proverbs could be used flexibly to reflect alternative views.

2. Proverbs in Cognitive Linguistics

Proverbs are concise statements of apparent truths and wisdom in colourful and formulaic language. They represent human experiences and express abstract social norms and moral concerns (Mieder 1993, 2004). Proverbs have a complex structure with linguistic, cognitive, psychological, and anthropological dimensions. The linguistic dimension makes it possible for proverbs to apply to states of affairs and to be culturally transmitted. The cognitive dimension concerns the use of proverbs in social interactions to make sense of lived experiences. The psychological dimension relates to the use of proverbs to categorise events and motivate thought and behaviour. The anthropological dimension represents the viewpoints and lifestyle of a given culture (Maalej 2009: 136).

Psycholinguistic research shows that proverbs have figurative interpretations and knowledge of the figurative meanings of proverbs is motivated by conceptual metaphors (Gibbs and Beitel 1995). The most influential account of proverbs in cognitive linguistics is probably that of Lakoff and Turner (1989). They argue that proverbs are metaphorically structured (see this volume). Lakoff and Turner's account of proverbs has been criticised on some levels (Honeck and Temple 1994; Maalej 2009; Buljan and Gradečak-Erdeljić 2013). First, this account restricts the application of proverbs to human affairs. Honeck (1997) holds that although proverbs are ordinarily about human concerns, they can be about anything. For example, the Persian proverb *tobeye gorg marge* 'a repentant wolf is a dead wolf' could be used to refer to a dog by a dog owner frustrated with his dog's habit of barking at strangers on the street, despite being trained not to do so. This shows, according to Honeck, that each proverb has a fundamental meaning that motivates its entrance into any kind of figurative meaning (op. cit.: 161). Second, it is too complicated because it makes use of a complex machinery to account for an already explained general principle stating that context determines the interpretation of proverbs (Buljan and Gradečak-Erdeljić 2013: 67–68). Third, the GENERIC IS SPECIFIC metaphor is too restricted to apply to all proverbs. Many proverbs do not abide by metaphoric mappings and admit only a literal interpretation, such as *a friend in need is a friend indeed* (Maalej 2009: 141).

The other criticism that could be levelled against Lakoff and Turner's account is that it shows the application of the generic-level structure to various situations only at the conceptual-cognitive level. The account shows that the generic structure is used in situations that present a similar generic structure. Nonetheless, the pragmatic link between the generic structure and the context of use seems to be missing in the cognitive linguistic account of proverbs. Proverbs may display features in context that cannot be obtained merely from the application of the generic structure to situations. The cognitive linguistic literature on proverbs abounds in studies that devote their attention to investigating the way the meaning of proverbs is obtained from the GENERIC IS SPECIFIC metaphor (Pourhossein 2016; Ben Salamh and Maalej 2018; Bletsas 2020, among others). In such studies, the analysis typically deals with (and is limited to) the metaphorical mappings that emerge from the conceptual pairing between the specific-level and generic-level schemas, as well as the type of source domains that are used, but rarely have cognitive linguists demonstrated how the generic meaning applies to concrete contexts of use. As a result, proverbs are pictured as static figurative structures that readily apply to context without considering any role for the communicative intentions of conceptualisers in local contexts. This chapter attempts to compensate for this shortcoming in the theory by paying more attention to the last link in the chain of association between the specific-level schema, the generic-level schema, and the specific situation to which the generic-level schema applies. In other words, while the chapter demonstrates the way the generic-level structure is obtained from the specific-level structure, it aims to show explicitly how the generic-level structure applies to the immediate context.

3. Method

Data were collected from a collection of popular Persian proverbs at www.daneshchi.ir. In addition to providing common interpretations for the proverbs, the website also offers vivid examples along with a detailed explanation of their experiential basis. Out of a large number of proverbs available on the website (approximately 450 proverbs), 17 proverbs were randomly selected. Next, each proverb was searched individually on Google coupled with the Persian phrases *enerjiye hasteyie* 'nuclear energy', *barnâmeye hasteyi* 'nuclear program', and *bomb e hasteyi* 'nuclear bomb'. Instances relevant to the topic were then recorded for each proverb. In total, 122 relevant instances were collected. The majority of the proverbs were found to be readers' comments on the news regarding Iran's nuclear program. However, a small percentage of the proverbs have been used by Iranian top officials, such as the Supreme Leader, Ayatollah Khamenei and the former president, Hasan Rouhani.

The categorisation of the data follows the main goals of the chapter. In order to find out which proverbs are selected for the conceptualisation of which target meaning in discourse, we need to identify the main theme of each proverb, based on the assumption that conceptualisers recruit proverbs generally according to whether the central theme of the proverb fits the target meaning they intend to communicate. Therefore, the recorded proverbs were first grouped according to their central theme. For example, *Shâhnâmeh âxaresh xosheh*, lit. 'it is the end of the *Shâhnâmeh* (story) that should be pleasant' and *salâh e mamlekat e xish xosrovân dânand*, lit. 'kings know what is best for their country' were placed in one category, as they both seem to warn of unpleasant consequences of unwise actions.

The proverbs were then categorised in terms of whether they represented the views of the proponents or opponents of the nuclear deal, or reflected both views. This is in line with the other goal of the chapter, which is to see how proverbs are used to make alternative conceptualisations of the same topic. The significance of discovering these alternative conceptualisations is that while it might demonstrate the flexibility of proverbs in applying to infinite number of situations (Lakoff and Turner 1989), it may also indicate the changes that are made to the generic meaning of proverbs in discourse context.

For the analysis of the Persian proverbs, following Lakoff and Turner (1989), the GENERIC IS SPECIFIC metaphor was used to derive the generic meaning of the proverbs from their specific-level schemas. The next step was identifying metaphors that emerged from the conceptual pairing between the specific-level and generic-level schemas. Criteria for identifying metaphors were (i) a contrast between the specific-level schema coded by the proverb and the generic meaning

Chapter 9. The role of Persian proverbs in framing Iran's nuclear program   235

that the proverb referred to and (ii) the possibility of understanding the generic meaning in comparison with the specific schema profiled by the proverb. For instance, at the specific level, the Persian proverb *sag e zard barâdar e shoqâleh* 'a yellow dog is the brother of the jackal' expresses the idea that even though a yellow dog and a jackal are superficially different animals, one should not assume that a yellow dog is less malicious based on the rationale that it is a kind of dog. The fact of the matter is that they are equally malicious. The generic meaning that is obtained from the specific-level schema (via the application of the GENERIC IS SPECIFIC metaphor) is that even though the two people in question are superficially different (one thought to be less malicious than the other is), they are in fact equally malicious. The metaphors that emerge from the conceptual pairing between the generic-level and specific-level structures are MALICIOUS HUMANS ARE YELLOW DOGS AND JACKALS, SIMILARITY IS BROTHERHOOD, THE SEEMINGLY LESS MALICIOUS PERSON IS THE YELLOW DOG, and THE SEEMINGLY MORE MALICIOUS PERSON IS THE JACKAL. Then, all uses of the proverb were examined to see how this generic structure applied to immediate contexts of use. As an example, the uses of the proverb *sag e zard barâdar e shoqâleh* revealed Joe Biden and Donald Trump to be the corresponding target domain elements metaphorically paired with the yellow dog and the jackal in the proverb respectively. This conceptualisation was used to convey the idea that Democratic and Republican presidents have adopted very similar malicious policies against Iran, despite their superficially different political affiliations. The same procedure was used to analyse all the proverbs in the dataset.

4. Data analysis

In this section, the Persian proverbs are presented in two main categories: the proverbs used by the supporters of the nuclear deal and the ones used by the opponents of the nuclear deal. Examples are also provided for the proverbs used by both sides. Proverbs within each category are further grouped according to their main themes. In total, fourteen themes were identified that are analysed separately. Table 1 provides the list of the proverbs along with their frequency of occurrence, Table 2 presents the identified themes, and the proverbs representing each theme (see Appendix).

4.1 Proverbs supporting the deal

Proverbs in this section reflect the viewpoints of the supporters of the nuclear deal. The proponents make use of four proverbial themes to support their views:

ingratitude, revelation of truth, warning of unpleasant consequences, and unnecessary trouble. Among these themes, warning of unpleasant consequences has been used by the opponents of the deal as well (see 4.1.1.1).

4.1.1 Warning of consequences

4.1.1.1 Shâhnâmeh âxaresh xosheh

lit. 'It is the end of the *Shâhnâmeh* that should be pleasant'.[1] The line of story in the *Shâhnâmeh* proceeds in such a way that it provides an initially positive evaluation of a given character or event, which changes into a negative and saddening one at the end. Thus, readers of the epic would be asked to postpone forming judgments of the character to the end of the story. This is the specific-level schema of the proverb. By means of the GENERIC IS SPECIFIC metaphor, the *Shâhnâmeh* is understood as events that start promising but end up with unpleasant consequences. It is via this generic structure that the speaker implicitly expresses pessimism over the outcome of an event. The main meaning communicated by the proverb is that it is wrong to see hope and feel joyful over temporary achievements, because the result determines winning or losing. In (1), the proverb has been used by one of the proponents of the deal to warn the Iranian government of the negative outcomes of increasing the level of uranium enrichment up to 60%. It also states implicitly that although this may initially sound like an important achievement, the political and economic consequences will nonetheless be harrowing in the long term. Iran's provocative nuclear activities (uranium enrichment up to 60%) are metaphorically seen as the starting point in the *Shâhnâmeh* and their dire political and economic consequences correspond to the end of the *Shâhnâmeh*.

(1) Shâhnâmeh âxarash xosh   ast vali bâlâgheyratan mardom e bichâreh va
    Shâhnâmeh its final pleasant is but please   people   of miserable and
    mostaz'af e irân râ   ham dar in miyân lahâz
    poor   of Iran OBJ-marker also in this between consider
    konid   (www.tabnak.ir, 21 Feb 2021)
    you do
    Lit. 'It is the end of the *Shâhnâmeh* that should be pleasant, but in the meantime please, take into account poor and miserable Iranians'.

---

1. The *Shâhnameh* ('Book of Kings', composed 977–1010 CE) is a medieval epic written by the poet Abolqasem Ferdowsi (l. c. 940–1020 CE) in order to preserve the myths, legends, history, language, and culture of ancient Persia. It is the longest work by a single author in world literature at a length of 50,000 rhymed couplets, 62 stories, and 990 chapters (www.worldhistory.org/shahnameh).

Proverb (1) has also been used by the opponents of the deal to warn the Iranians of the negative consequences of signing the nuclear deal in 2015. In (2), the commenter reacts negatively to people's joy on the streets right after the nuclear deal was signed between Iran and the world powers. In this context, the process of negotiating with the West over the nuclear issue is seen as the *Shâhnâmeh*, signing the nuclear deal is metaphorically conceptualised as the starting point in the *Shâhnâmeh*, and its unpleasant outcomes are viewed as the end of the *Shâhnâmeh*.

(2) Ba'dan mifahmid   barjam che balâie saretun   Avardeh.
    later   you will realise the deal what disaster your head has brought
    Shâhnâmeh azaresh xosh   e.
    Shâhnâmeh its final pleasant is
    Lit. 'You will realise later what disaster the deal has brought to you. It is the end of the *Shâhnâmeh* that should be pleasant'.

4.1.1.2   *Salâh e mamlekat e xish xosrovân dânand*

lit. 'Kings know what is best for their country'. The idea expressed at the specific-level schema is that each king or ruler knows what is good for his country and he should never let other kings or rulers interfere in his country's affairs. The generic meaning produced via the application of the GENERIC IS SPECIFIC metaphor is that everyone knows better than others what is good for him/her. In other words, each person is the king of his/her own life and nobody can impose upon him/her any idea or advice. Having full authority over one's own life is what is mapped from the source domain of KINGS (evoked by the word *xosrovân*) onto the target domain of ORDINARY HUMANS, giving the ORDINARY HUMANS ARE KINGS metaphors. Moreover, life is metaphorically conceptualised as a country ruled by a person. At the generic level, this proverb is used in situations in which the addressee seems to act unwisely and refuses to take advice from others. Therefore, the speaker gently advises the addressee to act more thoughtfully but leaves the final decision up to him. Nevertheless, depending on the context, the proverb could also be used to alarm or even threaten the addressee to take notice of the consequences of his acts, especially when the speaker believes that the addressee is taking a bad decision or acting unwisely. In (3), Alan Eyre, the former U.S. State Department Persian-speaking Spokesman has used the proverb to warn Iran of the risks of not taking important political decisions to finalise the deal (in 2015). Although the word *xosrovân* 'kings' is a plural noun and could be used metaphorically for addressing political leaders in Iran, it seems to be used metaphorically for addressing the Supreme Leader of Iran (THE SUPREME LEADER IS A KING), for he has the final decision on all critical matters of the state. The word *salâh*, lit. 'what is wise to do' metonymically alludes to signing the deal motivated by the GENERIC FOR SPECIFIC metonymy.

(3) *Vaght e tasmimgiri e qabl   az mohlat e pâyân e Mâh   e mârs*
    time of deciding   of before of deadline of ending of month of March
    farâresideh ast.   Salâh e mamlekat e xish xosrovân dânand ammâ be
    has   come. good of country of self kings   know   but to
    nazar   e man chenin natijeyi   be naf' e hameye tarafhâ va koll e
    opinion of me   such   conclusion to benefit of all   sides and all of
    donyâ bâshad   (www.khabarfarsi.com, 30 March 2015)
    world be
    Lit. 'It is time to take political decisions before the end of the March deadline passes. Kings know what is best for their country, but it seems to me that this result [signing the agreement] will benefit all sides [of the negotiation] as well as the whole world'.

4.1.2 Ingratitude

4.1.2.1 *Xar che dânad qeymat e noql va nabât*

lit. 'A donkey doesn't know the value of sweets and candies'. At the specific level, the proverb states that only donkeys do not like sweets and candies due to being foolish. Via the GENERIC IS SPECIFIC metaphor, the proverb refers to foolish people who do not appreciate the value of the valuables and cannot even distinguish what is valuable from what is not. It is worth noting that in Iranian culture donkeys symbolise foolishness. The conceptual pairing between the generic and the specific schema yields the FOOLISH HUMANS ARE DONKEYS and PRECIOUS ENTITIES ARE SWEETS AND CANDIES metaphors. In (4), the HUMANS ARE ANIMALS metaphor has been used to conceptualise the opponents of the nuclear deal in Iran as DONKEYS for lacking intellectual qualities to see the benefits of keeping the deal. Those taking stance against the deal are also criticised for discrediting the deal and raising naïve expectations that suggest the agreement should have dramatically changed the economic status of Iranians shortly after it was reached. The PRECIOUS ENTITIES ARE SWEETS metaphor brings the nuclear deal (as a precious entity) into correspondence with sweets and candies to provide a positive image of the deal and highlight it as a precious achievement in the way of establishing peace and helping the economy to grow again.

(4) *Mage mixâi   barjâm tu ye mâh   mo'jeze kone? Albate   râst goftan*
    if   you want the deal in one month miracle it does? of course right they said
    ke   migan   xar   che   dânad   qeymat e nogl   va
    that they say donkey what it knows price   of sweets and
    nabât   (www.yjc, 28 March 2016)
    candies
    Lit. 'How do you expect the nuclear deal to work wonders within a month? It is true that a donkey doesn't know the value of sweets and candies'.

4.1.3 Revelation of truth

4.1.3.1 Mâh posht e abr nemimânad

lit. 'The moon is not always covered by clouds'. This proverb is typically used in situations in which the speaker expresses doubt or disbelief as to the truth or validity of the information that is provided. The GENERIC IS SPECIFIC metaphor generates the meaning that truth will not remain hidden and will eventually be discovered. Through this metaphor, conceptual correspondences are set up between the moon and truth (TRUTH IS THE MOON), and between clouds and doubts (DOUBTS ARE CLOUDS). In (5), Majid Takht-Ravanchi, a member of Iran's negotiating team at the time responds to doubts raised as to whether the sanctions will be removed immediately. The proverb has been used to rule out indirectly the doubts and state that all the sanctions will be lifted at once. The proverbial metaphors TRUTH IS THE MOON and DOUBTS ARE CLOUDS apply to this scenario. Here, publishing the full text of the deal is the truth viewed as the moon and doubts about lifting all the sanctions at once are metaphorically seen as clouds covering the truth.

(5) *Majid taxt-ravânchi   dar pâsox   be ede'âye barxi maqâmât e âmrikâ*
    majid Takht-Ravanchi in response to claim of some officials   of the U.S.
    mabni bar tadriji budan e laqv   e tahrimhâ goft: belaxare matn e
    based on gradual be   of cancelation of sanctions he said finally text of
    tavâfoq   montasher mishavad va mâh   posht e abr
    agreement published it becomes and the moon behind of the cloud
    nemimânad   (www.farsnews.ir, 15 July 2015)
    won't stay
    Lit. 'In response to the claim of some U.S. officials that sanctions are going to be lifted gradually, Majid Takht-Ravanchi said, the text of the agreement will eventually be published and the moon is not always covered by clouds'.

4.1.4 Unnecessary trouble

4.1.4.1 *Sari ke dard nemikonad dastmâl nemibandand*

lit. 'A handkerchief is not tied to a head that does not ache'. In Iranian folk medicine, a handkerchief is tied around the head in order to relieve a headache. A handkerchief around the head is the symbol of headache in Iranian culture. Tying a handkerchief around the head when there is no headache is considered unwise or unnecessary and might mean to invite pain when in fact there is no pain. The application of the GENERIC IS SPECIFIC metaphor provides the generic meaning that you should not seek trouble when there is no trouble. The metaphorical correspondences that emerge from the pairing between the two schemas are TROUBLE IS HEADACHE and SEEKING TROUBLE WHEN THERE IS NO TROUBLE IS TYING A HANDKERCHIEF AROUND THE HEAD WHEN THERE IS NO HEADACHE. In (6), on the one hand, referring the nuclear deal to the Islamic Parliament for approval is regarded as seeking trouble, because the normal state of affairs is that Iran's National Security Council approves the nuclear deal. This idea is metaphorically analogous with the physical state of having no headache. On the other hand, providing the deal to the Islamic Parliament for approval would cause trouble and add to the complications of implementing the deal. This aspect of the target meaning corresponds to wrapping a handkerchief around the head when there is no headache.

(6) Tasvib   e barjâm dar shorâye âliye   amniyat e melli   kâfist.
    Approval of deal   in council supreme security of national enough-is.
    Sari   ke dard nemikonad râ   dastmâl
    a head that ache it does not OBJ-marker handkerchief
    nemibandand   (www.khabaronline.ir, 16 August 2015)
    they don't tie
    Lit. 'Approving the deal in the National Security Council is enough. A handkerchief is not tied to a head that doesn't ache'.

4.2 Proverbs opposing the nuclear deal

The proverbs in this section represent the viewpoints of the opponents of the nuclear deal. This category includes ten proverbial themes: unwise methods, recurring wrong acts, harm and malice, clumsiness/inability, empty promises, lauding one's own accomplishments, utmost adversity, cunning and greed, fairness, and unfulfillable wishes.

4.2.1 Harm and malice

4.2.1.1 Châhkan hamisheh tah e châh ast

lit. 'A pit-digger is always at the bottom of the pit'. The generic meaning of the proverb is that a person who harms others and wants bad for them will definitely be harmed. This generic meaning is produced by the GENERIC IS SPECIFIC metaphor. The application of this metaphor leads to the emergence of other metaphors, such as HARMING OTHERS IS DIGGING A PIT FOR THEM and THE CONSEQUENCE OF HARMING OTHERS IS REMAINING AT THE BOTTOM OF THE PIT. Example (7) pictures the situation where the nuclear agreement was about to be signed between Iran and 5+1 countries in 2015. According to the writer, the U.S. plot to isolate Iran through trade sanctions backfired and the Obama administration was the one that incurred the most loss. It was because other countries accompanying the U.S. in the execution of sanctions could readily resume investing in the Iranian markets, but the U.S. first must have gone through the legislative complications that stood in the way of returning to Iranian markets. In this example, the U.S. (the Obama administration) is metaphorically seen as the pit-digger, the plot to isolate Iran through sanctions is seen as the pit, and losing the Iranian markets is metaphorically viewed as remaining at the bottom of the pit.

(7) *Xod   e âmrikâ   ke bishtarin naqsh râ   dar e'mâl e tahrimhâ*
    the very of Americans that the most role   OBJ-marker in   exert of sanctions
    aleyhe irân dâsht barâye vorud be bâzârhây e irân bâ   mavâne' e
    against Iran had   for   enter to markets   of Iran with obstacles of
    saxttari ruberust   va nâxâsteh   in zarbolmasal e ma'ruf dar zehn
    structural it is facing and unintentionally this proverb   of famous in mind
    tadâ'ie mishavad ke châhkan hamisheh tah   e châh
    recall becomes that pit-digger always   bottom of pit
    ast   (www.eghtesadnews.com, 07 April 2015)
    is

Lit. 'The U.S., which had the main role in imposing sanctions on Iran, is now facing bigger obstacles [than other countries] in the way of entering the Iranian markets. That is when the famous proverb, a pit-digger is always at the bottom of the pit, is automatically recalled'.

4.2.1.2 Tobeye gorg marg ast

lit. 'A repentant wolf is a dead wolf'. The generic meaning produced via the application of the GENERIC IS SPECIFIC metaphor is that a vicious person will never stop being vicious. The metaphor results in setting up the following conceptual correspondences between the generic-level and specific-level schemas: VICIOUS HUMANS ARE WOLVES and THE POSSIBILITY OF A VICIOUS PERSON QUITTING HIS

VICIOUS BEHAVIOUR IS THE POSSIBILITY OF A WOLF QUITTING ITS VICIOUS NATURE. In (8), ferocity and cunning, as perceived features of the wolf, are metaphorically attributed to the present and past U.S. governments. Long precedence of U.S. sanctions against Iran within the past four decades has provided ground for the commenter in (8) to disbelieve that the newly elected president, Joe Biden, unlike his predecessors, is not going to adopt economic sanctions as an instrument of foreign policy against Iran. The impossibility of the U.S. changing its foreign policy is metaphorically understood through the impossibility of wolves changing their vicious nature. This is the main mapping of the metaphor THE U.S. IS A WOLF that conveys the central idea of the proverb in this context.

(8) Âncheh ke shavâhed neshân midahad fasl   e tâzei az   barjâm âqâz
    what   that evidence show   give   season of new from deal   start
    shodeh ammâ neshân nemidahad ke   âmrikâ âmâdeh bâshad ke
    become but   show don't give that the U.S ready be   that
    tobeh   konad balkeh bâ yek dolat   e jadid âmadeh tâ hamân
    repentance does but   with a government of new has come to the same
    ziyâdexâhihâye gozashteh râ bâ   faribkâri e jadidi bar mellat e irân
    overexpectations past   ra with deception of new   onto nation of Iran
    tahmil konad. Lezâ tobeye   gorg marg
    impose does.   thus repentance-of wolf death
    ast   (www.magiran.com, 18 April 2021)
    is

    Lit. 'Evidence shows that a new chapter has opened in the Iran Nuclear Deal but there is no evidence showing that the U.S. intends to repent. It rather shows that under a fresh government, the U.S. aims to re-impose avarice upon the Iranian nation with new deceptions. Therefore, a repentant wolf is a dead wolf'.

4.2.1.3 *Sag e zard barâdar e shoqâl ast*

lit. 'A yellow dog is the brother of the jackal'. At the specific level, the idea is that even though a yellow dog and a jackal are superficially different animals, one should not assume that a yellow dog is less malicious based on the rationale that it is a kind of dog. In fact, they have the same nature and are equally malicious. At the generic level (as a result of the application of the GENERIC IS SPECIFIC metaphor), the proverb refers to the situation where two superficially different people are believed to be equally malicious. The metaphors that emerge from the conceptual pairing between the generic and specific structures are MALICIOUS HUMANS ARE YELLOW DOGS AND JACKALS, SIMILARITY IS BROTHERHOOD, THE SEEMINGLY LESS MALICIOUS PERSON IS THE YELLOW DOG, and THE SEEMINGLY MORE MALICIOUS PERSON IS THE JACKAL. In (9), the HUMAN BEHAVIOUR IS ANIMAL

Chapter 9. The role of Persian proverbs in framing Iran's nuclear program 243

BEHAVIOUR metaphor is at play to conceptualise Joe Biden and Donald Trump as the yellow dog and the jackal respectively, as these two U.S. presidents are believed to have adopted very similar malicious policies against Iran, despite their superficially different political affiliations. More specifically, what motivates the use of the proverb is the assumption that U.S. presidents, no matter Democrat or Republican, have all utilised almost the same pressure mechanism (i.e., economic sanctions) to align Iran's foreign policy with their own national interests.

(9) Hattâ dar doreye   demokrâthâ az   in siyâsathâye Xabisâneye xod dast
    even in   period of Democrats from this policies   malicious of self hand
    bar nadâshtand. Har shaxi   re'is jomhur e ânhâ bâshad ebtedâ manâfe'
    on have not had. every person head republic of them be   first   interest
    e melli   e xod râ   dar nazar migirand va in râ bedânim ke
    of national of self OBJ-marker in look they take and this OBJ-marker that
    sag e zard   barâdar e shoqâl ast   (www.alef.ir, 05 November 2020)
    dog of yellow brother of jackal is
    Lit. 'Even during the presidency of the Democrats they did not give up their malicious policies. Whoever is elected president will give priority to national interests and we should remember that a yellow dog is the brother of the jackal'.

4.2.2 Unwise methods

4.2.2.1 Bâr e kaj be manzel nemiresad

lit. 'Slanting baggage never reaches home'. The specific schema pictures (probably) an animal setting off on a journey, carrying a slanting piece of baggage on its back. Since the baggage has not been positioned straight on the animal's back, it is very likely to fall to the ground before reaching the destination. By means of the GENERIC IS SPECIFIC metaphor, it can be interpreted as being impossible to achieve intended goals using improper methods. The TASKS/MISSIONS ARE BAGGAGE, IMPROPER METHODS ARE THE SLANTING POSITION OF THE BAGGAGE, and ACHIEVING GOALS IS REACHING HOME are the metaphors that construct the generic-level schema in terms of the specific-level schema of the proverb. In (10), Rouhani's government is criticised for negotiating with the West within the past eight years. The proverb applies to the context via the metaphor NEGOTIATING WITH THE WEST IS A JOURNEY. Moreover, the task in hand; i.e., the former government's attempt to reach an agreement with the West, is viewed as baggage. The central idea of the proverb in the context is metaphorically communicated by conceptualising the inapt method of dealing with the West as slanting baggage. The opponents of the deal claim that the strategy that Rouhani adopted in the negotiations with the West could not preserve Iran's full right to possess and develop its peaceful nuclear program. Besides, the U.S. exit from the deal, which is used as solid evidence to prove the futility of the negotiations, corresponds to not reaching the destination.

(10) *Hasht sâl   tul   keshid befahman   bâr   e kaj   be manzel*
    eight years length took to understand baggage of slanting to home
    nemireseh   (www.mashreghnews.ir, 15 July 2021)
    gets
    Lit. 'It took them eight years to realise that slanting baggage never reaches home'.

4.2.3 Recurring wrong acts

4.2.3.1 *Âdam e âqel az yek surâx dobâr gazideh nemishavad*

lit. 'A wise person is never bitten twice from the same hole'. The specific-level structure of the proverb contains one piece of advice: when a snake bites a person once, it is wise to keep away from the snake hole so that one would not be bitten for the second time. The generic meaning of the proverb is that a wise person should not make the same mistake twice. The GENERIC IS SPECIFIC metaphor maps ideas from the specific-level schema onto the generic-level schema, producing these metaphors: NEGATIVE CONSEQUENCES OF MAKING MISTAKES ARE SNAKE BITES, SUFFERING FROM THE CONSEQUENCES OF REPEATING THE SAME MISTAKE IS GETTING BITTEN AGAIN FROM THE SAME HOLE, and THE SOURCE OF MISTAKE IS THE SNAKE HOLE. In (11), Rouhani's government is ironically addressed as a wise person and asked to avoid resuming talks with the U.S. to revive the deal. The U.S. is metaphorically conceptualised as a SNAKE that has already bitten Iran once, referring to nuclear negotiations in 2015. The opponents of the deal believe that the 2015 deal has been a total loss for Iran, as the country could never use the economic and trade benefits of the deal while it had to curb its nuclear program and unilaterally remain fully committed. Therefore, negotiations with the U.S. to revive the deal would once again bring about loss, that is, Iran would be bitten for the second time (NEGOTIATIONS WITH THE U.S. ARE SNAKE HOLES, and LOSSES THAT IRAN SUFFERED AS A RESULT OF NEGOTIATING WITH THE U.S. ARE SNAKE BITES). From this viewpoint, Trump's withdrawal from the agreement in 2018 is further evidence that the opponents of the deal provide to argue against any diplomatic initiative to restore the nuclear deal in 2021.

(11) *Inkeh Irân xâstâre   mozâkereh bâ   âmrika nist   ham bar mabnâye adam*
that   Iran willing to negotiation with the U.S. is not also on basis   lack
e sedâqat e âmrikâiehâst. Âdame âqel az   yek surâx do bâr gazideh
of honesty of the Americans human wise from one hole   two time bitten
Nemishavad   (www.rc.majlis.ir, 12 July 2019)
does not become
Lit. 'The dishonesty of the U.S. is the reason why Iran is not willing to negotiate with it. A wise person is never bitten twice from the same hole'.

4.2.4 *Clumsiness/inability*

4.2.4.1 *Mush tu surâx nemiraft jâru be domesh mibast*

lit. 'The mouse couldn't get into the hole, yet it tied a broom to its tail'. The proverb is part of a fable in which a mouse finds a kitchen full of cheese and walnuts inside an old woman's house and decides to live in a hole in the kitchen. One day, the mouse wants to dust and clean its home (the hole). It finds a broom in the corner of the kitchen and thinks of finding a way to take the broom into the hole. The mouse thinks the hole is small, so it would not be able to carry the broom into the hole. Later, after some reflection, it eventually decides to tie the broom to its tail and get into the hole. When the old woman comes into the kitchen, she realises that part of the broom has stuck out of the hole. As she pulls out the broom, the mouse's tail comes off. The old woman laughs and says, "the mouse can't get itself into the hole, yet it ties a broom to its tail". At the generic level, this proverb describes people who are unable to deal with small problems and clumsily complicate them. This description is typically accompanied with a mocking tone. The proverb seems to be based on the CLUMSY HUMANS ARE MICE, FINDING SOLUTIONS TO PROBLEMS IS TRYING TO GET INTO THE HOLE, and A PERSON COMPLICATING A PROBLEM IS THE MOUSE TYING A BROOM TO ITS TAIL TO GET INTO THE HOLE metaphors. In (12), a commenter ridicules Joe Biden's remarks on his plans to incorporate Iran's ballistic missile program into the nuclear deal. The remark dates back to the time when Joe Biden was campaigning for the presidency against his Republican rival, Donald Trump. The proverb metaphorically conceptualises Biden as a mouse (BIDEN IS A MOUSE) in order to depict him as clumsy in handling the situation. Moreover, Biden's presumed inability to defeat Donald Trump and enter the White House corresponds to the mouse's inability to get into the hole, meaning that Biden was predicted to be unable to solve a small problem. Moreover, his plan to incorporate Iran's ballistic missile program into the nuclear deal if elected president is seen as adding an additional problem to the previous one. This aspect corresponds to the mouse tying a broom to his tail, conveying the idea that Biden is only clumsily complicating things.

(12) *Mush tu surâx nemiraft   jâru   be domeshmibast Aval bebin tuye kâx*
mouse into hole wouldn't go broom to its tail tied   first see   into palace
e sefid vâred mishi   ba'd ta'ien   taklif
of white enter you become then determine task
kon   (www.farsnews.ir, 03 January 2021)
you do

Lit. 'The mouse couldn't get into the hole, yet it tied a broom to its tail. Before deciding Iran's fate [in the negotiations], first, see if you can find a way into the White House.'

4.2.5 Empty promises

4.2.5.1 *Bozak namir bahâr miyâd kombozeh bâ xiyâr miyâd*

lit. 'Little goat! Don't die. Spring is coming and with it melons and cucumbers'. The proverb is based on a fable in which a boy cannot provide food to his little hungry goat. It is winter and there is no grass in the pasture nor is there any fodder in the stock. The little goat is constantly bleating about being hungry. The boy sympathises with the goat and promises to take it to the pasture to graze in the upcoming spring. This is the specific schema of the proverb that is used at a generic level to refer to situations in which a person makes empty promises to people in order to keep them vainly hopeful. The conceptual pairing between the two schemas yields the metaphors NAÏVE PEOPLE ARE LITTLE GOATS, EMPTY PROMISES ARE MELONS AND CUCUMBERS, and THE PROMISED TIME TO DO SOMETHING FOR A NAÏVE PERSON IS THE PROMISED TIME TO TAKE THE LITTLE GOAT TO THE PASTURE. In (13), supporters of the nuclear deal are mocked for being naïve and vainly hopeful that if Joe Biden is elected president, he will resume negotiations with Iran and lift sanctions right away. In this context, supporters of the deal are seen as goats and probably the EU countries are seen as the hopeful shepherds encouraging Iran to remain in the deal, in the hope that the newly elected U.S. president will return to the deal and lift all the sanctions. Moreover, lifting the sanctions by Biden is the empty promise that corresponds to melons and cucumbers. The use of the word *bozak* 'little goat' highlights the naivety of the supporters of the deal.

(13) *Hâmiyân e barjâm entezâr   dârand ke   bâiden bedune pishshart   be*
      supporters of the deal expectation have   that Biden without precondition to
      barjâm bargardad va   hameye tahrimhâ bardashteh shavand. Bozak
      the deal returns   and all   sanctions removed   become. Little goat
      namir   bahâr miyad   kombozeh bâ   xiyâr
      don't die spring will come melon   with cucumber
      miyad   (www.siasatrooz.ir, 23 December 2020)
      will come
      Lit. 'Supporters of the nuclear deal anticipate that Joe Biden will return to the [nuclear] agreement without preconditions and all the sanctions will be lifted. Little goat! Don't die. Spring is coming and with it melons and cucumbers'.

4.2.6 Lauding one's own accomplishments

4.2.6.1 *Hich mâstbandi nemigeh mâstam torsheh*

lit. 'No dairyman would ever say the yogurt he has made is sour'. The specific-level schema of the proverb relies on a stereotype. The stereotype is that dairymen generally refuse to inform their customers if the yogurt they have made is sour, and no matter what its quality is, they tend to speak highly of it. The generic meaning of the proverb is that it is wrong to expect from a person to speak lowly of his/her possessions, actions, and accomplishments. At the generic level, this proverb might be used to imply that the speaker is lying and deceiving the addressee(s). The application of the GENERIC IS SPECIFIC metaphor results in producing these metaphors: PEOPLE SPEAKING HIGHLY OF THEIR POSSESSIONS, ACTIONS, AND ACCOMPLISHMENTS ARE DAIRYMEN, LAUDING ONE'S OWN BAD ACTIONS AND PERFORMANCES IS PRAISING A SOUR YOGURT, and BAD OR DEFECTIVE IS SOUR. In (14), Javad Zarif's efforts to protect national interests in the negotiations is looked upon with depreciation. In this example, Zarif is metaphorically seen as a dairyman praising the sour yogurt he has made (i.e., the deal and his role in protecting national interests). Conceptualising Zarif as a dairyman serves the purpose of denigrating his position as the Foreign Minister as well as his role in signing the nuclear deal. Based on what the analogy offers, Zarif would never be expected to devalue the nuclear deal even if it were a bad deal. This aspect is analogous with the idea in the source domain that a dairyman would never be expected to speak lowly of his yogurt even if it were sour. The description of the yogurt as sour depicts the nuclear deal as a bad deal (BAD IS SOUR) and that the commenter disbelieves Zarif.

(14) *Har kesi jâye doctor zarif bud hamino migoft. Âxeh az*
every person place of Dr. Zarif was the same would say because from
qadim migan hich mâstbani nemigeh mâstam torsheh. Moteasefâneh
old times they say no dairyman doesn't say my yogurt is sour. unfortunately
âqâye zarif va tim e ishun dar mozâkerat e hasteyi natunestan hameye
Mr. Zarif and team of he in negotiations of nuclear couldn't all of
xotut e qermez e nezâm ro re'âyat
lines of red of state OBJ-marker observe
konan (www.khabarfoori.com, 15 July 2019)
they do
Lit. 'Anyone in Dr. Zarif's shoes would have said the same. There is an old saying that no dairyman would ever say the yogurt he has made is sour. Unfortunately, Mr. Zarif and his team in the nuclear negotiations couldn't observe all redlines of the state'.

4.2.7 Utmost adversity

4.2.7.1 *Bâlâtar az siyâhi rangi nist*

lit. 'There is no colour above black'. At the specific level, the proverb states that in the hierarchy of colours, black stands on the top as the most important colour. At the generic level, the proverb's meaning is that when adversities reach unbearable stages, things may not deteriorate any further. The application of the GENERIC IS SPECIFIC metaphor sets up correspondences between the two schemas, yielding the metaphor UTMOST ADVERSITY IS BLACK. In (15), the writer contends that the U.S. and EU countries have already imposed maximum pressure on Iran through crippling economic sanctions. Therefore, activating the snapback mechanism by the EU countries cannot exacerbate the situation for the Iranians and add to their adversity.[2] This idea is conveyed by the metaphor UTMOST ADVERSITY IS BLACK. Through this metaphor, black is conceived as the extreme point on the colour gradient, corresponding to the most adverse situation that the Iranians have already found themselves in and could find themselves in, later, due to the sanctions.

(15) *Keshvarhâye orupâyie irân râ be estefâdeh az az mekânism e*
countries European Iran OBJ-marker to use from of mechanism of
mâsheh tahdid kardehand. In keshvarhâ dar amal mâsheh râ
trigger threat they have done. this countries in practice trigger OBJ-marker
chekândehand va tanhâ qasd darand har tor shodeh dobâreh
they have hit and only intention they have every way has become again

---

[2]. The snapback mechanism is intended to automatically restore the U.N. sanctions on Iran that existed prior to 2015 in case of violations (www.foreignpolicy.com, 12 August 2020).

irân râ	*pâye*	*miz*	*e*	*mozâkereh*	*bekeshânand.*	*Bâyad be in*
Iran OBJ-marker	foot	of table	of negotiation	they pull.		must to this
dolatmardân motezaker		*gardid*	*ke*	*bâlâtar az*	*siyâhi*	*rangi*
officials		admonishment	became	that higher	from blackness	a colour
nist						
there isn't				(www.basirat.ir, 21 November 2019)

Lit. 'EU countries have threatened Iran to use the trigger mechanism. This is while these countries have actually already activated the mechanism and are just using psychological operations to bring Iran back to the negotiation table in any way possible, but they should be notified that there is no colour above black'.

4.2.8 Cunning and greed

4.2.8.1 *Salâm e gorg bi tama' nist*

lit. 'A wolf's hello is not without greed'. Wolves are known to be humans' enemies; therefore, it would be strange or suspicious to see a wolf behaving like a harmless domestic animal. The generic meaning of the proverb is that when an enemy shows kindness, care should be taken, as he may be using cunning and deceit to harm or take advantage of you. Because of the application of the GENERIC IS SPECIFIC metaphor, these metaphors emerge; CUNNING AND GREEDY HUMANS ARE WOLVES, THE ENEMY'S SUPERFICIALLY PLEASANT BEHAVIOUR IS THE WOLF'S SUPERFICIALLY INNOCUOUS BEHAVIOUR, and THE ENEMY'S CUNNING AND GREED IS THE WOLF'S CUNNING AND GREED. In (16), greed and cunning as characteristic features of wolves are metaphorically attributed to Russia via the metaphor A COUNTRY IS AN ANIMAL. The phrase *salâm e gorg* 'the wolf's hello' in Extract (16) metaphorically points to Russia's superficially constructive diplomatic engagements and efforts, especially endorsing the peaceful nature of Iran's nuclear program, which in fact aim to pursue Russia's interests in Iran, with no intention to contribute to peace whatsoever.

(16) | *Irâniyân va* | *hamvatanân e* | *aziz!* | *Rusiye dust* | *e* | *mâ nist.* | *Faqat bâj* |
|---|---|---|---|---|---|---|
| Iranians and | compatriots | of dear! | Russia friend | of | us isn't. | only blackmail |
| *mixâhad.* | *Salâm e* | *gorg bitama'* | | *nist* | (www.tabnak.ir, 09 December 2011) |
| it wants. | hello | of wolf without greed | | isn't | |

Lit. 'You dear Iranians and compatriots! Russia is not our friend. It just wants to blackmail [Iran]. A wolf's hello is not without greed'.

4.2.9 *Fairness*

4.2.9.1 *Ye suzan be xodet bezan ye jovâlduz be mardom*

lit. 'Prick yourself with a sewing needle before pricking others with a packing needle'. At the specific-level schema, people are advised to prick themselves gently with a small needle (a sewing needle) in order to get an idea of how painful it is to harm others with a bigger needle (a packing needle). The generic meaning of the proverb is that it would be fair to seek your own defects and to be self-critical first, before reproaching others harshly. It is typically used in situations in which a person unjustly criticises others for a wrong deed or moral defect when he himself possesses the very moral defects or demonstrates the very wrong behaviours. The metaphors that emerge from the application of the GENERIC IS SPECIFIC metaphor are REPROACHING IS PRICKING WITH NEEDLES, SELF-CRITICISING GENTLY IS PRICKING ONESELF WITH A SEWING NEEDLE, and REPROACHING OTHERS HARSHLY IS PRICKING OTHERS WITH A PACKING NEEDLE.

In (17), Emanuel Macron, the president of France, is harshly criticised for his remark over the necessity of adopting a strict approach against Iran in the negotiations for reviving the deal. This is while in the meantime, Macron himself was dealing with nationwide protests across France and had allegedly failed to control it. The metaphor REPROACHING IS PRICKING WITH NEEDLES is at work to remind Macron metaphorically of his unjust treatment. The generic meaning of the proverb applies to the specific situation to communicate the idea that Macron should foremost reproach himself for failing to deal with the protests in France. This idea is conceptually analogous with pricking oneself with the sewing needle (the smaller needle) so that he would get an idea of how painful it is to be reproached. It is only then that he will know how even more painful it is to prick others with a big needle (the packing needle). This aspect corresponds to harshly criticising Iran for not joining the negotiations to revive the deal.

(17) Ye suzan be xodet   bezan ye jovâlduz   be digari.   Boro mamlekat
 a needle to yourself you hit one packing needle to the other. go   country
 e behamrixteye xodet   ro   dorost
 of messy   yourself OBJ-marker right
 kon
 you do   (www.isna.ir, 08 January 2021)

Lit. 'Prick yourself with a sewing needle before pricking others with a packing needle. Go tidy up your own messy country'.

4.2.10 Unfulfillable wishes

4.2.10.1 *Shotor dar xâb binad panbeh dâneh*

lit. 'The camel dreams of eating cotton seeds'. At the specific level, it is said that camels love to eat cotton seeds but in reality they cannot eat them, because they live in deserts and cotton seeds are not planted there, hence they dream about eating them. At the generic level, the proverb is used ironically to convey to the addressee that what he/she has planned to do would never be fulfilled but would remain only sweet dreams. The impossibility of fulfilling dreams is the core meaning of this proverb. The application of the GENERIC IS SPECIFIC metaphor results in the emergence of the HUMAN WISHES/DREAMS ARE CAMEL DREAMS and UNFULFILLABLE WISHES ARE COTTON SEEDS. In (18), the Supreme Leader uses the proverb to state that the U.S. will never be able to demolish Iran's economy through sanctions. The West is likened to the camel, and the West's goal of isolating Iran and demolishing its economy by means of economic sanctions are metaphorically seen as dreaming of eating cotton seeds. These conceptual correspondences present these political goals or wishes as unfulfillable. In addition, the proverb demonstrates a speaker confident of his power and attempts (with a mocking tone) to undermine Iran's opponents in their ability to bring it to its knees.

(18) *Âmrikâieha   mixâhand dolat   e mâ râ   varshekasteh konand*
     the Americans want   government of us OBJ-marker bankrupt   it does
     va betore   kol   eqtesâd e irân râ   motelâshi   konand.
     and in the way general economy of Iran OBJ-marker demolished it does.
     Albate   bâyad beguyim shotor dar xâb   binad
     of course have to we say   camel in   sleep sees
     panbehdâneh   (www.khabaronline.ir, 31 July 2020)
     cotton seeds
     'The U.S. government plans to bankrupt our government and demolish the whole economy. However, I should say the camel dreams of eating cotton seeds'.

5. Findings and conclusion

The proverbs provide an elaborate account of the opponents' views but only a glimpse of the proponents'. One of the reasons could be that the opponents have used a larger proportion of the proverbial themes in the data. Another justification for the disproportionate use of the proverbs could be that probably the opponents of the deal have a stronger social base than that of the proponents. This might show that Iranians' support of the deal has decreased over time (Smeltz et al. 2021). The small size of the corpus might also have affected the distribution of the ideas represented by the proverbs.

Harm and malice stand out as the top themes in the opponents' discourse. This indicates the highly negative view of the opponents towards the 2015 deal, the West, and reviving the deal. In contrast, warning of negative outcomes stands out as the top theme in the discourse of the proponents of the deal, showing that diplomatic relations with the West and the impact of the sanctions on Iranians' lives matter most for the proponents. Naivety is the theme that both camps have used in their conceptualisations. The proponents call the opponents naïve for their over-expectations of the deal and the opponents call the proponents naïve for being hopeful that Joe Biden will lift all the sanctions and return to the deal. Both sides also make use of the warning theme in their conceptualisations. The proponents warn the Iranian officials of the negative outcomes of enriching uranium up to 60% and the opponents warn the proponents of the deal of the unpleasant consequences of signing the deal. The research also shows that in general the proponents of the deal use a milder language than the opponents do to express their views about the deal. Nonetheless, a larger corpus is needed to test the validity of these generalisations.

The majority of the source domains recruited for the metaphorical conceptualisations of aspects of Iran's nuclear program comes from the ANIMAL domain. The selection of the type of animals as metaphorical source domains is motivated by the particular viewpoints that distinguish the proponents and opponents of the deal in Iran. For the proponents of the deal, developing the nuclear program at the expense of the well-being of people sounds irrational, motivating the recruitment of the source domain of DONKEY to depict the opponents of the deal as lacking common sense. Moreover, at least for some of the proponents, Russia is seen as an Untrustworthy, greedy ally seeking its own interest in the game, motivating the use of wolves in the proverbial metaphors. This is the only animal source domain shared by both the proponents and opponents of the deal, though the opponents use this source domain only to conceptualise the U.S. and the West. The reason might be that for the opponents of the deal Russia is regarded as a reliable ally.

The opponents of the deal make extensive use of animals to conceptualise the U.S. government, the West, and the Iranian supporters of the deal. The opponents believe that the supporters of the deal in Iran are too optimistic, naively thinking that the deal will lead to a better relationship with the West and a significant improvement in the well-being of Iranians, motivating the use of GOATS as the source domain. But the opponents of the deal think that the U.S. will never change its strict policies against Iran and will continue to inflict harm upon the country through economic sanctions. In order to construct this specific attitude metaphorically, such wild animals as snakes, wolves, yellow dogs and jackals are utilised. In addition, the opponents claim that the economic sanctions are inefficient and it is unlikely that the sanction policy will keep Iran from pursuing its nuclear program. Moreover, the U.S. President Joe Biden is seen as unable to solve an international issue through negotiations. In order to highlight these views in discourse, CAMELS and MICE are used as metaphorical source domains. In general, the employment of these types of animals in the figurative conceptualisations ultimately serves the purpose of demonstrating the opponent camp as possessing more wisdom, strength, authority, and honesty. These positive characteristics are presented indirectly by demonising, undermining, and delegitimising the West, as well as their rival camp (i.e., the proponents of the deal) in Iran.

The proverbial metaphors reflect cultural overtones. First, the tangible trace of culture could be seen in the properties attributed to certain animals. The domain of ANIMALS has been extensively used in the data for offensive conceptualisations. The features attributed to goats (naivety), donkeys (lacking common sense), and mice (clumsiness) are prime examples of culture-specific conceptualisations that are used to convey undesirability or objectionability (Kövecses 2002) via the HUMAN BEHAVIOUR IS ANIMAL BEHAVIOUR metaphor. Second, Persian literature is the other important cultural source that is employed for much less offensive or more indirect criticisms via the proverbs. Persian poems are important sources of teaching proper speech and conduct. Therefore, the use of proverbs based on poems is to ensure that communication abides by the principle of politeness in order to maintain the face of the addressee(s). Third, social stereotypes about professions (as in the dairyman proverb) demonstrate how social views about certain professions find their way into proverbs to denigrate the social status of the addressee and disbelieve his/her speech. Fourth, Persian folk medicine (as in the handkerchief proverb) is yet another aspect of Iranian culture that has turned into a generic structure to conceptualise wider social problems. Fifth, the cultural model of *ta'ne* 'sarcasm' manifests itself in the proverb in which the speaker addresses the Iranian government as *âdam e âqel* 'a wise person' ('a wise person is never bitten twice from the same hole'), where it is actually used to criticise the former president for acting unwisely.

The analysis indicates that proverbs' scope of operation goes way beyond their conventional functions (i.e., presenting cultural desirables and undesirables). This research shows that proverbs can also be used to propagate pessimism, express sarcasm, threaten and humiliate opponents, and depreciate the addressee's performance. Some of the proverbs are involved in fabricating the outcome of the scenario in accordance with ideological wishes. For example, the piece of wisdom communicated by the proverb *bâlâtar az siyâhi rangi nist*, lit. 'there is no colour above black' justifies further rash actions (e.g., increasing the level of uranium enrichment), relying on the proverbial advice that adversity has a limit, no matter what the political actions are. This provides further evidence for the role of proverbs in the manipulation of thoughts and the content and courses of action in political space (Orwenjo 2009).

The analysis shows that the Persian proverbs represent varying degrees of criticism depending on the historical period (from 2003 to date) in which the nuclear program is discussed as well as the people or governments at whom the criticism is directed (e.g., Javad Zarif, Rouhani, EU countries, Donald Trump, or Joe Biden). In addition, rather than reflecting shared cultural values, the application of the Persian proverbs highlight shared ideological and political values and expectations. These findings attest the inevitability of paying attention to discourse context for more insightful investigations of proverbs in Cognitive Linguistics.

The application of the generic structure of the Persian proverbs to discourse context revealed dynamic aspects of the meaning of proverbs that metaphorical mappings at the conceptual level were unable to demonstrate. For example, the generic structure of some of the proverbs outside context present them only as gentle pieces of advice, nevertheless, they were used in context as threatening, sarcastic, or even insulting speech acts. This is evidence to support the idea that a more comprehensive account of proverbs may demand taking into account the link between the generic structure of proverbs and the contexts in which they are used.

Proverbs are shown to be appropriate tools for the conceptualisation of aspects of Iran's nuclear program as a complex issue with various dimensions. Proverbs encapsulate a bundle of integrated figurative conceptualisations that provide users with ready-to-use conceptual slots to apply to complex scenarios with multiple roles and relations. This might also account for why proverbial metaphors have been privileged for use over single conceptual metaphors. The proverbial metaphors examined are shown to perform a range of functions: they are employed to obscure facts and political reality, establish and stress ideological viewpoints on the nuclear deal, raise emotions and demonise the West.

The other important function of proverbs as revealed by the analysis is framing people, governments, and actions involved in the nuclear program. Previous studies have shown the framing power of metaphor, metonymy (Semino et al. 2016; Benczes 2018), and other figures of speech such as hyperbole and irony (Burgers et al. 2016). Since proverbs condense figurative structures (metaphoric and metonymic structures) and can be used both ironically and hyperbolically, a large-scale study of proverbs could demonstrate how all these structures are simultaneously involved in the conceptualisation of controversial or complex social and political issues.

References

Barajas, E. D. (2010). *The function of proverbs in discourse: The case of a Mexican transnational social network*. Berlin/New York: De Gruyter Mouton.

Belkhir S. (2012). Variation in source and target domain mappings in English and Kabyle dog proverbs. In S. Kleinke, Z. Kövecses, A. Musolff, & V. Szelid (Eds.), *Cognition and culture: The role of metaphor and metonymy* (pp. 213–227). Budapest: Eötvös Lorand University Press.

Belkhir, S. (2021). Cognitive linguistics and proverbs. In X. Wen & J. R. Taylor (Eds.), *The Routledge handbook of Cognitive Linguistics* (pp. 599–611). New York & London: Routledge.

Benczes, R. (2018). Visual metonymy and framing in political communication. In: A. Benedek, & K. Nyíri (Eds.), *Perspectives on visual learning: Image and metaphor in the new century*. Budapest: Hungarian Academy of Sciences.

Ben Salamh, S. B., & Maalej, Z. (2018). A cultural linguistics perspective on animal proverbs, with special reference to two dialects of Arabic. *Arab World English Journal for Translation and Literary Studies*, 2(4), 21–40.

Bletsas, M. (2020). Gendered metaphors in proverbs. A study on Italian and French. *Metaphorik.de*, 30, 11–37.

Buljan, G., & Gradečak-Erdeljić, T. (2013). Where cognitive linguistics meets paremiology: A cognitive-contrastive view of selected English and Croatian proverbs. *Explorations in English Language and Linguistics*, 1(1), 63–68.

Burgers, C., Konijn, E. A., & Steen, G. (2016). Figurative framing: Shaping public discourse through metaphor, hyperbole, and irony. *Communication Theory*, 26(4), 410–430.

Gaietta, M. (2015). *The trajectory of Iran's nuclear program*. New York: Palgrave Macmillan.

Gibbs, R., & Beitel, D. A. (1995). What proverb understanding reveals about how people think. *Psychological Bulletin*, 118(1), 133–154.

Honeck, R. (1997). *A proverb in mind: The cognitive science of proverbial wit and wisdom*. New Jersey: Erlbaum.

Honeck, R., & Temple, J. (1994). Proverbs: The extended conceptual base and Great Chain Metaphor theories. *Metaphor and Symbolic Activity*, 9(2), 85–112.

Joyner, D. H. (2016). *Iran's nuclear program and international law: From confrontation to accord*. Oxford: Oxford University Press.

Kövecses, Z. (2002). *Metaphor: A practical introduction*. New York: Oxford University Press.

Lakoff, G., & Turner, M. (1989). *More than cool reason: A field guide to poetic metaphor*. Chicago: University of Chicago Press.

Lemghari, E. (2019). A metaphor-based account of semantic relations among proverbs. *Cognitive Linguistic Studies*, 6(1), 158–184.

Maalej, Z. (2009). A cognitive-pragmatic perspective on proverbs and its implications for translation. *International Journal of Arabic-English Studies*, 10: 135–153.

Mieder, W. (1993). *Proverbs are never out of season*. Chicago: University of Chicago Press.

Mieder, W. (2004). *Proverbs: A handbook*. London: Greenwood Press.

Moreno, A. I. (2005). An analysis of the cognitive dimension of proverbs in English and Spanish: The conceptual power of language reflecting popular believes. *SKASE Journal of Theoretical Linguistics*, 2(1), 42–54.

Mousavian, S. H. (2012). *The Iranian nuclear crisis: A memoir*. Washington: Carnegie Endowment.

Orwenjo, D. O. (2009). Political grandstanding and the use of proverbs in African political discourse. *Discourse and Society*, 20(1), 123–146.

Pourhossein, Sh. (2016). *Animal metaphors in Persian and Turkish proverbs: A cognitive linguistic study*. Ph.D. diss. Hacettepe University, Ankara, Turkey.

Semino, E., Demjen, Z., & Demmen, J. (2016). An integrated approach to metaphor and framing in cognition, discourse, and practice, with an application to metaphors for cancer. *Applied Linguistics*, 39(5), 625–6451.

Smeltz, D., Farmanesh, A., & Brendan, H. (March 2021). Iranians and Americans support a mutual return to JCPOA. Chicago and Toronto. www.IranPoll.com/Publications/CCGA2.

Appendix

Table 1. List of Persian proverbs

Persian proverbs	Frequency
1. *Sag e zard barâdar e shoqâl ast* 'A yellow dog is the brother of the jackal'.	22
2. *Salâh e mamlekat e xish xosrovân dânand* 'Kings know what is best for their country'.	18
3. *Bozak namir bahâr miyâd kombozeh bâ xiyâr miyâd* 'Little goat! Don't die. Spring is coming with melons and cucumbers'.	14
4. *Shotor dar xâb binad panbeh dâneh* 'The camel dreams of eating cotton seeds'.	10
5. *Tobeye gorg marg ast* 'A repentant wolf is a dead wolf'.	10
6. *Âdam e âqel az yek surâx do bâr gazideh nemishavad* 'A wise person is never bitten twice from the same hole'.	9
7. *Shâhnâmeh âxaresh xosheh* 'It is the end of the *Shâhnâmeh* that should be pleasant'.	8
8. *Salâm e gorg bi tama' nist* 'A wolf's hello is not without greed'.	5
9. *Mush tu surâx nemiraft jâru beh domesh mibast* 'The mouse couldn't get into the hole, yet it tied a broom to its tail'.	4
10. *Xar cheh dânad qeymat e noql va nabât* 'A donkey doesn't know the value of sweets and candies'.	4
11. *Mâh posht e abr nemimânad* 'The moon is not always covered by clouds'.	4

Table 1. *(continued)*

Persian proverbs	Frequency
12. *Hich mâstbandi nemigeh mâstam torsheh* 'No dairyman would ever say the yogurt hehas made is sour'.	3
13. *Châh kan hamisheh tah e châh ast* 'A pit-digger is always at the bottom of the pit'.	3
14. *bâr e kaj beh manzel nemiresad* 'Slanting baggage never reaches home'.	2
15. *Ye suzan beh xodet bezan ye jovâlduz beh mardom* 'Prick yourself with a sewing needle before pricking others with a packing needle'.	2
16. *Bâlâtar az siyâhi rangi nist* 'There is no colour above black'.	2
17. *Sari ke dard nemikonad dastmâl nemibandand* 'A handkerchief is not tied to a head that does not ache'.	2

Table 2. Themes of the Persian proverbs

Themes	Proverbs translations
1. Unwise methods	'Slanting baggage never reaches home'.
2. Recurring wrong acts	'A wise person is never bitten twice from the same hole'.
3. harm and malice	'A pit-digger is always at the bottom of the pit'.
	'A repentant wolf is a dead wolf'.
	'A yellow dog is the brother of the jackal'.
4. Warning of unpleasant consequences	'It is the end of the *Shâhnâmeh* that should be pleasant'.
	'Kings know what is best for their country'.
5. Unnecessary trouble	'A handkerchief is not tied to a head that does not ache'.
6. Clumsiness	'The mouse couldn't get into the hole, yet it tied a broom to its tail'.
7. Empty promises	'Little goat! Don't die. Spring is coming with melons and cucumbers'.
8. Lauding one's own accomplishments	'No dairyman would ever say the yogurt he has made is sour'.
9. Utmost adversity	'There is no colour above black'.
10. Cunning and greed	'A wolf's hello is not without greed'.
11. Fairness	'Prick yourself with a sewing needle before pricking others with a packing needle'.
12. Unfulfillable wishes	'The camel dreams of eating cotton seeds'.
13. Ingratitude	'A donkey doesn't know the value of sweets and candies'.
14. Revelation of truth	'The moon is not always covered by clouds'.

PART IV

Proverbs and related phenomena in a cultural-cognitive linguistic framework

CHAPTER 10

The only good snowclone is a dead snowclone*
A cognitive-linguistic exploration of the frayed ends of proverbiality

Kim Ebensgaard Jensen
University of Copenhagen, Denmark

This chapter proposes that some snowclones (schematic stock phrases) display some degree of proverbiality to the extent that it can be argued that they occupy a grey zone between proverbs proper and semi-schematic idioms. Drawing on theoretical insights from construction grammar and cognitive-semantic approaches to socio-cultural cognition, this chapter also presents three case studies of snowclones within the English language that are based on corpus-data and corpus-linguistic methodology. More specifically, this chapter studies patterns of use, such as productivity, epistemic status marking, and co-occurrence with co-textual topics, of *the only good X is a dead X*, *one does not simply X into Y*, and *in X no one can hear you Y* so as to address their potential proverbial nature.

Keywords: construction grammar, cultural literacy, epistemic status, socio-cultural cognition

1. Introduction

A snowclone is a type of schematic stock expression that writers and speakers can use without having to exert much effort. An example is *X is the new Y* seen in *orange is the new black*, *gay is the new straight*, and *metal is the new pop*. Snowclones are often viewed as clichés associated with lazy writing. However, there is more to snowclones than laziness. They are *bona fide* grammatical constructions

---

* **Content warning:** Since one of the linguistic phenomena discussed in this chapter is often used in hate speech, a number of examples discussed in this chapter might be offensive or otherwise triggering to some readers. Note also that non-standard features of the data (such as typos and misspellings) are retained in the data examples discussed in this chapter.

that pair form with conventionalised meaning. Snowclones also have social currency serving as badges of cultural literacy and solidarity in social groups (Peters 2006b: 29) that require speakers to tap into linguistic and socio-cultural competence for appropriate use. Some even have features associated with proverbs.

Proverbs themselves reflect cultural literacy and are often intertwined with folklore, cultural didactics, belief systems, and encyclopaedic knowledge. So are proverbial snowclones: their use reflects underlying systems and processes of encyclopaedic and socio-cultural cognition. This chapter explores three potentially proverbial snowclones: *the only good X is a dead X* (1), *one does not simply X into Y* (2), and *in X no one can hear you Y* (3):

(1) The only good Boomer is a dead Boomer & the sooner we die the better.
(GLOWBE G CA ...elfarb.wordpress.com)[1]

(2) One does not simply walk into the Olympics and leave with four gold medals. Ambition is necessary. (NOW 17-07-14 US ESPN)

(3) The internet is spectacularly inhospitable to the grace notes of coy, hyper-intentional ambiguity and irony that marked the first wave of Morrissey's verbal career. Online, no one can hear you smirk.(NOW 16-06-23 US MTV.com)

We will refer to the snowclone in (1) as the *only good*-construction, while the one in (2) is referred to as the Mordor-construction and the one in (3) is called the Ripley-construction – named for the main character of the *Alien* franchise that introduced the snowclone. All three have independent declarative clause structures and can easily be used in a proverbial fashion as didactic comments that appear to draw on widely accepted general knowledge.

Drawing on construction-grammatical and socio-cognitive-semantic theory, this chapter addresses aspects of use of these snowclones hoping to illuminate their potential proverbial status. This study is best viewed as the first few shovels of soil from which hypotheses to be tested later might emerge. Therefore, while empirical and drawing on no less than three hypercorpora of English, the analytical methods applied are somewhat simplistic.

---

1. The corpora used in this study are the *Corpus of Contemporary American English* (COCA), *News on the Web* (NOW), and *Global Web-based English* (GLOWBE). Following the conventions of corpus-linguistic practice, each example is accompanied by a code that specifies the corpus and the source file.

2. Proverbial snowclones as constructions

Our main theoretical framework is usage-based construction grammar (Croft and Cruse 2004: 291–327; Hilpert 2019). In construction grammar as such (Fillmore et al. 1988; Goldberg 1995; Croft 2001), language is a system of signs pairing form and conventionalised meaning. Traugott and Trousdale (2014: 258) sketch out the basic principles:

> the basic unit of construction grammar is the sign. Grammar is conceptualized as a non-modular system, and therefore no one linguistic domain such as syntax is core. Constructions are made up of features: minimally, semantics, pragmatics and discourse function on the meaning side, and syntax, morphology and phonology on the form side … Constructions are organized at various levels of generality and may be formally specific or schematic or something in between. Schemas are abstract, sometimes wholly so …, sometimes partially so, but schematic constructions always involve slots with variables.

Language itself is viewed as a complex adaptive system (Beckner et al. 2009) where linguistic competence emerges as a global-level system from local-level patterns of interaction and, in a feedback loop, influences further usage-events. Patten (2014: 91) neatly summarises the usage-based model:

> On this model, humans are not innately programmed with grammatical knowledge; instead, all aspects of language are learned from the input (or rather from the speaker's linguistic experiences). Both language learning and language change involve the speaker inductively generalizing over instances to form mental schemas (or constructions) which are represented in the language system. On a usage-based model then, constructions are simply conventionalized chunks of linguistic knowledge … From this, it follows that the storage and organization of grammatical knowledge is dependent on, and can change according to, patterns of use.

The system is heterogeneously distributed such that "what is acceptable for some speakers may not be so for others" (Traugott and Trousdale 2014: 258). Structural redundancies can occur in the system in the form of different subconstructions. Contextual knowledge pertaining to the use of a construction is part of the language system and constitutes the external properties of a construction (Fillmore 1988: 36). The system, while stable and regulated by conventions, is not fixed but dynamic and adaptable to contextual and behavioural changes in local-level interactions.

2.1 Snowclones

A snowclone is an idiomatic constructional entity in which a fixed expression – the original model (Zwicky 2005) – is schematised into a more general pattern: "Snowclones are patterned figures of speech that empower swapping out words, phrases or images for one another without breaking the original pattern" (Hill 2018: 423). Traugott and Trousdale (2014: 270–271) describe this process as follows: "a fixed specific expression becomes less fixed by virtue of introducing a variable (a formal change), while the original meaning of the micro-construction generalizes (a meaning change)". Zwicky (2006) proposes the following outline of this process:

- **Pre-formula**: a number of specific expressions are uttered at the local level that are understood literally, requiring no special knowledge to decode.
- **First fixing**: a particularly attractive way of expressing the idea is uttered by someone that spreads in the speech community as a fixed form.
- **Variation on the fixed expression**: in subsequent usage-events, the fixed expression develops open slots through variations of it.
- **Snowcloning**: a schematic template of the expression emerges that contains one or more lexically open slots and a more or less identifiable communicative function.

The original model emerges in the first fixing phase, which arguably involves social factors like influence, outreach, and prestige; this is why many snowclones originate from popular culture. For instance, the original model of the snowclone *X? We don't need no stinking X!* is the line *Badges? We don't need no stinking badges!* from the popular 1974-movie *Blazing Saddles*; apparently, it can be traced back to the 1935-book *The Treasure of the Sierra Madre* (McFedries 2008: 27). Similarly, *I'm an X, not a Y!* evolved from a recurring gag in the original *Star Trek* series (O'Connor 2007a). A final example is *I, for one, welcome our new X overlords*, which stems from an episode of *The Simpsons* where a character says *I, for one, welcome our new insect overlords* (Peters 2006b).

While a snowclone has an original model, it can be used "without any appreciation of its origin; in fact, for many snowclones the original model is hard to determine" (Zwicky 2005). However, O'Connor (2007c) argues that "in order for a phrase to be a true snowclone, it will remind the hearer of the original source". Perhaps, since language is a heterogeneously distributed system, some speakers know the original model while others do not, and the snowclone has different cultural significance to different speakers. 'Snowclone' was introduced as a term by Whitman (2004) with reference to the bleached conditional *If Eskimos have N words for snow, then X have Y words for Z*. This was in response to calls by

Liberman (2003) and Pullum (2003a) for a term covering "a multi-use, customizable, instantly recognizable, time-worn, quoted or misquoted phrase or sentence that can be used in an entirely open array of different jokey variants by lazy journalists and writers" (Pullum 2003a).

Snowclones are sometimes regarded with disdain and viewed as clichés used by lazy writers and editors (e.g., Pullum 2004; Peters 2006a, b). However, Peters (2006b: 29) concedes that snowclones can have sociolinguistic meanings, serving as indicators of solidarity and cultural literacy within social groups, and McFedries (2008: 27) points to the fact that "many snowclones are firmly entrenched in mainstream culture". Peters (2006a: 14) reports that snowclones can be viewed as "poetic, rather than literal and pedestrian, language, so they add some interest and verve to writing and speech".

2.2 Proverbiality

Proverbiality is the degree to which an expression is perceived as a proverb. Taylor and Whiter (1967: viii–xii) lament the difficulty of clearly defining proverbs because the criteria are often vague. Indeed, proverbiality is not clear-cut in native speakers (Arora 1994; Gibbs 2001: 168) but a gradient entity defined by prototype features, some of which are listed below:

- **Didactics**: Proverbs are often advisory or didactic, calling upon various domains of conventional wisdom (e.g., Hoffman 2012; McArthur et al. 2018) and "well-known truths, social norms or moral themes" (Gibbs 2001: 168). Arora (1994: 4) writes that tradition and "the sense of historically-derived authority or of community-sanctioned wisdom that they convey" make proverbs work.
- **Axiomaticity**: Many proverbs express perceived universalities, eternal truths, or enduring themes "about everyday life because they allude to general, perhaps universal, principles about intelligent or reasonable human behavior" (Gibbs 2001: 169) and "serve to define and stereotype a range of domestic and interpersonal situations, and to transmit these cultural categories from generation to generation" (Cram 1994: 75). Consequently, "[t]he status of the proverb is similar to that of belief statements in general, and in particular to the axioms which underpin scientific systems of encyclopedic statements" (Cram 1994: 92).
- **Situational applicability**: A proverb is often applied in situations of perceived relevance to the axiom that it expresses (Abrahams and Babcock 1977: 417; Seitel 1976).

- **Familiarity**: Proverbs form a genre recognisable to language users (Arora 1994: 6). Gibbs (2001: 168) suggests that, in addition to fully fixed idioms, "certain fundamental proverb structures exist that have been the basis for hundreds of proverbs". He calls these proverbial markers and lists as examples *where there's X, there's Y, no X without Y, like X, one X does not make a Y* and *like X, like Y*.
- **Fixedness**: Proverbs may be fully fixed; however, as the notion of proverbial markers suggests, some merely require a syntactic scaffold to be recognised as proverbs.
- **Impersonality**: Proverbs "are typically "invoked" or "cited" rather than straightforwardly asserted" (Cram 1994: 75), quoting the collective and cultural wisdom of the community in question. While a proverb expresses the speaker's individual assessment of a situation, the assessment is construed as a judgment based on communal cultural values. Via their quotative nature, "proverbs may serve as impersonal vehicles for personal communication" (Ojo Arewa and Dundes 1964: 70).
- **Figurativity**: "Most proverbs are metaphorical" (Gibbs 2001: 168; see also McArthur et al. 2018; Hoffman 2012; Arora 1994: 11; Seitel 1976). However, Seitel (1976: 128) operates with a metaphorical proverb subcategory to contrast it with non-metaphorical proverbs. Arora (1994: 8) acknowledges the existence of apothegms: proverbs that are recognised as such by speakers despite not being figurative.

These features are intertwined, and, in some cases, difficult to disentangle. Moreover, several formal and rhetorical features have been proposed, such as shortness and plainness (Taylor and Whiter 1967: x), and Gibbs (2001: 168) lists the following as formal-rhetorical traits that are seen in many proverbs: meter, rhyme, slant rhyme, alliteration, assonance, personification, paradox, and parallelism.

Barring figurativity, formal features, and fixedness, all features listed above relate to the epistemic status of proverb. Epistemic status is the type of knowledge assigned to the proverb in usage-events as marked by co-textual features (or lack thereof). For instance, markers like *it is said that, they say, as the old saying goes*, or *according to the adage* present the expression as an impersonal quote (Ojo Arewa and Dundes 1964), while markers like *we all know, it is generally known*, or *everybody knows* treat the content of the expression as general knowledge or wisdom within the community. In cases where an expression appears in a bare declarative structure, its content is treated as what we call an unmarked fact – even if in reality, it expresses an opinion (M. van Leeuwen 2012: 98). The rhetorical effect is that, while very subjective, the utterance has more argumentative strength than had it included an opiner-marking matrix clause (Verhagen 2005: 107).

2.3 Proverbial snowclones

A subclass of snowclones displays proverbial behaviour. While many proverbs proper are folkloric (e.g., Seitel 1976; Ojo Arewa and Dundes 1964; Arora 1994), the familiarity and authority of proverbial snowclones is generated via their place in popular culture and they may be imbued with built-in irony, sarcasm, celebration, hostility and the like.[2] A proverbial snowclone may appear to have a didactic function, and, while it may take on the air of impersonality, it could still serve as a stance marker. Like proverbs proper, proverbial snowclones will often be restricted in terms of appropriate situations of use.

It is important to remember that proverbiality is gradient, understood such that some types of expressions are typical proverbs compared to others. Nontypical expressions may still be recognised as apothegms, proverbs or proverb-like expressions by speakers and may also overlap in function or otherwise share a number of features with proverbs proper. In this chapter, it is held that proverbial snowclones are less typical members of the proverb category, but still display enough proverbial features that they may be recognised and used as proverbs or at least in a proverb-like fashion.

3. Data and method

This chapter is corpus-based, drawing on the following corpora:

- *Corpus of Contemporary American English* (COCA): a 1-billion-word corpus of American English from the period 1990–2019
- *News on the Web* (NOW): a monitor corpus of English from online news items going back to 2010, this corpus contains, at the time of writing, around 13.2 billion words
- *Global Web-based English* (GLOWBE): a corpus of about 1.9 billion words from blogs and webpages, GLOWBE represents 20 varieties of English: American, Canadian, British, Irish, Australian, New Zealand, Indian, Sri-Lankan, Pakistani, Bangladeshi, Singaporean, Malaysian, Filipino, Hong Kong, South African, Nigerian, Kenyan, Tanzanian, and Jamaican English.

These corpora were selected due to their size, representativeness and recentness. Large hypercorpora provide a large data mass allowing for a number of hits, or occurrences, sufficient for systematic analysis. Moreover, while *COCA* only rep-

---

2. An interesting discussion, beyond the scope of this chapter, is where popular culture ends and folklore begins.

resents American English, the three corpora collectively represent many different national varieties and genres. The corpora all contain recent data, ranging from the 1990s to 2021, allowing for the inclusion of very recent usage-events into the analysis. The following search strings were used to retrieve instances of the three snowclones:

- *only good* construction: *only good NOUN+ BE a|an|the, only good _nn2 BE **
- Ripley-construction: *no one can _v?i you _v?i, no-one can _v?i you _v?i, nobody can _v?i you _v?i, noone can _v?i you _v?i*
- Mordor-construction: *one does not simply _v?i, you do not simply _v?i*

Note that none of the search strings finds all possible realisations of the snowclone in question. For instance, the two first search strings do not find variants where another adjective than *good* is used – see (12) for an example where *innocent* takes its place. In a more systematic large-scale study, such limitations would be severely problematic, and stricter search strategies would be required. Non-instances and duplicates manually discarded. Table 1 accounts for the post-pruning data.

Table 1. Overall frequencies

Snowclone	Hits
only good construction	421
Ripley-construction	357
Mordor-construction	269

A number of linguistic and extra-linguistic categories were identified and quantified. These were treated as association patterns: a unit's "systematic associations with other features" (Biber et al. 1998: 5). In a usage-based perspective, these are indicative of a construction's external properties. The patterns addressed in this study are:

- **Epistemic status**: The type of knowledge assigned to the content of the snowclone in the usage-event
- **Discourse function**: The discourse-pragmatic function that the snowclone plays in the usage-event
- **Co-textual topic**: The overall topic of discourse surrounding the snowclone in a usage-event

Construction-lexeme interaction patterns as well as other construction-specific patterns were also addressed. Appendix 1 lists the categories of epistemic status and discourse function, while Table 2 provides an overview of the co-textual topics observed in our data.

Table 2. Overview of co-textual topics

Co-textual topics	AGRICULTURE, THE *ALIEN* FRANCHISE, ART, ASTROPHYSICS AND OUTER SPACE, BUSINESS AND ECONOMY, CARS, CINEMA, COMMUNICATION, CONFLICT AND WAR, CRIME, CULTURE, NATURAL DISASTERS, EDUCATION, FAMILY, FASHION AND APPAREL, GASTRONOMY, GEEK CULTURE, HOUSEKEEPING, LATRINARY AFFAIRS, LOCATIONS AND PLACES, THE *LORD OF THE RINGS* FRANCHISE (INCL. OTHER RELATED LITERARY WORKS BY TOLKIEN), MEDICINE AND HEALTH, MEMES, MUSIC, NATURE, OCCUPATIONS AND JOBS, PERIL, PERSONAL DEVELOPMENT AND PSYCHOLOGY, PETS, PHILOSOPHY, POLITICS, RADIO, RELIGION, SCIENCE, SHOPPING, SOCIETY, SPORTS, TECHNOLOGY, TELEVISION, THEATRE, TRAFFIC, TRAVEL AND TOURISM

Some topics could be subsumed under others. For instance, ASTROPHYSICS AND OUTER SPACE could be subsumed under SCIENCE, and both the *ALIEN* and *LORD OF THE RINGS* FRANCHISES could be subsumed under GEEK CULTURE.

Fixedness being a proverbial feature and snowclones having undergone schematisation, productivity seems relevant to address. Productivity is here understood such that a schematic structure that can be realised by several forms is more productive than one that can only be realised by few forms (Bybee 2010): a construction with many hapax legomena (and a high type frequency) is productive while one with few hapax legomena (and a high token frequency) is not. Shibuya (2015) argues that lexical richness measures are also applicable as measures of productivity. In this study, productivity is addressed via what I call productivity profiles. These are matrices of productivity measures of all schematic positions in a construction. For the purpose of this study, while more complex measures exist (e.g., Baayen's (2008) lexical growth curves), standardised type-token ratios (STTR) were applied. STTRs are according to Baker et al. (2006: 151)

> achieved by obtaining the type/token ratio for, say, the first 2,000 words in the corpus (or however many words are specified), then the next 2,000 words, then the next and so on. The standardised type/token ratio is calculated by working out the average of all of these separate type/token ratios, providing a more representative figure.

STTRs were calculated for each schematic slot based on raw lists of units occurring in each slot. This particular study operates with chunks of 100. The output of an STTR analysis is a number between 1 and 100: the closer to 100, the higher the degree of productivity.

4. *Only good* as a marker of social attitude

This snowclone is derived from the original model *the only good Indian is a dead Indian* – an instance of hate speech attributed to American Civil War General Philip Sheridan (O'Connor 2007b). It has appeared in various western-themed media and literature. Its general schematic syntactic structure can be represented as follows:

$$[^S \textit{the only good } N1_i] \, [^V BE] \, [^{SC} DET_{indef} \, PrM \, N2_i]$$

The subject (S) is realised by *the only good* followed a head noun (N1) while the verbal (V) is a form of *BE*, and the subject complement (SC) is an indefinite noun phrase (99.5% of all instances have indefinite determiners; only 0.5% have definite ones) followed by a unit that premodifies (PrM) a head noun (N2). N1 and N2 are coreferential (indicated by *i*) via lexical repetition:

(4) The only good Communist is a dead Communist.
 (NOW 20-12-25 IN businessinsider.in)

(5) The only good media is a truthful media.
 (GLOWBE US B …hiddenharmonies.org)

(6) The only good vigilante is a fictional vigilante and The Punisher is one of the best examples. (NOW 17-11-17 US Den of Geek US)

However, as seen in (7), coreferentiality may also be achieved via anaphoric *one*. 95.4% of all instances of N1 and N2 are in the singular, while only 3.6% are in the plural. Semantically, the snowclone selects a category expressed by N1 and N2 and specifies that, in order to qualify as desirable or acceptable, the member must meet the criterion of having the attribute expressed by PrM. The S arguably has generic reference while the SC has specific reference.

How productive is this schema? Table 3 presents the STTR-based productivity profile of this snowclone.

Table 3. Productivity profile of the *only-good* construction

Position	STTR
N1	59.25
N2	52.2
PrM	22.27

N1 is slightly more productive than N2. PrM is less productive than N1 and N2. N1 and N2 fall within a mid-range of productivity suggesting that, while there might be many hapaxes, there are also some lexemes with high token frequencies. Figures 1 and 2 provide an overview of the distribution of lexemes in these two positions.[3]

Figure 1. Lexemes in N1

Unsurprisingly, given the original model, *Indian* is the most frequent lexeme in N1 and N2. In many cases, this owes to speakers directly reciting the original model.[4] The difference in productivity between N1 and N2 is due to pronominal

---

3. EMPTY indicates that the position is not filled (or filled by Ø).
4. There is a similar reason why *Democrat* is so frequent.

Figure 2. Lexemes in N2

one appearing in N2 in many cases (accounting for 16.67% of all tokens in N2) with anaphoric reference back to N1:

(7) You communist heathen you can burn in hell as well because the only good communist is a dead one (COCA 2012 WEB theblaze.com)

Moreover, most lexemes in N1 and N2 refer to categories of people based on, for instance, ethnicity, nationality, religious or political orientation as well as vocation or other activities. This indicates the slots may be somewhat semantically restricted: part of speakers' knowledge of the *only good*-construction is its semantic preference (Begagić 2013) for social category labels:

(8) "The only good Arab is a castrated Arab," I was told by my lab partner in Zoology. (COCA 2012 BLOG muslimvoices.com)

(9) It has been said that the only good lawyer is a dead one.
(NOW 16-02-21 US Catch News)

(10) The only good Zionist is a dead Zionist. (NOW 13-03-12 GB Daily Mail)

In all three examples, the lexemes in N1 and N2 prompt hearers to engage in social categorisation to identify the referents, thus accessing relevant information within a shared system of social categories. It is not far-fetched to speculate that the snowclone serves the purpose of othering (the process of constructing an US/THEM relationship while typically also judging the THEM negatively). The social category labels may be downright derogatory:

(11) Eughhh! A Kraut is a Kraut is a Kraut. And the only good Kraut is a dead Kraut. (NOW 12-01-23 GB Daily Mail)

(12) Just as in the Vietmam War, where the policy was "The only Good Gook is a Dead Gook", we now have "The only Innocent Suspect is a Dead Suspect".
(GLOWBE GB B guardian.co.uk)

(13) Only good injun is a dead injun. (GLOWBE LK G dbsjeyaraj.com)

This is not surprising, as the original model counts as an instance of hate speech. Thus, in prototypical uses, N1 and N2 signal social categories while less prototypical ones signal other types of categories as seen in (14)–(16). Figure 3 shows that *dead* has a very high token frequency in PrM. Like the original model, the snowclone serves mainly to judge the social category negatively through a hyperbolic wish for the death of members of that category. Since the social label categories in N1 and N2 appear in the singular, but have generic reference, the snowclone involves the socio-discursive, and in my opinion also cognitive, process of genericisation (T. van Leeuwen 1995: 46–48) in which reference is made to an entire social category. The snowclone largely retains the negative other-evaluating communicative function of the original model: it is prototypically used as a discursive tool of hate speech. Both original model and snowclone have a built-in morbid irony in that the only desirable members of the category are ones that are no longer alive. Consequently, while not outright metaphorical, core uses of this snowclone do display some level of figurativity, but possibly not enough to elevate it out of the apothegm category.

Chapter 10. The only good snowclone is a dead snowclone **273**

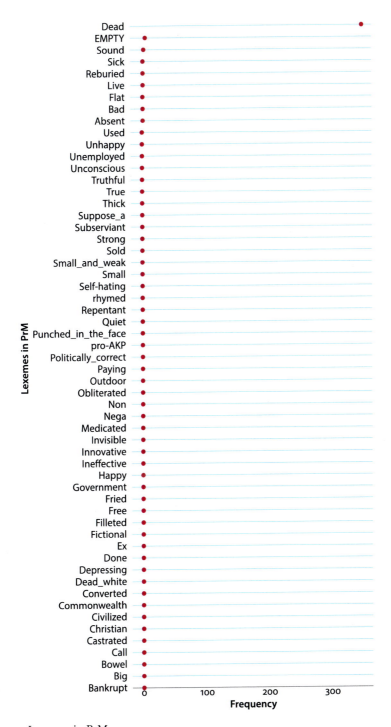

Figure 3. Lexemes in PrM

As Figures 1 and 2 suggest, this negative evaluation is extended to non-human entities:[5]

(14)   the only good carp is a dead carp   (GLOWBE AU G …ishingmonthly.com.au)

(15)   To most people, the only good fly is a dead one.
(NOW 15-07-30 GB The Guardian)

(16)   The only good Brexit is a dead Brexit.   (18-09-23 GB Metro)

(17)   To many people, the only good bug is a dead bug. And even though insects may not be the most cuddly creatures on the planet, some can actually help you grow your garden better.   (COCA 2004 MAG Child Life)

The evocation of a category and negative judgment thereof are retained, but the category is not a social category. Still, it seems that, in a case like (16), where the category is an animacy-less one, personification still occurs due to *dead*.

There is a minority of cases where the negative evaluation is less hyperbolic (18–20) or absent (21–23):

(18)   because the only good cop is an absent cop, Black, brown or white
(NOW 17-11-29 CA Toronto Star)

(19)   The only good landlord is a bankrupt one…
(NOW 17-11-28 NZ Interest.co.nz)

(20)   the outright apologists for religiobabble clearly feel the only good atheist is an invisible one, this lot appears to me to feel the only good
(GLOWBE US G freethoughtblogs.com)

(21)   The only good customer is a paying customer, and if you don't ask, you might not   (GLOWBE NZ G sharkpatrol.co.nz)

(22)   But according to Rousseau, the only good death is an unconscious death, and that biotechnology could easily achieve.   (COCA 2003 ACAD PerspPolSci)

(23)   at least the only good dollar is a strong dollar.
(COCA 2018 SPOK PBS_Business)

Unlike (16), (22–23) do not seem to involve personification, as PrM is filled by adjectival forms that do not presuppose high animacy. Presumably, speakers are aware of the status of this snowclone as a tool of hate speech and othering, and that this function is expanded and, in some cases, even subverted, in less central uses. This arguably requires cultural literacy in speakers.

---

5. Here, it is relevant to mention that the reason why *bug* is somewhat prominent is due to a line from the *Starship Troopers* movie, in which Earth is fighting an interplanetary war against a race of giant insects, being referred to several times in the data.

Chapter 10. The only good snowclone is a dead snowclone

Turning to the potential proverbial status of this snowclone, let us first have a look at its epistemic status (see Table 4).

Table 4. Distribution of epistemic status categories in the *only-good* construction

Epistemic status	Frequency	%
advice	1	0.24
assumption	1	0.24
axiom	4	0.95
belief	8	1.90
fact	3	0.71
general knowledge	13	3.09
opinion	32	7.60
other-assigned belief	95	22.57
other-assigned opinion	178	42.28
possibility	1	0.24
revelation	1	0.24
unmarked fact	84	19.95

The unmarked fact category has the third highest occurrence. Here, the snowclone appears in a declarative sentence such that, while arguably expressing the opinion of the speaker, it is treated as expressing a fact (24–26). Opiner-markers are completely absent here. Contrast this with the opinion category in which the speaker openly signals that the snowclone is an opiner (27–29).

(24) Shove your mthr fkn racist comments up I ((. The only good bigot is a dead one. Lets start with you bigot.   (GLOWBE US G …s.washingtonpost.com)

(25) Free verse is no more than cut-up prose, and the only good poem is a rhymed poem.   (COCA 2010 ACAD Writer)

(26) We had to make it look good. The only good witness is a dead witness. Good shot. Let's get the diamonds.   (COCA 2002 MOV All About The Benjamins)

(27) I tend towards the temperate view that the only good cyclist is a dead one.   (GLOWBE GB B bikebiz.com)

(28) You really want to know what I think?
Yes.
I think the only good alien's a dead alien.   (COCA 2013 TV Falling Skies)

(29) And as far as I am concerned the only good patriotism is a civilized one.
(NOW 11-09-10 PH Inquirer.net)

The examples in (24-26) have higher degrees of proverbiality because they express what opinions is really as if they were indisputable facts in commentary on the situations in which they appear. For instance, *the only good bigot is a dead one* in (24) seems to take for granted that its content is an established objective fact upon which the threat that appears in the following sentence builds. This is not the case in (27-28). Here, the co-textual markers *I think* and *as far as I am concerned* indicate that the instances of the snowclone merely signal the speakers' opinions. The two most common categories are other-assigned belief and other-assigned opinion, as seen in (30) and (31) respectively:

(30) Traditionally the wolf has been the sworn enemy of the livestock farmer and shepherd, Spanish country lore holding that the only good wolf was a dead wolf. (NOW 13-03-01 GB Financial Times)

(31) Lurking in the area is also the zombie hunter Max who insists that the only good zombie is a dead zombie. (GLOWBE NZ G moria.co.nz (1))

Here, the snowclone is primarily construed as an expression that has proverbial status within a community that excludes the speaker. That is, speakers will use it to signal an axiom, perceived fact, belief, or something similar only to distance themselves from it by assigning it to another individual or to another community. Thus, this use expresses negative stance towards a worldview as an other-assigned opinion. The co-textual topics associated with the snowclone in our data are CONFLICT AND WAR, POLITICS, RELIGION, and SOCIETY, as seen in Table 5.

Many of these topic patterns already come with systems of social categorisation, alignment and othering, making them ripe for negative judgments of social categories that one finds disagreeable (arguably at the core of hate speech). Turning to the distribution of discourse-pragmatic functions, as seen in Figure 4, the most common function is the comment one.

We see the comment function in several of the examples listed above, in which a speaker appends an instance of the snowclone as commentary on a topic or situation, bringing to the forefront the speaker's dislike for a category that relates to the topic or situation.

Table 5. Distribution of co-textual topics in the *only-good* construction

Topic	Frequency	%
AGRICULTURE	1	0.24
ART	7	1.66
BUSINESS AND ECONOMY	3	0.71
CARS	1	0.24
CINEMA	5	1.19
COMMUNICATION	4	0.95
CONFLICT AND WAR	63	14.96
CRIME	7	1.66
EDUCATION	3	0.71
GASTRONOMY	4	0.95
GEEK CULTURE	12	2.85
HOUSEKEEPING	2	0.48
MEDICINE AND HEALTH	3	0.71
MEMES	6	1.43
NATURE	53	12.59
OCCUPATIONS AND JOBS	4	0.95
PERSONAL DEVELOPMENT AND PSYCHOLOGY	3	0.71
PETS	4	0.95
POLITICS	98	23.28
RELIGION	27	6.41
SHOPPING	1	0.24
SOCIETY	85	20.19
SPORTS	5	1.19
TECHNOLOGY	7	1.66
TELEVISION	7	1.66
TRAFFIC	6	1.43

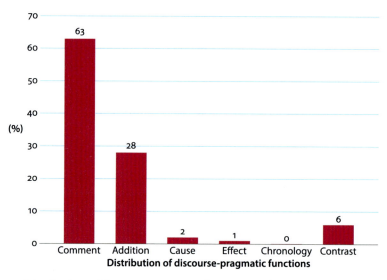

Figure 4. Distribution of discourse-pragmatic functions in the *only-good* construction

5. Difficulties in Mordor

The Mordor-construction is derived from a line in the 2001-film *Lord of the Rings: Fellowship of the Ring* in which the character Boromir explains how well guarded and dangerous Mordor is. The construction *one does not simply X* predates this movie though, and a quick Google ngram search documents uses as far back as the 1870s. Some examples are *One does not simply attempt to cure a confession* (1901), *To be seen, one does not simply show one's self; one gesticulates* (1927), and *But while this is the ultimate goal for the very gifted man, one does not simply vault into that position, not even if one is a child prodigy* (1949). Similarly, the corpora used in this study document examples that predate *Lord of the Rings*. Arguably, this construction was around before *Lord of the Rings* but was made popular by that franchise. As a construction, it has the following syntactic structure:

$[^S one] \ [^{V\text{-}} does] \ [^{PRN} \ [^A not] \ [^A simply] \ [^{\text{-}V} MV_{inf}] \ [X]]$

Several elements are fixed: the subject *one* (the possibility of other generic pronouns being used cannot be excluded), the auxiliary verb *does* and the two adverbials *not* and *simply*. It is in the latter portion of the predication (PRN) that we find schematicity. The infinitive main verb (the hyphens before and after V indicate discontinuity) and what follows – here referred to as X – are the schematic positions in this snowclone. Semantically, the snowclone appears to express a scenario in which TROUBLE-FREE MOVEMENT INTO A PARTICULAR LOCATION is negated.

Table 6 accounts for the productivity profile of the Mordor-construction.

Table 6. Productivity profile of the Mordor-construction

Position	STTR
MV_{inf}	57.66
X	82.78

The STTR of X is based on everything appearing after MV_{inf} as one string rather than on the individual words in the string. The X-position has a quite high STTR score. This makes sense given that the position is realised by large strings of words for the most part, meaning that there will be more hapaxes throughout. As expected, *into Mordor* has the most tokens with a frequency of 47 (17.34%). The MV_{inf} position is moderately productive, suggesting a similar behaviour to the N1 and N2 positions in the *only good*-construction. As seen in Figure 5, that is indeed the case with *walk* forming the basis of multiple tokens while many of the other lexemes are hapaxes.

While this snowclone has a declarative structure, there is variation in transitivity. It appears with the following transitivity patterns:

(33) One does not simply become a Karen.
(NOW 20-06-04 ZA 2oceansvibe.com) [copula]

(34) One does not simply tell the companies how they will operate.
(COCA 2012 WEB paidcontent.org) [ditransitive]

(35) One does not simply change just by glancing through, and no one can change a person. (COCA 2012 WEB mytwodollars.com) [intransitive]

(36) In Denmark, one does not simply let the new year happen. You go on the offense and jump into it.
(NOW 20-12-28 US The Washington Post on MSN.com) [*let*-concessive]

(37) One does not simply tackle Josh Papalii one-on-one.
(NOW 20-11-04 AU theroar.com.au) [monotransitive active]

(38) One does not simply get set up on Word Press, configure a few plugins, sit back and get rich. (GLOWBE ZA G memeburn.com) [monotransitive passive]

(39) One does not simply add lazygamer to Bloodborne memes.
(NOW 14-08-12 ZA Lazygamer) [complex transitive w. adverbial]

Figure 5. Lexemes in MV_{inf}

(40) One does not simply call a Canadian province an American state and not expect to get some feedback.
(NOW 21-02-25 CA huffingtonpost.ca) [complex transitive w. object complement]

(41) One does not simply walk into *that* Mordor.
(NOW 13-11-13 GB Wired.co.uk) [intransitive w. adverbial]

The distribution is accounted for in Table 7.

Table 7. Distribution of transitivity patterns in the Mordor-construction

Transitivity pattern	Frequency	%
copula	5	1.86
ditransitive	3	1.12
intransitive	10	3.72
let-construction	1	0.37
monotransitive active	111	41.26
monotransitive passive	2	0.74
complex transitive w. obligatory adverbial	3	1.12
complex transitive w. object complement	1	0.37
intransitive w. spatial adverbial	133	49.44

The fact that intransitives with spatial adverbials are frequent is to be expected due to *into Mordor*, itself a spatial adverbial, being the most repeated X-unit. However, monotransitive actives come very close. As a construction, this snowclone may prefer these two transitivity patterns as external properties. Examples (33–41) suggest a more schematic version of the semantics outlined above: rather than expressing negation of TROUBLE-FREE MOVEMENT INTO A PARTICULAR LOCATION, the snowclone more generally expresses negation of a TROUBLE-FREE ACTION as such. Monotransitivity typically involves two-participant situations in which an AGENT, or AGONIST, exerts energy upon a PATIENT that may or may not exert ANTAGONISTIC ENERGY (Talmy 1988), thus requiring more effort from the AGENT. The Mordor-construction is thus arguably semantically compatible with monotransitives.

In terms of epistemic status, this snowclone is most frequently used to signal unmarked facts (see Table 8).

(43) Discovery also borrows Mirror, Mirror's logic that one does not simply travel to the Mirror Universe, but must switch places.
(NOW 18-01-09 GB Den of Geek UK)

Table 8. Distribution of epistemic status categories

Epistemic status	Frequency	%
axiom	6	2.23
fact	3	1.12
general knowledge	2	0.74
other-assigned belief	1	0.37
other-assigned opinion	1	0.37
possibility	2	0.74
revelation	1	0.37
unmarked fact	253	94.05

(44) I respect the necessity for a diversity of tactics in tackling this issue – after all, one does not simply walk into Mordor.
(NOW 13–10–28 US Waging Nonviolence)

(45) If you're looking to bone up on the mythos before diving in, you may think it's a pretty easy task. Just a couple of films, right? Nope. One does not simply walk into Shimizu's sprawling world. There are 12 full-length feature films to get through (and that's not even taking into account the short films, the mobile content, the novelisations, the manga and the Wii game)...
(NOW 20–01–15 GB denofgeek.com)

Like the *only good*-construction, instances of the Mordor-construction construe their contents as indisputable objective facts rather than subjective judgments of difficulty. In terms of discourse-pragmatic function, as Figure 6 shows, the most common ones are the comment and contrast functions.

Here are some examples of the comment function:

(46) Wild Star is an extremely promising game, with some of the most fun combat around (ask anyone who's played Wild Star then went back to World of Warcraft – one does not simply go back to not double jumping).
(NOW 20–03–24 GB denofgeek.com)

(47) Being a geek isn't a superficial thing. One does not simply walk into a geek convention, or put on a certain style of clothing, or a costume, and become a geek.
(GLOWBE US G whatever.scalzi.com)

The comment function presents the speaker's commentary on a situation judging its level of difficulty as if it were an objectively inherent to the situation. In (46), the preference for double jumping and the difficulty it presents to a player who has transitioned back from *Wild Star* to *World of Warcraft* is construed as a gen-

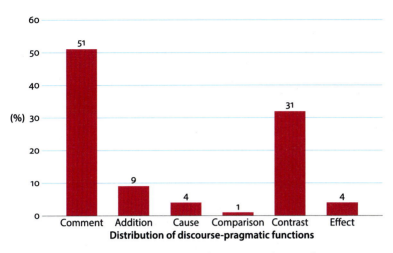

Figure 6. Distribution of discourse-pragmatic functions in the Mordor-construction

eral experience shared by all players who have made that switch. It elevates the experience from an individual one to a communal one. Example (47) construes the road to geekdom as one that demands more dedication than investing in particular apparel and participating in certain events. Presenting this as an unmarked fact, (47) elevates the speaker's opinion on what qualifies a person as a true geek to being a rule that defines all of geekdom. In (48–50), we see some instances of the contrast function:

(48) One does not simply establish once and for all an essential body of religious knowledge that is "good enough" for being a Muslim. Rather, good Muslims pursue religious understanding and persistently attempt to shape one's life according to the will of God. This is an on-going struggle (cihad), as many observant Muslims reminded me.   (COCA 2008 ACAD AnthropoIQ)

(49) One does not simply appear in Australian Spectator; one is inducted after having passed tests of conservative soundness such as being a Liberal staffer and Murdoch journalist (e.g. Tom Switzer, Christian Kerr) or having been a Liberal MP of many years' standing   (GLOWBE AU B …hepoliticalsword.com)

(50) Mama! They must take ship. It is an island. One does not simply walk into Murano.   (COCA 2014 FIC Bk:ValourVanity)

This function contrasts the perceived trouble-free scenario with the, in the speaker's perspective, realistic more difficult scenario. Example (49) is particularly interesting as it is an example of what could be called the *one does not simply X, one does Y* contrastive construction (whose function is arguably identical to the contrasting uses of the Mordor-construction). As mentioned earlier, in the corpora used for this study, there are examples of this construction that predate the Mordor-construction (and a Google ngram search similarly documents earlier uses). Thus, clearly, *one does not simply X* was an operational construction before *Lord of the Rings* transformed it into snowclone and meme. With this in mind, one might speculate that it is an aspect of the pre-formula that has been assimilated by the snowclone. In any case, both functions amount to this particular snowclone in proverbial uses serving a quite clear didactic function imparting information upon the addressee that the speaker does not expect the hearer to have, essentially serving to provide a lesson on difficulty. In terms of figurativity, this construction seems to be balancing on the ledge between metaphorical proverb and apothegm. The construction displays some degree of figurativity due to an analogous relationship between entering Mordor and the difficulty of the evaluated situation. Yet, most instances cannot justifiably be classified as metaphorical proverbs, as the underlying semantic scenarios themselves, while analogous, are not metaphorical as such.

Lastly, let us look at the distribution of co-textual topics (Table 9).

Table 9. Distribution of co-textual topics in the Mordor-construction

Topic	Frequency	%
AGRICULTURE	1	0.37
ART	1	0.37
ASTROPHYSICS AND OUTER SPACE	2	0.74
BUSINESS AND ECONOMY	15	5.58
CARS	6	2.23
CINEMA	13	4.83
COMMUNICATION	5	1.86
CONFLICT AND WAR	1	0.37
CRIME	2	0.74
CULTURE	3	1.12
EDUCATION	3	1.12
FAMILY	2	0.74
FASHION AND APPAREL	3	1.12
GASTRONOMY	9	3.35
GEEK CULTURE	32	11.90
LORD OF THE RINGS FRANCHISE	31	11.52
MEDICINE AND HEALTH	3	1.12
MEMES	25	9.29

Table 9. *(continued)*

Topic	Frequency	%
MUSIC	4	1.49
OCCUPATIONS AND JOBS	8	2.97
PERIL	1	0.37
PERSONAL DEVELOPMENT AND PSYCHOLOGY	3	1.12
PHILOSOPHY	2	0.74
POLITICS	26	9.67
RADIO	1	0.37
RELIGION	6	2.23
SCIENCE	4	1.49
SHOPPING	4	1.49
SOCIETY	3	1.12
SPORTS	21	7.81
TECHNOLOGY	8	2.97
THEATRE	2	0.74
TRAVEL AND TOURISM	19	7.06

The snowclone often appears in the context of GEEK CULTURE and the LORD OF THE RINGS franchise; this is not surprising, given the source of the original model. This might hint at the sociolinguistic function of snowclones (Peters 2006b): by using the snowclone in contexts in which it is appropriate, such as discussions relating to GEEK CULTURE and LORD OF THE RINGS (often considered part of GEEK CULTURE), one signals membership of the geek community and/or the *Lord of the Rings* fan community. Arguably, then, usage and full appreciation of this snowclone requires cultural and social literacy in two ways:

- speakers must know its socially accepted situational applicability
- speakers must know its topical linkage to the *Lord of the Rings* franchise

SPORTS and MEMES are also somewhat frequent co-textual topics. One reason why MEMES is a frequent topic is that the snowclone often appears in discussions of its own status as a meme, and, in most of these instances of what is essentially metalinguistic discussions, the snowclone naturally is used non-proverbially. SPORTS is at first blush perhaps a bit surprising. However, given that the snowclone serves to negate effortlessness and emphasise difficulty, its use in sports discourse is not a mystery.

6. Screaming in space and bread with Ripley

This snowclone is derived from the original model *in space no one can hear you scream*, a tagline for the 1979 horror science fiction film *Alien* (Pullum 2003b, O'Connor 2007c). Its syntactic structure can be laid out as follows:

[^{A} PP] [^{S}*no one/no-one/nobody*] [^{V}*can* MV$_{inf}$1] [*you*] [^{V} MV$_{inf}$2]

A variant on this structure occurs occasionally in the data in which the place adverbial is not fronted:

(51) Truly nobody can hear you scream in an empty cinema-auditorium
(NOW 16-07-29 GB BBC New)

This use is not particularly common, though, constituting only 1.73% of all occurrences.

O'Connor (2007c) suggests that this snowclone is not particularly productive. Table 10 seems to support this claim.

Table 10. Productivity profile of the Ripley-construction

Position	STTR
A	23.01
S	3.57
MV$_{inf}$1	1.44
MV$_{inf}$2	22.00

MV$_{inf}$1 is limited to *hear* and *see*, with the former accounting for 98.88% of all occurrences. There is a considerable number of hapaxes in MV$_{inf}$2, but *scream* still makes up 77.59% of all occurrences with many of the other lexemes being VOCAL SOUND EMISSION verbs such as *giggle*, *meow*, *sneeze*, and *snore* (see Figure 7). We do see verbs that do not express VOCAL SOUND EMISSION though:

(52) In space, no one can hear you sweat. Friday, apparently, was the little-known National Trivia Day, and when asked, Star Wars star Mark Hamill had a gem of movie trivia to share. When asked on Twitter by a fan for a bit of trivia, Hamill revealed, "Because of a record heatwave in England when we filmed the original." (NOW 19-01-06 AU CNET)

(53) In space, no one can hear you drool. Which is handy if you're playing the dashingly designed Galaxy on Fire THD in orbit (but, less helpful if you're on a bus). (NOW 12-05-15 GB Pocket Gamer)

Chapter 10. The only good snowclone is a dead snowclone **287**

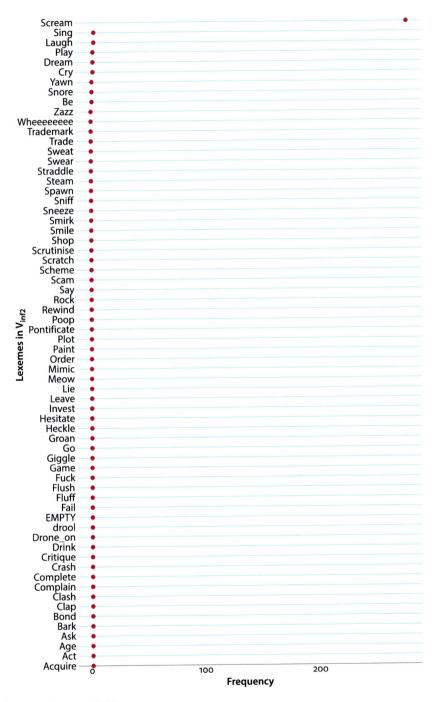

Figure 7. Lexemes in $V_{inf}2$

(54) Hey, Pete, is it true that in space, no one can hear you poop?
(COCA 2010 TV Better Off Ted)

In connection with snowclones' linkage to their original models, O'Connor (2007c) goes as far as stating that she "believe[s] this is a violation of snowclonehood, because the further it gets from having something in common with scream, the less likely it is to evoke the movie quote". We must remember, however, that linkage back to the original model may be less tangible than this and might take the form of co-textual topics as well. Thus, uses without VOCAL SOUND EMISSION verbs are not necessarily violations but rather non-prototypical uses.

Table 11 shows that, just like the Mordor-construction and the *only good* construction, this snowclone is used most often as an unmarked fact, as seen in (52).

Table 11. Distribution of epistemic status categories of the Ripley-construction

Epistemic status	Frequency	%
assumption	6	1.31
belief	1	0.22
category	1	0.22
fact	24	5.25
fantasy	3	0.66
general knowledge	17	3.72
possibility	5	1.09
prediction	1	0.22
quote	13	2.84
revelation	6	1.31
unmarked fact	380	83.15

Fact and general knowledge are also somewhat common: the snowclone is often used to assign general factuality to the contents of its instances. Note also, it is used 13 times (2.84%) in impersonal quotational contexts:

(55) Deep in outer space, millions of miles from civilisation, they say no-one can hear you scream. (NOW 10–06–01 GB BBC News)

(56) As the old saying goes, "in space, no one can hear you scream." (NOW 13–11–04 US EarthSky)

(57) I don't believe it's true what they say; that in space, no one can hear you fluff a note. (NOW 13–01–25 AU Limelight Magazine)

While 2.84% is not a lot, the fact that there are usage-events in which this snowclone is quotatively marked is indicative of some speakers perceiving it as a proverb. There seems to be some degree of familiarity here, and all 13 instances are presented as impersonal quotes of the kind that Ojo Arewa and Dundes (1964) argue to be a feature of proverbiality. An interesting twist, however, is seen in (57) which the repository of general knowledge that is assigned to the community represented by *they* in *what they say* is actually challenged by the speaker.

The most frequent unit in the A-position is the original model's *in space* making up 72.83% of all occurrences. In addition, there are other instances where outer space is retained as a location but expressed through other means like *on an asteroid*, *in a vacuum* or *in a black hole*. This supports O'Connor's (2007c) suggestion that this position prefers space-themed PPs. However, we do see other locations in this position. Some of these evoke similar images of ISOLATION:

(58) At sea, no one can hear you scream   (NOW 19–06–14 IE The Bookseller)

(59) In lockdown, no one can hear you scream   (NOW 21–02–01 US syfy.com)

Others do not do that as such, but – interestingly – the construction nevertheless seems to impose the sense of isolation upon them:

(60) Turns out that in Kent, no one can hear you scream.
(NOW 17–08–01 GB Metro)

(61) At Comic-Con, no one can hear you scream (if you're hidden inside a space suit)   (NOW 17–07–27 ZA Memeburn)

This might indicate that the concept of ISOLATION is a conventional semantic feature inherited from the original model, such that NON-SPACE themed elements that appear in the A-position are coerced into adopting it while other concepts associated with OUTER SPACE are discarded. In addition to OUTER SPACE, another somewhat prominent theme here is the INTERNET:

(62) In cyberspace, no one can hear you scream: The plight of a BT 'fast' broadband user.   (NOW 14–11–15 GB The Guardian)

While (62) is an example of the notion of ISOLATION being imposed upon the preposition phrase *in cyberspace*, there are cases where, rather than ISOLATION – or maybe as a further semantic extension of ISOLATION – it seems that the construction draws on ANONYMITY and THE FREEDOM FROM THE PRYING EYES OF OTHERS. Another factor is likely to be the presence of *space* as the second element in the compound noun *cyberspace*. Below is an example:

(63) And even if you don't attract a single one of them then, well, who cares? In cyberspace no-one can see you fail. Offline, not only is your potential audience restricted by geography but you're also competing with laziness, weather, forgetfulness, traffic and the fact that no-one cares about your damn hotels-and-booze memoir (GLOWBE GB G guardian.com)

Seeing that this use recurs a few times, we might speculate that this more positive construal of the effects of ISOLATION could be a subconstruction of the Ripley-construction. When considering discourse-pragmatic function, an additional nuance emerges.

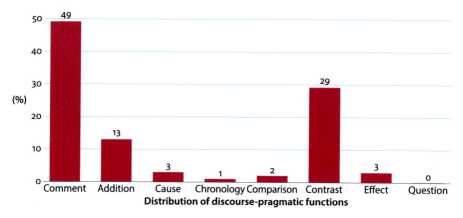

Figure 8. Distribution of discourse-pragmatic functions in the Ripley-construction

As seen in Figure 8, the comment function is the most frequent. Also interesting is the second-most frequent function – namely, contrast-marking. Consider the following examples:

(64) In space, no one can hear you scream – but they can hear you scream in movie theatres, where the Alien movies have given us an awful lot of shocks and scares. (NOW 17-05-16 AU CNET)

(65) In space, no one can hear you scream, but at home, everyone can. (NOW 16-12-24 US Consequence of Soun)

(66) In space, no one can hear you scheme. But here on Earth, plans to go where few have gone before are getting louder by the minute. (NOW 17-05-23 US Fox News)

In these cases, the Ripley-construction presents a generally assumed fact or knowledge, serving as background against which something that challenges it is highlighted and contrasted. This use is similar, but not identical, to what we saw in (57). A variant exists in which the challenge serves as ground while the establish fact is highlighted:

(67) *John Carter* is one of those films that is so stultifying, so oppressive and so mysteriously and interminably long that I felt as if someone had dragged me into the kitchen of my local Greggs, and was baking my head into the centre of a colossal cube of white bread. As the film went on, the loaf around my skull grew to the size of a basketball, and then a coffee table, and then an Audi. The boring and badly acted sci-fi mashup continued inexorably, and the bready blandness pressed into my nostrils, eardrums, eye sockets and mouth. I wanted to cry for help, but in bread no one can hear you scream. Finally, I clawed the doughy, gooey, tasteless mass desperately away from my mouth and screeched: "Jesus, I'm watching a pointless film about a 1860s American civil war action hero on Mars, which the inhabitants apparently call Barsoom. I can't breathe." (GLOWBE GB G guardian.com)

This quite innovative use of the snowclone appears in conjunction with a textual mega-metaphor, in which the ADVERSE EFFECT WATCHING A BAD SCIENCE FICTION MOVIE has on the VIEWER is conceptualised as BAKING BREAD. This evokes the image of the VIEWER'S HEAD BEING ENCASED IN A LOAF OF BREAD. The writer first mentions their desire to scream for help, but this is contrasted with *in bread no one can hear your scream*, highlighted against the entirety of what we, drawing on Langacker (2001), can call the current discourse space (i.e., all the concepts that are activated at a particular point within a discourse). Moreover, the snowclone is likely to evoke in culturally literate readers the original model and the *Alien* franchise such that a particular social allegiance between the writer and the reader emerges through their mutual implied knowledge of the original model. Moreover, culturally literate readers are also likely to identify the connection between the snowclone and the *John Carter* movie in that both *Alien* and *John Carter* belong to the science fiction genre. A full appreciation of this use of the snowclone requires quite in-depth knowledge of this area of popular culture.

As mentioned earlier, there is a preference for space-themed contexts. This is also reflected in the co-textual topics (see Table 12).

Table 12. Distribution of co-textual topics in the Ripley-construction

Topic	Frequency	%
ALIEN FRANCHISE	69	19.33
ART	4	1.12
ASTROPHYSICS AND OUTER SPACE	49	13.73
BUSINESS AND ECONOMY	5	1.40
CINEMA	39	10.92

Table 12. *(continued)*

Topic	Frequency	%
COMMUNICATION	4	1.12
CONFLICT AND WAR	1	0.28
CRIME	2	0.56
NATURAL DISASTERS	1	0.28
FASHION AND APPAREL	4	1.12
GASTRONOMY	3	0.84
GEEK CULTURE	51	14.29
LOCATIONS AND PLACES	34	9.52
MEDICINE AND HEALTH	4	1.12
MEMES	2	0.56
MUSIC	11	3.08
PERIL	1	0.28
POLITICS	9	2.52
PERSONAL DEVELOPMENT & PSYCHOLOGY	2	0.56
SCIENCE	5	1.40
SHOPPING	1	0.28
SOCIETY	1	0.28
SPORTS	4	1.12
TECHNOLOGY	41	11.48
TELEVISION	4	1.12
THEATRE	1	0.28
LATRINE AFFAIRS	3	0.84
TRAFFIC	1	0.28
TRAVEL AND TOURISM	1	0.28

ASTROPHYSICS AND OUTER SPACE figures are used prominently with a frequency of 49 (13.73%). Other prominent topics are the *ALIEN* FRANCHISE, GEEK CULTURE, CINEMA, and TECHNOLOGY. TECHNOLOGY co-texts are often tied in with INTERNET TECHNOLOGY. As a snowclone, then, the Ripley-construction is not only formally tied to its original mode. It is also linked to the original model through co-textual topical patterns such as the *ALIEN* franchise, of course, but also adjacent ones like GEEK CULTURE and CINEMA.[6]

---

6. It should be mentioned that several instances of this snowclone are replications of the original model, many of which are direct quotes of the original tagline – in fact, no less than 24.7% (nearly a fourth) of all occurrences are cases like that.

8. Concluding remarks

The present chapter has presented an exploratory study of three snowclones and discussed, in a cognitive-linguistic perspective, their potential proverbiality. Our analysis has shown that, among the three proverbial snowclones, there are a number of differences and similarities. All three constructions are arguably proverbial snowclones located on the fringes of the proverb category, as they display some proverb features, but not enough to make them proverbs proper. The *only good*-construction is an apothegm, despite its inbuilt irony. The main proverbial features of this construction are its presentation of its content mainly as an objective fact, thus displaying some degree of axiomaticity, and that it is linked with particular types of topics, thus also having situational applicability. Being a tool of hate speech, this construction cannot be properly understood in terms of its cognitive semantics without reference to social cognition as it draws on socio-cultural knowledge structures and processes including the socio-cognitive processes of othering and social categorisation as well as negative social attitudes. Arguably, these processes underpin all types of hate speech, so it should come as no surprise that they also apply here. Like the *only good*-construction, the Mordor-construction seems to mainly be used as a means of presenting an individual judgment as an objective fact, also giving it some degree of axiomaticity. However, it appears to have more of a didactic advisory orientation in that it negates a perceived effortlessness. It often reveals to the hearer, as a fact, that the realistic version of the scenario is much more difficult than the hearer thinks. Like the *only good*-construction, this snowclone displays apothegm features; yet, it seems that analogy is a central element of the semantics of this construction. Of the three, the Ripley-construction may be the most proverbial snowclone, as it seems to display more features of proverbiality. Axiomaticity must be a feature, as instances of the construction serve to present their contents as undisputable facts. Moreover, it also displays the lowest degree of productivity and thus the highest degree of fixedness. It is particularly interesting that some speakers seem to assign quotative impersonality to it, suggesting that the Ripley-construction might be on the way to becoming a proverb proper, and that in its current state, at the very least it serves as a proverbial marker.

While by no means the final words – to the point that I will concede that many of the findings presented here must be taken with a grain of salt – it is hoped that the study has shown that snowclones can overlap with proverbs and apothegms, in some cases serving the some of the same functions. Specifically, like proverbs proper, proverbial snowclones require in-depth cultural literacy from language users, as they seem to be used as rhetorical devices that either draw on belief systems, presenting them as encyclopaedic knowledge, or construe their contents as if they had the epistemic status of facts or widely accepted general knowledge. Having probably raised many questions, this chapter has hopefully inspired readers to view snowclones – proverbial or otherwise – as worthy objects of cognitive-linguistic research that might contribute to our understanding of socio-cultural cognition.

References

Abrahams, R. D., & Babcock, B. (1977). The literary use of proverbs. *The Journal of American Folklore*, 90(358), 414–429.

Arora, S. (1994). The perception of proverbiality. In W. Mieder (Ed.), *Wise words: Essays on the proverb* (pp. 3–29). London: Routledge.

Baayen, R. H. (2008). *Analyzing linguistic data: A practical introduction to statistics using R*. Cambridge: Cambridge University Press.

Baker, P., Hardie, A., & McEnery, T. (2006). *A glossary of corpus linguistics*. Edinburgh: Edinburgh University Press.

Beckner, C., Ellis, N. C., Blythe, R., Holland, J., Bybee, J., Ke, J., Christiansen, M. H., Larsen-Freeman, D., Croft, W. A., & Schoenemann, T. (2009). Language is a complex adaptive system. *Language Learning*, 59(s1), 1–26.

Begagić, M. (2013). Semantic preference and semantic prosody in the collocation *make sense*. *Jezikoslovje*, 14(2/3), 403–416.

Biber, D., Conrad, S., & Reppen, R. (1998). *Corpus linguistics: Investigating language structure and use*. Cambridge: Cambridge University Press.

Bybee, J. (2010). *Language, usage and cognition*. Cambridge: Cambridge University Press.

Cram, D. (1994). The linguistic status of the proverb. In W. Mieder (Ed.), *Wise words: Essays on the proverb* (pp. 73–97). London: Routledge

Croft, W. A. (2001). *Radical construction grammar: Syntactic theory in typological perspective*. Oxford: Oxford University Press.

Croft, W. A., & Cruse, D. A., (2004). *Cognitive linguistics*. Cambridge: Cambridge University Press.

Fillmore, C. (1988). The mechanisms of construction grammar. In S. Axmaker, A. Jassier & H. Singmaster (Eds.), *Proceedings from the Fourteenth Annual Meeting of the Berkeley Linguistics Society* (pp. 35–55). Berkeley, CA: Berkely Linguistics Society.

Fillmore, C., Kay, P., & O'Connor, M. C. (1988). Regularity and idiomaticity in grammatical constructions: The case of LET ALONE. *Language*, 64(3), 501–538.

Gibbs Jr., R. W. (2001). Proverbial themes we live by. *Poetics*, 29, 167–199.

Goldberg, A. E. (1995). *Constructions: A construction grammar approach to argument structure*. Chicago: Chicago University Press.

Hill, I. E. J. (2018) Memes, munitions, and collective copia: The durability of the perpetual peace weapons snowclone. *Quarterly Journal of Speech* 104(4), 422–443.

Hilpert, M. (2019). *Construction grammar and its application to English*. Second edition. Edinburgh: Edinburgh University Press.

Hoffman, D. (2012). Proverb. In R. Greene, S. Cushman, C. Cavanagh, J. Ramazani & P. Rouzer (Eds.), *The Princeton encyclopedia of poetry and poetics* (pp. 1122–1123). Princeton, NJ: Pinceton University Press.

Langacker, R. W. (2001). Discourse in cognitive grammar. *Cognitive Linguistics*, 12(2), 143–188.

Liberman, M. (2003). Egg corns: Folk etymology, malapropism, mondegreen,???. *Language Log*. URL: http://itre.cis.upenn.edu/~myl/languagelog/archives/000018.html Accessed June 29, 2021.

McArthur, T., Lam-McArthur, J., & Fontaine, L. (2018). *The Oxford companion to the English language*. Second edition. Oxford: Oxford University Press.

McFedries, P. (2008). Snowclone is the new cliché. *IEEE Spectrum* (February 2008), 27.

O'Connor, E. (2007a). (Dammit Jim,) I'm an X, not a Y! *The Snowclone Database*. URL: https://snowclones.org/2007/08/06/dammit-jim-im-an-x-not-a-y/ Accessed June 29, 2021.

O'Connor, E. (2007b). The only good X is a dead X. *The Snowclone Database*. URL: https://snowclones.org/2007/12/13/the-only-good-x-is-a-dead-x/ Accessed August 18, 2021.

O'Connor, E. (2007c). In X, no one can hear you Y. *The Snowclone Database*. URL: https://snowclones.org/2007/07/05/in-space-no-one-can-hear-you-x/ Accessed August 19, 2021.

Ojo Arewa, E., & Dundes, A. (1964). Proverbs and the ethnography of speaking folklore. *American Anthropologist*, 66(6), 70–85.

Patten, A. L. (2014). The historical development of the *it*-cleft: A comparison of two different approaches. In N. Gisborne & W. B. Hollmann (Eds.), *Theory and data in cognitive linguistics* (pp. 87–114). Amsterdam & Philadelphia: John Benjamins.

Peters, M. (2006a). Not your father's cliché. *Columbia Journalism Review*, 45(2), 14.

Peters, M. (2006b). Attack of the clones. *Psychology Today*, 39(4), 29.

Pullum, G. (2003a). Bleached conditionals. *Language Log*. URL: http://itre.cis.upenn.edu/~myl/languagelog/archives/000049.html Accessed June 29, 2021.

Pullum, G. (2003b). Phrases for lazy writers in kit form. *Language Log*. URL: http://itre.cis.upenn.edu/~myl/languagelog/archives/000061.html Accessed August 19, 2021.

Pullum, G. (2004). Snowclones: Lexicographical dating to the second. *Language Log*. URL: http://itre.cis.upenn.edu/~myl/languagelog/archives/000350.html Accessed June 29, 2021.

Seitel, P. (1976). Proverbs: A social use of metaphor. In D. Ben-Amos (Ed.), *Folklore genres* (pp. 125–143). Austin, TX: University of Texas Press.

Shibuya, Y. (2015). Lexical and constructional richness of adjectives. Presented at the 13th International Cognitive Linguistics Conference, Northumbria University, Newcastle-upon-Tyne, July 2015.

Talmy, L. (1988). Force dynamics in language and cognition. *Cognitive Science*, 12, 49–100.

Taylor, A., & Whiting B. J. (1967). *A dictionary of American proverbs and proverb phrases 1820–1880*. Cambridge, MA: The Belknap Press of Harvard University Press.

Traugott, E. C., & Trousdale, G. (2014). Contentful constructionalization. *Journal of Historical Linguistics*, 4(2), 256–283.

van Leeuwen, M. (2012). Rhetorical effects of grammar. *Critical Approaches to Discourse Analysis across Disciplines*, 5(2), 85–101.

van Leeuwen, T. (1995). The representation of social actors. In C. R. Caldas-Coulthard & M. Coulthard (Eds.), *Texts and practices: Readings in critical discourse analysis* (pp. 32–70). London: Routledge.

Verhagen, A. (2005). *Constructions of intersubjectivity*. Oxford: Oxford University Press.

Whitman, G. (2004). Phrases for lazy writers in kit form are the new cliché. *Agoraphilia*. URL: http://agoraphilia.blogspot.com/2004_01_11_agoraphilia_archive.html#107412842921919301 Accessed June 26, 2021.

Zwicky, A. (2005). Critical tone for a new snowclone. *Language Log*. URL: http://itre.cis.upenn.edu/%7Emyl/languagelog/archives/002555.html Accessed June 30, 2021.

Zwicky, A. (2006). Snowclone mountain. *Language Log*. URL: http://itre.cis.upenn.edu/~myl/languagelog/archives/002924.html Accessed June 30, 2021.

Appendix. Epistemic status and discourse-pragmatic function categories

Category	Subcategory	Definition
Epistemic status	advice	The unit is overtly co-textually marked as advice given to the recipient by the speaker, drawing on a pool of communal knowledge that the speaker has access to
	assumption	The nit is overtly co-textually marked as expressing something that is generally assumed or theorised to be a fact
	axiom	The unit is overtly co-textually marked as reflecting a general socially or otherwise accepted axiom, principle, or rule
	belief	The unit is overtly co-textually marked as expressing a general belief
	category	The unit is overtly co-textually marked as expressing a category or portion of knowledge
	fact	The unit is overtly co-textually marked as expressing a factual truth
	fantasy	The unit is overtly co-textually marked as expressing an imagined state-of-affairs
	general knowledge	The unit is overtly co-textually marked signalling generally accepted knowledge
	opinion	The unit is overtly co-textually marked as expressing the speaker's opinion
	other-assigned belief	The unit is overtly co-textually marked as indicating a belief held by a group the does not include the speaker or an individual that is not the speaker
	other-assigned opinion	The unit is overtly co-textually marked as signalling an opinion held by a group the does not include the speaker or an individual that is not the speaker

Appendix. *(continued)*

Category	Subcategory	Definition
	possibility	The unit is overtly co-textually marked as expressing a possibility or something otherwise hypothetical
	prediction	The unit is overtly co-textually marked as predicting a future event
	quote	The unit is overtly co-textually marked as an instance of a general saying or adage
	revelation	The unit is overtly co-textually marked as expressing otherwise generally knowledge, facts, or truth revealed to the speaker
	unmarked fact	The unit appears in a declarative structure, thus presenting its content as a fact rather than a possibility, an opinion or something otherwise non-factual or weakly factual (see M. van Leeuwen 2012)
Discourse-pragmatic function	comment	The unit serves as a comment on the overall topic of the stretch of discourse in which it appears
	addition	The unit provides content added to other content in the discourse
	condition	The unit expresses the condition under which something happens or the cause that makes something happen
	chronology	The unit expresses a scenario that is chronologically related to another scenario
	comparison	The unit is compared, and found to be similar, to other content in the discourse
	contrast	The unit is contrasted to other content in the stretch of discourse in which it appears
	effect	The unit expresses a scenario that is the effect or result of a cause or condition
	question	The unit serves to ask a question about, rather than comment on, the topic of the stretch of discourse in which it appears

CHAPTER 11

A cultural linguistic study of embodied Hungarian proverbs representing facial hair

Judit Baranyiné Kóczy
University of Pannonia, Veszprém, Hungary

This chapter offers a Cultural Linguistic analysis of the conceptualisations of BEARD and MOUSTACHE in Hungarian proverbs. While FACIAL HAIR is an underexploited field in paremiology, the chapter argues that it is an appropriate concept for capturing the cultural aspects of the figurative language collections of proverbs. The study analyses 31 proverbs selected from five collections, where the identification process of cultural conceptualisations involves conceptual analysis combined with drawing on other linguistic evidence and culturally relevant ethnographic data. The results show that the seven target concepts (PERSONALITY, MANLINESS, INDEPENDENCE, PATRIOTISM, AGE, DIGNITY, and WISDOM) are interconnected in the Hungarian cultural model of MAN, and MOUSTACHE has a dominance and more positive value in cultural cognition as compared to BEARD. The study shows how the theoretical framework and methodological tools of Cultural Linguistics can be used in studying the cultural elements of proverbs and how they can enhance the understanding of their linkage to cultural models.

Keywords: cultural conceptualisations, facial hair, metaphor, metonymy, proverb

1. Introduction

Proverbs are phraseological sentences expressing collective wisdom and moral judgement, which encapsulate a segment of cultural knowledge in a concise way. The diverse paremiological approaches from the perspective of Cognitive Linguistics, be they investigating their metaphoricity within the Cognitive Metaphor Theory (Lakoff and Johnson 1980; Lakoff and Turner 1989; Kövecses 2005a), or studying their usage-based aspects, need to consider that proverbs are strongly interwoven with the cultural context in which they emerge. In accordance with this observation, the present chapter takes the vantage point of Cultural Linguistics (Sharifian 2011, 2017) to explore proverbs, and analyses a selected group of Hungarian proverbs that exhibit embodied cognition, particularly ones that feature the body-parts *szakáll* 'beard' and *bajusz* 'moustache'. The aims of the study are the following:

1. to study the linkage and learn some of the aspects in which facial hair is reflected in Hungarian proverbs and show a way to analyse proverbs using cognitive linguistic and cultural linguistic terminology; thus making a manifold contribution to Cultural Linguistics and Cognitive Linguistics.
2. to show how cultural conceptualisations – cognitive processes that embody group-level cognitive systems such as worldviews (Sharifian 2011: 5) – can be identified and analysed in proverbs. In this way, this research adds to the theoretical framework and methodological tools of paremiology in studying the cultural aspects of proverbs.
3. Finally, to gain a better understanding of values and masculinity in Hungarian culture.

It is argued that the figurative usages of the two basic types of facial hair – BEARD and MOUSTACHE – reside in different cultural conceptualisations according to the Hungarian proverbs. The study substantiates that MOUSTACHE holds a stronger position in the Hungarian worldview than BEARD; moreover, it has an overall positive assessment in its figurative usages whereas BEARD can entail both positive and negative connotations.

The chapter is structured as follows: Section 2 offers an overview of the status of proverbs from the perspective of cognitive linguistics and, more specifically, Cultural Linguistics, and posits the notion of *cultural conceptualisation* in their cultural-conceptual analysis. It is followed by a brief account of the sociocultural functions of facial hair in some cultures including the Hungarian context (Section 3). After the description of the data and methodology (Section 4), the figurative extensions of both BEARD and MOUSTACHE are presented along with their underlying cultural conceptualisations (Section 5). The final part is devoted to the summary of the results and the conclusions with respect to the cultural-conceptual analysis of embodied proverbs.

2. Proverbs, conceptualisation and culture

The various kinds of linguistic approaches to proverbs agree that they are fixed, phraseological expressions that represent wisdom or truth grounded in moral issues or social norms (Norrick 1985; Mieder 1993; Gibbs and Colston 2012; Belkhir 2014). Mieder (1985:19), defines a proverb as "a short, generally known sentence of the folk that contains wisdom, truth, morals, and traditional views in a metaphorical, fixed and memorisable [memorable] form and that is handed down from generation to generation". This definition leads to the emergence of at least three types of elements within proverbs: their structural, semantic, and discursive-pragmatic nature, including their prominent role in cultural transmission. From a structural perspective, in Norrick's (1985:3) view, proverbs unite "properties of the word and the sentence as morphologically complex form-meaning units" as well as "properties of the sentence and the text". This is because they "occur in larger texts such as everyday conversations, newspaper editorials and sermons; and they occur as texts complete in themselves, e.g., as group slogans, house inscriptions and along with other sayings in anthologies". In contrast with idiomatic expressions, "a proverb is a complete sentence that is often metaphorical and used to convey some wisdom or accepted truth" (Belkhir 2014:133), and their concise structure has an important role in ensuring their memorisability that helps their frequency and distribution among the members of a language community. Second, regarding their semantic content, proverbs are "traditional items of folklore" (Norrick 1985:28) in that they communicate collective wisdom; i.e., experiences, beliefs and prejudices of the community that often come from before the era of industrialisation (Norrick 2014). Another important feature of proverbs is that they are essentially figurative by nature, and their metaphorical meanings can be unfolded in relation to the socio-cultural contexts where they are used (Belkhir 2019). Finally, concerning their discursive functions, proverbs are often adopted in everyday interactions and free conversations, and commonly have an evaluative function and a didactic tone (Norrick 1985:28). Their frequent usage ensures their salient position in discourse and that they are recognised as 'proverbs' thus distinguishing them from other sentences.

2.1 The cognitive linguistic approach to proverbs

In the cognitive linguistic framework, idiomatic expressions are taken as well-entrenched lexical items that have a unit status in both the cognitive-structural as well as the semantic sense (Langacker 1987:93). Their entrenchment also explains that they are stored as units in the mind (Komlósi 2005:115). In relation to the main objective of Cognitive Linguistics, namely, to unfold 'meaning' by investigating the processes that participate in cognition (Croft and Cruse 2004), idioms are first and foremost viewed as carriers of figurative language (e.g., Lakoff and Turner 1989; Gibbs 1994; Gibbs et al. 1997; Kövecses 2002). In other words, the formulation of metaphorical content that governs their interpretation or understanding is primarily in the focus of interest. In Gibbs's (1994: 268) words,

> People make sense of idiomatic speech precisely because of their ordinary metaphorical knowledge which provides part of the link between these phrases and their figurative interpretations. There is now much evidence from cognitive linguistics and experimental psychology to support the idea that idiomatic language retains much of its metaphoricity.

According to Maalej's (2009) and Belkhir's (2014) overviews, the cognitive linguistic approach to proverbs was mainly confined to Cognitive Metaphor Theory (e.g., Lakoff and Turner 1989), where the Great Chain of Being Metaphor model and its underlying metaphor, GENERIC IS SPECIFIC were identified as keys to explain how proverbs refer to a multitude of situations through representing an individual one. The Great Chain of Being Metaphor models how human characteristics are understood metaphorically in terms of low-level forms of beings (Lakoff and Turner 1989: 204). In a similar vein, the 'wisdom' and 'accepted truth' conveyed by the specific-level representations of proverbs are manifested in their generic-level schemata and structure. Maalej (2009) proposes a mapping-based classification of proverbs by making a distinction between mapping-free, single-mapping and multiple-mapping proverbs. He also argues that some proverbs may be cross-linguistically similar on the SPECIFIC level, while having different GENERIC-level grounds, which can be explained by cultural alterations (Maalej 2009: 148). The Cognitive Metaphor Theory was also claimed to be insufficient for grasping their cultural content and cross-cultural similarities or variances because proverb meaning is understood in relation to the social-cultural contexts wherein they are used (Belkhir 2014, 2019). To address this need, Kövecses (2005a) has introduced the advanced model of CMT called Cultural Cognitive Theory to explain how the variations of source and target domains and conceptual mappings can account for metaphor diversity.

The cultural-conceptual analysis of proverbs can be further refined by a usage-based approach (Békei 2012), because proverbs may have several levels of meanings or they may even show substantial differences in various discourse contexts. The meanings of proverbs very often cannot be specified without regard to their context (Szemerkényi 1994: 58). An example of this is Békei's (2012: 4) corpus linguistic study of the Hungarian proverb *Nem esik messze az alma a fájától*, lit. 'Like father, like son' (*An apple does not fall far from the tree*), where she convincingly shows that the same proverb may have positive, negative or neutral values depending on the context.

Closely related to the cultural elements of proverbs, the aforementioned 'wisdom' grounded in moral judgement is a core element of the meanings of proverbs.

Proverbs are statements targeting certain phenomena about which moral evaluation has already been established in the cultural community. The basis of moral judgement is what is generally accepted as 'good' or 'beneficial' by the members of the group (Kocsány 2002: 23), therefore proverbs have a major role in preserving and transmitting the value system of a cultural community (Szemerkényi 1994: 82–3). It follows from the figurative nature of proverbs that both the source domains and the target domains manifested in them may have strong cultural implications. The notion 'cultural conceptualisations' was introduced as a central concept within the cognitive-linguistic discipline of Cultural Linguistics (Sharifian 2017) with the aim to integrate cognitive semantic analysis with insights of various types of cultural disciplines including cultural anthropology, ethnography, folk theory, philosophy, religious studies etc.

2.2 The interconnectedness of language, culture and conceptualisation – a cultural linguistic view

The study of cultural conceptualisations in language lays central emphasis on understanding the interconnectedness of language, culture and conceptualisation, and its basic argument is that conceptualisation does not entail merely cognitive processes that operate in individuals, but they also apply to group-level cognition. In this context, 'culture' is defined in relation to conceptualisation and meaning: it can be interpreted as a particular worldview that is characteristic of a group of people living together in a particular social, historical, and physical environment and interpreting their experiences in a more or less unified manner (Kövecses 2005b: 136; Sharifian 2017: 26). People who are members of the same culture, can successfully participate in the 'meaning making process' that involves various cognitive acts such as producing, understanding, identifying, evaluating phenomena appropriately in a given cultural context (Kövecses 2005b: 136–137). Cultural conceptualisations are encoded in linguistic elements (grammar, semantics, and pragmatics) and may be apparent in non-linguistic cultural artefacts: cultural events, rituals, gestures, emotions, images etc. While cultural conceptualisations can be captured and studied via a linguistic approach, cultural cognition is a latent and dynamic system of implicit knowledge that is shared, negotiated, and renegotiated among the members of a cultural community (Sharifian 2017). In this emergent system, cognition results from the continuous interactions between the group members.

Cultural conceptualisations instantiate the elements of a cultural community's worldview in the forms of categories, schemas, and metaphors/metonymies. Cultural categories are culturally constructed conceptual categories, e.g., objects, events, settings, mental states, properties, relations (Glushko et al. 2008: 129).

Another set of conceptualisations covers cultural schemas, namely, beliefs, norms, and expectations of behaviour, e.g., event, emotion, or role schemas (e.g., gender roles). The notion of 'cultural schema' is broadly similar to 'cultural model' that can be described as skeletal outlines of knowledge, "presupposed, taken-for-granted models" (Quinn and Holland 1987: 4) shared among a group of people. Cultural models bring together various semantic components, associations and values that belong to an entity or situation, and they are grounded in folk knowledge; i.e., everyday collective experiences. Finally, cultural metaphors (worldview metaphors, see Sharifian 2017: 60) are conceptual metaphors (cross-domain mappings) that are based on cultural models related to folk medicine, worldview, or a spiritual belief system (Sharifian 2017: 4).

2.3 Cultural conceptualisations in proverbs

Unveiling cultural conceptualisations is central to the study of embodied language. Within the broad understanding of embodiment, which emphasises the fundamental role of the human body in shaping the conceptual system and language use (Johnson 1987; Gibbs 2006), "embodiment via body parts", i.e., how single body-parts in various languages are exploited for abstract processes, is extensively studied to highlight cross-cultural differences (Yu 2001; Niemeier 2008; Sharifian et al. 2008; Maalej and Yu 2011; Kraska-Szlenk 2014; Baranyiné Kóczy 2020a, 2020b, 2023). The various studies have shown that embodiment is motivated by both bodily and cultural factors, where physiological embodiment is in interaction with cultural embodiment (Maalej 2008). Body-part terms lend themselves to a large amount of figurative language that is grounded in conceptual metaphors and metonymies that are very often triggered by physical experience. The most common extensions of body-part terms to internal (human-related) abstract concepts are EMOTIONS, KNOWLEDGE/REASONING and SOCIAL INTERACTIONS and VALUES (Kraska-Szlenk 2014). The metonymic link between the experience of an emotion and its associated physical experience, symptom or effect has a direct basis, whether it is grounded in a biologically valid process (such as a heartbeat) or in folk belief (e.g., A DROP IN BODY TEMPERATURE FOR FEAR) (Kövecses 1990, 2000, 2005a). Folk beliefs simplify biological concepts, e.g., BLOOD is a metonymy for all kinds of genetic relationships between individuals of the same family (Charteris-Black 2001). Body-part metaphors and metonymies are connected in and governed by systematic configurations named cultural models (e.g., Yu 2001; Sharifian et al. 2008) that rely on complex scenarios, such as the cross-linguistically present metaphor HONOUR (RESPECT, DIGNITY) IS FACE (Yu 2001; Ukosakul 2003; Kraska-Szlenk 2014). It has developed at the intersection of two conceptual metaphors: the FACE (FACIAL MANIFESTATION) FOR EMOTION metonymy (Yu 2001) and the GOOD IS UP metaphor, where the perceptions about one's emotions through facial expression were extended to one's personality in social interactions, resulting in the cultural concept of 'social face' (Kraska-Szlenk 2014: 30). Embodied metaphors often develop from metonymies through a gradual process along the schema 'from concrete to abstract'. Metaphor and metonymy are therefore viewed as a continuum of related processes (Kövecses and Radden 1998; Radden, 2000) that is reflected in Goossens's (1990) notion 'metaphtonymy' meaning metaphor-metonymy interactions.

The different texts based on collective experience can be conceived as different types of repositories of cultural cognition because cultural models "may leave their mark on a language long after they have disappeared from the consciousness of its speakers" (Wolk 2008: 309). In the Hungarian context, Baranyiné Kóczy (2022) has shown how the cultural metaphors in Hungarian folk songs exhibit cultural experiences of folk communities. In a similar vein, proverbs also serve as 'collective memory banks' that communicate, store and (re)transmit components of cultural cognition, where their cultural content can be investigated in a systematic and structured way through cultural conceptualisations (Dabbagh 2016). Cultural conceptualisations in fixed idiomatic expressions and proverbs have been investigated in connection with animals (Fiedler 2016; Ben Salamh and Maalej 2018; Nosrati 2019; Belkhir 2021), where references to cultural influences upon conceptualisations of animals were highlighted. Body-parts in proverbs have been studied in various languages (Yu 2001; Wolk 2008; Maalej and Yu 2011; Siahaan 2011; Berggren 2018), in which the cross-cultural variances of proverbs were often attributed to cultural models of body-parts. For example, the Hungarian proverb *Más szemében meglátja a szálkát, a magáéban a gerendát sem*, lit. 'He sees a speck in others' eyes but fails to notice a rafter in his own eye' encapsulates various components of the moral model of the EYE (Baranyiné Kóczy 2021).

Even though FACIAL HAIR is a definitive part of the cultural model of MAN in various cultures (Maxwell 2015; Gray et al. 2020), the figurative extensions of BEARD and MOUSTACHE have been relatively neglected in cognitive linguistic research. The reason is that body-part semantics considers FACIAL HAIR a non-prototypical element of the category of BODY-PARTS, owing to its variability. However, this characteristic makes it a prominent symbolic element of human appearance in several cultures. Such a contradiction is presented by the fact that the most extensive collection of Hungarian idiomatic expressions on body-parts contains references neither to *szakáll* 'beard' nor to *bajusz* 'moustache' (Bárdosi 2013). On the contrary, Szilágyi (2013) collected around 470 synonyms, dialectic expressions, and collocations used for describing a moustache in Hungarian that indicates its importance in the Hungarian worldview.[1]

3. BEARD and MOUSTACHE in cultural cognition

Both hair and facial hair have a major role in giving an impression about a person that may be positive such as respect, admiration, sexual attraction, comradeship, or negative like disgust, contempt, or disparagement. Facial hair can be considered as part of the face that is "the body-part that is most distinctive of a person", "the focus of human interaction" that "shows our emotions and feelings" (Yu 2001: 1). Yu (2001) has shown that the metaphoric and metonymic expressions based on the nature of the face in Chinese are used to understand abstract concepts like EMOTIONS, CHARACTER, RELATIONSHIPS, DIGNITY, and PRESTIGE. In Hebrew, it is the face as subject (rather than the whole body as in English) that undergoes the emotional experience (Kidron and Kuzar 2002). However, while there is an "observable association between facial expression and emotion, face does not reveal aspects of one's character or social standing, i.e., there is no causal chain linking face to either of them" (Marmaridou 2011: 29).

Facial hair is a secondary sex characteristic that develops at puberty, it contains value for attractiveness, and it can be an indicator of a male's overall condition in terms of age, physical strength, health and social dominance (Dixson and Brooks 2013; Gray et al. 2020). A number of historical, cultural, anthropological, and ethnographic studies concerned the role of facial hair in human history and culture, its symbolic meaning connected to life stages, socio-cultural events, religious rituals, or how it has become a means of expression about one's ideological and political views (Maxwell 2015). Throughout history, facial hair was a "badge of allegiance" (Peterkin 2001: 28), and it came with several layers of meaning. In the Western cultural context, until the spread of Christianity, facial hair was widely promoted, either as a religious requirement, or as a status symbol, whereas shaving and hair cutting were viewed as acts of betrayal and humiliation (Peterkin 2001: 17–19). Prominent rulers often guided cultural traditions of facial hairstyle, and during the reign of various kings, decrees were issued that ordered or forbade facial hair and set requirements for its appropriate style.

In some cultures, the beard has been a symbol of masculinity and male sexual potency throughout history because the potential to grow thick hair is a male trait.

---

1. I am indebted to Péter Szilágyi, founding member of the Hungarian Moustache Society, for providing me extensive language data as well as reference works for an ethnographic account of the 'Hungarian moustache'.

Wearing a beard has been influenced by custom, law, religion and fashion trends; where growing or removing it had a meaning within the actual cultural context (Sherrow 2005: 56). In general, growing a beard expressed manliness, health and honour, and sometimes wisdom, goodness, sorcery and diabolism. However, in cultures where shaving was a cultural norm, it could express deep mourning by letting it grow wild and unruly (Peterkin 2001: 22), or a disregard for convention and conformity (Sherrow 2005: 278).

Similarly, wearing a moustache was connected to religion, social custom, occupation, or fashion, and in some countries, different styles of moustaches were associated with military men, or the size and shape of a moustache indicated one's social status or group membership. Again, the choice to wear or not to wear a moustache could also be a statement of one's objection to a political system (Sherrow 2005: 277–278). Facial hair is present in various proverbs across the world, as the *World proverbs* website indicates. This website lists 87 proverbs representing beard, but only three referring to moustache, which may at least suggest that beard is more often exploited for figurative meanings than moustache.

The role of facial hair in the Hungarian cultural model of MAN was emphasised in ethnographic studies (Herman 1902, 1906; Paládi-Kovács 1997). The etymology of the two words shows that facial hair has been present in Hungarian cultural cognition for more than a millennium. The word *szakáll* 'beard' is a loanword from the pre-Conquest times (the Hungarian conquest of the Carpathian Basin at the turn of the 9th and 10th centuries) from Ottoman-Turkish *sakal* that can be traced back to the verb **saqa-* 'hang down' (Zaicz 2006: 765–766). This loanword testifies both linguistic and cultural contacts of Hungarians and Turkish: "The Magyars [Hungarians], Finno-Ugric in origin, inseparably amalgamated with Turkic tribes thousands of years before the Conquest, and this duality determined the basic tone of their culture even before the Conquest" (Balassa and Ortutay 1979: 572). However, the origin of *bajusz* 'moustache' is unknown (Zaicz 2006: 50). The moustache style trends that characterised Hungary for a millennium were strongly dependent on Western and Eastern influences. Traditionally, having a beard and a moustache in Hungary was a privilege of nobility and married men; therefore, it indicated social hierarchy and adulthood because marriage was a milestone in reaching adulthood. Commoners generally wore a moustache from the 15th century, but under the Austrian influence in the 18th century, Hungarian peasants were obliged to shave both their beards and moustaches, because the authorities levied a 'beard fine' (*szakállbírság*) viewing facial hair as a revolt against Austrian dominance over Hungary, a marker of patriotism (Maxwell 2015). After the 1848–49 revolution against Austrian dominance, the 'Kossuth-beard' (named after Lajos Kossuth, a prominent figure of the revolution) became highly popular as a political statement for Hungarian independence and a symbol of the passive resistance.

In the 19th century, the nobility and the military spread the fashion of moustache again. Hungarian moustaches variously symbolised class inclusiveness, martial manliness, patriotism, anti-monarchist liberalism, public service, and masculine privilege (Maxwell 2015). In 1902, Herman defined the Hungarian national character traits such as pride, honour, and respectability with respect to moustache (Herman 1902). He also published a paper on the traditional names, descriptions, and illustrations of 26 Hungarian moustache types (*The Hungarian moustache*, see Herman 1906). The most typical form of moustache that characterises the Hungarians is the 'handlebar' shape worn by various famous Hungarian noblemen, politicians, poets etc. in the 19th century.

The cultural meaning of moustache is still to some degree present in Hungarian cultural cognition, which is, for example, marked by the activities of the *Hungarian Moustache Society* and other frequent gatherings for men wearing whiskers that embrace the cultural traditions of grooming a moustache and the symbolic meanings related to it. To some men, wearing a moustache still gives a sense of being Hungarian: "Many people wear a moustache because it is a Hungarian tradition, and it is a way of expressing their Hungarian identity" (Bárány 2016). In a report about one of the 'moustache gatherings' a participant explained about wearing a moustache means being a man and being Hungarian: *Egyszer azt jelenti, hogy férfi vagyok, másodszor azt jelenti, hogy magyar vagyok* 'First of all, it means that I am a man, secondly it means that I am Hungarian' (Molnár and Marjanovic 2021). The concept of HUNGARIAN MOUSTACHE also exists outside Hungary, which is shown in the fact that the 'Hungarian style' is one of the six sub-categories at the largest facial hair competition worldwide, the *World Beard and Moustache Championships* ([Article about categories and judging]).

4. Data and methodology

This section discusses the linguistic data of the analysis, the selection method of proverbs, some issues regarding the meanings of proverbs, other kinds of linguistic data used for supporting the argumentations, and the method of the study. The language dataset of the present research (31 types of proverbs in total) was selected from six dictionaries and collections of proverbs: *Magyar közmondások könyve* (Book of Hungarian proverbs, Erdélyi 1851), *Magyar közmondások és közmondásszerű szólások* (Hungarian proverbs and proverb-like sayings, Margalits 1896), *A magyar nyelv értelmező szótára VI.* (Dictionary of the Hungarian Language Vol. VI, Bárczi and Országh 1962), *Magyar szólások és közmondások* (Hungarian proverbs and sayings, O. Nagy 1966), *Szólások és közmondások* (Proverbs and sayings, Szemerkényi 2009), *Szólások, közmondások eredete* (The origin of sayings and proverbs, Bárdosi 2012), and from the website of the *Hungarian Moustache Society*. The dictionaries of proverbs present several meanings of the given proverbs, however, the situations and contexts where they are used are not detailed, with the exception of Szemerkényi (2009). There are also very few references to the origin of certain proverbs or idioms that could explain both their cultural background (scenarios) and the linkage between proverbs. In Bárdosi (2020), a single brief description can be found on the conceptual link between BEARD and FINANCIAL CREDIT, but none related to MOUSTACHE.

The cultural relevance of the proverbs featuring *szakáll* 'beard' or *bajusz* 'moustache' can be captured with varying degrees and some of them do not apply to human faculties (see Section 5). The criteria for the selection of the 31 proverbs were that (i) they must include the body-part terms *bajusz* or *szakáll*; (ii) the facial hair terms are used metonymically or metaphorically for person-bound target concepts (unlike (1–3)); (iii) the proverbs as types represent a group of variants.

The process of analysis is the following: the meanings of the proverbs are explained by using the descriptions found in the collections, after which the metonymic or metaphoric cultural conceptualisations of BEARD and MOUSTACHE are identified. In the next step, the explanation of the connection between source and target concepts is supported by other linguistic data (idiomatic expressions) and by drawing on ethnographic (social, political, etc.) insights from reference works (Herman 1902, 1906; Paládi-Kovács 1997) or reports, in order to unveil the evaluative connotations to the proverbs. The focus of analysis is set on the source concepts of the conceptualisations (FACIAL HAIR) because the data is gathered around these concepts. According to the conventions of Cultural Linguistics, the 'A AS B' formula is used for metaphor identification. In the study, the fuzzy boundaries of the conceptualisations and the linkages between them are also highlighted; e.g., the connection between AGE and WISDOM. On the ground of the results, the similarities and differences in the conceptualisations of BEARD and MOUSTACHE are discussed with reference to their status in the cultural cognition of Hungarians.

5. Cultural conceptualisations of BEARD and MOUSTACHE

This section presents the cultural conceptualisations of *szakáll* 'beard' and *bajusz* 'moustache' as they can be identified in the Hungarian proverbs. It must be noted that some proverbs do not reflect strong culture-specific elements such as Examples (1a)–(c).

(1) a. *ritka szakál kóc nélkül.*
rare beard knot without
Lit. 'a beard without a knot is rare'.
b. *az éles borotva friss-en bán-ik a szakáll-lal.*
the sharp razor fresh-ADV treat-PRS.3SG the beard-INS
Lit. 'a sharp razor trims the beard quickly/easily'.
c. *könnyü a bajusz-t meg-pöndörit-eni.*
easy the moustache-ACC PREV-twirl-INF
Lit. 'a moustache is easy to twirl'.

These observations are grounded in the everyday experiences related to wearing and grooming a beard or a moustache and they are applied to external domains. The first one is that beards need to be kept regularly, the second one is that a good equipment (as opposed to a blunt razor) can help trimming, and in the third proverb, the shape of a moustache with upward curling edges is highlighted. In the figuratively extended sense, (1a) means that 'every situation entails a problematic issue', (1b) asserts that 'every problematic situation can be tackled by appropriate means', while (3) condemns easy success. In each proverb, the physiological characteristic of facial hair is highlighted, and neither the source nor the target conceptualisations exhibit much cultural content (an exception is (1c) where the typical shape of the Hungarian moustache is represented). Those proverbs that express folk beliefs related to weather, for example, are not included in the analysis either (2a)–(b).

(2) a. *meg-ráz-za még szakáll-á-t Gergely.*
PREV-shake-PRS.DEF.3SG yet beard-POSS.3SG-ACC Gergely
Lit. 'Gergely will shake his beard'.
'it is expected to snow on St. Gergely's day'.
b. *Orbán meg-ráz-ta a szakáll-á-t.*
Orbán PREV-shake-PST.DEF.3SG the beard-POSS.3SG-ACC
Lit. 'Urban shook his beard'.
'it was snowing on St. Urban's day'.

Both proverbs reside in the folk superstition that weather is governed by the will of the celestial powers, particularly when snow occurs and when a saint, whose names day is around that time, shakes his grey beard. Hence, (2a) and (2b) report the traditional observation that despite the spring weather it snows occasionally on St. Gergely's Day (12 March) and even on St. Urban's Day (25 May).

The following sections focus on and discuss person-bound cultural conceptual target domains ("conceptual keys", see Charteris-Black 2001), namely, PER-

SONALITY, INDEPENDENCE, MANLINESS, PATRIOTISM, AGE, DIGNITY and WISDOM that are presented in the order of which have a clear metonymic basis or have a more abstract metaphorical profile. The analyses aim to highlight which conceptualisations are shared by both types of facial hair and which are dominated by either of them or can be even attributed to either of them exclusively. The cultural-semantic linkages between the conceptualisations are made explicit throughout the study.

5.1 FACIAL HAIR FOR PERSONALITY

The generic-level conceptualisation representing facial hair is FACIAL HAIR FOR PERSONALITY, which appears in two variants of a popular proverb. This conceptualisation is based on the APPEARANCE FOR PERSONALITY metonymy that has a strong experiential basis in form of facial gestures, mimics or others.

(3) a. *az-t gondol-od, hogy csak szőr a bajusz?*
 that-ACC think-PRS.DEF.2SG that just fur the moustache
 Lit. 'do you think that a moustache is just any hair?'
 'don't you know that a moustache has a meaning?'
 b. *nem csak szőr a magyar bajusz.*
 not just fur the Hungarian moustache
 Lit. 'the Hungarian moustache is not just any hair'.
 'wearing a moustache has a meaning'.

Proverbs (3a)–(b) have at least two meaning layers, one with a more general meaning and another one with a more specific meaning. According to the general meaning, the physical appearance of people and objects may have important symbolic references to their internal characteristics or content. In the specific sense, the prominent status of moustache as a property of an ideal Hungarian man is brought into the limelight. In the first place, it indicates that there is a rich array of meanings behind men's moustaches. The difference between (3a) and (3b) is that *bajusz* 'moustache' is first contrasted with other types of body hair (*szőr*), whereas in the second proverb it is the *magyar bajusz* 'Hungarian moustache' viewed in opposition to body hair (*szőr*). It applies to both cases that in Hungarian 'hair' is expressed by two lexemes, *haj* and *szőr*. The first one, *haj* denotes the one on the scalp that is considered in the case of women an essential element of beauty. Women having thick hair are often referred to as having *hajkorona* (lit. hair-crown), which indicates the positive values attached to *haj*. The second lexeme *szőr* means animal hair as well as body hair, but itis primarily associated with animals; therefore, it implies a lower value than hair. Both beard and moustache fall under the category of *arcszőrzet* 'facial hair', lit. 'face-fur', associating them with the 'lower-level' category. Based on this, proverb (3a) formulates that moustache has a privileged position among other types of *szőr* 'hair', whereas (3b) further emphasises the special status of moustache (unlike beard) for Hungarians. The FACIAL HAIR FOR PERSONALITY metonymy can be further specified to MOUSTACHE FOR PERSONALITY and MOUSTACHE FOR PATRIOTIC PERSONALITY, which mark the prominent status of moustache in the Hungarian cultural cognition. Remarkably, no such proverbs representing beard can be found in the dataset.

5.2 FACIAL HAIR FOR MANLINESS

In this metonymic conceptualisation, facial hair is posited as paramount to manliness in the Hungarian worldview.

(4) a. nem is   ember az, aki az-t   a   kis szőr-t   el   nem
       not even man   that who that-ACC the little fur-ACC PREV not
       bír-ja!
       bear-PRS.DEF.3SG
       Lit. 'one who cannot wear that little facial hair cannot be considered a man!'
   b. bajusz   és szakáll férfi-ember-t   illet-ø.
       moustache and beard   masculine-man-ACC suit-PRS.NDEF.3SG
       Lit. 'moustache and beard make a man'.
   c. ott   kezdőd-ik   az ember, ahun a bajusz.
       there begin-PRS.DEF.3SG the man   where the moustache
       Lit. 'one becomes a man when his moustache starts growing'.

The reference to 'little facial hair' (moustache) in (4a) implies that it is a symbol of manliness. As Szilágyi (2013: 34) notes, around the beginning of the 20th century, in the Szeged region of Hungary, moustache was called *embörcímör* (lit. 'man's emblem') meaning that for men, it symbolised all the attributes of 'manliness' in the eyes of the members of the society. Proverb (4b) has at least three meanings: the first one emphasises the aesthetic function of facial hair (both moustache and beard), the second one is that facial hair gives a man dignity and authority, and the third one indicates that young men were not allowed to conduct certain activities in the traditional communities. The Hungarian language distinguishes categorically these two phases in men's life by using separate lexemes: *legény* means 'young man' whereas *férfi* or *ember* denote a '(mature) man'. This is the core idea of proverb (4c): it either means that true men wear a moustache or that becoming a mature man begins with growing a moustache (i.e., when it starts sprouting). As explained in Section 3, marital status was a milestone for young men to proceed from the life stage of *legény* to *férfi/ember*. The various simultaneous meanings of proverb (4c) indicate that MANLINESS incorporates different values, including physically attractive appearance, dignity within one's local community, and it is connected to a certain age and life stage.

Some proverbs also foreground a moustache as a marker of a sexually attractive man.

(5) a. *bajusz   alól   édes a csók.*
       moustache below.ELA sweet the kiss
       Lit. 'the sweetest kiss is the one from below a moustache'.
    b. *a csók bajusz   nélkül olyan, mint a   leves só nélkül.*
       the kiss moustache without thus   like the soup salt without
       Lit. 'a kiss without a moustache is like soup without salt'.

(5a) and (5b) report that for a woman, a kiss is only pleasant with a moustachioed man. The reference to 'salt' in (5b) is based on the conception that salt is an essential ingredient for delicious food. The figurative sense of SALT AS ESSENCE is strongly embedded in Hungarian cultural cognition, e.g., in the phrase *az élet sója*, lit. 'the salt of life' meaning 'the spice of life' or the personality trait *sótlan*, lit. 'one who contains no salt' that is used for a boring personality. Another example that can be given is the Hungarian folk tale entitled *A só* 'The salt' (it is translated to English as 'The salt princess'; folk tales with a similar story exist in other folk cultures as well). It is about a princess who told her father that she loved him like salt, a compliment that was, at first, strange to the king and offended him, but later, he realised how essential salt was for living and apologised to her. Again, the MOUSTACHE FOR A SEXUALLY ATTRACTIVE MAN metonymy does not appear in connection with beards.

5.3   FACIAL HAIR FOR INDEPENDENCE

Another masculine quality loosely connected to the conceptualisation of MANLINESS is INDEPENDENCE. Only one proverb representing the INDEPENDENCE AS FREE BEARD cultural metaphor could be found in the collections, however, it is present in several idioms (6a)–(b).

(6) a. *a   szabad szakáll-ra   él-ő   ember-t kerül-d.*
       the free   beard-SUBL live-IMPF.PTCP man-ACC avoid-SBJV.DEF.2SG
       'avoid the men who live irresponsibly'.
    b. *szabad szakáll-ra   él-ø.*
       free   beard-SUBL live-PRS.NDEF.3SG
       'he lives fully independently/ irresponsibly'.

c. *saját szakáll-á-ra   tesz-ø   valami-t.*
   own beard-POSS.3SG-SUBL do-PRS.NDEF.3SG something-ACC
   'he does sg. at his own risk, without permission'.

While the idioms (6b)–(c) do not necessarily entail a negative evaluation towards having a 'free beard', the proverb (6a) warns us that such a person is considered harmful or dangerous from a collective perspective. Independence is associated with stubbornness, irresponsibility, and having one's own rules. This conceptualisation is related to the FINANCIAL CREDIT AS BEARD conceptualisation that is found in idioms (see 7) but no proverbs were found.

(7) *más-ø   szakáll-á-ra   isz-ik.*
    other-GEN beard-POSS.3SG-SUBL drink-PRS.NDEF.3SG
    'he drinks at someone else's financial responsibility'.

The FINANCIAL CREDIT AS BEARD metaphtonymy traces back to the cultural belief that, in the past, a beard was considered as part of one's personality (see FACIAL HAIR FOR PERSONALITY) and soul. The beard was paramount to one's dignity, strength and personal value; therefore, when someone borrowed money and pledged his beard, it meant that he was in severe financial trouble. For this reason, a beard became a symbol of those kinds of loans that had to be repaid on moral basis (O. Nagy 1966: 335–336). Assuming that the FREEINDEPENDENCE AS BEARD cultural metaphor relates to (or derives from) FINANCIAL CREDIT AS BEARD, the metonymic motivation of their instantiations in idiomatic expressions can be captured in the cultural schema of TAKING A LOAN.

5.4 FACIAL HAIR FOR PATRIOTISM

The largest number of proverbs in the data transmit the idea that moustache is considered an emblem of men of the Hungarian nation. Some of them emphasise that the nationality of Hungarian men can be recognised by their moustache (8a)–(b), which assert an external point of view.

(8) a. *Ritka, mint a magyar   bajusz   nélkül.*
       rare like the Hungarian.man moustache without
       Lit. 'As rare as a Hungarian without a moustache'.
    b. *Nincsen   kocsis   ostor nélkül, magyar   ember bajusz*
       be.not.PRS.3SG coachman whip without Hungarian man moustache
       nélkül.
       without
       Lit. 'No coachman without a whip, no Hungarian without a moustache'.

As Dziewońska-Kiss notes (2016: 124), proverbs with a similar structure can also be found in other languages such as Polish (*Miłość bez zazdrości jest jak Polak bez wąsów*, lit. 'Love without jealousy is like a Polish man without a moustache'); however, she also lists various examples that make moustache an essential component of the Hungarian male model but not of the Polish one. The proverbs (9a)–(c) show the natural link between Hungarian men and moustache from an internal perspective: they express the personal motivation for Hungarian men to wear a moustache in order to become attractive (9b, see MANLINESS) or to acquire self-esteem and dignity (9c). In (9c) *eb* 'dog' represents a worthless person based on A VILE MAN IS A DOG metaphor in the Hungarian proverbs (Papišta 2018). This proposition presents the role of moustache in moral recognition in the Hungarian cultural worldview, which is based on the metonymic chain MOUSTACHE FOR APPEARANCE ⇒ APPEARANCE FOR (VALUABLE) PERSONALITY.

(9) a. *bajusz kell-ø a magyar-nak.*
      moustache need-PRS.3SG the Hungarian.man-DAT
      Lit. 'a Hungarian needs a moustache'.
   b. *magyar ember bajusz-szal szép.*
      Hungarian man moustache-INS beautiful
      Lit. 'a Hungarian man is handsome with a moustache'.
   c. *eb a magyar bajusz nélkül.*
      dog the Hungarian moustache without
      Lit. 'a Hungarian man is a dog without a moustache'.

A certain cluster of proverbs also considers the quality of the Hungarian moustache and according to them, the thick (10a) and large one is appreciated. The meaning of (10b)–(c) is that a Hungarian man's moustache is typically very long and it can even hang down into one's drink, so after drinking he has to lick off the leftover from his moustache.

(10) a. *szőr-ös, mint a magyar bajusz.*
       hair-ADV like the Hungarian moustache
       Lit. 'it is as hairy as the Hungarian moustache'.
   b. *bajusz-á-ról másodszor isz-ik a magyar.*
       moustache-POSS.3SG-DELA twice drink-PRS.NDEF.3SG the Hungarian.man
       Lit. 'a Hungarian man drinks from his moustache for the second time'.
   c. *a bajusz-os kétszer isz-ik.*
       the moustache-ADJ twice drink-PRS.NDEF.3SG
       Lit. 'a Hungarian man drinks twice'.

These examples show that a moustache gives a sense of community/patriotism to Hungarians as well as that it is an essential element of the cultural model of MAN in Hungarian culture.

5.5 FACIAL HAIR FOR AGE

According to this conceptualisation, both BEARD and MOUSTACHE are figuratively extended to represent AGE, which has a direct experiential basis. A GREY BEARD is a conventional metonymy for a MAN OF MATURE AGE (based on AGING BODY FOR AGE) as in (11). The Hungarian equivalent of 'grey beard' is *ősz szakáll*, where *ősz* is a specific word used to mean 'white hair'.

(11) *becsül-d   meg az ősz szakáll-t!*
respect-SBJV.DEF.2SG PREV the grey beard-ACC
Lit. 'respect the grey beard'.
'show respect to the elderly men!'

In proverb (11), the appreciation for the elderly implies that mature age has a positive connotation. This conceptualisation is also linked to WISDOM (see Section 5.7) because, according to common experience, wisdom is acquired by getting old. In (12), it is the moustache that represents an aged person, but most probably it is used in the context of relatively young men's gatherings, therefore moustachioed men are opposed to bare faced, i.e., not bearded ones. This proverb was originally used in a company of men where they circulated the same drinking vessel, and it formulated the courtesy custom that the older one can drink first. The generic sense of the proverb is that 'the elder one deserves priority over the younger ones in certain activities' where AGE has a positive connotation.

(12) *bajusz-ra   jár-ø.*
moustache-SUBL go-PRS.NDEF.3SG
Lit. 'one deserves it for his moustache'.
'the elder should drink first'.

In connection with AGE, beard and moustache are contrasted in a popular proverb (13a), where the conceptualisations BEARD FOR THE OLD AND WISE PERSON and MOUSTACHE FOR THE YOUNG AND UNEXPERIENCED PERSON are captured. Another version of this proverb is (13b) which contrasts a moustachioed man with a downy chinned young man. In this context, a higher value is placed on a moustachioed man than on a downy lad. Both proverbs are used to express that in situations of multiple competing opinions the words of the older carry more weight, and in this regard, the DIGNITY AS FACIAL HAIR conceptualisation is the underlying one that develops from the FACIAL HAIR FOR AGE and AGE FOR DIGNITY metonymies.

(13) a. *fél-re   bajusz,   jön-ø   a szakáll!*
         aside-SUBL moustache come-PRS.3SG the beard
         Lit. 'move aside moustache, the beard is coming!'
         'listen to the old and wise one!'
     b. *fél-re   pehely, jön-ø   a bajusz!*
         aside-SUBL down   come-PRS.3SG the moustache
         Lit. 'move aside, down, the moustache is coming!'
         'listen to the old and wise one!'

Although these examples show that beards have an overall positive connotation with regard to AGE, the Hungarian idioms related to AGE are dominantly negative and they associate it with too long time or boringness (14a)–(c). The figurative extension of BEARD to BOREDOM again has a metonymic basis as shown in (14a), where the link between TIME (represented by a growing beard) and BOREDOM are disclosed. In (14b)–(c), however, we can observe the metaphorical usage of BEARD because it is used in connection with inorganic entities, moreover, abstract concepts.

(14) a. *szakáll-a   nő-tt   a vár-akozás-tól.*
         beard-POSS.3SG grow-PST.3SG the wait-NOM-ABL
         Lit. 'he had a beard grown from waiting'.
     b. *szakáll-as vicc.*
         beard-ADJ joke
         'old, boring joke'.
     c. *en-nek   már   szakáll-a   van.*
         this-GEN already beard-POSS.3SG be.PRS.3SG
         'this is a very old/boring issue'.

According to an ethnographic report (Paládi-Kovács 2000), AGE was positively associated with communal values in the Hungarian traditional peasant communities. This had an evident link with growing facial hair in the case of men. In traditional Hungarian peasant communities, "participation in social life, and even more so in decisions affecting the lives of the wider and narrower groups, was usually linked to a certain age, social status and marital status" (Paládi-Kovács 2000: 398–399) and "elderly people – especially elderly men – had the highest prestige in society" (op. cit.: 405). The various stages of growing a moustache were landmarks of life stages from childhood to adolescence as well. Both the moustache growth stages and the quality of one's moustache had direct consequences for language use within the communities, e.g., in various regions of Hungary, moustache had a significant role in determining compliment forms in everyday discourse. The Hungarian language – similar to German, for example – distinguishes two basic personal pronouns and verb conjugations in second person singular. Addressing someone as *te* 'you' (often translated to English as "address somebody by his/her first name") is considered informal, and it is used to address children, people with lower social ranking, or ones whom we are on familiar terms with. One can be formally addressed in various ways depending on his/her social status, position, familial relations that were strictly regulated in the past. The verb conjugation used for formal addresses was third person singular, which reflected some sort of polite distance between the people. According to Gelencsér (1972: 50), in some regions,

> The younger children started addressing formally a lad with the sprouting moustache. The unmarried girls, even if they had called a lad by his first name, started using the formal form when his moustache begin to sprout. [...] Moustache was highly respected, so young girls continued to call by their first names those blond men whose hair looked sparse, even when they grew older.

In sum, both BEARD and MOUSTACHE are extended to AGE in the proverbs; however, BEARD is applied to OLD AGE (BEARD FOR ELDERLY MAN) whereas MOUSTACHE represents COMING OF AGE (MOUSTACHE FOR ADULTHOOD). When they are contrasted, however, the beard indicates maturity. AGE is generally conceptualised as a positive characteristic that is due to the socio-cultural status of elderly men in traditional Hungarian communities, where becoming of age and growing old was associated with gaining wisdom that entailed certain rights and privileges in the group: according to the proverbs, the 'primacy in some social activities' was such a benefit. Hence, AGE is further extended to DIGNITY: BEARD FOR DIGNIFIED MAN and MOUSTACHE FOR DIGNIFIED MAN. However, it has been shown that BEARD is sometimes used with a negative value, especially when its growth expresses TIME and consequently BOREDOM.

5.6 DIGNITY AS FACIAL HAIR

The role of facial hair in marking one's special and esteemed position within society can be further grasped in the DIGNITY AS BEARD AND MOUSTACHE conceptualisation that relies on the DIGNIFIED APPEARANCE FOR DIGNITY metonymy. Among Hungarians, a moustache was regarded as an aesthetic property of men, which lent them a dignified outlook. According to Herman's sub-categories of the Hungarian moustache, they were often named after different types of cattle-horn (Herman 1906) based on the analogy of their shapes. This is presented in idiom (15):

(15) úgy áll-Ø   a   bajsz-a,   mint az öreg bika-Ø
      thus stand-PRS.3SG the moustache-POSS.3SG like the old cattle-GEN
      szarv-a.
      horn-POSS.3SG
      Lit. 'his moustache is shaped like the horn of an old bull'.

In this idiom, both the size and the shape of one's moustache is emphasised to be crucial for an attractive appearance. Comparing a moustache to a cattle-horn has a positive implication because it alludes to the 'Hungarian Grey', a much-appreciated animal in Hungary for centuries. The grey cattle breeding (also known as the 'Hungarian Steppe Cattle') was an ancient breed of domestic beef cattle indigenous to Hungary and the leading economic sector in the country. In the minds of Hungarian people, the 'Hungarian Grey' was the manifestation of dignity and strength among bread animals, partly due to its large horn. In this cultural context, comparing a man's moustache to the cattle horn was a reference to one's majestic appearance and an expression of appreciation.

The distinguished position of men wearing a moustache can also be found in proverbs. Example (16) reports that a moustache is an emblem of a precious member of the community.

(16) meg-es-ik   az még bajusz-os   ember-en   is.
      PREV-happen-PRS.3SG that still moustache-ADJ man-SUPPRESS too
      'it may happen even to distinguished people'.

The proverb is used as an expression of comfort to somebody who has made some mistakes or some misfortune happened to him. It has a rough meaning like 'do not worry, it can happen to anyone'. As a generally agreed wisdom, it can be formulated as 'bad issues can affect anyone'. In this sentence, moustachioed men are posited at the top of the hierarchy of the members of a community. The meaning of dignity is elaborated further in proverb (17) which alludes to an honourable and morally impeccable person.

(17) se   bajusz-a,   se   pénz-e.
      neither moustache-POSS-3SG nor money-POSS-3SG
      'he has neither moral nor financial credits'.

Proverb (17) goes in line with Szemerkényi's (2009: 100) statement,

> For centuries, moustache was part of the costume of a man. Its form varied from region to region, from age to age, and according to social status. The ones who didn't have a moustache stood out from the others and didn't fit in with society's expectations. Such a person was assumed to have no money.

This observation can be understood as a proverb based on the implied knowledge that those people who lost both their financial and moral credits are peripheral members of the community.

In contrast with MOUSTACHE, the conceptualisation DIGNITY AS BEARD could not be found in any proverbs, only idioms (18a)–(d). In each of the following examples, DIGNITY is closely linked to HONOUR that can be best observed in (18c) and (18d).

(18) a. *csak szakáll-á-ra   néz-ve   tisztel-endő.*
only beard-POSS.3SG-SUBL look-ADV respect-FUT.PTCP
Lit. 'he can be respected only for his beard'.

b. *ad-nak   a szakáll-am-ra.*
give-PRS.3PL the beard-POSS.1SG-SUBL
Lit. 'they give sg. on for my beard'.
'they respect me'.

c. *szakáll-am-ra   mond-om.*
beard-POSS.1SG-SUBL say-PRS.DEF.1SG
Lit. 'I say it on my beard'.
'on my honour / you can believe me'.

d. *meg-becsül-t-e   szakáll-á-t.*
PREV-honour-PST-DEF.3SG beard-POSS.3SG-ACC
Lit. 'he valued (his own) beard'
'he was fair'.

5.7 WISDOM AS FACIAL HAIR

In Section 5.4 the conceptual link and cultural background of AGE and WISDOM has been described and exemplified by two proverbs, both in the meaning 'Listen to the old and wise one!' This metaphor emerged from the belief of traditional folk communities where aging and becoming wise were viewed as hand-in-hand processes (Turai 2009). In Hungarian folk culture, the conceptual connection of (MATURITY) AGE ⇒ EXPERIENCE ⇒ WISDOM is apparent in several proverbs. A moustache may indicate becoming an adult (19a) as well as growing very old, in the first case it is metonymically represented by a sprouting moustache whereas in the second case by a grey one (19b).

(19) a. *előbb nő-ø   a bajusz,   aztán ér-ik   az ész.*
first grow-PRS.3SG the moustache then mature-PRS.3SG the brain
Lit. 'first grows the moustache, then the brain gets mature'.
'reaching adulthood does not mean becoming wise'.

b. *későbbre ősz-ül   a bajusz,   mint a   haj.*
later   grey-PRS.NDEF.3SG the moustache than the hair
Lit. 'one's moustache gets grey later than his hair'
'mental ageing comes later than physical ageing'.

Example (19a) asserts that reaching adulthood is by no means becoming knowledgeable. On the contrary, proverb (19b) is used to give comfort to those elderly men who complain about their body getting tired or painful as part of aging, by emphasising that they are still intellectually fit. In this way, two metonymies are incorporated in it: HAIR FOR PHYSICAL CONDITION and MOUSTACHE FOR INTELLECTUAL CONDITION. Accordingly, moustache seems to have an ambiguous connotation in proverbs; however, one should observe that (again) the sprouting moustache carries a relatively negative evaluation.

Turning to proverbs of BEARD, the conceptualisation BEARD AS WISDOM can be found in a negative form. This shows that people do not consider men with large beards necessarily wise (see also idiom (20.a)). These proverbs and idioms imply that while certain positive values are attached to beard, they question them at the same time.

(20) a. *nagy szakáll senki-t   tudós-sá   nem tesz-en.*
big beard nobody-ACC scholar-TRANSL not make-PRS.NDEF.3SG
Lit. 'a big beard does not make anybody wise'.
b. *szakáll-á-ba   száll-t-ø   az esz-e*
beard-POSS.3SG-ILLA sink-PST-3SG the brain-POSS.3SG
Lit. 'his brain sank into his beard'.
'he lost his mind'.

6. Conclusion

The present study focusing on the figurative usages of BEARD and MOUSTACHE in Hungarian proverbs identified seven metaphorical or metonymic target domains: PERSONALITY, MANLINESS, INDEPENDENCE, PATRIOTISM, AGE, DIGNITY, and WISDOM. The analyses of the metaphorical meanings of proverbs reflected on how various elements of culture can be detected in the sentences, and on the values associated with each conceptualisation.

The FACIAL HAIR FOR PERSONALITY metonymic conceptualisation is only apparent in connection with moustache and it is linked to PATRIOTISM and a sense of community. The same holds for the FACIAL HAIR FOR MANLINESS conceptualisation, but other related, though negative 'manly' traits are attributed to the beard in INDEPENDENCE AS BEARD and FINANCIAL CREDIT AS BEARD. The third conceptualisation, MOUSTACHE FOR PATRIOTISM is the most elaborated one that posits the MOUSTACHE as a characteristic 'facial emblem' of Hungarians and it gives a strong sense of patriotism and moral virtue for Hungarians. The preferable shape and size of the Hungarian moustache are also communicated via proverbs, as part of the cultural model of MAN. Both types of FACIAL HAIR have metonymic extensions to AGE, but the status of MOUSTACHE is context-dependent. BEARD is generally applied to OLD AGE, whereas MOUSTACHE represents COMING OF AGE. When the two are contrasted, it is always the elder one who embodies a higher value (a privilege in certain activities), in line with the distinctive position of elderly men in Hungarian traditional communities. However, BEARD also represents LONG TIME and BOREDOM that have a negative content. Both MOUSTACHE and BEARD are also applied to DIGNITY, however, while MOUSTACHE is unarguably positively evaluated, BEARD has an ambiguous, often ironic reference. The conceptualisation WISDOM AS FACIAL HAIR was argued to be in close association with AGE, and it was exemplified in contrastive examples of MOUSTACHE and BEARD, where – in contrast with MOUSTACHE – BEARD was reported not to indicate wisdom on a natural basis.

The present research asserts a qualitative analysis of Hungarian proverbs drawing on a cultural linguistic methodology, and proves that an unambiguous dominance of MOUSTACHE over BEARD is outlined in them. On the one hand, proverbs present a considerable distinction between the two types of facial hair in Hungarian cultural cognition in that MOUSTACHE is reported to be a requirement for a (sexually) attractive man, a definitive and positively valued element of the Hungarian cultural model of MAN, and it is also linked to the cultural identity of Hungarians. On the other hand, BEARD appears to be linked to MANLINESS in various cultures, but not so much in the Hungarian context. Such metaphoric meanings as WISDOM, INDEPENDENCE, or FINANCIAL INDEPENDENCE are frequently presented in propositions exhibiting BEARD with a negative overtone. On the contrary, the moustache is only negatively viewed when it is sprouting, meaning that one has not acquired manly traits yet. In sum, the list of proverbs and the ethnographic insights show that it is the MOUSTACHE and not the BEARD that is a constitutive element of the cultural model of MAN in the Hungarian cultural cognition. The limitation of this observation is that some conceptualisations are more bound to idiomatic expressions than to proverbs, which indicate their entrenchment in Hungarian cognition, but they seem to be rarely used with a moral-evaluative function.

The study also commented on the linkages of different conceptualisations and their common metonymic grounds that incorporate cultural elements. The interconnection of the various conceptual target domains (MASCULINITY, AGE, DIGNITY, WISDOM, INDEPENDENCE, and FINANCIAL INDEPENDENCE) in the Hungarian cultural cognition has been explained. According to the ruling conventions of the folk communities, in the cultural model of MAN, manliness was naturally connected to mature age, familial status, independence of households, wealth, and dignity, all of which virtues entitled one to participate in decision making within the community. As the analysis shows, all these attributes are related to MOUSTACHE rather than BEARD.

The research argues that the representations of MOUSTACHE and BEARD in the proverbs can often be considered as cultural conceptualisations because they carry culture-specific elements that can be anchored to other linguistic and non-linguistic data extracted from various sources of the Hungarian culture (idioms, reports, social events, moustache, competitions etc.). The comparative study of BEARD and MOUSTACHE evidently shows that MOUSTACHE has an overall positive diverse evaluation while BEARD has a contradictory one. Moreover, MOUSTACHE has more conceptualisations, a more detailed description, and it is considered as a truly Hungarian element of culture, having a characteristic shape that does not hold for BEARD. Only in the context of AGE is the quality of BEARD elaborated. The contrastive analysis of the two concepts indisputably shows that the figurative extensions of such naturally connected body-parts as BEARD and MOUSTACHE have diverse positions in cultural cognition, including salience, values, associations etc., and most importantly, their varying relevance to cultural models.

In sum, the chapter aimed to show that the cultural linguistic approach to proverbs and its way of studying the systematic organisation of cultural conceptualisations can enhance a deeper understanding of the cultural aspects of proverbs, and in this way, it both contributes to cognitive linguistic, particularly cultural linguistic research as well as paremiology.

References

Balassa, I., & Ortutay, G. (1979). *Hungarian ethnography and folklore*. Budapest: Corvina Kiadó.

Bárány, J. (2016). *Nem ér majd össze a bajszuk [Their moustaches won't touch]*. Felvidék.ma. https://felvidek.ma/2016/09/nem-er-majd-ossze-a-bajszuk/

Baranyiné Kóczy, J. (2020a). Light-blooded, blood-fumed and blood-rich: Cultural conceptualizations of vér 'blood' in Hungarian. In B. Lewandowska-Tomaszczyk, V. Monello, & M. Venuti (Eds.), *Language, heart and mind: Studies at the intersection of emotion and cognition* (pp. 137–158). [(Łódź Studies in Language]. Bern: Peter Lang.

Baranyiné Kóczy, J. (2020b). Keeping an eye on body-parts: Cultural conceptualizations of the 'eye' in Hungarian. In I. Kraska-Szlenk (Ed.), *Body-part terms in conceptualization and language usage* (pp. 215–245) Amsterdam & Philadelphia: John Benjamins.

Baranyiné Kóczy, J. (2021). The moral eye: A study of Hungarian *szem*. In I. Kraska-Szlenk, & M. Baş (Eds.), *Embodiment in cross-linguistic studies: The 'Eye'* (pp. 45–69) [Brill's Studies in Language, Cognition and Culture] Leiden: Brill.

Baranyiné Kóczy, J. (2022). Cultural metaphors in Hungarian folk songs as repositories of folk cultural cognition. *International Journal of Culture and Cognition*, 22(1–2), 136–163.

Baranyiné Kóczy, J. (2023). More than emotions: Cultural conceptualizations of *szív* 'heart' in Hungarian. In J. Baranyiné Kóczy, & K. Sipőcz (Eds.), *Embodiment in cross-linguistic studies: The 'heart'* (pp. 75–107) [Brill's Studies in Language, Cognition and Culture]. Leiden: Brill.

Bárczi, G., & Országh, L. (1962). *A magyar nyelv értelmező szótára VI. [Dictionary of the Hungarian language VI.]*. Budapest: Akadémiai Kiadó.

Bárdosi, V. (2012). *Magyar szólások, közmondások adatbázisa [Database of Hungarian proverbs and sayings]*. Budapest: Tinta Könyvkiadó.

Bárdosi, V. (2013). *Lassan a testtel! Emberi testrészek a magyar szólásokban, közmondásokban [Not so fast! Human body-parts in Hungarian proverbs and sayings]*. Budapest: Tinta Kiadó.

Bárdosi, V. (2020). *Szólások, közmondások eredete [The origin of sayings and proverbs]*. Budapest: Tinta Kiadó.

Békei, G. (2012). A közmondások pragmatikai vizsgálata [A pragmatic investigation of proverbs]. In A. Parapatics (Ed.), *Félúton 7*. http://linguistics.elte.hu/studies/fuk/fuk11/.

Belkhir, S. (2014). Cultural influence on the use of DOG concepts in English and Kabyle proverbs. In A. Musolff, F. MacArthur, & G. Pagani (Eds.), *Metaphor and intercultural communication* (pp. 131–145). London: Bloomsbury.

Belkhir, S. (2019). Animal-related concepts across languages and cultures from a cognitive linguistic perspective. *Cognitive Linguistic Studies*, 6(2), 295–324.

Belkhir, S. (2021). Cognitive linguistics and proverbs. In X. Wen & J. R. Taylor (Eds.), *The Routledge handbook of cognitive linguistics* (pp. 599–611). New York & London: Routledge.

Ben Salamh, S. B., & Maalej, Z. (2018). A Cultural linguistics perspective on animal proverbs, with special reference to two dialects of Arabic. *Arab World English Journal for Translation and Literary Studies*, 2(4), 21–40.

Berggren J. (2018). *Embodiment in proverbs: Representation of the eye(s) in English, Swedish, and Japanese*. Ph.D. diss., University of Malmö, Malmö.

Charteris-Black, J. (2001). Blood sweat and tears: A corpus based cognitive analysis of 'blood' in English phraseology. *Studi Italiani di Linguistica Teorica e Applicata*, 30(2), 273–287.

Croft, W., & Cruse, D. A. (2004). *Cognitive linguistics*. Cambridge: Cambridge University Press.

Dabbagh, A. (2016). Cultural linguistics as an investigative framework for paremiology: comparing *time* in English and Persian. *International Journal of Applied Linguistics*, 27(3), 577–595.

Dixson, B. J., & Brooks, R. C. (2013). The role of facial hair in women's perceptions of men's attractiveness, health, masculinity and parenting abilities. *Evolution and Human Behavior*, 34, 236–241.

Dziewońska-Kiss, D. (2016). A nő és a férfi nyelvi képe a magyar és a lengyel nyelvben (a frazeológiai kapcsolatok tükrében) [The linguistic image of woman and man in the Hungarian and Polish language (in light of phraseology)]. *Studia Slavica Savariensla*, (1–2), 120–126.

Erdélyi, J. (1851). *Magyar közmondások könyve [Book of Hungarian proverbs]*. Pest, Kisfaludy-Társaság. https://www.arcanum.com/hu/online-kiadvanyok/Szolasok-regi-magyar-szolasok-es-kozmondasok-1/erdelyi-janos-magyar-kozmondasok-konyve-2E62/

Fiedler, A. (2016). Fixed expressions and culture: The idiomatic MONKEY in common core and West African varieties of English. *International Journal of Language and Culture*, 3(2), 189–215.

Gelencsér, S. (1972). Népi megszólítások és a tiszteletadás nyelvi formája a Kapos mentén [Linguistic forms of folk address and dignity in the Kapos region]. *Somogyi Honismereti Híradó (Kaposvár)*, 1, 50–52.

Gibbs, R. W. (1994). *The poetics of mind: Figurative thought, language, and understanding*. Cambridge: Cambridge University Press.

Gibbs, R. W. (2006). *Embodiment and cognitive science*. Cambridge: Cambridge University Press.

Gibbs, R. W., & Colston, H. L. (2012). *Interpreting figurative language*. Cambridge: Cambridge University Press.

Gibbs, R. W., Strom, L. K., & Spivey-Knowlton, M. J. (1997). Conceptual metaphors in mental imagery for proverbs. *Journal of Mental Imagery*, 21(3–4), 83–109.

Glushko, R. J., Maglio, P., Matlock, T., & Barsalou, L. W. (2008). Categorization in the wild. *Trends in Cognitive Science*, 12(4), 129–135.

Goossens, L. (1990). Metaphtonymy: The interaction of metaphor and metonymy in expressions for linguistic action. *Cognitive Linguistics*, 1(3), 323–340.

Gray, P. B., Craig, L. K., Paiz-Say, J. et al.. (2020). Sexual selection, signaling and facial hair: US and India Ratings of Variable Male Facial Hair. *Adaptive Human Behavior and Physiology*, 6, 170–184.

Herman, O. (1902). *A magyar nép arcza és jelleme [The face and character of the Hungarian nation]*. Budapest: Természettudományi Könyvkiadó Vállalat.

Herman, O. (1906). A magyar bajusz [The Hungarian moustache]. *Magyar Nyelv*, 2, 85–91.

Johnson, M. (1987). *The body in the mind. The bodily basis of meaning, imagination and reason*. Chicago: The University of Chicago Press.

Kidron, Y., & Kuzar, R. (2002). My face is paling against my will: Emotion and control in English and Hebrew (Special issue: The Body in description of emotions. Issue editors: N. J. Enfield and A. Wierszbicka). *Pragmatics and Cognition*, 10, 129–157.

Kocsány, P. (2002). *Szöveg, szövegtípus, jelentés: A mondás, mint szövegtípus [Text, text type and meaning: Proverb as a text type]*. Budapest: Akadémiai Kiadó.

Komlósi, L. I. (2005). A jelentésszerkezet dinamikája mentális műveleteink tükrében: kísérlet a szókapcsolatok kognitív szemantikai osztályozására [The dynamics of meaning structure in the light of our mental operations: an attempt at a cognitive semantic classification of word combinations]. In A. Kertész, & P. Pelyvás (Eds.), *Általános Nyelvészeti Tanulmányok XXI*. (pp. 89–126). Budapest: Akadémiai Kiadó.

Kövecses, Z. (1990). *Emotion concepts*. Berlin & New York: Springer-Verlag.

Kövecses, Z. (2002). *Metaphor. A practical introduction*. Oxford: Oxford University Press.

Kövecses, Z. (2005a). *Metaphor in culture: Universality and variation*. Cambridge: Cambridge University Press.

Kövecses, Z. (2005b). A broad view of cognitive linguistics. *Acta Linguistica Hungarica / Acta Linguistica Academica*, 52(2–3), 135–172.

Kövecses, Z., & Radden, G. (1998). Metonymy: developing a cognitive linguistic view. *Cognitive Linguistics*, 9(1), 37–77.

Kraska-Szlenk, I. (2014). Semantic extensions of body-part terms: common patterns and their interpretation. *Language Sciences*, 44, 15–39.

Lakoff, G., & Johnson, M. (1980). *Metaphors we live by*. Chicago: University of Chicago Press.

Lakoff, G., & Turner, M. (1989). *More than cool reason: A field guide to poetic metaphor*. Chicago: University of Chicago Press.

Langacker, R. W. (1987). *Foundations of cognitive grammar. vol. I. Theoretical prerequisites*. Stanford, California: Stanford University Press.

Maalej, Z. (2008). The heart and cultural embodiment in Tunisian Arabic. In F. Sharifian, R. Dirven, N. Yu, & S. Niemeier (Eds.), *Culture, body, and language: conceptualizations of internal body organs across cultures and languages* (pp. 395–428). Berlin & New York: Mouton de Gruyter.

Maalej, Z. (2009). A cognitive-pragmatic perspective on proverbs and its implications for translation. *International Journal of Arabic-English Studies*, 10, 135–154.

Maalej, Z., & Yu, N. (2011). *Embodiment via body-parts: Studies from various languages and cultures*. Amsterdam & Philadelphia: John Benjamins.

Margalits, E. (1896). *Magyar közmondások és közmondásszerű szólások [Hungarian proverbs and proverb-like sayings]*. Budapest: Kókai Lajos.

Marmaridou, S. (2011). The relevance of embodiment to lexical and collocational meaning: The case of *prosopo* 'face' in Modern Greek. In Z. Maalej, & N. Yu (Eds.), *Embodiment via body-parts. Studies from various languages and cultures* (pp. 23–40). Amsterdam & Philadelphia: John Benjamins.

Maxwell, A. (2015). 'The handsome man with Hungarian moustache and beard'. *Cultural and Social History*, 12(1), 51–76.

Mieder, W. (1985). A proverb is a short sentence of wisdom. *Proverbium*, 2, 109–143.

Mieder, W. (1993). *Proverbs are never out of season*. Oxford & New York: Oxford University Press.

Molnár, R., & Marjanovic, M. (2021). A bajusz azt jelenti, hogy férfi vagyok [A moustache means that I am a man]. *Telex*. https://telex.hu/video/2021/08/23/bajuszfesztival-kiskunfelegyhaza-verseny-bajuszkiraly

Niemeier, S. (2008). To be incontrol: Kind-hearted and cool-headed. In: F. Sharifian, R. Dirven, N. Yu, & S. Niemeier (Eds.), *Culture, body, and language: Conceptualizations of internal body organs across cultures and languages* (pp. 349–372). Berlin & New York: Mouton de Gruyter.

Norrick, N. R. (1985). *How proverbs mean: Semantic studies in English proverbs* (Trends in Linguistics 27). Berlin, New York, & Amsterdam: Mouton De Gruyter.

Norrick, N. R. (2014). Subject area, terminology, proverb definitions, proverb features. In H. Hrisztova-Gotthardt, & M. A. Varga (Eds.), *Introduction to paremiology* (pp. 7–27). Warsaw: Mouton De Gruyter.

Nosrati, V. (2019). *Cultural conceptualisations of animal expressions in Persian*. Ph.D. diss., Monash University, Melbourne.

O. Nagy, G. (1966). *Magyar szólások és közmondások [Hungarian proverbs and sayings]*. Budapest: Gondolat Kiadó.

Palády-Kovács, A. (1997). *Magyar Néprajz IV. Életmód [Hungarian ethnography. vol. IV: Lifestyle]*. Budapest: Akadémiai Kiadó.

Paládi-Kovács, A. (Ed.) (2000). *Magyar néprajz VIII. Társadalom [Hungarian ethnography. vol. VIII: Society]* (pp. 396–412). Budapest: Akadémiai Kiadó.

Papišta, Ž. (2018). Feledésbe merült kutyák: A magyar *kutya* vezérszavú frazémák archaikus rétege kognitív nyelvészeti megközelítésben [Dogs forgotten: The archaic layer of Hungarian phrasemes representing the keyword *kutya* 'dog' from a cognitive linguistic perspective]. *Tanulmányok*, 57, 133–150.

Peterkin, A. (2001). *One thousand beards. A cultural history of facial hair*. Vancouver: Arsenal Pulp Press.

Quinn, N., & Holland, D. (Eds.) (1987). *Cultural models in language and thought*. Cambridge: Cambridge University Press.

Radden, G. (2000). How metonymic are metaphors. In B. Antonio (Ed.), *Metaphor and metonymy at the crossroads. A cognitive perspective* (pp. 93–108). Berlin & New York: Mouton de Gruyter.

Sharifian, F. (2011). *Cultural conceptualisations and language: Theoretical framework and applications*. Amsterdam & Philadelphia: John Benjamins.

Sharifian, F. (2017). *Cultural linguistics*. Amsterdam & Philadelphia: John Benjamins.

Sharifian, F., Dirven, R. Yu, N., & Niemeier, S. (2008). (Eds.), *Culture, body, and language: Conceptualizations of internal body organs across cultures and languages*. Berlin & New York: Mouton de Gruyter.

Sherrow, V. (2005). *Encyclopedia of hair: a cultural history*. Westport & London: Greenwood Press.

Siahaan, P. (2011). HEAD and EYE in German and Indonesian figurative uses. In Z. Maalej, & N. Yu (Eds.), *Embodiment via Body-parts. Studies from various languages and cultures* (pp. 93–114). Amsterdam & Philadelphia: John Benjamins.

Szemerkényi, Á. (1994). *„Közmondás nem hazug szólás" (A proverbiumok használatának lehetőségei)* ["Proverbs are no lies" (Possibilities of using proverbs)]. Budapest: Akadémiai Kiadó.

Szemerkényi, Á. (2009). *Szólások és közmondások [Proverbs and sayings]*. Budapest: Osiris Kiadó.

Szilágyi, P. (2013). *„Mert nem csak szőr a magyar bajusz"*: Kis magyar bajusz-hon-ismeret ["Because the Hungarian moustache is not just any hair": A small Hungarian study of moustache]. *Honismeret*, 2, 33–36.

Turai, T. (2009). *Öregek társadalomnéprajzi vizsgálata [A socio-ethnographic analysis of the elderly]*. Ph.D. diss., Eötvös Loránd University, Budapest.

Ukosakul, M. (2003). Conceptual metaphors motivating the use of Thai 'face'. In E. H. Casad, & G. B. Palmer (Eds.), *Cognitive linguistics and non-Indo-European languages* (pp. 275–303). Berlin & New York: Mouton de Gruyter.

Wolk, D. (2008). Expressions concerning the heart (libbā) in Northeastern Neo-Aramaic in relation to a classical syriac model of the temperaments. In F. Sharifian, R. Dirven, N. Yu, & S. Niemeier (Eds.), *Culture, body, and language: Conceptualizations of internal body organs across cultures and languages* (pp. 267–318). Berlin & New York: Mouton de Gruyter.

Yu, N. (2001). What does our face mean to us? *Pragmatics & Cognition*, 9(1), 1–36.

Zaicz, G. (2006). *Etimológiai szótár: Magyar szavak és toldalékok eredete [Dictionary of etymology: The origin of Hungarian words and suffixes]*. Budapest: Tinta Kiadó.

Web sites

World Beard and Moustache Championships. https://www.worldbeardchampionships.com/categories

Proverbs about Beard. *World Proverbs.* (listofproverbs.com) https://www.listofproverbs.com/keywords/beard/

Proverbs about Moustache. *World Proverbs.* (listofproverbs.com) https://www.listofproverbs.com/keywords/moustache/

CHAPTER 12

"We are in the same storm, not in the same boat"
Proverbial wisdom in environmental debates

Anaïs Augé
University of Louvain, Belgium

The chapter proposes to investigate the implications of the proverbial phrase *to be in the same boat* in international debates about climate change. The study exposes the endorsed or disputed uses of the proverb. I analyse its exploitation by different discourse producers who convey different opinions. The data are extracted from various texts and speeches produced (or translated) in English. This research illustrates how the proverb can be exploited to fit different cultural traditions and different environmental concerns. The aim of the chapter is to identify the different arguments promoted by the use of the proverb. It also highlights the aspects of the proverb that may not correspond to the reality of climate change. This gives rise to argumentative exploitations using related metaphorical expressions. With reliance on cognitive metaphor theories (Lakoff 1993, 2004, 2010), and on metaphor scenarios in particular (Musolff 2004, 2016, 2019a), the occurrences discussed below demonstrate how the metaphorical image of the EARTH IS A CONTAINER has been challenged through the depiction of the EARTH IS A BOAT. Indeed, the source concept BOAT comprises particular characteristics that can cause division among discourse producers to the extent that climate change debates may revolve around the use and misuse of the proverb. The chapter demonstrates that the proverbial phrase *to be in the same boat* involves precarious implications in environmental discourse.

Keywords: to be in the same boat, climate change, argumentation, Cognitive Linguistics, metaphor

1. Introduction

This chapter proposes to highlight the implications of the phrase *to be in the same boat* when it is applied in an environmental context. The qualification of a metaphorical phrase as a proverb may be a complex task for metaphor scholars. The conceptualisation of THE EARTH IS A BOAT (as implied by the phrase *to be in the same boat*) is associated with different historical references and cultural beliefs. These references and beliefs justify an interpretation of the phrase as a proverb. In addition, the occurrence of the proverb *we are in the same boat* in the context of international meetings involves another layer of analysis concerning its argumentative function. In such a context, political arguments might appear as a "wisdom or accepted truth" (Belkhir 2014: 133) when applied to the topic of climate change. Sperber and Wilson (1995) define the function of a proverb as being "attributable not to any specific source but to people in general" (Sperber and Wilson 1995: 238–239). Indeed, the political discussion of a scientific topic, such as the environmental crisis, characterises scientific references as the language of truth (see Musolff 2019a); i.e., scientists study the phenomenon and conduct a range of experiments to produce certain results that can then be communicated to the public. This emphasis on knowledge and scientific truth can be promoted in politics, and proverbial wisdom can shed light on the accuracy of the political statements. This proverbial wisdom conveys a sense of unity, implying "we sink or swim together" (Robertson 2012). This sense of unity may still be conveyed by the less complex metaphorical mapping THE EARTH IS A CONTAINER (Romaine 1996). Indeed, a large body of work demonstrated that the target domain EARTH might map with a large variety of CONTAINER source concepts like TRAIN, PLANE, or even SPACESHIP (Muir 1994; Charteris-Black 2004; Musolff 2004; Deese 2009; Cibulskiene 2012; Robertson 2012; Charteris-Black 2019; Silaški and Durovic 2019). The present research investigates the characteristics of the source concept BOAT in order to identify the arguments it may promote in the political context (as opposed to the arguments promoted by other CONTAINER source concepts). For this purpose, I study proverbial occurrences in texts describing the environmental crisis. The topic of climate change is of particular interest because it defines a global threat requiring international cooperation. The extracts discussed below establish how the proverbial phrase *to be in the same boat* can depict different experiences of climate change. These extracts show that certain characteristics of the source concept BOAT can illustrate particular experiences of climate change. In the next section, I provide more details about climate change metaphors and proverbs in political contexts. I then describe the data selected for this research. In the first part of the analysis, I analyse arguments that endorse the image of HUMANITY AS THE CONTENT OF THE SAME BOAT. This is followed by the study of more complex depictions of the BOAT. In such cases, the source concept is exploited to endorse or criticise the image of THE SAME BOAT. The final discussion exposes the implications of the phrase *to be in the same boat* in the context of international debates.

2. Climate change, politics, and metaphors

2.1 Climate change metaphors

Climate change is a complex topic. Metaphors are needed in order to communicate about the crisis. Indeed, through the conceptual mapping of a complex, scientific target domain, such as atmospheric gases, with a more concrete, familiar source domain, such as BOAT, metaphor users can explain climate change to a larger audience (Lakoff 1993). This process may be necessary because recipients are asked to alter their life style in order to reduce pollution and its impact on the planet.

Firstly, scientists have produced theoretical and pedagogical metaphors (Boyd 1993) to name their environmental discoveries (e.g., *the greenhouse effect*, see Augé 2021) and to explain their findings to the largest number (e.g., *the carbon footprint*, see Nerlich and Koteyko 2010; Nerlich and Hellsten 2014; Augé 2022).

Secondly, climate change metaphors have been studied with attention paid to the arguments they may promote in particular contexts. Indeed, the environmental actions required to control the threat may generate various debates opposing climate activists to sceptical communities (Augé 2021). For instance, Nerlich (2010; see also Shaw and Nerlich 2015) demonstrates how the use of RELIGION metaphors can promote sceptical arguments depicting science as untrue. Nerlich and Koteyko (2010: 39–48) focus on the economic aspect of climate change in the British press. They observe two metaphorical frames – CARBON GOLDRUSH (e.g., "Bioprospectors' (...) *quest* for green gold") and CARBON COWBOY (e.g., "the fast growing but increasingly criticized carbon offset industry is at risk of being discredited by *cowboy* operators"). These involve ethical considerations about carbon offsetting. This study reveals that the same process (offsetting) can be perceived through different –but semantically related– source domains while conveying different arguments regarding ethics.

Third, several existing surveys aimed at identifying the metaphorical theme that is the most likely to convince recipients to reduce pollution. Notably, these studies distinguish metaphors that can promote actions, such as, the WAR metaphor (e.g., "When will Americans start to *combat* excessive energy use and *kill* the problems?"), from metaphors that do not effectively reflect the danger represented by the environmental threat, such as the RACE metaphor (e.g., "When will Americans *go after* excessive energy use and surge ahead on problems?") (Flusberg, Matlock and Thibodeau 2017: 772). Nay and Brunson's (2013: 165) survey focuses on the WAR and MEDICINE metaphors. They study the effects of such metaphors on the participants' opinions on the management of forests. Their results contradict the findings of the aforementioned survey. They conclude that

WAR metaphor does not influence support for any particular solution (tree burning or felling).

These significant findings establish the ideological function of metaphors in climate change discourse. Yet, the linguistic literature on climate change metaphors in political and international contexts seems more limited. This chapter thus proposes to contribute to this existing body of research by investigating the arguments promoted by the phrase *to be in the same boat* in international debates about the environmental crisis.

2.2 Proverbs and metaphors in political debates

This chapter demonstrates that the source domain BOAT has been significantly exploited in environmental debates. Politicians have used the proverb *we are in the same boat* in order to advertise certain points of view on climate change. In turn, the proverb has been re-used by opponents to discredit existing arguments. In such contexts, the ideological stances alter the conceptual mapping so that it corresponds to the metaphor user's political background. For instance, in his review of environmental political speeches, Lakoff (2010) suggests that the politicians who favour the enactment of climate policies do not show good mastery of argumentation through metaphors. However, sceptical speakers and U.S. Republicans (Lakoff 2004, 2010) rely on effective metaphors to communicate about such policies. Lakoff concludes that these different metaphorical uses may be the reason behind the fact that not enough climate policies have been voted (2010: 73).

Indeed, politicians use metaphors to sound right, legitimise their decisions, and persuade the population that their policies are good for the country (Charteris-Black 2011: 15; Williams 2015: 271). These help them to advertise a link between their political and individual interests (Ly 2013: 152). An illustration of this argumentative strategy can be observed in Bamberg's study (2004: 357). He demonstrates that metaphors can depict a figurative opposition in discourse between heroes and villains. This opposition arises from the creation of a "storied world" where characters' goals are evaluated to define different camps, one of which the recipients are invited to join (Labov 2006: 37; Jucker 2010: 71; Hanne 2014: 13). Focusing on the argumentative role of proverbs, Charteris-Black (2019) and Musolff (2019b) show that the phrase *having your cake and eating it* has played a significant role in the political communication related to Brexit; this proverb has been exploited in various ways to either endorse or criticise (e.g., "Stop it, Boris! This recycling is pasta joke. If you carry on, Liam Fox will want a pizza the action. Or you'll be moved to the Minestrone of Defence" quoted after Musolff 2019b: 138) Boris Johnson's decision and pro-Brexit arguments ("My policy on cake is still pro having it and pro eating it" quoted after Musolff 2019b: 136).

Concerning climate change debates, Shaw and Nerlich (2015:38) identify a particular strategy to discuss energy policies: transition to environmentally friendly energy is either characterised as being painless or aggressive, depending on the stance adopted in the texts. Both of these metaphorical characterisations rely on the source domain WAR-COMPROMISE. The source domain has been exploited in a way that fits the discourse producer's opinion. In addition, politicians may rely on metaphors to reassure recipients and downplay the risks associated with climate change (Lakoff 2004). For example, Lakoff (2004: 22) refers to the legislation named the *Clear Skies Act* whose outcome would increase pollution rates while the metaphor (*clear*) suggests an absence of polluting gases. In the next section, I focus on the CONTAINER-TRANSPORT metaphor and its exploitation in discourse.

2.3 The JOURNEY, TRANSPORT, and BOAT metaphors

Existing studies on metaphors in environmental debates demonstrate that politicians tend to favour conventional metaphorical expressions and conceptualisations (Ly 2013). The WAR and JOURNEY metaphors have been identified in discourse: these metaphors are used to unify the population by picturing climate change as a MUTUAL ENEMY. They also describe a DISTANCE THAT HAS BEEN COVERED and an opposition between the WRONG and the RIGHT TRACKS (Ly 2013: 152–164).

The EARTH IS A BOAT metaphor can be related to the JOURNEY metaphor that also involves MEANS OF TRANSPORT, PASSENGERS, and a DESTINATION. Atanasova and Koteyko (2017) observe the frequent use of JOURNEY metaphors in *The New York Times* online editorials to advance pro-climate change arguments (conceptualisations of efforts and solutions to solve the issue). They find that the focus is on the JOURNEYING (the means to reach a certain destination) rather than on the DESTINATION itself. Asplund (2011) focuses on the PACE OF THE JOURNEY described in Swedish farm magazines discussing climate change. She highlights that efforts of adaptation are regularly conceptualised through motion verbs such as *break*, *crash*, and *creep*, and metaphorical expressions related to SPEED. These metaphorical expressions emphasise the need to SLOW climate change and convey a feeling of urgency to find solutions. From a different perspective, Deignan (2017) notes the frequent use of JOURNEY metaphors related to a particular TRAJECTORY in the descriptions of scientific diagrams related to environmental experiments.

With attention paid to TRANSPORT metaphors, the conceptualisation of the EARTH AS A SPACESHIP has been a relevant metaphorical theme in environmental debates. Muir (1994) explains that this metaphor originates in Richard Buckminster Fuller's (theorist) book *Spaceship Earth* published in 1969 (quoted after Muir

1994). In this book, the Earth is conceptualised as an INTERSTELLAR VEHICLE CRUISING through the galaxy (1994: 148). Muir suggests that the SPACESHIP EARTH metaphor is associated with the conceptualisation HUMANITY AS A CREW ON THE SHIP (e.g., Disney Channel's use of the metaphor; 1994: 149). According to Deese's research (2009: 70–71), the SPACESHIP EARTH metaphor was part of American environmental discourse in the 1960s and 1970s. The metaphor has emerged as a result of the Cold War and scientific improvements that improved our understanding of the Earth.

The metaphorical MARITIME JOURNEY (comprised in the proverb *to be in the same boat*) highlights the progressive aspect of environmental damages. The metaphorical reference to the BOAT can highlight the negative aspects of political decisions (to characterise the opposing party's JOURNEY; Charteris-Black 2004: 163; Cibulskiene 2012: 149–150; Charteris-Black 2019: 145–146; Silaški and Durovic 2019: 4), with the identification of the SHIPWRECK scenario-version (Musolff 2004: 55–59). The source domain BOAT has been observed in British political discourse and its frequent use has been justified with references to British maritime history (Charteris-Black 2004: 162, 2019: 145; Silaški and Durovic 2019: 4). For instance, the then British Prime Minister Winston Churchill used the phrase *to be in the same boat* in his speeches to unify the British population against Nazi Germany (quoted after Mieder 1997: 44). *The Brewer's dictionary of phrase and fable* (Dent 2018) establishes that the phrase is a reference to "the perils faced by people in small boats at sea". It depicts a difficult situation that the metaphor users and recipients experience (Dent 2018).

The present research investigates the different uses of the phrase in international settings. The extracts demonstrate that the phrase is not restricted to British history. For instance, one may consider the Chinese version of the proverbial phrase. This version refers to the story of two opposing soldiers who are forced to cooperate in order to travel "in the same small boat" (Sun Tzu 5th century BC – trans: Butler-Bowdon 2010; see also McCreadie 2008). Hence, the international relevance of the phrase suggests particular implications in climate change discourse: the global threat requires political leaders to cooperate in order to control the danger.

In the following section, I describe the relevant approaches to analyse the proverbial phrase, and I provide more details about the texts that have been selected for the present research.

3. Relevant approaches and selection of data

This chapter aims at identifying the varying use of the phrase *to be in the same boat* in discussions of climate change. This stems from the hypothesis that the phrase conveys a certain wisdom that may be disputed in the context under study. Indeed, climate change represents a global phenomenon affecting the world population. Yet, it does not represent the same danger for all countries and places. For instance, southern countries and northern and southern hemispheres may be more at risk of temperature increases than places like Europe and the United States. Littoral places may be more at risks of flooding than inland places. High-income countries may be more ready to face climatic threats than lower income countries. In addition, pollution mainly affects areas where industrial activities take place. These observations thus significantly contradict the image of *the same boat*. This contradiction is of particular interest since it may give rise to argumentative uses of the phrase in environmental debates.

In order to analyse the argumentative uses of the phrase *to be in the same boat*, I rely on the identification of metaphor scenarios (Musolff 2004, 2016, 2019a, 2019b). Scenarios involve assumptions about the source concept: this source concept becomes part of a metaphorical script to promote a certain evaluation of the topic (Musolff 2016: 30–31). Scenarios are not limited to the exploitation of the source domain; they are included in contexts that involve various arguments about the target. For example, the BOAT scenario may involve a SHIPWRECK (2004: 55–6). Hence, the political context of use may reveal particular assumptions regarding the historical background and stories associated with the phrase. Politicians may also exploit the source domain BOAT in order to adapt the phrase to particular environmental experiences.

The focus on argumentative exploitations of the proverb in environmental debates is associated with a particular selection of relevant occurrences for the research. Here, occurrences are defined as relevant when these refer to the metaphorical image THE EARTH IS A BOAT, and when these are employed within a text that explicitly emphasises a particular argument regarding climate change. For instance, when contextual information were lacking (like in short headlines or shortened quotes) the related occurrence was not selected for the present study. The Metaphor Identification Procedure (Steen et al. 2010) was also used to test the metaphorical meaning (as opposed to the literal meaning) of each occurrence. The occurrences selected for the present research emerge from a large variety of texts retrieved from newspapers (*The Guardian, The Telegraph, Washington Post, Canberra Times, The Globe and Mail, The Star*), communications from Non-Governmental Organisations (Extinction Rebellion, Greenpeace, Friends of the Earth), politicians' speeches (Conference of the Parties), and communications from the United Nations and the World Health Organisation. These texts have been collected as part of a project that investigates a larger range of metaphors in climate change discourse (Augé 2023). The language used in the texts is English. Besides, other languages are represented (such as French, Chinese, Dutch, or German) with translated occurrences produced by the discourse producers.[1] These translations – in the form of citations used in the text – may thus be ideologically oriented to fit the stance adopted by the discourse producers in English, although the present chapter does not tackle these translation issues. These texts include the phrase *climate change* or *global warming* in their titles or headlines. The period of the publications of the texts is situated between 1984 and 2021.[2]

The extracts I discuss below are related to the use of a particular metaphor; i.e., EARTH IS A BOAT that occurs in some of the texts collected as part of this project. These have been of particular interest because they promote a particular viewpoint on climate change: they describe national experiences of climate change, political oppositions, international solidarity, religious perspectives on the phenomenon, and support to climate refugees. Yet, these do not limit the wide range of arguments conveyed through the image of *the same boat*. The aim is to demonstrate how discourse producers may endorse or question the wisdom related to the proverb. Table 1 below provides more details about the data associated with this research.

I offer a qualitative analysis of the expression and its context, downplaying systematic patterns (Tognini Bonelli 2001: 65–81) in climate change discourse. As demonstrated in Table 1, the uneven characteristics of the texts produced in different languages, in different genres, and at different periods do not allow me to produce a quantitative comparison (approximate number of texts analysed in the corpus-based project: 27,643).[3] Additionally, among the 2,331 metaphorical occurrences selected for the corpus-based project (Augé 2023), the occurrences of THE EARTH IS A BOAT metaphor are limited to 53 instances. This represents 2, 27% of the metaphorical expressions discussed in the project.

---

1. These translations are performed by discourse producers when they cite an external individual in the text. In the case of official speeches from politicians, the translations are performed by professional interpreters.
2. This period was established after a research on the *Nexis* database (n.d.) that determined that the phrase 'climate change' was popularised for the first time in 1984.
3. This corpus-based project is discussed in Augé (2023), texts are regularly added to address modern concerns. A corpus-based approach is defined according to Tognini-Bonelli's definition (2001: 81; see Charteris-Black 2019 for an empirical use of this approach to corpora).

Table 1. General overview of the data

Sources	Newspapers	Non-governmental	Politicians' speeches	(Other) international organisations
(from 1984 to 2021)	Nexis (n.d.) URL: nexis.com	Official websites of the organisations and official archives URLs: greenpeace.org foei.org extinctionrebellion.uk cop26coalition.org worldwildlife.org wcs.org	Nexis (n.d.); Conferences of the Parties official websites URLs: nexis.com unfccc.int unece.org ukcop26.org	United Nations and United Nations Environment Program official websites; World Health Organisation official website URLs: un.org unep.org who.int
EARTH IS A BOAT: number of occurrences (total: 53)	15	20	11	7

The next section focuses on the texts that endorse the image of *the same boat*. It establishes how this image is promoted. It also determines how different communities endorse this image.

4. We are in the same boat: Same boat, different arguments

The image of a single global boat allowing humanity as whole to get *on board* is an effective way for metaphor users to involve all recipients in the storyline they describe. This storyline depicts climate change from the particular viewpoint of the metaphor user. In the texts that endorse the proverbial wisdom, the image of *the same boat* seems tightly linked to arguments favouring climate actions. Alternatively, this may be used to criticise political inaction towards climate. In the extracts presented below, the metaphorical phrase is used to reflect and value peace and international agreements. The image of *the same boat* with humanity ON BOARD is used as a familiar proverbial reference. One might expect a DESTINATION TO BE REACHED following the BOARDING. Yet, the focus is rather on the characteristics of the JOURNEY and the PASSENGERS. Metaphor users identify the

PASSENGERS OF THE BOAT who may have favoured a SEPARATE JOURNEY but who agree to (or have to) TRAVEL TOGETHER following the impact of the environmental crisis. For example, in a recent instance from Jamie Shea, the former Deputy Assistant Secretary General at NATO refers to climate change to promote the benefits of international cooperation, as in:

(1) The Earth Day summit, involving 40 leaders from the world's major nations, demonstrated that even in a more competitive and fractured security environment, multilateralism can still work when, (…) as with piracy and now climate change, *everybody finds themselves in the same boat* and realises they can't solve their own problems without effective, and extensive, international cooperation. (Jamie Shea, 30/04/2021)

In this extract, the image of *the same boat* is used to present a pre-condition to international cooperation (multilateralism). Jamie Shea states that events such as climate change have brought countries together to face a global danger. The argument promoted here is not so much related to the need to address a global threat internationally. Instead, it highlights the positive impact of international cooperation in a modern, divided world. For instance, in the last sentence of the extract, the metaphor user refers to nations' respective problems (that cannot be solved at the national level), but does not characterise the nature of these problems. The general stance adopted in this sentence implies that international cooperation is, according to Jamie Shea, an essential feature in the resolution of every national concern. The image of *the same boat* is here not related to the JOURNEY-MEANS OF TRANSPORT-DESTINATION. It is used as a figurative device with historical background that can be understood and reflected in the statement. This reference to proverbial wisdom presents the positive consequences of international cooperation and evolution, and it downplays national or individual interests. In other words, when individuals are found on the same small boat (Dent 2018), they face the same problems and move at the same pace. This shows that the proverbial wisdom does not require to be described explicitly: Jamie Shea does not need to elaborate on the BOAT imagery to produce a link with his topic of discourse; i.e., the Earth Day summit.

In different cases, the image of *the same boat* is part of a eulogistic description of the ecosystem. The BOAT does not only include humanity but also every living species on the planet. Such occurrences insist on the global perspective associated with the conceptualisation EARTH IS A BOAT, implying that BOARDING is not an option (as it was described in the extract aforementioned). This is illustrated in Extract (2) presented below:

(2) *We are all in the same boat*, humans born and still not born, animals born and still not born, the whole of the great Seder Bereshit, the Order of Creation that God declared very good. *Whether we continue to paddle through calm waters is up to us.*
   (Rabbi Lawrence Troster, Ethical responsibility and Climate change, 13/07/2011)

In this extract from Rabbi Lawrence Troster's statement (an eco-theologian and environmental activist), the image of *the same boat* is associated with religious depictions of life and creation ("the Order of Creation"). This association comprises various implications regarding the BOAT storyline and the religious dogma. Indeed, the image of the SHARED BOAT is used to illustrate the particularities of God's creation. For instance, the exploitation of the proverb depicts humanity as a single species, among other existing animals whose individuals are deprived of identifying attributes (such as social status, nationalities, etc.; "humans born and still not born"). Therefore, like in the preceding extract from Jamie Shea, the BOAT is used to symbolise unity and equality. The stance is more explicit in the last sentence of the above extract where the source domain is exploited to warn about the danger of climate change, caused by human activities. The activist describes the *calm waters*. Unlike the conceptualisation of the SHARED BOAT, we see that the conceptualisation of the WATERS is distinguished from religious appreciation. This is perceptible in the metaphorical reference to "paddling" that defines a typical activity conducted by the human species, i.e., God has created the world ("the Order of Creation") but the world evolves as a consequence of human activities ("paddling"). Therefore, the image of *the same boat* is slightly altered to depict the CALM MARITIME JOURNEY ON A SHARED BOAT as a divine process that may evolve in certain ways following PASSENGERS' activities and behaviour ("up to us"). This extract represents an effective use of religious conceptualisations: it implicitly prevents recipients from believing that a higher authority is responsible for the climate crisis (see the sceptical use of RELIGION metaphor in Nerlich 2010). Instead, it emphasises humans' responsibility to protect their MEANS OF TRANSPORT adapted to their evolution, related to its divine origins.

In different texts, the image of *the same boat* emphasises the positive effects of reconciliation between opposing political leaders. The BOAT depicts a (climatic) situation that forces these leaders to TRAVEL TOGETHER; i.e., they need to act together to control an environmental threat. This is illustrated in Extract (3) presented below.

(3) Trump, Trudeau *in same boat* as sea ice melts around them.
   (Bill McKibben, *The Globe and Mail*, 02/03/2017).

This extract is an exemplary instance of topic triggering. Topic-triggering can be noticed in instances relying on conventional metaphors: "an aspect of the topic under discussion inspires the choice of the metaphorical source domain that is evoked via the metaphorical expressions used in the text" (Semino 2008: 27). For example, *The Guardian* referred to the conflict between South Africa and Morocco over control of Western Sahara as a *Diplomatic desert*, where desert applies to both the lack of diplomatic relationships, and to the literal desert of Sahara (Semino 2008: 27). In the present extract, the source domain BOAT is associated with the image of *the same boat*. This image highlights the noticeable characteristics of the agreement involving two opposing political leaders. The source domain BOAT is also part of a pun that includes the proverbial phrase in a description of ice melting; water, around the United States and Canada. Indeed, the occurrence of the phrase *to be in the same boat* in climate change discourse does not only reflect an endorsement or criticism of environmental arguments; it can also fit the characteristics of the target domain that comprises rise of sea levels, melting of glaciers, and impacts of fishing industry. These characteristics provide a very large ground for the mapping characterising the EARTH (affected by climate change) as a BOAT.

The historical background and cultural stories associated with the image of *the same boat* may also represent a rhetorical tool in international politics. Notably, several occurrences from the corpus refer to the BOAT-related story that is adapted to describe the countries involved in the political meetings. For instance, the Chinese version of the BOAT story has been mentioned in American texts describing environmental discussions between the leaders of these two nations. This is illustrated in Extract (4) presented below.

(4) The US President was just following the 'go Mandarin' fashion modelled by US Secretary of State Hillary Clinton in February 2009, when she trotted out ancient four-character sayings like *tongzhou gongji*, literally, same boat, help (each other) cross (the water) when she only meant to celebrate mutual dependence. But US Treasury Secretary Timothy Geithner put it more plainly: *fengyu, tongzhou* : (Same) stormy weather, same boat. (...) the PRC (People's Republic of China) leaders are very concerned with energy security. That is now widely perceived in the West through the distorting prism of climate change, widely read as code for global warming caused by man-made emissions of greenhouse gases   (Defense and Foreign Affairs Analysis, 18/11/2009)

The occurrence of the *same boat* is a meta-representation of the Chinese BOAT proverbial story that is mentioned by the American politicians in order to, on the one hand, promote cooperation, and on the other hand, act as a rhetorical device that demonstrates the metaphor user's interest in the Chinese culture. The reference to the Chinese culture is perceived through the cultural story of the opposing soldiers sharing a small boat (McCreadie 2008). Regarding the journalist's stance, this meta-representation is criticised at several levels: first, the emphasis is put on the politicians' approximate knowledge of the language and story ("trotted out"). Second, this description of the approximate use of the proverb by the two politicians is linked with the journalist's comment regarding Hilary Clinton's aims, CROSSING THE WATER, in comparison with Timothy Geithner's: FACING STORMY WEATHER. Hence, the source concept BOAT is exploited to define different political goals and achievements through the depiction of the OBSTACLES politicians are ready to overcome through cooperation. Third, in the last instance of the proverb, the plain tone adopted by Timothy Geithner (according to the journalist) conveys a different image of *the same boat*. While this image was almost eulogistic in previous extracts, the politician's statement relies on the image of *the same boat* as a reminder of shared responsibility. This may be caused by the journalist's interpretation or by the translation from Chinese to American English, or by the mention of a STORM related to the global impact of climate change. The STORM defines a sudden threat that requires the CREW to act in order to protect the BOAT. Therefore, the unassertive tone associated with Hilary Clinton's statement promotes an optimistic view on collaboration whereas the plain tone adopted by Timothy Geithner echoes a more pragmatic stance that places the BOAT in an ad-hoc situation. The adaptation of a foreign proverb can thus represent an ideological tool to illustrate different political commitments.

This section established the varying arguments related to the endorsement of the image of *the same boat*. The next section focuses on the occurrences that dispute this eulogistic picture.

5. Sink or swim: Same storm, different boats

The image of *the same boat* can be associated with a eulogistic and concrete description of cooperation. Yet, this description is significantly challenged by the reality of climate change. Some discourse producers may focus on a global threat, but others may highlight that its consequences differ depending on the economy, politics, and industrialisation of the countries. In such cases, metaphor users refer to a SHARED BOAT THAT IS SINKING, A STORM that endangers the MARITIME JOURNEY, or even a BOAT THAT IS TOO SMALL FOR ALL HUMANS TO GET ON BOARD. For instance, some extracts still endorse the image of *the same boat* but exploit the source domain to criticise the PASSENGERS' behaviour. This is illustrated in Extracts (5) and (6) provided below.

(5) Climate change *puts us all in the same boat, one hole will sink us all.* Global warming does not respect borders. A mindset shift is required if world leaders are to save us from ourselves.　　(Kofi Annan, *The Guardian*, 10/12/2009)

(6) *While we are all in the same boat, not all have a say in how to steer it,* he [Ban Ki Moon] said of the current economic architecture, stressing that that was not just a matter of democracy and legitimacy, but a crucially important factor in addressing the many pressing issues currently demanding the world's attention, such as climate change.　　(*States News Service*, 28/06/2011)

In these two extracts, the two metaphor users endorse the depiction of a SHARED BOAT. However, this depiction is distinguished by additional BOAT-related characteristics that act as pre-conditions for the MARITIME JOURNEY to be beneficial.

In Kofi Annan's statement (the former Secretary General of the United Nations), the BOAT is characterised as a SINKABLE CONTAINER. This characterisation highlights the fragility of the concept EARTH-BOAT that contains humanity. Kofi Annan first indicates that a personified version of climate change ("puts us") has captured humanity and imprisoned it in a BOAT-CONTAINER. This scenario-version emphasises that cooperation is not a *desirable* process any more (as it was described in the extracts presented in the previous section), it becomes a *mandatory* process that is imposed upon humanity. Hence, the stance in this extract is much more alarmist than in other extracts referring to a MARITIME JOURNEY ON CALM WATERS (see previous section). Kofi Annan exploits the characteristics of the HUMAN CONTAINER as a BOAT to mention the danger represented by the WATERS ("sink"). In other words, the BOAT here acts both as a PRISON following the personification of climate change as an EVIL-MINDED CHARACTER, and as a CONTAINER NECESSARY FOR HUMAN LIFE ("sink"). The historical and cultural background related to the BOAT story is still at play: the description of the HOLE involves shared responsibilities to take care of the BOAT.

These shared responsibilities are discussed in Ban Ki Moon's statement (former Secretary General of the United Nations). In his statement, the BOAT represents the relationship between economy and climate change. The source domain is exploited to highlight the fact that one may need particular knowledge and a licence to STEER THE MARITIME MEANS OF TRANSPORT. This exploitation is related to Ban Ki Moon's description of two highly complex concepts: economy and climate change. In this scenario-version, the conceptualisation is twofold: on the one hand, the target domain ECONOMY is mapped to the source domain BOAT. On the other hand, climate change is implicitly assimilated to a forthcoming danger that the BOAT may face during the MARITIME JOURNEY ("not just a matter of democracy and legitimacy…the many pressing issues…"). Ban Ki Moon implicitly mentions this forthcoming danger to explain that the population needs an EXPERIENCED

SAILOR. Therefore, the historical and cultural background of the *same boat* story is slightly challenged: Ban Ki Moon attributes special responsibility to qualified SAILORS to secure humanity within the BOAT. This effectively argues in favour of a more sustainable economy.

While these two statements still favour an optimistic (yet slightly alarmist) view on the evolution of climate change (the BOAT can still TRAVEL), other metaphor users promote a much more dramatic version of the scenario. In such cases, the image of *the same boat* is disputed, and the focus is on the unsuitable characteristics of the BOAT(s). This is illustrated in Extract (7) presented below.

(7) But with public confidence in climate science taking such a knock in recent months, what will it take to convince the public that urgent action really is required to reduce greenhouse gas emissions or, as is Lovelock's preference, *to adapt and prepare the lifeboat for a changing climate*? (...) Lovelock freely admits that, at 90, he won't be around to see the results of the "experiment humans are currently conducting with the atmosphere. It's what, in part, gives him the licence to speak with such frankness.

(*The Guardian*, Leo Hickman, 30/03/2010)

In this extract from *The Guardian*, the journalist distinguishes two alternatives to deal with climate change. He opposes emission reduction to adaptation. He refers to the latter with the LIFEBOAT scenario-version that is attributed to James Lovelock. Lovelock (2007) is an environmental scientist, famous for his Gaia theory that gives power to nature and describes climate change as the realisation of Nature's (or Gaia's) intended actions. Consequently, humans are attributed a passive role in the control of the environmental crisis. Their role, according to Lovelock, is to PREPARE A LIFEBOAT: this indirectly indicates that the Earth is conceptualised as a DAMAGED CONTAINER that cannot carry humans any more. The LIFEBOAT scenario-version identifies climate change as a MARITIME ACCIDENT that endangers the lives of the PASSENGERS.[4] The stance is thus much more dramatic than in Kofi Annan's and Ban Ki Moon's respective statements: the PASSENGERS cannot remain in the present EARTH-CONTAINER. This dramatic storyline is contrasted with the journalist's alternative solution: "reduce greenhouse gas emissions". The progressive evolution of climate change allows the PASSENGERS time to adopt this solution (the LIFEBOAT can still be avoided). The LIFEBOAT represents an alternative CONTAINER whose characteristics comprise less desirable features; i.e., it is a MEANS OF TRANSPORT used for survival. Additionally, the DES-

---

4. The results provided by the British National Corpus (from *Sketch Engine*, Kilgarriff 2014) for the search term *lifeboat* show that this word is part of contexts describing various ranges of accidents, like *ambulance, hospitals, flooding, death*, and *victim*.

TINATION OF THE LIFEBOAT adds undesirable features to Lovelock's solution: "the lifeboat for a changing climate". The journalist's opposition between the LIFEBOAT scenario-version and emission reduction strongly promotes the latter, presented as a self-evident choice. Consequently, the lack of adapted environmental decision appears absurd.

The image of the *same boat* can be challenged further, notably in NGO discourse advocating in favour of climate justice. The notion of climate justice is a significant feature of environmental NGO discourse that asks political leaders to consider the uneven consequences of climate change worldwide (Schlosberg and Collins 2014). Unsurprisingly, this notion of climate justice directly contradicts the image of the *same boat*: cooperation is still favoured, but BOATS and MARITIME JOURNEYS differ following a number of factors. This description of DIFFERENT BOATS is best illustrated in Extract (8) provided below.

(8) *We are not all in the same boat:* We, the COP26 Coalition, have come together united under *the common cause of climate justice*. We are a collaboration of civil society organisations including trade unions, direct action networks, climate justice groups, environment and development NGOs, faith groups, students and youth, migrant and racial justice networks. *Same storm, different boats: quite literally this is the fight for our lives and our livelihoods.*
(COP26 Coalition, Coalition Statement 2, 01/11/2020).

This extract has been selected from the publications produced by the Non-Governmental Organisation COP26 Coalition. The focus is on the notion of climate justice. The metaphor users highlight the existence of DIFFERENT BOATS distinguished by the various social status, occupations, nationalities, and skin colours of the PASSENGERS. Yet, this depiction of DIFFERENT BOATS still promotes the benefits of cooperation. Indeed, the DIFFERENT BOATS here inform the readership about the various characteristics of the world population. The conceptualisation explains that some humans can afford WELL-SUITED BOATS whereas other humans may only afford SMALL BOATS. This distinction may be emphasised by the mention of climate migrants in the beginning of the extract, in which case the (SMALL) BOATS source domain is used as a topic-triggering device. The NGO relies on this distinction to explain that global cooperation is needed: PASSENGERS ON BOARD OF LARGER BOATS MUST HELP PASSENGERS ON BOARD OF SMALLER BOATS. This argument is reinforced in the remainder of the extract that refers to a STORM that BOATS have to face. One might infer that the pre-existing climate crisis has attributed particular BOATS to particular PASSENGERS, and the evolution of climate change has put all PASSENGERS (of BIGGER and SMALLER BOATS) at risk ("our lives"; "our livelihoods"). Yet, this evolution does not impact the activists' argument: the STORM is mentioned to represent the common "fight" for survival. Therefore, the activists do not so much argue for cooperation, but for solidarity.

This section demonstrated how the image of the *same boat* has been challenged by metaphor users. The focus has been on the danger faced during the MARITIME JOURNEY that requires all PASSENGERS to take care of the BOAT(s). Alternatively, metaphor users may mention the existing DAMAGES OF THE BOAT(s), and rely on the proverb to promote particular solutions: emission reduction or international solidarity. In the next section, I discuss the implications of these various exploitations, and I provide some concluding remarks about the variation of the *same boat* storyline.

6. Discussion and concluding remarks

This chapter has established the rhetorical role of the proverbial phrase *to be in the same boat* in a plurality of debates about climate change. The wisdom associated with the *same boat* imagery is highly relevant to interpret metaphorical uses and exploitations in politically-oriented texts. Indeed, the story of two opponents sharing a small boat and being forced to cooperate in order to face stormy waters (Sun Tzu 5th century BC; McCreadie 2008; Dent 2018) is implicitly referred to in the extracts discussed here.

Firstly, this story may be used by metaphor users to playfully describe agreements involving political opponents (like in the case of Donald Trump and Justin Trudeau). Secondly, the wisdom associated with the boat-related story helps metaphor users to convey a eulogistic view on the BOAT that suggests, in relation to the target domain EARTH, that human life can thrive through cooperation. Thirdly, some metaphor users focus on the characterisation of the PASSENGERS AS OPPONENTS and describe the danger of a divided world with reference to the FRAGILITY OF THE BOAT, and the DANGER OF THE MARITIME TRAVEL. This perspective may also be part of sarcastic statements depicting absurd images of PASSENGERS' BEHAVIOUR ON BOARD (like in the case of James Lovelock's LIFEBOAT). Fourthly, the opposition between different PASSENGERS can be exploited: this division is not systematically expressed in terms of ANTAGONISTIC RELATIONSHIPS (PASSENGERS AS ENEMIES), but in terms of different attributes. Metaphor users mention the ability of certain communities to face threats as opposed to other communities.

Therefore, the extracts presented in this chapter contradict certain claims made in existing literature regarding the association between the source domain BOAT and the more generic metaphor (Lakoff 1993, Kövecses 2010) of the JOURNEY (Atanasova and Koteyko 2017). Indeed, the association of the *same boat* storyline with descriptions of climate change leads metaphor users to focus on division and cooperation, on PASSENGERS' CONTRIBUTION ON BOARD, and in particular, on the DANGER OF THE MARITIME JOURNEY. Therefore, the significant threat represented by climate change might prevent metaphorical references to a JOURNEY or a DESTINATION: the main arguments are related to the STORM to come and to PASSENGERS' ability to survive. Some extracts still allude to a MARITIME JOURNEY with reference to "calm waters", in cases where the metaphor users promote an optimistic view on climate change mitigation.

The historical background of the phrase *to be in the same boat* can also be perceived through implicit references to WAR. Indeed, the story involves soldiers and opponents travelling in the same boat. The storyline has been adapted to climate change discourse. In such cases, a personified or materialised version of the phenomenon is identified as HUMANITY'S ENEMY (in Kofi Annan's statement). The opposition that is part of the BOAT-related story promotes international solidarity that may sometimes be forced upon humanity. Hence, the BOAT scenario may represent an effective alternative to the use of WAR metaphors in the communication of global crises (Ly 2013; Nay and Brunson 2013; Hanne 2014).

Finally, extracts demonstrated that the BOAT source domain might be selected in climate change discourse for other reasons than its historical implications. The characteristics of the source concept may favour topic-triggering processes (Semino 2008). The danger related to sea level rise and melting of glaciers can map with the concept WATER, implied in the depiction of a MARITIME JOURNEY. Hypothetically, the BOAT source domain may also adequately alarm about the situation of climate migrants, trapped in a boat while they fled dangerous climatic conditions experienced in their countries.

To conclude, the occurrences of the proverbial phrase *to be in the same boat* demonstrated how climate change debates might sometimes revolve around the use and misuse of a metaphorical statement. These debates flourish in cases where the statement is associated with proverbial wisdom that may be disputed following political stances, cultural versions, and adaptation to present-day concerns. Therefore, proverbial stances in (environmental) debates may not always unify participants; these may become effective rhetorical devices to promote one's arguments.

References

 Asplund, T. (2011). Metaphors in climate discourse: An analysis of Swedish farm magazines. *Journal of Science Communication*, 10(4): 1–8.

Atanasova, D., & Koteyko, N. (2017). Metaphors in online editorials and op-eds about climate change, 2006-2013: A study of Germany, the United Kingdom, and the United States. In K. Fløttum (Ed.). *The role of language in the climate debate* (pp. 71-89). London: Routledge.

Augé, A. (2021). From scientific arguments to scepticism: Humans' place in the GREENHOUSE. *Public Understanding of Science*, 31(2), 179-194.

Augé, A. (2022). How visual metaphors contradict expectations about verbal metaphors: A cross-linguistic and multimodal analysis. *Metaphor and the Social World*, 12(1), 1-22.

Augé, A. (2023). *Metaphor and argumentation in climate crisis discourse.* New York: Routledge.

Bamberg, M. (2004). Considering counter narratives. In M. Bamberg, & M. Andrews (Eds.). *Considering counter-narratives: Narrating, resisting, making sense* (pp. 351-373). Amsterdam & Philadelphia: John Benjamins.

Belkhir, S. (2014). Cultural influence on the use of DOG concepts in English and Kabyle proverbs. In A. Musolff, F. MacArthur, & G. Pagani (Eds.). *Metaphor and intercultural communication* (pp. 131-147). London: Bloomsbury Academic.

Boyd, R. (1993). Metaphor and theory change: What is 'metaphor' a metaphor for? In A. Ortony (Ed.). *Metaphor and thought.* Second Edition. (pp. 481-532). Cambridge: Cambridge University Press.

Charteris-Black, J. (2004). *Corpus approaches to critical metaphor analysis.* London: Palgrave Macmillan.

Charteris-Black, J. (2011). *Politicians and rhetoric: The persuasive power of metaphor.* London: Palgrave Macmillan.

Charteris-Black, J. (2019). *Metaphors of Brexit: No cherries on the cake?* London: Palgrave Macmillan.

Cibulskiene, J. (2012). The development of the JOURNEY metaphor in political discourse: Time-specific changes. *Metaphor and the Social World*, 2(2): 131-153.

Deese, R.-S. (2009). The artefact of nature: Spaceship Earth and the dawn of global environmentalism. *Endeavour*. 33(2): 70-75.

Deignan, A. (2017). Metaphors in texts about climate change. *Ibérica*, 34, 45-66.

Dent, S. (2018). *Brewer's dictionary of phrase and fable.* Twentieth edition. London: Chambers Harrap.

Flusberg, S.-J., Matlock, T., & Thibodeau, P.-H. (2017). Metaphors for the war (or race) against climate change. *Environmental Communication* 11(6), 769-783.

Hanne, M. (2014). An introduction to the "warring with word" project. In M. Hanne, W.-D. Crano, & J.-S. Mio (Eds.). *Warring with words: Narrative and metaphor in politics* (pp. 1-57). New York & London: Psychology Press.

Jucker, A.-H. (2010). "Audacious, Brilliant! What a strike!": Live text commentaries on the internet as real-time narratives. In C. R. Hoffmann (Ed.). *Narrative revisited: Telling a story in the age of new media* (pp. 57-79). Amsterdam & Philadelphia: John Benjamins.

Kilgarriff A. (2014). *Sketch Engine*, URL: sketchengine.eu

Kövecses, Z. (2010). *Metaphor: A practical introduction.* Oxford: Oxford University Press.

Labov, W. (2006). Narrative pre-construction. *Narrative Inquiry* 16(1), 37-45.

Lakoff, G. (1993). The contemporary theory of metaphor. In A. Ortony (Ed.). *Metaphor and thought* (pp. 202-252). Cambridge: Cambridge University Press.

Lakoff, G. (2004). *Don't think of an elephant! Know your values and frame the debate: The essential guide for progressives.* Vermont: White River Junction, Vt.: Chelsea Green.

Lakoff, G. (2010). Why it matters how we frame the environment. *Environmental Communication*, 4(1), 70–81.

Lovelock, J. (2007). *The revenge of Gaia: Why the earth is fighting back – and how we can still save humanity.* London: Penguin.

Ly, A. (2013). Images and roles of the European Union in the climate change debate: A cognitive approach to metaphors in the European parliament'. In K. Fløttum (Ed.). *Speaking of Europe: Approaches to complexity in European political discourse* (pp. 151–71). Amsterdam & Philadelphia: John Benjamins.

McCreadie, K. (2008). *Sun Tzu's the art of war: A 52 brilliant ideas interpretation.* Oxford: Infinite Ideas Limited.

Mieder, W. (1997). *The politics of proverbs: From traditional wisdom to proverbial stereotypes.* Madison, WI: University of Wisconsin Press.

Muir, S.-A. (1994). The web and the spaceship: Metaphors of the environment. *Et cetera: A Review of General Semantics*, 51(2), 145–152.

Musolff, A. (2004). *Metaphor and political discourse: Analogical reasoning in debates about Europe.* Basingstoke: Palgrave Macmillan.

Musolff, A. (2016). *Political metaphor analysis: Discourse and scenarios.* London: Bloomsbury Academic.

Musolff, A. (2019a). How (not?) to quote a proverb: The role of figurative quotations and allusions in political discourse. *Journal of Pragmatics*, 155, 135–144.

Musolff, A. (2019b). Factual narrative and truth in political discourse. In M. Fludernik, & M.-L. Ryan (Eds.). *Narrative factuality* (pp. 351–67). Berlin: Mouton de Gruyter.

Nay, C. G., & Brunson, M. W. (2013). A war of words: Do conflict metaphors affect beliefs about managing unwanted plants? *Societies*, 3, 158–169.

Nerlich, B. (2010). Climate Gate: Paradoxical metaphors and political paralysis. *Environmental Values*, 14 (9), 419–442.

Nerlich, B., & Hellsten, I. (2014). The greenhouse metaphor and the footprint metaphor: Climate change risk assessment and risk management seen through the lens of two prominent metaphors. *Technikfolgenabschätzung: Theorie und Praxis*, 23(2), 27–33.

Nerlich, B., & Koteyko, N. (2010). Carbon gold rush and carbon cowboys: A new chapter in green mythology? *Environmental Communication*, 4(1), 37–53.

Robertson, T. (2012). *The Malthusian moment : Global population growth and the birth of American environmentalism.* Rutgers: Rutgers University Press.

Romaine, S. (1996). War and peace in the global greenhouse: Metaphors we die by. *Metaphor and Symbolic Activity*, 11(3), 175–194.

Schlosberg, D., & Collins, L. (2014). From environmental to climate justice: Climate change and the discourse of environmental justice. *WIREs Clim Change*, 5, 359–374.

Semino, E. (2008). *Metaphor in discourse.* Cambridge: Cambridge University Press.

Shaw, C., & Nerlich, B. (2015). Metaphor as a mechanism of global climate change governance: A study of international policies, 1992–2012. *Ecological Economics*, 109, 34–40.

Silaški, N., & Durovic, T. (2019). The JOURNEY metaphor in Brexit-related political cartoons. *Discourse, Context and Media*, 31, 1–10.

Sperber, D., & Wilson, D. (1995). *Relevance*. Oxford: Blackwell.
Steen, G.-J., Dorst, A.-G., Berenike Herrmann, J., Kaal, A.-A., Krennmayr, T., & Pasma, T. (2010). *A method for linguistic metaphor identification*. Amsterdam & Philadelphia: John Benjamins.
Sun Tzu (5th century B.C.). *The art of war*. Trans. Butler Bowdon, T. (2010). Hoboken: Wiley.
Tognini Bonelli, E. (2001). *Corpus linguistics at work*. Amsterdam & Philadelphia: John Benjamins.
Williams A. (2015). Metaphor as tools for enrolment: A case study exploration of the policy press release genre in regards to the Alberta Super Net. In J. B. Hermann, & T.-B. Sardinha (Eds.). *Metaphor in specialist discourse* (pp. 271–296). Amsterdam & Philadelphia: John Benjamins.

Online resources and data availability statement

Data are available at

Conference of the Parties: unfccc.int; unece.org; ukcop26.org
COP26 Coalition: cop26coalition.org
Extinction Rebellion: extinctionrebellion.uk
Friends of the Earth: foei.org
Greenpeace: greenpeace.org
Nexis (n.d.): nexis.com
United Nations: un.org
United Nations Environment Programme: unep.org
World Health Organisation: who.int
World Wild Fund: worldwildlife.org
Wild Life Conservation Society: wcs.org

Index

A
Akan language 147, 207, 210
Alien franchise 261, 291–292
Alteration 11, 92, 98, 101
anti-proverbs 11, 4, 92–93, 102
    Anglo-American 88, 94–97
    and wellerisms 94–95, 103
apothegm 265–266, 272, 293
    proverbial 89
Arabic language 13, 100, 136, 137
Axiom 264, 276
axiomaticity 264, 293

C
Cause and Effect pattern, in proverbs 56, 181, 194, 195, 197
CCT (Cultural Cognitive Theory) 8, 13, 301
Chinese language 34, 105, 335, 340
CMT (Conceptual Metaphor Theory) 6–8, 10, 12–15, 71, 75, 135, 180, 203
    tools of 17
    literature 29, 33
    claim of 65
    challenges to 82
    as an approach to metaphor identification 138
COCA (Corpus of Contemporary American English) 266
cognition 5, 7, 19, 33, 302
    and culture 1, 2, 18
    and emotion 178
    cultural 302, 304, 306
    embodied 6, 8, 133, 136, 299
    social 176, 293
    socio-cultural 261, 294
cognitive ideals hypothesis 176
Cognitive Linguistics 1, 65, 114, 116, 179, 204
    as an interdisciplinary perspective 2, 13
    and construction grammar 2, 20
    and Cultural Linguistics 1, 8, 17, 140, 149
    and paremiology 9, 91
    fundamental terminology of 5–8
    pre-corpus 18
    proverbs within 3, 12, 13, 17, 19, 26–28, 42, 67, 136, 137, 232–233, 300–302
cognitive model 3, 6, 11, 16, 29, 58, 91, 137, 140, 179
    of love 93
    approach 195
Cognitive Sociolinguistics 2, 114
complex adaptive system, language as a 262
conceptual pathways 14, 33
conceptualisation: cultural 1, 7, 10, 72, 132, 133, 299, 302–304
    metaphorical 1, 15, 35, 66, 75
Conference of the Parties 334
construction grammar 20
    and cognitive semantics 17, 261
    usage-based 262
context: African 134, 137
    in CMT 14, 34
    in ECBT 12, 135
    in ECMT 14, 28, 31, 34–38
    and meaning making 8, 68
    and contradictory proverbs 68–69
    and metaphorical proverbs 36–38, 89
    historical 129
    of GEEK CULTURE 285
    socio-cultural 9, 10, 19
    and semantic ambiguity 11
contextual factors 34–35
contiguity 43
contradiction, proverbial 66–69, 71, 76, 78, 81–83
co-textual features 265
Croatian language 41, 50, 55, 56
Cultural Linguistics, and Cognitive Linguistics 299
cultural literacy, and proverbs 261
    and snowclones 261, 264, 274, 293
cultural model 6
cultural schema, in Cultural Linguistics 7, 137
    and cultural model 303
    L1 134

D
Danish language 99, 101
didactic function, of proverbs 19, 42, 48
    of proverbial snowclones 266, 284
didactics 261, 264
discourse function 267
domain mappings, source-target 13, 44
Dutch language 99, 103, 335

E
ECBT (Extended Conceptual Base Theory) 12, 28, 135, 176, 178
echoes, proverbial 53
ECMT (Extended Conceptual Metaphor Theory) 14, 31
    as a new framework of CMT 37
    aspects of 28
    introduction to 28
Egyptian language 104
embodiment 8
    extended 1
English language: British 93, 124
    American 93, 94, 267
epistemic status, of proverbs 265
    of snowclones 267, 281
experiential basis 8
experiential gestalts 29

Extinction Rebellion 334

F
figurativity: in relation to proverbs 16, 176, 178, 180–181, 194, 195, 197, 265
  in relation to snowclones 284
Finnish language 104, 105
fixedness: as a proverbial feature 5, 265, 268
  in proverbs and snowclones 20
  in the Ripley-construction 293
frame 14, 28–30
  and mental space 30
framing 52, 66, 83, 254
free-mapping proverbs/aphorisms 180
French language 104, 105, 113, 115
Friends of the Earth 334

G
GCMT (Great Chain Metaphor Theory): components of 12, 177–178
  in proverb interpretation 140, 206
  vs. ECBT 135, 176, 178
German language 41, 50, 51, 90
GLOWBE (Global Web-based English) 266
Great Chain of Being Theory 12, 46, 76, 140, 149, 177, 178
Greek language 179, 182, 183, 195
Greenpeace 334
Grice, Herbert Paul 12, 48, 68, 177

H
hapax legomena 268
hate speech 260, 269, 272, 274, 276, 293
  social categorisation in 276, 293
Hausa language 99
heterogeneously distributed system, language as a 263
Honeck, Richard P. 176–177, 187, 197, 232–233

Hungarian language 41, 99, 305, 307
Hyperbole 88, 178, 254
Hypercorpora, representativeness of 266

I
ICMs (Idealised Cognitive Models) 5, 7, 91
  types of 91
  of love 91
idiom 4–5, 17, 19, 42, 46, 179, 210, 300
image schema, and embodied cognition 6–7
  and ICMs 7
  and frames 30
  level in the schematicity hierarchy 28
  in proverbs 136
impersonality, in proverbs 265
  in proverbial snowclones 266, 293
Indian language 101
Irish language 99, 104

J
Japanese language 97, 99

K
Kabyle language ix, 13,

L
Latin language 99, 113, 115
LDOCE (Longman Dictionary of Contemporary English) 115, 117
Lebanese language 99
little texts, proverbs as 52
Lovejoy, Arthur Oncken 177

M
Mali language 101
marker, proverbial 265, 293
  co-textual 276
mental space 30
Metaphor Identification Procedure 334
metaphor: conceptual 6, 8, 28–36
  contextualist view of 34–36
  correlation-based 35, 37

GENERIC IS SPECIFIC 12, 26, 28, 46, 90, 177, 193, 233–236
GREAT CHAIN 10, 76, 77, 146
  proverbial 9, 13, 36, 37, 239, 252, 253
  resemblance-based 27, 37
  stereotypical 15, 66, 71–82
metaphorical mappings 6, 7, 30, 44, 233, 254, 329
metaphorical variation 1, 10
metaphoricity 5, 41, 73, 76, 138, 143, 298, 301
metonymic mappings 6, 44
metonymic presupposition 51
metonymic shifts 20, 42, 44, 46, 58
metonymy, illocutionary 49
SPECIFIC FOR GENERIC 15, 19, 46, 58
models of love: the "alternative" 94
  the ideal 94, 103, 179
  the typical 94, 103, 179–181, 187
Monkrani language 101

N
Nexis Uni 116
NOW (News on the Web) 261, 266

O
OALD (Oxford Advanced Learner's Dictionary) 115, 117, 119
ODP (Oxford Dictionary of Proverbs) 115, 117
OED (Oxford English Dictionary) 15, 114–117, 129
othering 272, 274, 276, 293

P
paremiography 9
paremiological minimum 53
paremiologists 9, 19, 91
paremiology 3, 9
Peruvian language 99
Phraseology 4
productivity 17, 268
productivity profile 268

proverb transformation 54, 92, 95, 96, 100, 102
proverb truncation 20, 52, 53, 54, 55
proverbial phrase 4, 17–20, 94, 135
  to be in the same boat 329, 339, 344–345
proverbiality 264, 266, 276, 293
  indicators of 3, 5, 41, 88–89, 107, 29, 293
proverbs: and anti-proverbs 15, 92, 96, 100, 105, 107, 108
  and apothegms 293
  borrowed 114, 129
  contradictory 15, 66–70, 82
  defining 3–4, 41, 113, 132–133, 232, 299–300
  delineating 4, 19
  French-derived 114, 121, 124, 129
  Latin-derived 114, 121, 126, 129
  meaning of 11, 89, 176, 232–234, 254, 301
  metaphorical and non-metaphorical 16, 89, 138, 197, 203, 205
  multilevel view of 31–34, 37
  truncated 18, 52, 54, 56, 58
  origin of 4, 19
  pre-cognitivist research into 1, 2, 9, 19

R
Russian language 41, 99, 104

S
scenario 7, 29, 334
  illocutionary 49
  love 195
  BOAT 334, 342, 345
schematicity hierarchy 14, 19, 28, 33
Scottish language 104
shared schematic structure 28
Sharifian, Farzad 1, 7, 17, 132, 299
Shona language 100
similarity 8, 43–44, 70, 203
  literal 28
  structural 27
  in meaning 70
  in the conceptualisation of love 92–93, 108
simile 44
situational applicability 264, 285, 293
snowclones, analysis of 17
  as a tool of hate speech and othering 274
  definition of 260–261, 263
  delineating 4, 19
  discourse-pragmatic function of 267, 276
  Mordor-construction 261, 267
  only good construction 261, 267
  originating from popular culture 263
  original model of 263
  proverbial 17, 20, 261, 262, 266

Ripley-construction 261, 267
schematisation 268
sociolinguistic function of 285
socio-cognitive analysis, of proverbs 112
Socio-cognitive Linguistics 113
specific-generic mapping 46
speech act, indirect 20, 48–49, 58
STTR (Standardised Type-token Ratio) 268
Swahili language 99

T
Tajik language 41, 54
Taylor, Archer 3
themes, of proverbs 9, 17, 234–236, 240, 252
  in proverb alterations 92, 95
topic 35
  co-textual 267, 276, 284–285, 288
  of discourse 36–37
topic-comment 43
Trench, Richard Chenevix 9
Turkish language 101

U
usage-based model 42, 47, 262
usage-event 262–263, 265, 267, 289
Uzbek language 41, 54, 57

W
wellerisms 94, 102–103, 106–107